Siam in Crisis

The Thai Inter-Religious Commission for Development (TICD)is an organization which seeks to promote the exchange of ideas and knowledge on development between various religions.

First published 1980

© 1980 S.Sivaraksa

Revised Edition published 1990

© 1990 S.Sivaraksa

Artwork by Dear Book Co., Ltd. Tel. 2349374
Printed in Bangkok by Rung Seang Printing House Tel. 437-2947
Manuscript editor : Harold F. Gross
Editors of revised edition : Ken Scott and Paul Wagner

Front cover designed by Pichai Lertsuwansri
Lay-out   by   Song Sayam Co., Ltd.
                   113-115 Fuang Nakhon Rd.
                   (o.p. Wat Rajibopit), Bangkok 10200,
                   Tel. 222-5696-8
Back-cover : The author with bust of Phya Anuman Rajadhon, his mentor, at Buddhaisavariya Hall in the National Museum, Bangkok, when the government commemorated the late Chao Khun's centennary 14 December 1988.
Distributed by   Suksit Siam
                 1715 Rama IV Road
                 Bangkok 10500

300 Baht (paperback)
400 Baht (hard cover)

Siam in Crisis

A Collection of Articles by

S.Sivaraksa

Revised 2nd Edition

Santi Pracha Dhamma Institute

Thai Inter-Religious Commision for Development (TICD)
Bangkok 2533/1990

Contents

Preface to the First Edition
Notes from the Author on the Second Edition

PART I : Introduction
Editor's Introduction to First Edition (Harold F. Gross)............2
Editor's Introduction to Second Edition (Ken Scott)...................4
About the Author and His Poem (Herbert P.Phillips).................6

PART II : Personalities
H.R.H Prince Naris 16
H.H Prince Dhaninivat: Seven Cycles of Life 20
Phya Anuman Rajadhon : A Common Man or A Genius 23
M.R. Kukrit Pramoj Whom I Know 36
The Life and Work of Prince Damrong Rajanubhab 47
Direck Jayanama 71
Preecha Arjunka 73
Thomas Merton 75
Alexandra David - Neil 78
Vikas Bhai 83
Surendra Chakrapani 86
Shigeharu Matsumoto 89

PART III : Background to Understanding Thai Politics
The Privileged Elite Versus The Common Man (1965) 94
Students' Role in Society (1966)...97

The Avoidance of Basic Social Problems (1969) 101
Democracy in The Future (1967) 106
Charting Our Course (1967) 111
Siam Versus The West (1967) 114
Siam: The Move Away From Military Dictatorship (1973) 118
Interview by Wolfgang Schmidt (1977) 126

PART IV : Western Contributions to Thai Studies
American Influence on Books, Magazines and
    Newspapers in Siam 134
Political Science – A Siamese Response
    to Western Studies 158

PART V : New Crisis : Viewpoint from The Late 1980's
On Southeast Asian Modernization (1987) 166
The Religion of Consumerism (1988) 175
The Problem of Ethnic Minorities and State:
    Burma and Siam (1988) 188
Arguments for Real World Development:
    a Buddhist Perspective (1989) 201

PART VI : Aspects of Thai Buddhism
Buddhadasa Bhikkhu:
    A Religious Innovator of Undying Fame 224
Visakha Puja 2509 in Suan Mokkha 228
An Interview with Buddhadasa Bhikkhu 231
Conversations with an Abbot 249
Buddhism and Social Values 253
Renewal : A Buddhist Perspective 268
Paññānanda Bhikkhu 272
Dhammavitaka Bhikkhu 281
Phra Dhammacetiya : In Memoriam 283
Artistic Venture at Wat Thongnopakhun 285

PART VII : Siam – SE Asia – Japan
The Siam Society 290
Thai Dilemma 298
Resistance for Reconstruction 300
Networking & Co-ordinating 306
Japan in Asia 310

APPENDICES : On The Author And His Views
The Dominant Figure : Sulak Sivaraksa 314
The Meaning of Peace 317
A Buddhist in Bangkok 322
Is Foreign Money Good for Thailand? 325
Santi Asoke: Symptom, Not Sickness 327
East Meets West – A Dialogue 332
A Socially Engaged Buddhism 335
The Mirror of Siam 345
Living At Sulak's 352
Review of The First Edition 357
Interpreter of Two Cultures 360
Western Culture Unmasked 364
The Making of the Thai Intellectual Tradition 367

This book is gratefully dedicated to my *Farang* friends, especially in Europe and North America, who helped me, my family and my compatriots in many respects throughout the period of the dictatorial regime during the Thanin Kraivixien Government (6 Oct. 1976 – 20 Oct. 1977) when most liberal intellectuals were politically, socially and economically oppressed in various degrees.

Crisis has come to mean that moment when doctors, diplomats, bankers and assorted social engineers take over and liberties are suspended. Like patients, nations go on the critical list. *Crisis*, the Greek term that has designated "choice" or "turning point" in all modern languages, now means "driver, step on the gas".

Crisis now evokes an ominous but tractable threat against which money, manpower and management can be rallied. Intensive care for the dying, bureaucratic tutelage for the victim of discrimination, fission for the energy glutton, are typical responses. Crisis, understood in this way, is always good for executives and comissars, especially those scavengers who live on the side effects of yesterday's growth : educators who live on society's alienation, doctors who prosper on the work and leisure that have destroyed health, and politicians who thrive on the distribution of welfare which, in the first instance, was financed by those assisted. Crisis understood as a call for acceleration not only puts more power under the control of the driver, while squeezing the passengers more tightly into their safety belts, it also justifies the depredation of space, time, and resources for the sake of motorized wheels, and , it does so to the detriment of people who want to use their feet.

But crisis need not have this meaning. It need not imply a headlong rush for the escalation of management. Instead, it can mean the instant of choice, that marvelous moment when people suddenly become aware of their self-important cages and of the possibility of a different life. And this is the crisis that , as choice, confronts both the United States and the world today.

Ivan Illich : *Toward A History of Need* (1977).

...And in those days all men and beasts
Shall surely be in mortal danger,
For when the Monarch shall betray
The Ten Virtues of the Throne,
Calamity will strike. The omens,
Sixteen monstrous apparitions:
Moon, stars, earth, sky shall lose their course.
Misfortune shall spread everywhere.
Pitch-black the thundercloud shall blaze
With Kali's fatal conflagration.
Strange signs shall be observed throughout
The land, the Chao Phraya River shall boil
Red as the heart's blood of a bird.
Madness shall seize the Earth's wide breast,
Yellow the colour of the leading sky.
The forest spirits race to haunt
The city, while to the forest flee
The city spirits seeking refuge...
The enamel tile shall rise and float
The light gourd sink down to the depths.

Translated from a Thai poem of the seventeenth century by B.Anderson in *Bulletin of Concerned Asian Scholars*, vol. 9 no. 3, July 1977.

This kingdom was known as Siam until 1939, when it was changed to Thailand. Then it reverted to the original name in 1946. Two years after the *coup d'état* of 1947 it was decreed that the country would be called Thailand, and it remains so officially. Ironically the kingdom has since been ruled by one dictator after another with very brief liberal democratic intervals. The name, Thailand, signifies the crisis of traditional Siamese Buddhist values. Removing from the nation the name it has carried all its life is in fact the first step in the psychic dehumanization of its citizens, especially when its original name is replaced by a hybrid, Anglicized word. This new name also implies chauvinism and irredentism. For this reason, the author of this book prefers to use the name Siam.

Preface to the First Edition

In 1973 I collected my English articles, mimeographed and bound in a volume, called *Siam through the Looking Glass – A Critique,* copies of which were offered to friends and for sale in limited number. It is now out of print.

In 1976 I was invited by the Thompson Memorial Lecture Committee to deliver a series of lectures in Chiengmai on *Religion and Development*. The Church of Christ in Thailand published the text of my talk in Thai, which was reprinted by the Ven. Phra Dhammacetiya in honour of the Buddhist Patriarch of the North. The book had been translated into English by Francis Seely of the Dhamma-Logos Group in Chiengmai. I understand that the CCT will publish the English version in due course.

During the winter term of 1978, I was a Visiting Professor at the Centre for Religious Studies, University of Toronto. At the end of my teaching period, I was invited to take part in a Colloquium—*Multiple Loyalties: Buddhism and Christianity in Crisis* – together with Wilfred Cantwell Smith, Roger Hutchinson and Abe Masao. At that Colloquium, I gave a paper on "Buddhism and Society : Beyond the Present Horizons".

The Centre was so kind that it not only accepted my paper for publication, but also offered to put my other lectures and articles together in a special volume entitled *A Buddhist Vision for Renewing Society*. Willard G. Oxtoby, Director of the Centre, and David W. Chappell, Professor of Buddhist Studies, at the Department of Religion, University of Hawaii, were responsible for that volume. William L. Bradley, President of the Edward H. Hazen Foundation, and great-grandson of the famous Protestant missionary in the reign of King Mongkut, kindly wrote an appreciation of the volume.

Apart from these three gentlemen, there are quite a number of friends in Europe and North America who helped me in many respects while I was not able to be in Siam during the 1976 – 1978 period, due to the political upheaval at home. Some invited me to stay with them in their own homes for quite some months. They even put up with Thai friends who visited me for days or weeks! Some invited me to teach, to speak and to write. They also helped me in editing my articles and polishing my English. For all their service I am truly grateful.

Since *Siam through the Looking Glass* is now out of print and *A Buddhist Vision for Renewing Society* deals mostly with Buddhist perspectives, I feel I ought to supplement it with a locally produced volume, dealing mostly with Thai affairs. Harold F. Gross of Wattana Wittaya Academy in Bangkok liked my idea and kindly helped in editing this volume for me. He took some articles from *Siam through the Looking Glass* plus my newly-written material.

I am grateful to him as well as to Herbert H. Phillips, Professor of Anthropology at the University of California, Berkeley, who not only wrote about me earlier in his famous article "The Culture of Siamese Intellectuals", which is now included in *Change And Persistence in Thai Society : Essays in Honour of Lauriston Sharp* edited by G.W. Skinner and A.T. Kirsch (Cornell University Press) 1975, but he also invited me to teach at the Department of South and Southeast Asian Studies, in his University, during the Spring Quarter of 1977. Dr. Phillips is now editing a new volume called *Thai Thoughts : A Decade of Change* to be published by the University of California Press. He kindly let me publish his translation of my poem together with his introduction to it.

I should also like to acknowledge my gratitude to other editors and publishers alike whose names appear at the end of each article, for allowing me to publish or reprint the articles here. The date is also supplied to each airticle so that the reader will know precisely the time when it was written.

The paper on Prince Damrong was prepared for the Kyoto Symposium on Intellectual Creativity in Endogeneous Culture (13-17 November 1978) organized by the United Nations University, Human and Social Development Progamme. It was later delivered at the Siam Society, Bangkok, on 15 May, 1979. The article on American Influence on Thai Books, etc. is to be published by Greenwood Press, Westport, Connecticut, in a volume entitled

For Better Or Worse: The American Influence in the World.

Although I wrote mainly in English, that language is not my mother tongue. Furthermore, some of these articles have been translated by many hands, some of whom I do not even know. Because of this limitation, some of my thoughts are not expressed here so clearly. I hope, however, that this volume contains something of value to the readers who are not familiar with the Thai language. If it can contribute something towards an understanding of Siam – her perspective and predicament – I feel it is worth our effort in presenting this volume to our foreign readers.

S.S.S.
10-VI-79

Notes from the Author on the Second Edition

Since the publication of *Siam in Crisis* in 1980, I have published a few other volumes in English, such as *Religion and Development*, *A Buddhist Vision for Renewing Society*, *Siamese Resurgence* and *A Socially Engaged Buddhism*, two of which have second editions. There would seem to be no more need to reprint *Siam in Crisis*, but quite a few guide books on Thailand mention this book, so foreign visitors keep on asking for it. A few friends therefore suggested that there would be no harm in a new edition, provided that some obsolete articles were deleted as well as adding a few recently written articles by me.

I agreed with the idea and asked Ken Scott to be the editor. I feel he has done the work thoroughly. However, I took the liberty of adding a few more writings. Hopefully, the new edition is more readable than the old one.

Although a decade has elapsed since *Siam in Crisis* first appeared in print, my view on my country and the region has not changed significantly. In fact the crisis in ethical and cultural values seems to be worsening. Yet there is a good sign of hope that more people are now committed to liberating themselves and their societies in a nonviolent way, using spiritual tradition critically and mindfully. I hope the return to the sacred as opposed to secularism, materialism and consumerism, may be a good landmark for a better society in the future.

This new edition is timely, in away, as this country is now at its fiftieth anniversary since the name Thailand was imposed on us by the dictatorial regime of P.Pibulsongkram on 24 June 1942.

As the first edition of this book was dedicated to my Farang friends who helped me during my exile, due to the bloody coup of

October 1976, I must add that when I was charged with *lesé majesté* in 1984, with the maximum sentence of 45 years (if convicted), not only Farang and Siamese, but many Asians too were very helpful in getting me free. I am very grateful to all these *kalaynamitta* (good friends) all over the world.

I should also like to thank my own colleagues in various organizations who have been very patient and faithful in working with me, and last but not least, my own family, especially my wife, who has endured me for 25 years!

As for those who assisted me in seeing this volume through the press, I should like to mention Paul Wagner and Nicholas P. Kohler as well as all my Siamese staff members at the Thai Inter Religious Commission for Development and Santi Pracha Dhamma Institute who tirelessly worked behind the scene to get *Siam in Crisis* ready for the public in a handsome and (hopefully) error-free new edition. For all their untiring effort, I am grateful.

S.S.S.
27 - XI - 89

I
INTRODUCTION

EDITOR'S INTRODUCTION TO THE FIRST EDITION

When writing a book one aims at being accurate. If an author is writing about or forecasting the future he can do so with a certain impunity, knowing that his work will be published and (hopefully) sold before his predictions can be proved true or false by the march of time. It therefore takes a certain degree of courage to publish what was written some time ago, if time has since falsified, in whole or in part, what was foreshadowed therein. It also demands humility on the author's part. None of us can be right all the time, but some of us would like to make out that we are, and would therefore suppress that which shows that we are, after all, fallible.

In gathering together some of his miscellaneous writings over a period of 14 years (1965-1978) Acharn Sulak Sivaraksa has displayed such courage and humility.

Sulak Sivaraksa has been known for many years as an informed and concerned commentator on many aspects of Thai life and affairs. He combines in his thinking the traditional and contemporary, the insight of a trained legal mind and an innate empathy with the thinking of his fellow-countrymen, an incisive assessment of what is going on around him, tempered by a realization that change requires fundamental adjustments in human attitudes that take time to mature and produce results. If he consistently uses the old name, Siam, for his country, known to most of us as Thailand, it is because he cannot let go the values from the past which that name embodies. Yet his education overseas and his worldwide contacts make him responsive to those trends in modern thinking which are universally valid.

All his work and thought, moreover, is permeated by his profound loyalty to the Buddhist faith. This loyalty is not merely verbal or intellectual, but finds expression in those acts of piety and humaneness which indicate the reality and truth of that faith for him. This volume contains a number of essays which reflect that underlying approach to life.

There is another advantage in collecting together the occasional pieces such as are found here. The historian wants to know, not only what has happened, but how those who lived through the events saw and evaluated them. It does not matter if these reflections on contemporary events are completely accurate, or whether the hopes and fears they aroused all came to pass. For these reflections, hopes and fears are themselves part of the raw material out of which the future is shaped. Those pieces in this book which relate to the contemporary events of the period for which they were originally written should be read in this light. They tell us what people at that time thought, more particularly what one shrewd observer thought, and this in itself may provide a clue to the way the future later evolved.

Someone has written,
"And I honour the man who is willing to sink
Half his present repute for the freedom to think."

Sulak Sivaraksa is this kind of man. He is not unmindful of what others think, but this is not the mainspring of his writings or his actions. The major concern is to express the truth as he sees it, and to let results take care of themselves. It is this which gives to these essays their appeal and their abiding interest.

Harold F. Gross

INTRODUCTION
TO THE SECOND EDITION

In the decade after the first edition of *Siam in Crisis* there has been a divergence between Thai society and Sulak Sivaraksa's position. And his pen has not been still : "... I do not agree with that form of development which aims at quantity, and not even that form of development which has as its objective the improvement of the quality of human life, yet still stresses material things. In reality, the latter, too, diminishes the quality of human life."

As a social critic thus concerned with real development in a Buddhist society, Sulak cannot leave recent changes alone. An interview and four new essays from 1987-89 consequently reassert Sulak's Buddhist and humanitarian position in response to the social changes of the late 1980s. The new essays include: On Southeast Asian Modernization (1987), The Religion of Consumerism (1988), The Problem of Ethnic Minorities and State: Burma and Siam (1988), Buddhism and Social Values (1988) and Arguments for Real World Development : A Buddhist Perspective (1989). Sulak has lost none of his idealism, using allies from "small is beautiful" Schumacher to Thich Nhat Hanh, the Vietnamese monk to prove that his Buddhist alternative – the middle way – is socially viable.

On the "debit" side, nine essays – mostly short political observations from the 1960's – have been omitted from the second edition. The six remaining essays of Part III – Background to Understanding Thai Politics – are the residual best of Sulak's responses to select events in Thailand during the 1960's and 70's.

Many of Sulak's readers, however, like him best when he is turning over the soil of Siam's recent past, introducing unlauded figures of minor royalty, enigmatic monks of wisdom, and lesser known literary personalities. Such readers will consequently be pleased to find that Parts II and VI – Personalities, and Aspects of Thai Buddhism – remain virtually untouched, although seven more personalities, including a few friends of the author, have been added to Part II. In these essays a strong sense of nobility is evident, Sulak writing with great warmth about what is in effect his heroes' lives. These essays are debts of honour to people whose work – mostly unappreciated at the time – has had a formative influence on his own outlook.

Finally, Part VII, Siam-SE Asia-Japan, contains several new articles of regional interest, and the Appendices present the author and his views as others see him, from an assortment of angles: book reviews, interviews, newspaper articles and even a house-guest.

By criticizing the sacred cow of modern Thai development and espousing often unfashionable opinions, Sulak is assuring his position on a lonely path, a path similar perhaps to that his heroes found themselves walking on. It is not an extreme course. It is merely the middle way made to look extreme by modern Thai society racing headlong into new crises on its own divergent highways.

Ken Scott
April 1989

ABOUT THE AUTHOR

While in no sense extraordinary, Sulak Sivaraksa is a person who from early childhood has been enraptured by the values and great men of his culture.

Sulak was born in 1933, the son of chief clerk of a Western import - export firm, and was educated at Assumption College in Bangkok before leaving for England at the age of nineteen. Even before reaching adolescence, he had gone through most of the available writings of Prince Damrong Rajanubhab, the architect of Thailand's system of modern education and public administration; another of his childhood heroes was Prince Narisara Nuwatiwongse, designer of Bangkok's Marble Temple and Thailand's greatest composer-musician of the early twentieth century period. Prince Damrong's impact on him was sufficiently great that more than thirty years later Sulak undertook a study (actually funded by the Ford Foundation) of Prince Damrong's contributions to Thai intellectual history.

Sulak spent nine years in England studying history, philosophy, literature and law. On his return to Thailand, he became the principal disciple of Phya Anuman Rajadhon – philologist, ethnographer, and literary critic, and at the time the doyen of the Thai scholarly world. He also came under the informal protection of Prince Dhaninivat, Regent of Thailand and President of the Privy Council, and Prince Wan who had just retired from the presidency of the General Assembly of the United Nations. The halo of patronage provided by these two most senior and prestigious princes was later to prove critical in ensuring Sulak's safety while out on his numerous sallies against the inadequacies of a changing Thai society. Very few people or institutions escaped Sulak's evaluation – including the King (in a metaphor comparing him with King Chulalongkorn) and M.R. Kukrit Pramoj. Sulak's criticisms of Kukrit have continued intermittently for many years and have yet to elicit a direct reply. While he occasionally praises his self-selected adversary, the thrust of his view is that Kukrit is a fallen idol – a pretentious, and thus false version of the "great man" of Thailand. While all of this might seem somewhat juvenile, it in fact relates to precisely the same issues raised in Sulak's poem, What Kind of Boat? e.g., how is excellence, success, pretense, and fraud to be identified and judged?

During the middle and late 1960's the principal forum for Sulak's views was the *Social Science Review* which he established, operated, and developed into Thailand's major intellectual magazine. Reflecting the times and its character – but also Sulak's character – the magazine was successfully apolitical during his tenure as editor. It was not until Suchart Sawadsri assumed editorship in the late 1960's that the thrust of the journal began to change and it very quickly became the major source of Thai protest against the Vietnam War. While serving as editor, Sulak also established the first university bookstores in Thailand and did considerable travelling in provincial and rural Thailand stirring up apolitical intellectual controversy.

In recent years, Sulak has established his own publishing house, translated several books into Thai and written several of his own, the latter tending to be increasingly 'political' in nature, e.g., addressing the reality of Marxism, he lauds it for its commitment to social justice but condemns it for its indifference to the spiritual needs of man. With the passage of time, his intellectual style has also become increasingly mellow. The latter is in part a function of the fact that in recent years he has become the major liaison figure linking the intellectual life of Thailand with the intellectual life of the international world. He is the "favourite" lecturer or discussant on humanities and Buddhism in Thailand at international conferences, and during 1977-78 he taught Thai Studies and Buddhist Studies at Berkeley, Cornell, and the University of Toronto.

Sulak's influence, however, will always be greatest within Thailand. Although he is the spokesman for no "school" and has had perhaps fewer disciples than his fame would warrant, he has had a profound personal impact on a number of people whose work appears in this book – particularly Suchit Wongthed, Suchart Sawadsri, and Angkarn Kalayaanapong. (They are the source of this information, not he.) Suchit – whose own writing reflects strikingly different interests and values – cites Sulak's integrity, his knowledge and appreciation of premodern Thailand, and his communication of both the propriety and joy of being daring, as his most valuable legacy.

Herbert P. Phillips

WHAT KIND OF BOAT ?

There are so many good boats.
Why are they not used for crossing the river?
Instead they choose the boats that leak.
And when a good job is really needed,
They find only imposters to do the work.
            - - An old Siamese saying

Among the Thai people in this era
    The degree alone is the symbol of success.
Masks are worn to deceive others
    And to gain congratulations and approval.
The more one struts, the more credible one is,
    The larger the boasts, the greater the expertise.
Bosses busy themselves in this and that[1]
    While uncontrolled subordinates create havoc.
When not at their meetings

---

1. The busyness of bosses is in part prompted by their need to prove (or, more precisely, to go through the motions of "proving") that they have the expertise to deal with all problems and in part by the need to demonstrate that they are always seeking opportunities to expand their responsibilities, power, and little empires.

> They sit picking at their buttons, smirking their insipid smiles.[2]

They call their plagiarism "creative writing"
> And present it to the boss as proof of their merit.

The boss reads it, and cannot possibly understand
> But he does not dare to say anything.

For to open his mouth would betray him as a Phuu Yai Lee,[3]
> Proclaiming his stupidity for all the world to hear.

The subordinates speak their "foot fit,"[4]
> With English and American swagger.

The more they speak, the more credible they seem,
> Even better than *farang* at what they know.

Oh, *farang*—they are really quite stupid,
> Always believing the bravado of their older Thai brothers.[5]

Whatever we want, they give.
> Just talk big—they will fall for it.

---

2. The symbolism of "meetings" in Thailand is akin to the symbolism of being "in conference" in the United States: it is meant to suggest something secretive, inviolable, and terribly important, although it also has a latent element of fraudulence, e.g., that the purpose of the meeting is really quite unimportant or that a participant is simply using it as a cover for doing something or being somewhere else. Button picking is the perfect posture of the person who is doing (as well as thinking and feeling) nothing. The insipid smile is the act of someone who is simply too lazy to do anything more.

3. The hero of the most popular song of this period.

4. This is a contraction of "foot, fit, four, five" which is a phrase of Thai gibberish used to mock the sounds of spoken English.

5. By referring to the Thai as "older brothers," the authour is making their bravado more persuasive or credible to native Thai readers.

If you ask only for a little bit, they think you are flattering them and do not need it.

But if you ask for something grand, it suits their disposition.
Whether the project is feasible
Or whether it is absurd—that is not what matters.
What matters is the way you act.
Act big and you will get what you want.
Creating academies with a snap of the fingers,
It is an easy thing, in fact the simplest thing, to do.
Once you have the money...
Are there really any other problems? Just let me know.
Teachers? Oh, that is no issue.
What is important are the curricula and the children.
Have loads of them and make them all jazzy.
Degrees? We will give them away with generosity.[6]
Everybody is happy.
There will be no suffering, no difficulty.[7] How could there be?
Teachers with degrees from abroad.
Give them money. They will come running.
To teach those courses with the Indian names, [8]
Those weird words that required research expeditions to be discovered.

---

6. The terms here are the same terms that are used to describe the giving of alms when making Buddhist merit.

7. Again, the author uses the Buddhist canonical terms for "suffering" and "difficulty".

8. The term here for "Indian" is "Khaeg," a word that is always charged with a bit of ridicule. While the author is referring to names taken from Pali and Sanskrit, names that ought to be respected for their sacred qualities, he is also deriding the way they are adulterated and misused. Thus, to speak of Pali and Sanskrit as "Khaeg languages" is like referring to Latin as "that Wop language."

While the translations from *farang* are done verbatim,
    And are passed off as new books.
The graduates that result from all of this,
    Whether bright-eyed or dull-witted,
Are in the end all levelled off.
    They all are given the same degrees.
The big shots of this world
    Act as if they are skilled in everything—from the beginning to the end,
Each a universal expert
    With hundreds of responsibilities—and that is hardly a little.
Where do they get the eyes?
    To see who is who?
To see whether it is a good boat or a leaky boat.
    To them, they are all the same—just boats.

Translated by Herbert P. Phillips and Vinita Atmiyanandana

เรือดี ๆ ก็มีไม่ขี่ข้าม

เอาเรือรั่วน้ำมาข้ามขี่

อยากได้การงานดี ๆ

เอาคนผี ๆ มาใช้งาน

(ภาษิตเก่า)

คนไทยสมัยนี้	ดูดีกรีจึงเป็นผล
สวมหน้ากากหลอกคน	อนุโมทนาสาธุการ
ยิ่งอวดก็ยิ่งโก้	ยิ่งโม้ก็ยิ่งชำนาญ
ปล่อยลูกน้องจุ้นจ้าน	นายมัวแต่สาระแน

ถ้าแม้นไม่เข้าประชุม	ก็นั่งเกาะกระดุมยิงฟันแหง
เขียนหนังสือก็คือแปล	อวดนายใหญ่ไปอีกที
นายอ่านแล้วไม่เข้าใจ	พูดไปก็จะไม่ดี
เดี๋ยวกลายเป็นผู้ใหญ่ลี	อวดโง่เขาจะโพทะนา
ยิ่งลูกน้องพูดฟุตฟิต	สำเนียงอังกฤษอเมริกา
ยิ่งเก่งยิ่งเข้าท่า	ฝรั่งมันจะรู้อะไร
ฝรั่งหรือก็คือโง่	ฟังคำโม้ของพี่ไทย
อยากได้ก็เป็นให้	ขอให้เขื่องเรื่องโวหาร
ถ้าขอแต่น้อย ๆ	ว่าสำออยไม่ต้องการ
ใหญ่โตมโหฬาร	เป็นชอบอัธยาศัย
โครงการจะทำได้	หรือไม่ได้ไม่เป็นไร
ขอเพียงทีท่าใหญ่	ก็จะสมอารมณ์หวัง
นิรมิตวิทยาลัย	เรื่องง่าย ๆ สบายจัง
ได้เงินแล้วจะรัง	เกียจอะไรให้บอกมา
ครูหรือคือเรื่องเล็ก	สำคัญเด็กกับวิชา
มีให้มากให้หรูหรา	ปริญญาประเคนเข้าไป
ทุกคนก็มีสุข	จะเกิดทุกข์ยากอะไร
ครูนอกเอาเงินให้	ก็ขี้คร้านวิ่งมาสอน
ชื่อวิชาภาษาแขก	คำแปลก ๆ เที่ยวแซกซอน
แปลฝรั่งเป็นตอน ๆ	มาลงไว้ในหนังสือ
บัณฑิตที่ออกมา	จะตาสว่างหรือตาปรือ
ผลสุดท้ายก็ครือ ๆ	เพราะดีกรีมีเหมือนกัน

ผู้ใหญ่ในพิภพ ออกเจนจบสารพัน
คนเดียวท่านชำนัญ งานนับร้อยน้อยเมื่อไร
ที่ไหนจะมีตา มารู้ว่าใครเป็นใคร
เรือดีเรือรั่วไซร้ มันก็อ้ายเรือนั่นเอง

II
PERSONALITIES

H.R.H PRINCE NARIS

Exactly 100 years ago today there was born into the world, a son of King Mongkut, the fourth of the Chakkri Dynasty, whose name was Citracareon, which means "Improving One's Character". The name proved prophetic, for throughout his long life, Citracareon improved his character constantly, although the name was soon forgotten when he was created a Krom and given the name of Narisara Nuwattiwongse, which became more popularly Prince Naris.

A story had it that when he pursued his religious training as a monk at Wat Bovornives, Citracareon thought of remaining in holy orders for the rest of his life. But when the new King Chulalongkorn heard of this, he went personally to the monastery and asked his brother to return to lay life. And although he obeyed, the teaching of the Lord Buddha was always for him as a layman "the Guide, the Light and the Lamp". While he was alive he was loved, respected, and admired by his fellow countrymen.

But today we are not celebrating the centenary of his birth because of his personality. We are paying tribute to a son of Siam who has contributed much to her culture.

A younger son of King Mongkut, Naris was born on April 28, 1863, during the last six years of his father's reign. His secular education was undertaken by tutors in the Palace School. But, unlike his more famous brother, Prince Damrong, he never learned to write or speak English well, although the two brothers at one time shared the same English tutor – Francis George Patterson, successor to that well known lady, Anna Leonowens.

Naris's interests lay elsewhere, in the sphere of Siamese art and literature, and he preferred the ancient languages of the East to the living and useful languages of the West. However, he knew enough English to read textbooks on the subjects in which he was interested. Later in life, he produced a translation from the ancient Khmer language which surprised everyone, and scholars regard it as the best work in its field.

In art and literature, Naris had a chance to shine at an early age, for, in 1882, Bangkok was to have its centenary celebration. The young King Chulalongkorn, being a progressive man, wanted his numerous half brothers – all of whom were even younger than himself – to share the responsibility for the reconstruction of Wat Pra Kaew, the Temple of the Emerald Buddha. Prince Naris, then still in his teens, took charge of rebuilding the Gandhara Buddha Tower, which housed an image for the rain-calling ceremony. He personally painted the inner wall of this tower and inlaid mother-of-pearl in the front door of the Royal Pantheon. He also supervised the making of two demons facing the Consecrated Assembly Hall. And, like the rest of his half brothers, Naris wrote two long poems describing the Ramayana episodes which were painted along the cloister of the Temple Royal.

Although Naris served King Chulalongkorn as Minister in four successive portfolios, the most permanent marks he left in that long and prosperous reign were his paintings and designs. The prince was well aware that western civilization was creeping in through the back door of Siam, so he tried his best to preserve the arts and crafts of his country.

In one of his letters to his king he said, "What I am trying to do is to show that our old masters are inferior to none. I am only following their footsteps. At least I want to claim that even in the reign of your Majesty there still exists an artist who can paint in the old Siamese fashion." Alas, is there an artist now who can make such a statement with justification?

Naris was not, however, old fashioned in the decadent sense of the word. One only has to look at Wat Benjamabopitr – the Marble Temple (to cite but one) – to find out how modern, and yet how traditional his design is. Every piece of his work, even a tiny little official seal like the Garuda, is so Siamase and so alive. And he created many of them, ranging from palaces, pavilions, temples and crematoriums to gaols. All his half brothers teasingly styled him "the Great Constructor of Siam." And Chulalongkorn once said to him, "As a designer, I must admit, you have a place in my heart."

When the prince was promoted by King Vajiravudh to the rank of Kroma Pra, his new title included a phrase which may be rendered as follows: " an accomplished artist of great success, with a profound knowledge of various forms of art ; a gifted writer, archaeologist, composer and choreographer of excellence." This should suffice to show what a rare and gifted artist, what a true genius, the prince was.

Phya Anuman, one of our leading scholars, who has the honour to address the Regent today on the opening ceremony of the centenary celebration, has this to say of Naris. "The works he left us with are not only a priceless treasure to the Thai people but a precious gift to the whole world. They belong to the category of the high arts."

Unlike Prince Damrong, Naris was not known to the multitude. He preferred the quiet life of a country gentleman to the busy life of an administrator in town. While his contemporaries were building mansions in the city after the European fashion, Naris bought a Siamese homestead and lived among farmers whom he regarded as friends. Yet, when official duty called him to manage the affairs of state, he did it rather well, although he seemed to regard it as a mere necessary evil.

In the reign of King Prajadhipok, he rose to the rank of Supreme Counsellor of State, which was next in importance only to the sovereign himself. Soon after the change of regime in 1932, he was appointed Regent when the King was abroad. And he carried out this difficult position, in his old age, with justice and courage. For this service the King sent him the following telegram on the day he abdicated:

" I beg you to accept this present of gold and silver trees from me as a mark of my profound reverence and admiration for your fortitude and courage in the face of great difficulties, also as a humble offering to show my boundless gratitude for your ever true loyalty to myself and the Royal House. I humbly beg you to forgive me for any trouble and sorrows that I may have caused you to feel."

To this telegram, Naris replied in a manner which gives us a glimpse of his modesty and humility.

"In reply to your telegram, I am too overcome to find words to express my deeply touched feelings. It is my intention to offer the gold and silver trees which Your Majesty graciously presented to me as tribute to the memory of our august ancestors at the Pantheon."

After his retirement, till his death in 1947, Naris had more time to devote to writing songs and to painting. Although he no longer created great objects like the Marble Temple, nor was he asked to write important songs like the Royal Anthem, for which he had supplied words in the reign of Vajiravudh, he nevertheless carried on designing fans for monks, all of which had certain artistic and religious value. Another of his hobbies was to correspond with "fellow students", notable among these being his own brother, Damrong. Their correspondence was published last year to mark the latter's centenary. This year, the University Press of the Social Science Association is bringing out five volumes of Naris's correspondence with Phya Anuman, one of the greatest living scholars of Siamese customs. Other volumes will include the Prince's works in painting, architecture, and drama. While he was alive, the Prince never blew his own trumpet, so the majority of his countrymen hardly realized his significance. These books, one hopes, will help the Siamese of this generation to look back to the past, and feel proud of a son of Siam, who has contributed so much to Siamese culture.

Bangkok World Sunday, April 28, 1963.

H.H PRINCE DHANINIVAT: SEVEN CYCLES OF LIFE

Thirty-two years ago Prince Dhani wrote his Memoirs in English entitled *Kings I Have Served*. He showed his manuscript to a friend, who remarked that the book seemed to have been planned along the lines of an autobiography, but the author became almost obliterated as the narrative proceeded and eventually disappeared altogether. Had the book been published, we of the younger generation would still have learned a great deal about His Highness. It is disappointing to learn that the manuscript has been lost. Quite a few of us had since begged the learned author to write his Memoirs again in whatever form or language. We were gratified, therefore, when we received a present from him on his last birthday anniversary in the form of the very book we wanted. He had just completed the seventh cycle of his birth; hence the title of his memoirs.

I believe the lost manuscript in English dealt only with Kings Vajiravudh and Prajadhipok, whereas the present volume in Thai covers the whole period of his life, starting from the reign of King Chulalongkorn, whom he knew as a child, living in the Grand Palace with his grandmother, and who sent him to Europe on a grant from the privy purse. Prince Dhani was fortunate enough to meet King Chulalongkorn when he visited England in 1901, and he started his long and distinguished career during the last years of Rama V's reign.

During the first part of the author's life, we have several glimpses of the good old days. He was very much attached to his grandmother, who was Mistress of the Robes in the Royal Household, and so we learn a lot about life in the Grand Palace. Those who wish to study this side of the story more seriously should read the biography of his grandmother which has now been reprinted in His Highness's Collected Works in Thai.

The author's attachment to his grandmother almost made him decide to remain in the Buddhist novitiate permanently instead of disrobing to go abroad. After his Rugby and Oxford days, it was because of this yearning to be in the company of the old lady again that he refused the offer to join the Foreign Office, and thus missed the opportunity of further study in France. He really wanted to study archaeology, but Siam then, as now, needed civil servants more than scholars. This being so, Prince Dhani decided to work as a provincial administrator, starting from a low level, rather than to be a diplomat or a courtier, moving in high society. His reason was that to know one's country well, one ought to be in the provinces. His first assignment was at Ayudhaya, where he not only had a chance to meet provincial people, but also had the opportunity to be involved in the archaeological excavations under the Governor-General, Phya Boran, who was also an able scholar in matters concerning the old capital.

By this time, Prince Dhani had lost both his parents, and when King Chulalongkorn passed away, Queen Saowapha, who now became the Queen Mother, made him her private secretary. Whether the author liked it or not, this post paved the way for him to serve closely under King Vajiravudh, who regarded Prince Dhani as a friend and a fellow scholar. Everyone knows that the King was very generous with his courtiers, many of whom asked for special favours, in cash as well as in kind. Prince Dhani managed to remain poor all through this reign, despite the fact that he held no less a position than the King's foreign secretary and assistant secretary-general to His Majesty, equivalent to the present-day Minister of the Prime Minister's Office.

Soon after King Prajadhipok's coronation, Prince Dhani became Minister of Public Instruction. It is a pity that he was not in this office long enough to inject his ideals and ideas into the educational system, for after the 1932 *coup d'état* everything in this country seemed to go wrong, especially in education. The author rightly refers to the promoters of the *coup* as Hiranyakasipu. Those of us who read the *Mahabharata* and the *Puranas* know such a character well and it need not be elaborated on here.

Luckily, Prince Dhani was not detained or put in prison, a fate that befell quite a number of his cousins. His release from the cabinet gave him ample time to do his gardening which he loved, and to do research work in Siamese literature, history and archaeology. His writing both in Thai and English began seriously after this retirement. He also devoted more time to the Siam Society, of which he was the first Siamese president. His contributions to the *Journal of the Siam Society* and his activity in the society need not be mentioned here, and he carried on with the Society even after his return to high office in the present reign.

Although a lot of information is given regarding the work he has done as Regent, Grand Counsellor of State and President of the Privy Council, the full implications of the work will have to wait for the future historian or biographer to evaluate.

In these Memoirs the author's own self is not quite obliterated, but he writes in a very modest way. The whole story is told concisely and clearly, the only criticism is that it is too short. Any topic in the book could very well be expanded into a chapter by itself; especially that concerning his family which is rather thin. But we know that Prince Dhani had many official duties and social functions to attend; the mere fact that he could spare the time to write these *Seven Cycles of Life* in the midst of a very active life should leave us grateful. Despite the fact that the book was written in a short period of time by a man in his eighties, it is accurate and written in beautiful Siamese prose. If His Highness will not write his Memoirs in English, this book ought to be translated into English.

PHYA ANUMAN RAJADHON
A COMMON MAN OR A GENIUS

When I accepted the invitation to give a talk and pay homage to the late Phya Anuman Rajadhon to mark the interval of one month after his death, it was with mixed feelings. On the one hand I felt highly honoured, but on the other I felt rather uneasy about it. I knew that I would not be able to express what I felt. I always maintain that it is never very difficult to talk about something one does not know, for if time is available one can always do a bit of research and make something out of it. It was Lao Tzue who said that he who knows does not talk, while he who talks does not know. To speak about something one knows well and admires very much is difficult indeed, for one could not be satisfied unless one were able to transmit the knowledge and understanding to the hearers to the depth and the degree that one desires.

I consider myself very privileged to have known Phya Anuman Rajadhon so well, and to have been in such close acquaintance with him that I feel bold enough to boast that among his disciples of later days I was among those closest to him. For one thing we were neighbours, and also for reasons of work I saw a good deal of him until, I could almost say, the very end of his life.

I can say with confidence that I know almost every facet of his life and work of the last period, and the better I got to know him, the more I loved and revered him. But over and above all this I, together with my family, owe him many personal kindnesses. It is therefore difficult for me to talk about his qualities without strong personal bias.

Originally the Librarian of the National Library suggested to me the title of "Phya Anuman Rajadhon-a Memorial Lecture." Her idea was to leave it broad so that I could choose to treat any aspect of his excellence that I was able to think of. Then I heard and read what so many people, ranging from friends and pupils who attended his funeral rites to newspaper columnists, had to say about him, extolling his talents, calling him a genius, so much so that Siriraj Hospital Medical School made a request for his brains for medical students to study. Some, for example, said he was extraordinarily intelligent and was endowed with virtually superhuman talents as an administrator, as a scholar, as a writer and as a teacher. I kept my ears open to these eulogies and pondered upon them. If I myself and each of his other pupils were to take an aspect of his genius as described by various people and give a talk on it, the result would be a really long series of lectures and all this without touching on his virtues as a husband, a son and a father, each of which role could easily be developed into a talk.

On the subject of Phya Anuman Rajadhon as a scholar, I am in agreement with Professor William Gedney of Michigan University who, although he was not formally a pupil of Phya Anuman Rajadhon, counted himself one. In his preface to *Life and Ritual in Old Siam* Gedney sums up the qualities of Phya Anuman Rajadhon so well that I would like to quote his words in the following paragraph :

"Phya Anuman Rajadhon occupies, or rather has created for himself, a position in the field of Thai letters and scholarship which is unique and paradoxical. Though he is not an academician by training, his scholarly attainments have made him one of Siam's most highly respected university professors. Though he is not an anthropologist, no one has made so great a contribution as he to the study of traditional Thai culture. Though he is not primarily a student of language and literature, no one can proceed very far in Thai philological or literary studies before he has to seek enlightenment from the contributions which Phya Anuman has made in these fields. Though he is not a product of Western education, hardly anyone has done more than he to introduce and popularize Western learning among the Thai. Though he is much more than a popular writer, one could hardly find a professional writer in Siam who can match the grace and wit of his prose style. Most astonishing of all, though he is not a Thai by ancestry, no student of Thai culture, history, literature and language, has displayed greater devotion to these fields."

It is not only his pupils who sing the praises of the late Phya, neither is it only after his death that he is extolled. Everyone who knew him had always been aware of his extraordinary talents and moral excellence. "Dhanyavan", a writer, and a contemporary of his, whose real name was Phra Sombati Dhanyapol, and who was a close friend of his, at one time said : "Phya Anuman is really a monk in a layman's garb." We all like our friends to praise us, but it is surely rare to be paid such compliments. Perhaps it was this kind of high praise that prompted Sathirakoses to write the third part of his Memoirs, almost all of which was about wenching. From reading the Memoirs it would be virtually impossible to detect the qualities of a "monk" in the author, for on those pages the author does not reveal his own qualities but concentrates on revealing the good points of all his friends and acquaintances. His praises, I must add, are all sincerely meant. He neither exaggerates nor flatters.

In the appendix to the First Part of the Memoirs, the reader meets and gets to know a number of writers and scholars - ranging from Prince Damrong downwards. In *Phra Saraprasert As I Knew Him* the reader has an opportunity of meeting Phya Anuman's dearest friend and of appreciating almost all of Nagapradlpa's qualities. But no where in these writings is the reader given a chance to know that Nagapradlpa revered his friend to the extent of kneeling down to salute him at his feet, although the friend was only his senior by one year. And it was not from Phya Anuman that I learnt this truth.

Many men, some of higher birth, some of more advanced years, some with higher academic qualifications, have been loud in Phya Anuman's praises. Among them was Prince Prompong Adhiraj, his direct superior at the Customs Department, who gave him a photograph signed "to my friend Phya Anuman." It is not often that a prince signs a photograph thus for a commoner, and anyone interested in seeing this photograph can find it in the Anuman Rajadhon Library, on the third floor of the building.

Prince Naris, a prince of even higher rank, who was not connected with Phya Anuman through official duties, visited him in his home and referred to him as his "fellow scholar". From this "fellowship" sprang five volumes of *Notes on Knowledge* – the work which is the richest source of information on Thaiology ("Thai Vidhya"). The term "Thai Vidhya" is my own coinage, by analogy to the terms "China Vidhya" and "Bharata Vidhya" first used by Phya Anuman Rajadhon, who paved the way for future research work in this field for his pupils. As for Thaiology, we need not look far to find it, we only have to look to Phya Anuman.

Within this decade there has been no book published which would give wider or deeper knowledge on Thaiology than *Notes on Knowledge* by the two scholars. Even in this 20th Century it is not possible to find another such mine of knowledge. Scholars of future days wishing to make a study of Thai features and characteristics, however far they may have gone in their own study, must inevitably resort to this work.

All I have said so far has been an attempt to point out that Phya Anuman Rajadhon had almost always been recognized as a man of genius. Mr. Norman Maxwell, his first boss, might have been the first person to realize this, for he got to know him well before anyone else. His own father, on the other hand, may have discerned signs of genius in his son before that. This we cannot tell, because in his writings Phya Anuman praises his father without revealing his father's opinion of him, as he usually does with all his acquaintances.

I myself never asked him if he considered himself a genius, but from our conversations it was obvious that he did not consider himself especially intelligent to the extent of having unusual brains. He often said that as far as knowledge of Thai studies was concerned, Prince Dhani undoubtedly was the most learned man and the greatest authority. For brainpower and intelligence, especially in creating new words, Prince Wan, according to him, was top. The present Minister of Education, he said, was far more clever and far more quick-witted than he, and this was not because he was younger in years, he added. The former Minister he regarded as the only academician in the field of belles-lettres other than himself. Even with his pupils he would single out this one as being eminent in the field of literature, that one in anthropology, that one in history, etc. He would say of one that he had a quick mind, of another that he was a profound scholar though a little slow on the uptake, and so on and so forth. He paid tribute to people who succeeded him in the Department of Fine Arts, each according to their special qualities and standard.

Of himself he said he was a slow thinker. His writings, he said, lacked depth. On the topic of the beauty of his language, he said he owed a great debt to Nagapradlpa. Concerning his scholarly writings he said, both verbally and in writing, that he decided to write down the fruit of his studies simply because it was his hope that scholars of future generations would produce better things. Only a week before he died, he said to me that by international standards of scholarship his book on philology had no right to be published, but it got published in order to pave the way for future development. I realized that he mentioned that in order to prompt me to support the publication of the work of one particular person. I am happy to say that I quoted his words at the meeting at which the question whether this work should be published or not was considered, and we won by one vote. So the Siam Society has now agreed to sponsor the publication of this work. This episode shows that even when nearing his end he was concerned about helping younger people.

Phya Anuman Rajadhon often said that his works would sooner or later become out-of-date,that they were, like all else in this world, subject to the Law of Impermanency. This was his sincere opinion. It was no surprise, therefore, that when the Anuman Rajadhon Library was organized last year, it was so difficult to lay hands on his early writings. He himself could not remember what he had written, or which books had gone through how many editions. He had no idea and it was of no interest to him who printed his works or into whose pockets the royalties went. Even his medals, his honorary degree certificates and so forth, were not properly kept. And I should think it would be difficult to find a photograph of him in academic gown or in full uniform.

So, it would seem obvious that Phya Anuman regarded himself as an ordinary man. His way of life consistently conformed to this view. He was simple in his living habits, had no ambition, and while careful with his money he was most generous to other people. He dispensed gifts of knowledge, and of affection, as well as material gifts to all and sundry without ever expecting anything in return.

As regards intellectual power, he again considered himself no more than as ordinary man. His attainment of the rank of Phya – and he could almost be said to have been the youngest man to reach that height – although he only had grade IV of Assumption College behind him in the way of formal education, his attainment of the highest honours the King could give, his record of high official positions, as well as his achievements as an author, to him were just things of this transient world, to which he was not very much attached.

His insistence that he was just an ordinary man does not in the least mean that he had an inferiority complex about his humble background. On the contrary, while paying due respect to those of high birth including members of "Rajinikul" families (i.e. families that have produced queens), such as the Bunnag family, he was proud to be what he was, without being haughty. He never felt any shame in making it known that he was a son of a Nai Lee alias Mali, and his mother was called Hia. His clan name was Sae Lee, and his first name was Kwang Yong. Sometimes he would boast jokingly that if we were to take account of lineage then he had among his ancestors poets, philosophers and even emperors, for Lao Tzue belonged to the Lee family, Lee Po was a great poet and Lee Si Bin was a great king known far and wide as emperor Tang Tai Chong. (And if we were to go back further his lineage would probably be traced back to Adam and Eve.)

If one is to put emphasis on family background, then Phya Anuman must be considered one of the first generation of Thais who succeeded in establishing families. Both Sathirakoses and Anuman Rajdhon are names originating from him. In writing the Memoirs, he gave reasons for writing this work in a Preface concluding like this, "...That was how the Memoirs came to be written. They were not written because, out of a sense of self-importance, I wanted to write my own biography." No, all through his life, Phya Abnuman was free from self-importance. He was what he was, always.

In *Spirits and Gods (Peesang Devada)* he wrote the following words in the Dedication "I decided to write and publish this work to commemorate the cremation of my mother. When she was alive my five younger sisters and I were able to do our filial duties towards her with our deepest gratitude. This thought is a source of consolation to us all. Our dear mother has now departed from us, gone to some unknown region, some mysterious territory. Naturally we feel a deep sense of loss, a feeling which only time can alleviate. But it will take a long time. The depth of gratitude one owes to one's mother, felt so profoundly in one's own heart, is not something that can be expressed in words. Usually a cremation memorial book contains a biography of the deceased, but there are some that do without. I have decided to adopt the latter procedure. My mother was just an oridinary woman born of an ordinary family. If I were to include her biography it would have nothing of interest to offer the reader. It would only be of interest to me –

the fact that I was privileged to be her son."

From his own words the reader could not get a clear idea of his strong sense of gratitude towards his parents. In the Memoirs one senses this quality of the author but only vaguely. There is nothing there to tell us of the extent of the patience and endurance of his conduct towards his parents, particularly his mother. I used to think that Prince Damrong was the only son who had to go and pay respects to his mother everday before he went to work. Phya Anuman Rajadhon never told me that he did the same. Such behaviour must be utterly unknown to the people of our time. In spite of his effort to act as a link in transmitting virtues of the past to the present, many must have passed away irrevocably with him. However, certain aspects of his life story should help to stimulate younger men to emulate him and thus help to hand down our traditional values to future generations, creating an unbroken stream of cultural progress.

It should be clear from what I have said so far that to other people Phya Anuman Rajadhon was a genius, while in his own mind he was just an ordinary man. There was one man, however, who saw him as both, and that was Phya Sarabhaipipat, a school fellow from the Assumption College days and a fellow writer who later was dismissed from government service at about the same time as Phya Anuman, (although one was a fully fledged politician and the other tried to have as little to do with politics as possible). Phya Sarabhai tells us that in their school days, Phya Anuman did not show particular signs of brilliance. He completed only Standard IV which was not the top class in school. It was Prince Damrong who predicted that Phya Anuman would become a great scholar, and Phya Sarabhai admits that Phya Anuman did become a great scholar.

Can one call a great scholar or a learned man a "genius" ("acchariya")? The word "acchariya" is a Pali word, and its Sanskrit counterpart "Asacaraya" we know, means a marvel, something out of the ordinary. If a man of ordinary parentage who was not particularly brilliant at school, growing up in an atmosphere of gambling and other vices, among friends given to quarrelling, drinking and wenching, and starting his career in a hotel and the Customs House where there were plenty of opportunities to make something on the sideline – yes, even in those days, though much less than now – if such a man could survive and firmly establish an honourable family and was able to render invaluable services to his country and the world of scholarship, should one not consider him a wonder?

My close acquaintance with Phya Anuman, my understanding and knowledge of his character and personality, together with my familiarity with biographies of great men, have given me a firm belief that geniuses are born out of the ordinary way of life. Gandhi's autobiography (translated by Karuna Kusalasai and perhaps the last work to receive a preface by Phya Anuman) shows us what an ordinary man Gandhi was, how he had to fight ordinary temptations in life and in what ways he sought to overcome them. Prince Naris and Prince Damrong may have been born princes of royal blood, but if we considered their attitudes to life we would see that they really were ordinary men at heart. Those of you who have read Prince Damrong's biography may remember the episode describing how, when he first went to Suan Kularb Palace, upon being asked rudely who he was by some half sister, he answered, with his hands joined in salute, simply, "My name is Dis." Just like that, although the person who questioned him was a younger girl. His is a good example which shows what a simple, ordinary man he was at heart. As for Prince Naris, it was clearly evident that he lived his life as an ordinary man from beginning to end. His intent was for ever on doing good, giving service and not wasting time. These princes were considered great scholars and geniuses ("acchariya"). The world is maintained, society is maintained, surely by geniuses who retain the characteristics of ordinary men.

Geniuses with dazzling qualities, full of extraordinary attributes, tend to forget themselves and become overconceited. We see such phenomena in biographies of great politicians, dictators, military leaders and some perverse men. (We need not mention the name of a certain Field Marshal of this country.) Rather let us pause to think about Alexander the Great, Napoleon and Rasputin and to consider what kind of geniuses these men were, yet we will harp upon the lives of these men and hold them up as examples.

Geniuses of the other kind – ranging from our Lord Buddha and including Phya Anuman – though they be geniuses of varying degrees, have one trait in common : they retain the characteristics of ordinary men. Even subsequent to his Enlightenment, Lord Buddha lived simply, sitting under trees, sleeping on bare ground.

Most people are interested in lives which are larger than life-size. Very often lives of men of extraordinary talents are lacking in simple virtues. Many great men have lived empty and lonely lives. Their works might have been great, but what they have achieved is bound to be superceeded in the future. It is said that Lord Lutherford of England made a great discovery in physics in 1932, but surely during the thirty odd years between that time and now far greater achievements have been made. Einstein may have given the world a great discovery, but if Einstein had not been born the world would one day or other have discovered the theory of relativity. It is therefore advisable, when judging a man of great distinction to always take into account his moral virtue. There are a great number of men of moral excellence scattered about who are not remarkable in any way – practising (meditative) monks, dedicated teachers, honest and scrupulous government officials etc. These people manage to proceed along their paths of virtue and duty because of their simple ways and simple attitudes to life. We need such people. They are neccessary for the survival of society but they live unknown, unrecognized. At the same time people with mediocre qualities who think themselves geniuses and try to achieve startling effects do harm, not only to themselves but also to the society as well.

In the case of Phya Anuman Rajadhon, he had unusual talents and fundamental goodness, in addition to being an ordinary man at heart. The combination made him more than a genius and more than just a good man with simple moral virtues.

If someone were to ask what turns an ordinary man into a genius, a definitive answer to the question could not be derived out of a study of Phya Anuman's life. The more widely one studies biographies of great men, the more difficult it would be to formulate an answer to that question. As a Buddhist I believe that a genius must be endowed with Dharma. In the case of Phya Anuman Rajadhon, the predominant Dharma qualities were the "Four Wheels" which are compared to the four wheels of a vehicle, which help it to move along the path of progress. The first is merit achieved in past lives, without which it would be no good among corrupted influence and temptations. We all know how easy it is to choose the right or the wrong path, and so what direction one takes in one's life must be to some extent a result of past deeds. As a child Phya Anuman was not very clever at school; he picked quarrels, liked to fight and even got wounded at one time and was branded for life with a scar. As a young man he visited brothels, went out with drunkard friends. Yet he survived unscathed. It is without any doubt that he must have been saved by grace achieved in past lives. I have never believed this so firmly until now.

The second of the Four Wheels is the ability to conduct oneself rightly. All through his life Phya Anuman Rajadhon tried to conduct himself according to the rules of right and wrong. Though he entered brothels he refused to have relations with fallen people. As an official in the Customs Department where, as I said earlier, there were ways and means for doing well for oneself, he never strayed.

The third is association with worthy men. All through his life Phya Anuman Rajadhon associated with good men - starting with Father Colombet of the Assumption College, then moving to Mr. Norman Maxwell of the Customs Department, Prince Prompong Adhiraj, Phra Saraprasert, Prince Naris and so forth. All these men he counted good friends. To all of them he considered himself indebted because they gave him knowledge and shone light on his path of life. To Phya Anuman Rajadhon, then, association with right men was of great importance.

The fourth is right surrounding. True enough, in his childhood and youth Phya Anuman was surrounded by vices of many kinds, as I mentioned earlier. But because he conducted himself well and associated with people who had beneficial influence on him, the otherwise harmful surroundings became fascinating settings, of which he gave an enjoyable account in the Memoirs.

All the four Dharma qualities were possessed in full by Phya Anuman. And there were other qualities as well. He was endowed with mindfulness, a strong sense of gratitude and tolerence, all of which helped to abate any tendencies towards evil that may have been in him. He was, for example, a man of quick temper, but with the help of Dharma his conduct was irreproachable all through.

If one were to ask him what made him the man he was all through his life, the answer could be found in the Memoirs in which he quotes the following motto of someone else:

"Good health, knowledge and understanding, work and friendship. These are the things of supreme value in life"

GOOD HEALH. His health was excellent all through his life. He took great care of his physical welfare. He never drank, never went to bed late and every day had a run starting at four o'clock in the morning. When he was Directer-General of the

Department of Fine Arts he walked home everyday from Phramaru Ground to Dejo Road. As a result he never had to be in hospital until the very end when he entered the hospital for the first and last time.

KNOWLEDGE AND UNDERSTANDING. Whatever he wrote it was out of desire to know, to understand something. When he wanted to understand other people's faiths, *Friends' Religions* was produced. He wanted to learn about the lives of Thai peasants and farmers and local customs in different regions of the country, so he proceeded to find out and the result was the *Thai Customs* series. When he was asked to teach philology, a book on Thai philology was produced. When he was given the post of Director-General of the Fine Arts department, aware of his lack of knowledge in the arts field, he fully exploited the Department which he considered a great source of artistic authority and learnt as much as he could. On western art Professor Silpa Birasi gave him much help and what he learnt was turned into book form under the title of of *Understanding Art*. Phra Devapinimit helped him on the subject of Siamese art, along with many other knowledgedable people. He originally knew nothing about court life and customs, but Phya Devadhiraj was able to teach him a great deal. All this learning took place because Phya Anuman felt himself to be ignorant and wanted to learn. He would seek knowledge from anyone who, he knew, had something to tell him, from the most high ranking prince, Prince Naris, down to his own servants. The knowledge he obtained he turned into writing.

WORK. His whole life was the life of a working man with tremendous capacity for perseverance. When asked where he found spare time to do things, he answered that he got free time out of full time. I think there is much food for thought in that saying. Many people with time on their hands tend to while it away, achieving nothing. Many of us feel that we have no time to spare simply because we spend it all on useless activities – on administrative chores, socializing, in amusements – but Phya Anuman never did any of these things. If he went out it was to seek knowledge, to learn, in order to write about it later on. It is no wonder then that he should have left behind a greater body of work than anyone else of this age.

FRIENDSHIP. He always maintained it was of great value. His whole life was filled to the brim with goodwill and friendliness - towards all his acquaintances, whether they be colleagues or junior staff members, all of whom he praised, encouraged, helped and honoured. For his pupils he was always a source of encouragement He said that just as he wanted, as a father, his sons to do better than he, so as a teacher he desired to see his pupils go further. He never envied his pupils. His desire was that there should prove greater authourities, more profound scholars than he, and this attitude definitely had beneficial results. Holding friendship to be of great value, he was generous to all; his gifts to all and sundry were not only of the material kind, but also were gifts of knowledge and affection. He was able to give so freely and liberally because he was a contented man. He was happy with what he had, and in this way he always felt rich, never poor or wanting.

When we say that Phya Anuman was rich, we do not mean that he possessed great wealth. On the contary he died leaving less than 100,000 baht in his bank account - and this in an age when a late cabinet Minister leaving 16 million baht after his death was described as poor.

Phya Anuman acted in accordance with his words, in conformity with all the things he held in theory. He was an honest, upright man who was stable in his path of virtue. He was able to communicate with both the old and the young, that is to say both with his contemporaries and those of the younger generations. Indeed he was an important link which bridged the past and the present, and thus helped to pave way for the future. He was a highly developed and civilized man, and he wanted to help others along the same path. On the concept of civilization he spoke some unforgettable words, among the ruins of Ayudhaya, when we celebrated the Second Centenary of the Recapture of the City. I quote his words:

"Those who hope to achieve civilization should look back as far as they look forward. It is not only in the realm of the present that our duties and responsibilities lie, but also toward the past and the future. Only thus can continuous progress be achieved. The creations of the past, especially things of beauty, which have been handed down to us, we must preserve. We should also create more for the future. Do not let those who come after have cause to reproach us with failure to build up what is good and beautiful for them. In this rapid age of progress, let us always remember that it is not sufficient to look forward. We must also take into account the past upon which the present and future progress is based and which contributes to balanced future development."

The life of Phya Anuman Rajadhon was a well balanced one. Physically he was in good health all through his four score years plus. It was the life of a man with self-knowledge and understanding of his society. It was a life entirely devoted to work, most of which was the kind of work he loved and was happy to do. It was a life full of goodwill. In brief, it was the life of a cultured man - an ordinary man who was at the same time a genius.

That such a man has been born in Siam is a source of pride for us all. Younger men and women have not had an opportunity of knowing him as my generation knew him. But the last verse of *The Hitopadesa* - a beautiful Thai version by Sathirakoses and Nagapradlpa, should give them an idea of what Phya Anuman Rajadhon was like. I would like, therefore, to end this profile quoting the last verse from *The Hitopadesa*:

"Men of good conduct who have achieved no concrete results of their endeavour for the world to see, should be judged by their effort. Although it may not have obvious results to show, it is important to fully understand the nature of the work of a man."

Visakha Puja 2514 (1971).
The Buddhist Association of Thailand.

M.R. KUKRIT PRAMOJ WHOM I KNOW

Many people have said to me personally, or written to other newspapers, that our publication does not show any interest in some distinguished writers such as M.R. Kukrit Pramoj. Before I reply in the affirmative or negative to this accusation, I should like to refer the subscibers of the Review to the first issue of the Review in which mention was made of M.R. Kukrit Pramoj in the Thai section (pages 69 and 91), and in which we published the translation which he did jointly with M.R. Seni Pramoj, in the English section (pages 85-88). The publication in both languages resulted in a lengthy story afterwards so that as an editor, I gave up the idea of troubling him by requesting an article or of criticizing his works. I should like to relate briefly the cause and result.

The English article published concerns King Mongkut, translated and adapted by the two Pramoj brothers, so as to offer correct information on King Mongkut to foreigners, who would not then have misconceptions about the King, as supplied by Anna Leonowens, the American play, and the Hollywood film. In fact, the translation had been duplicated and distributed to various libraries some time ago, and some foreigners had quoted long passages in their writings. I believed that it would be an honour for the Social Science Association Press to publish the translation and so I wrote letters to request permission from the two translators. The following day I received a written reply from M.R. Seni Pramoj that he would be pleased to let us publish the translation, but permission should also be given by his brother. I waited for an answer from the younger brother, but no written reply came. Later he remarked to others that I behaved like an Englishman in going so far as to write to him on such a trivial matter; that he and I knew each other, and I could very well lift the telephone to speak to him. He had no objection and was pleased to give permission. On hearing this, I was very glad, believing that he felt kindly towards me; but I had never thought that in behaving humbly like a Thai and refraining from telephoning an elderly person, I would be accused of behaving like a European. Had I telephoned, I would then be accused of being fresh, not knowing the high and low in social circles, and behaving again like a Farang. As a matter of fact, a person working in a publishing house should have an agreement in a written form with a writer or a translator. As I studied law, I should be even more strict on such matters. But I was not; I continued in a Thai way to believe a person's words easily, especially when a highly distinguished person gave permission for his copyright. I was delighted, and published extracts in the first issue of the Review, with a footnote stating that the article would later be published in a book form (footnote on page 88). One fine day, however, M.R. Kukrit sent a letter to me referring to the fact that though previously he had agreed to have his translation published, since that time a publishing press in Singapore had decided to publish this work, and so he requested me to stop my publication of the translation. Although I had already set the type, I had to respect the owner of the manuscript. Thus, I had the type unset, since the book would be published abroad, which would mean the publication would be better than if it was done here. However, my mention of him in the article on the centenary celebration of Prince Naris's birthday in SSR vol.1 No.1 turned out to have an unexpectedly explosive result, and even more unexpected when considering that M.R. Kukrit himself has criticized many people for a long time, sometimes with prejudice and sometimes with reason. I made only a one-sentence criticism of him; he should not have been so angry with me as to use a strong language to reproach me. Moreover, the language I used in my criticism was chosen with great care, and I even tried to comply with the Buddhist saying as selected by M.R. Kukrit to be published daily in his newspaper *Siam Rath*.

The consequence of the article published in the first issue of the Review seems to be the severance of my relation with M.R. Kukrit Pramoj, or to use M.R. Kukrit's favourite figure of speech, the matter was the last straw that breaks the camel's back. It is only appropriate therefore to relate the beginning of my acquaintance with M.R. Kukrit. I am one of the majority of the Thai people who was born in Siam when the system of government had already been changed. I cannot remember what it was like at the beginning of the change; every time I recall the past, it seems that the country was inclined more and more towards dictatorship. There were constant arrests. Although I was born in a family of a commoner, and had nothing to do with the members of the Royal Family in those days, nor anything to do with those in power afterwards, we used to remark that the country was going downhill. When I grew up, I noticed the strong happenings, since I was old enough to witness the regime under which people were mauled and shot to death when there was martial law; then the peril of "Follow the leader, and the nation will be safe", "Wearing hats as a sign of progress", when the people were ordered not to wear "Pa Nung" (Thai trousers), not to chew betel, but to kiss their wives before going to work etc. Then came the period when the Prachatipat Party removed the yoke. I shall not discuss whether this political party was good or bad, but I admit that when the Government was formed, and members were sent to seek votes for the election, they were mostly distinguished and honourable persons – M.R. Kukrit among them. Although I never had the right to vote (and when I was old enough to vote, the system of government by votes had already been banished), I had been interested in the election since the time of N. Nen being nominated candidate. Later I was even more excited and interested, and followed the news of our representatives in the Parliament as if they were our own relatives. I took particular interest in M.R. Kukrit who had a bigger role than any other. When he resigned from the House of Representatives, at the same time as Junior Lieutenant Sampan Kandhachawana, on account we all regarded him as having lofty and strong ideals (but later he accepted appointment as a member of the Interim Assembly, a post which brought him a salary four times higher than the previous one. No matter how he explains this action, I have never understood it, even now).

Although he changed camp and became a cabinet minister in the government under the premiership of a former dictator, I still had faith in his sincerity, and sympathized with him even more when he wrote to explain his action ("Why I volunteered to be a cabinet minister"). Then when he took up journalism, I became an addict to his witty remarks, his ideas, and his long stories published in serial form, whether it be *Huan Nang, Jocho a Lifetime Premier, Many Lives* or *Four Reigns*. At that time there were not so many lectures and debates as nowadays; not so many broadcasting stations, no television, no seminars. Whenever he went to give talks at Chula, Thammasat, Vajiravudh, Wat Bovornnives etc., I would be there to listen to him. I admired him for choosing young men to work with him. I believed that he was the only person outside government circles who would lead the whole nation, and that he would be able to establish relations with foreign countries on an equal basis. At that time I had hopeful dreams that if I had any new project, I could consult M.R. Kukrit first; if he approved of it, then the project would be sure to succeed. This kind of dream is probably cherished still by the younger generation. Even some foreigners used to entertain the same hope; some even said that M.R. Kukrit ought to lead entire Southeast Asia with his ideas and thinking. We cannot blame M.R. Kukrit alone for our disappointment, since we counted too much on him.

Even when I went to study in England, I still followed the work of M.R. Kukrit Pramoj. Whenever there were any rumours about his personal life, I defended him and asked the people to understand him, that he is not a person with whom one can easily get acquainted due to his unhappy personal life. I considered myself his "fan", and claimed to know and understand all his works to the point of understanding his philosophy of life in his works. I even recognized M.R. Kukrit disguised as some of the characters in his works. And when I became more expert, and was able to detect any faults of M.R. Kukrit, I felt so pleased and proud. Some of my friends in England thought that I was too ardent an admirer of M.R. Kukrit, and reminded me of the original source of *Many Lives*. *Red Bamboo* which was published later was more evident. I made an excuse that the original source of a book is of no importance. What is important is the characters and how far their lives and spirit are Thai. At that time I admitted that I did not like *Red Bamboo,* but still admired *Many Lives*. However, I felt rather uneasy about his not revealing the original source of his idea of the story. Was he trying to keep the knowledge a secret? However, a person who could create a character such as Mae Ploy deserved all the excuses. At least I used to think so every time I felt angry with M.R. Kukrit.

Even after I completed my university course and worked at the B.B.C., my admiration for M.R. Kukrit never decreased, although I had never met or spoken to him. An elderly friend of mine at the B.B.C. warned me that when I got to know him and speak to him, my admiration would not be so ardent. He said that

Mom Kukrit is good when he writes for people to read, or speak to an audience; but when one holds a tete-a-tete, he would show contempt for the other man to an almost unbearable degree. I did not altogether believe my friend's words, and thought that as he was M.R. Kukrit's contemporary, he was probably jealous of M.R. Kukrit. A person such as I should not mind his acting superior or being contemptuous. And then came an opportunity for me to meet M.R. Kukrit Pramoj.

By that time the B.B.C. had cancelled the Thai programme, and I earned my living teaching at London University. But when His Majesty the King paid a State Visit to England, the B.B.C. put on a special programme during the Visit, and asked me to take on a temporary job. The B.B.C. invited M.R. Kukrit Pramoj to be on the programme with us. The first thing I had to do was to welcome him at the airport on behalf of the B.B.C. But since he was a distinguished personality who travelled ahead of the royal party, the Ambassador was on hand to welcome him in the V.I.P. room, and I did not need to say much to him, not until we reached the office. At that time *The Times* had just published a series of articles entitled "Important men in Asia on whom interest should be focussed", among whom was M.R. Kukrit Pramoj. A B.B.C. man showed M.R. Kukrit the article; M.R. Kukrit laughed in his face and said, "I know, I am one of the twenty-eight important men". When I chatted with him and mentioned that a professor at the University would like to invite him to a luncheon, he accepted the invitation and spoke graciously to me.

It was strange that at the lunch party at a French restaurant in Soho, attended by two officials of the Foreign Office, a newspaperman from the *Daily Telegraph*, a staff writer from Chatham House, the host, the guest of honour and myself, the guest of honour was the only one to speak in a voice which could be heard by everyone present in the restaurant. I can still remember the subjects he talked about that day. Nobody disagreed with him, nobody contradicted him; everyone made additional remarks. Our guest of honour seemed very pleased.

As for me, I thought he was play acting rather than holding an ordinary conversation. We left the restaurant and M.R. Kukrit and I went by car to the broadcasting house. On the way I asked him a question on the points on which I disagreed with him, especially on Thai dress. He said that the Thais are better off than any other nationality in Asia, since we can wear either European or

Thai dress as we like, unlike the Burmese, Laotians and Cambodians who are nationalists and refuse to wear foreign dress. In my opinion we are hopeless; that it was not true when he said that a Thai could wear Thai dress if he wanted to ; that for him it was all right to do so, but generally speaking, even if a person wanted to wear a *pa muang* (Thai trousers), he would not dare to since most people had been forced to stop wearing it, except some members of the Royal Family. Most of us therefore had to adopt European clothing, which in my opinion is a pitiful fact. He answered me graciously, and showed no trace of play acting, and conversed politely with me, so that I felt that if M.R. Kukrit coud only stop play acting, he could be a very kindly elderly man towards the young. But as soon as there was an audience, he would again resume his play acting. This was so, for as soon as we reached the B.B.C., there were less than ten people there, but he started acting superior to me, although he had been very polite to me all the way.

The following happened: a Thai friend of mine who was not well versed in using the royal language could not select the correct term for translating "The King's activities" into Thai. I said immediately that the term "Phra Raj Koraneeyakit" should be used. M.R. Kukrit interrupted me at once and said, "Karn Sadej Phra Raj Damnern" was better. Of course my friend would believe the words of a distingished person rather than those of his contemporary. However, I still believe until now that my answer was more correct, as "Phra Raj Koraneeyakit" includes various royal movements - sitting, taking a bath, taking meals, even sleeping. While His Majesty stayed in England, he would be undertaking "Phra Raj Koraneeyakit". The term 'Sadej Phra Raj Damnern" cannot include all the actions mentioned. I had previously met a few elderly persons. The good ones never disgraced a younger person. If an elderly man saw that a younger person was in the wrong, he would tell him quietly, giving reasons why his version was better. M.R. Kukrit did not spare my feelings at all, although his version of the translation was not as good. When we were on the air, we all spoke seriously. However, M.R. Kukrit began by saying, "It must be past eight o'clock at night in Bangkok. The listenters are probably chasing away mosquitoes. There are none here etc." The rest of us thought the remark rather strange. If this was a Thai way of making people laugh, then we must have been too long in England to understand them.

We thought the remark unsuitable for the occasion, and revealed poor taste for a short-wave special programme on the occasion of the Royal State Visit which was very important. However, at the end of the programme, M.R. Kukrit was all smiles and was very pleased with his words.

At that time I thought that if it could be arranged for M.R. Kukrit to meet about ten bright students studying in England, it would be profitable to all. However, he cancelled it. This was understandable, since we were all tired out even before the end of the State Visit. Later the Secretary of the Debate Committee of Samaggi Samagom (Thai Students' Association) invited him to hold a discussion with students. He made a short introduction, then asked the students to ask questions. When no one did, he intimidated us, with the result that I had to put a whole lot of questions to him one after another. I scored some points. He said, "You have buried yourself here, and have not sent any writing to me." This remark caused a member to ask him whether he would publish a story sent to him, since rumour had it that the newspaper of which he was director usually threw away writings by outsiders. He answered, "I did not mean that I would publish all articles sent to me. What I said just now was meant especially for Khun Sulak, since I consider that he knows how to write. It does not mean that everyone present here can write." I considered his words a kind of blessing, since although I could not bear M.R. Kukrit in many respects, I considered him a source of principles in the literary field.

Because of the invitation, on my return home I intended that if an opportunity arose, I would write and send a story to his newspaper; but it was not my habit to impose myself on anyone. So when I met him at a party at the residence of a member of the Royal Family, I mentioned that I should like to pay my respects to him. The reply was. "Oh! I don't receive visitors whether at home or at my office. People come and bother me incessantly." Although I could guess that he was being sarcastic for a director general standing nearby, I accepted that he had uttered the negative words, and that was final. There would be no visit.

What shocked me most when I had an occasion to come face to face with M.R. Kukrit Pramoj was not when he intimidated me in front of the Claridge's Hotel in London, or when he spoke abusively about other people at the Hague, or when he glanced sidewise at me with disapproval at the residence of members of the Royal Family, but what happened at the residence of the US Ambassador in Bangkok. When he heard that I was working for foreigners, he made a passing remark that the country seemed to be in the same state as that during the reign of King Narayana, when the Thais were extremely pro-European; that soon there would be a Phra Petraja to subdue them. I thought it rather strange, since he had just returned from abroad where he had taken part in a film and had earned something from foreigners.

These words were nothing new to me. But after dinner, he behaved as if he were trying to win favour from someone younger than he but who was holding a high position, and that was something I could not tolerate, especially when he spoke as if he was angling for an invitation to teach philosophy in a university. He said that nobody could be compared to him when it came to teaching, which was probably true. He went on to say that as long as that person was in the same position, he would continue to teach, otherwise he would resign. Did he want to teach for the sake of only that person, or for the benefit of education of the young? What was most unbearable was the fact that he had once declared openly in London amidst the students there that he had given up teaching altogether; that even if invited he would refuse to teach, since his academic knowledge had all gone down the drain and he had no time to prepare himself; that it would be better to let the younger generation who had just completed their studies teach. How his words uttered this time differed from what he had previously said! Was it possible that M.R.Kukrit Pramoj went back on his own words? I have been looking for an answer, but have not found it.

All the events that happened have made me give up patience in trying to continue to win favour from M.R. Kukrit. After all I am also a human being full of obstinacy and prejudice, just like any other. On recalling the past, I came to a conclusion that it would be better for him and I to go our own ways. It does not mean that I intend to show disrespect towards him, or consider myself his equal; especially when I consider that there is hardly anybody in Siam who is so able as M.R. Kukrit. It is not appropriate for a man of a younger generation to destroy him. However, I must admit that I am sorry to see such a person as he refusing to look favourably on us sometimes.

Many of us are ready to admit that he is more intelligent, more able, more experienced in life and more skilled than any of us in almost every field. What we cannot understand is why he draws the bridge so as not to allow the young to cross over to him. Perhaps he may think that we lack the perseverance necessary to climb up to him, and there may be some truth in it, but whoever has come across M.R. Kukrit's unreliable disposition will find it very difficult to exercise patience more than once.

Those of us who have organized seminars, radio or T.V. programmes, or published books etc. do not wish or dare to invite M.R. Kukrit to take part because of this reason. Many people have found out for themselves that at the first meeting M.R. Kukrit would look down upon the intelligence of a younger person; and if it is someone who makes use of his intelligence, then M.R.Kukrit would disapprove of him and would not tolerate him. M.R. Kukrit wrote an article in 1943 (in "The Three Generations") that he once looked to the younger people, "but what can one expect of them?" since they all count on him to lead. He explained in detail that there was only one person younger than he and who was able to show some light but did so only for a short while, and then the light disappeared. Since that light was very bright and came from very high, M.R. Kukrit shuts his eyes and refuses to receive the dim light from the younger people, particularly from anyone who is inferior to him by birth.

M.R. Kukrit is content to remain in the circle of his equals by birth, and even then M.R. Kukrit must be the most prominent; or among those with equal talents in the art of using their hands and feet; even those who use the art of speech must accept that they are inferior to M.R. Kukrit before M.R. Kukrit associates himself with them. Is it because M.R. Kukrit considers himself an artist? Can an artist do no wrong? M.R. Kukrit does not associate himself with the intellectuals who are younger because he is afraid that they would realize what kind of a person M.R. Kukrit really is.

It is better for him to wear a mask. Once he has taken off the mask of Toskan, he can still wear other masks. Since he can act in a film, a likay, a play and a masked play, why can he not act in his real life? The review in *The Times* on the role of the Prime Minister of Sarkan stated that this character was well portrayed, since the actor did not have to pretend, but he acted a part in real life. For M.R. Kukrit, there is probably no difference between real life and imaginative life.

M.R. Kukrit regards reality as unreal, and vice versa. If we use the form of the philosophy of the Zen sect, this is an advanced Dharma. Perhaps it is because of this that he cannot bear the younger generation, since they look at life too seriously, consider themselves superhuman enough to improve the society. M.R. Kukrit is particularly impatient of those younger men who count on M.R. Kukrit to lead the way, since M.R. Kukrit has seen failure in society during various epochs and various regimes, and does not wish to initiate any more grand schemes. But M.R. Kukrit cannot reach the state of complete deliverance, since M.R. Kukrit gives great consideration to his ego.

The person whom M.R. Kukrit loves most is M.R. Kukrit; the highest ideal of M.R. Kukrit is Kukritism. M.R. Kukrit loves Siam because it is his birthplace, the land of his ancestors, and what is more important, a land where the people are ready to listen to him, to believe him. Even if there is a madman who is brave enough to bring him to his senses, to contradict him or challenge his secured position, M.R. Kukrit may employ sharp words to pound him into dust at any time, even though that person may mean well and may have the same trend of ideas as M.R. Kukrit. It is of no importance that the destruction of that person may be against the Buddha's teachings, since the ultimate aim of M.R. Kukrit is Kukritism.

Do not hope against hope to change M.R. Kukrit's way of thinking. Do not hope that he will associate himself with us and give us advice. He has built for himself an ivory palace; let him continue his way to enjoy happiness. Whoever may remain, whoever may go, whichever government may be in power, M.R. Kukrit will remain. Although M.R. Kukrit does not teach in a university and does not have to write texkbooks, the Thai people will still admire and believe him, as long as the Thai people dislike reading texts and seeking knowledge for themselves. When M.R. Kukrit is gone, it is of no importance whether the newspaper he has created, the writing he has written and the work he has completed, will continue to exist; whether this Siam will continue its existence is of no concern to M.R. Kukrit. After all when he was a monk he was given an ordained name of Pamojkaro, the Laughing One, why shouldn't he continue to laugh at people?

What has been said so far may be rather strong, as if no regard has been given to the good deeds of M.R.Kukrit. But in fact whoever reads this article carefully will realize that I am of the opinion that M.R. Kukrit has done a lot of good, but he has also done a lot of damage. There is in a person both virtues and vices. Even the politicians who have governed the country during many periods have left some good deeds behind them. In considering to what extent a person is good or bad, it is important to consider his basic ability, and also whether he thinks more of the public or of himself, and to what extent. Finally, how far does he adhere to his ideal? A person who is not intelligent and has received little education should deserve more sympathy than one who is intelligent and who had opportunities and better environment.

The Thai original first appeared in *Social Science Review* Sept. 1965. Vol.3. No. 2. The English version was first published in *Siam through the Looking Glass* 1973.

THE LIFE AND WORK OF PRINCE DAMRONG RAJANUBHAB (1862-1943)
as an Historical Testimony of Endogenous Thai Intellectual Creativity

I

At present, the absence of endogenous Thai intellectual creativity seems to be rather obvious. The prevailing fashion of the day tends to rely more on the transfer of knowledge, especially from abroad, rather than on self reliant creativity or conservation of the national identity. The country's philosophy is to follow the western capitalistic goals of development, economically, socially and culturally. Without popular participation or freedom of expression, the country is bound to stagnate and members of the younger generation lose their respect for their seniors – a group of second and third rate hypocrites who are in charge of the country at various levels. They only care for their own wealth and are without any real concern for social justice or the well-being of the multitude, who are exploited more and more by the unjust social system within the country, as well as from abroad. Neither do they plan positively or seriously for the future of the country. Anyone who really cares for society and his own intellectual independence is alienated from the present political system. He is either not allowed to take any part in the development process of his country, or is forced to live abroad or in the jungle– ot to mention the prison.

In order to understand the meaning of the present state of affairs in contemporary Thailand, one should study an historical testimony of endogenous Thai intellectual creativity, immediately prior to the present, in order to see how such a country managed to maintain its unique Thai identity, culturally and politically, despite the fact that in the 19th century, and up to the early part of this century, Western imperialism was very strong and Siam, unlike Japan, was very small and militarily very weak. Yet, while quite a number of Siam's neighbours, which were formerly colonies and protectorates of the imperial powers, liberated themselves from the intellectual colonialism of their former masters by being proud of their own self-reliant creativity, the Thai are now sinking into blindly following Western materialistic development goals without critical evaluation.

II

H.R.H. Prince Damrong Rajanubhab, a great Thai historian, statesman and man of letters, declared in 1927[1], after several decades of Siamese encounter with European powers, that the Thai national identity arose from three main national characteristics, namely:

(a) the Thai loved freedom and wished to preserve their independence at any cost;

(b) they disliked violence in any form; and

(c) they were clever at bringing out whatever was good and useful from any cultural stream of influence.

Before we examine these three points, let us look at Siam and Prince Damrong historically. H.R.H. Prince Damrong was a son of H.M. King Mongkut (1851-68), famous abroad as the King in Margaret London's *Anna Leonowen and the King of Siam,* which became a famous musical, *The King and I.* In fact, Mongkut deserves more respect and serious treatment from scholars than that which Hollywood and popular authoresses have shown by caricaturing him [2]. Indeed it was he who preserved Thai political independence at the expense of unequal treaties with the West. He was prepared to lose some of his territories to the French in order to preserve the unity of his kingdom. In other words, he was willing to lose something in order to be able to preserve what, to him, was essentially and endogenously Thai. This is very much what Buddhism taught him, as the Buddha reminded his follow-

---

1 Prince Damrong Rajanubhab: *Laksana Kanpokkrong Pathet Sayam Tae Boran* (Ancient Forms of government in Siam) Bangkok, 1927.

2 A.B. Griswold: "The Historian Debt to King Mongkut" in *His Majesty King Rama The Fourth Mongkut,* Bangkok 1968.

ers that a wise man must sacrifice that which is not essential for the essence; he must sacrifice the smaller for the greater happiness. Mongkut's contemporaries in Vietnam and Burma failed to do this. Their failure was not due entirely to their ultra-conservatism or the wickedness of oriental despotism, as it is usually portrayed in Western textbooks. Mindon of Burma (1852-78), for instance, did not want to give an inch to the British for fear that they would eventually expand further at the cost of the total collapse of what he regarded as endogenous Burmese culture, which was linked closely to Buddhism. King Mindon was as devout a Buddhist as Mongkut, but he seemed to have failed to apply the Buddha's teaching to the sociocultural development alternatives in the changing world of his time. As late as 1910, when Bali lost its independence to the Dutch, we can see a ruling prince's argument thus: "It has become much clearer to me. I have looked about me and I cannot believe there is a country on earth as beautiful as Bali. I cannot give it away to foreigners or sell it. I cannot and may not. What would they make of it once it was in their hands? They do not know our gods and they do not understand the laws by which mankind must live. They would pull down the temples, and the gods would forsake our island, and soon it would become as barren and ugly as the deserts of China. They would grow sugar cane but not as our peasants do - just enough to sweeten their food and for their children to enjoy. They would cover the whole country with sugar cane and boil it down into sugar in large buidings, until the villagers stank of it, and they would take the sugar away in great steamers to change it into money. They would plant ugly trees in rows and draw rubber from them: they would lay the sawahs waste, and cut down the beautiful palms and fruit trees to make room for their towns. They would turn our peasants into slaves and brutes, and leave them no time for cock fights and festivals and music and dancing. Our women would have covered their breasts as if they were whores, and no one would wear flowers in their hair anymore or bring offerings to the temples. They would squeeze the joy from the hearts of our children, and tear the patience and tolerance and gentleness from their natures, and make them bitter and unkind and discontented, as the white men are themselves."[3]

---

3   Vicky Baum: *A Tale from Bali* OUP, Kuala Lumpur 1970.

Mongkut, on the other hand, wanted "to bring his country into line with those more advanced countries of the West, and to inspire the people with the spirit of patriotism, something hitherto unknown to them. Yet the King was wise enough to found nearly all the component parts of the new ceremonial on rites drawn from the stock of Siamese religion and culture – the material that lay ready at hand and was most easily understood by the people."[4]

The above quotation is in direct contrast to the one immediately before it, yet it was written by a British sociologist in 1931, from the definite viewpoint of the "more advanced countries in the West". Mongkut never used such a term. He cautioned his people to change in order to survive as an independent nation, because it was the time to do so. He used the word *Lokasannivasa*, which might loosely be translated as a new *Weltanschaung* - a new world view. His fluency in English - the first instance of this among oriental monarchs - and his understanding of the West was secondary to his command of Pali - the language of Theravada Buddhism - and his Thai culture.

Before his time, Thai Buddhism was much mixed up with Hinduistic practices and popular animism. The monkhood was not very strict in applying Buddhist disciplines to their daily life. Buddhist meditation was largely geared towards the manipulation of supernatural power rather than for the wisdom of release from wordly suffering. Scholars were concerned with commentaries and sub-commentaries composed in Ceylon, Burma and Siam, rather than with the authentic words of the Buddha. Thai history, too, was limited to Ayudhaya, the immediate kingdom prior to Bangkok. Ayudhaya in fact accepted much of Khmer civilization at the expense of pristine Buddhist teaching and endogenous Thai culture, especially with regard to magic, kingship and social classes, including slavery, though a rigid caste system never managed to creep into Siam.

Mongkut went back to the original sources of Theravada Buddhism by studying the words of the Buddha, as expressed in the Pali Canon. He regarded the original text as the final court of appeal in Buddhist doctrine, regarding commentaries and sub-

---

4 H.G. Quartich Wales : *Siamese State Ceremony*, London 1931.

commenteries as supplementary sources of evidence. Since he was 26 years in the monkhood prior to becoming king, he could reform the Sangha properly from within. While he was a monk, he travelled incognito among his people and went on foot as part of Buddhist austerity practices to the ancient capital of Sukhothai much further north than Ayudhaya, where he discovered the ancient inscription of King Ramkamhaeng, who introduced the Thai script in 1283.

From that inscription, he learned that the endogenous Thai culture was similar to the teaching of pristine Theravada Buddhism, i.e., the "god-king" (devarájá) concept was alien to the first Thai kingdom as it was to the original Pali canon. Both regarded men and women as free and almost equal. The king was taken to be a father of the nation. It was due to his meritorious deeds in past lives as well as in the present one that he could reign, for the justice, peace and well-being of his people. He was not ordained by gods to do so, nor was he a god incarnate. He could be blamed for everything which went wrong in his kingdom, including flood and famine, which mignt be due to his unrighteous conduct[5]. If the people had grievances, they could see their king at any time as the king installed a gong at the palace gate for them to beat, and he would come and listen to them. On ordinary days he would sit on a throne in the palm groves to give his counsel and pass his judgement on worldly affairs for the benefit of his subjects. On holy days, a Buddhist monk *(bhikkhu)* would sit there in his stead to give spiritual comfort to the faithful[6]. If the King could not carry out his regal duty properly, he could be removed from office like any other person.

When Mongkut ascended the throne in 1851, he tried to put his knowledge and experience into practice as much as possible,

---

5 S. Sivaraksa : "Buddhism and Society : Beyond the Present Horizons", a lecture delivered at the Center for Religions Studies, University to Toronto, March 1978, to be published by the University as a pamphlet.

6 King Ramgamhaeng's inscription has been translated into English by Prince Wan, into French by G. Coedes, and Y.Ishii made a thorough study of it at the Center of Southeast Asia Studies, Kyoto University.

bearing in mind the rapidly changing world outside his kingdom and the multitude of his people who still clung to the old beliefs and world-view inherited from Ayudhaya, so that whatever he did, it had to "lay ready at hand and was most readily understood by the people".

Mongkut was versed in Western astronomy as well as in traditional astrology. His children also inherited some of his talents. What he could not achieve himself, however, he planned would be accomplished by his sons in the years to come. He was very conscious of the need for this, because he succeeded his brother, Rama III, at the advanced age of 47. Having lived a celibate life for over 26 years, his first royal duty was to have enough offspring to care for the kingdom. This he was able to do, for he produced 82 royal children. His subjects were very grateful to him for doing so. Most of them were of high calibre, for instance, Chulalongkorn (1868-1910) who succeeded his father to the throne, could accomplish most of what Mongkut had dreamt of, including the abolition of slavery, of flogging, torturing and other outdated customs, as well as a thorough administrative reform of the entire kingdom. Prince Patriarch Vajiranana managed to spend his entire life in the Buddhist brotherhood and eventually became Supreme Head of the Holy Order. He carried out what his father had left undone when he gave up the monkhood to become king. The Prince's contribution to Thai Buddhism and Buddhist education has been of permanent value to the Sangha (Buddhist Church) as well as to the State. Prince Devawongs became a most famous diplomat, especially in times of crisis, at a time when there were many threats from Western colonial powers. He was Foreign Minister for 38 years. Most people did not realize that the Prince was well versed in astronomy as well as astrology. Prince Naris was a great artist, architect, musician and philologist. Prince Pichit was an able local administrator and a poet. Prince Sommot was a noted scholar and Prince Svasti was a leading lawyer, while Queen Saowapa was as able as, if not more able than, her brothers. In this paper, we shall confine ourselves with only one of these royal children, Prince Damrong Rajanubhab.

Before dealing with Damrong himself, we should bear in mind that Mongkut was well aware of the then socio-cultural development alternatives in the changing world of his time, for this is very much expressed in the teaching of the Buddha. Anyone who is not aware of a changing world is bound to be in peril! Mongkut wanted endogenous Thai intellectual creativity to withstand negative influences from outside, and constraints as well as counter-actions from within, for he believed in the uniqueness of Theravada Buddhism and the endogenous Thai identity. He himself had learnt hard lessons by spending so many years in the Holy Order, learning Latin from the French Roman Caltholic bishop and English from American missionaries. Both wanted to replace his Buddhism and his Thai cultural identity with Christianity and Western civilization and technology. He combated them with his Thai Buddhist virtue and adopted their technology for his own purposes. For instance, his Buddhist tolerance and his strong faith in Buddhsim made him allow American missionaries to preach the Gospels in his own temple in exchange for their teaching him English. He taught the French bishop Pali and Sanskrit in exchange for Latin. He also purchased a printing press from the missionaries to produce Buddhist tracts and pamphlets, otherwise his Buddhist followers could only read Christian literature in print[7].

He did not want his children to travel the long road which he had done. Through education, he could shorten the path of self-realization for them. They could be proud of their own culture and identity and at the same time know how to adapt it to suit the changing values entrusted to them from abroad. English books, however, claimed that engaging a British governess and tutor to teach the royal children was his great achievement, which in fact is not the case. These teachers certainly helped; yet most Thai are grateful to their teachers, however slight the teachers' contribution has been[8].

In order to understand this properly, one ought to realize that the most important part of the education that Mongkut imprinted on the minds of his children and people around him was he himself, for he was a charismatic leader. From all accounts in the Thai language, he was loved, respected and admired by his

---

7 S. Sivaraksa: "American Influence on Books, Magazines and Newspapers in Siam". a paper delivered at the Smithsonian Institution, Washington D.C. 1976, See infra.

8 A.H. Leonowens : *An English Governess at The Court of Siam*, London 1870.

children, for his truthfulness, his knowldege, his scholarship, his able administration, and above all for his loving care to all his children. His children realized that it was not easy for him to be responsible for the state, the Sangha and the family at the same time - and such a large family too. Yet he seemed to have done very well. He was known to his children for his impartiality to them all and his minute attention to the personal comfort of each of them. They all wanted to imitate him. Although he was sometimes criticized by his children, it was done with the utmost respect.

Love and loyalty to him was not only confined to members of the royal family (including his many half-brothers, uncles and cousins, who did not feel the same with previous reigns) but also extended to courtiers, officials and monks as well as ordinary people who knew him. One uncle had a strong grudge against him, yet after the uncle's death (by being convicted of treason during the previous reign), Mongkut looked after his children personally. Even missionaries who attacked him in print, loved and respected him. He confessed that missionaries annoyed him. They wanted him to adopt their way of life, the "superior" technology of the "more advanced countries of the West", which his subjects could not appreciate. Yet he was tolerant, remained friendly with them, and was very helpful to them when they were in need.

With these strong pillars of love and respect that Mongkut imprinted on his children and contemporaries, endogenous Thai intellectual creativity could be nourished.

Apart from the King himself, the cultural surroundings and social influences at work around them made the young princes proud of their upbringing, their Buddhsim and their Thai identity. Their traditional education within the wall of the grand palace as well as in the Buddhist monasteries contributed very positively towards endogenous intellectual creativity in the years to come. Besides, their mothers - mostly commoners and devout lay Buddhists, very loyal to their husband - were another great asset. In the case of Damrong, he wrote in his Memoirs that it was due to his mother that he never told lies, never visited prostitutes, nor ever stole. Their relatives and friends too, played a good role in their development. The Buddhist concepts of Good Friends is very important for one's education. The Buddha said, "As at dawn light is shining forth, this is the first mark of sunrise. Likewise a good friend is the first mark of the dawn of the Noble Eightfold Path".

The foreign teachers to royal children could also be regarded as good friends, with a difference, for their ideas brought forth something new, which could be contrary to the fundamental concept of endogenous Thai culture. However, being so deeply rooted in their own culture and civilization, the princes were confident in being able to extract what was good and useful from the West. This was especially so in the case of Damrong.

III

Prince Damrong was, in a sense, a direct link between old Siam and new Thailand. His royal father laid some foundation stones in the direction of the new era of Western contact, yet Damrong's birth and upbringing as well as his education through the palace tutors and the monkhood was very much in the old Siamese tradition. He was not quite six years old when his father passed away, yet he remembered his kindness to him vividly. His half brother, King Chulalongkorn, acted as a father to him, although he was not quite ten years his senior. However, in the royal family, seniority was taken very seriously, and the new King was just and kind to his many brothers and sisters. He tried to imitate his august father as much as possible, so there was much love, respect and comradeship among the royal brothers, who contributed so much to Thai intellectual creativity. It is true that some of the princes received English lessons for a few years. The impact on the whole would not have been that great, yet through the English language they were aware of the outside world, which could be of great benefit to their country and which could also bring them peril as they had already witnessed in Burma and Vietnam. Prince Svasti, in particular, who was the only one among his brothers who went as far as Oxford for his further education, was very much outspoken against Western materialism and Western imperialism. Prince Dammrong, however, was more moderate. He acknowledged his indebtedness to his British tutor, George Francis Patterson, (the only foreign teacher he had) who taught him at an early age.

When Chulalongkorn succeeded his father to the throne in 1868, he was only fifteen years old. At first the king was powerless since power was in the hands of the Regent and the old nobility, so the young princes and members of the younger generation among the nobility formed themselves into a sort of political party, which slowly gathered momentum. Its members were sufficiently strong by 1873 to take the lead in urging radical reforms. They wanted to pursue their own creativity at the expense of the decadent out-dated values belonging to the older generation. They began by issuing their own newspaper *Darunowat*, which published a considerable amount of foreign news, proverbs, sciences and articles about the fine arts, fables, poetry and drama, as well as general news and much comment on, and discussion of, reforms that they felt needed to be undertaken in Siam. They formed the Young Siam Society of which Chulalongkorn's full brother, Prince Phanurangsi, was president[9]. This was the first time that Chulalongkorn's full brothers and half-brothers had a forum to test their intellectual creativity. Since they were all aware of negative foreign influences from outside and the constraints and counteractions from members of the older generation who still clung to power, their intellectual pursuit was endogenous and moderate: yet sometimes it was very challenging, especially to the powers-that-were.

Darunowat itself was published from July 1874 to June 1875 by one of the King's younger brothers, Prince Phrom. It was succeeded by the daily newspaper, *Court* (September 1875 to September 1876) published within the palace walls by eleven of the King's younger brothers, all of whom became famous in the Siamese literary world, as well as for bringing about modern administration both in the Sangha and the State. Damrong took a part, especially in the latter newspaper. Without any doubt these young princes were influenced by periodicals and books published by American missionaries. Unlike their father's generation, they were no longer interested in publishing counter attacks on Christian propaganda. Their publications were much superior, in accuracy and scholarship, to those produced by the foreigners.

Later Chulalongkorn founded the Vajirañāna Library in memory of his father who had started collecting books and archeological objects from ancient capitals like Ayudhaya and Sukhothai. His younger brothers and sisters took turns in serving as commitee members, and the Vajirañāna Library really became a national library and museum. Until then the history of Siam prior to the fourteenth century was practically unknown. It was

---

9 David K. Wyatt : *The Politics of Reform in Thailand*, Yale University Press, 1969.

due to the valuable research of a small group of enthusiasts, mostly members of the Royal Family, deciphering the annals of neighbouring states and lithographic inscriptions found in various parts of the kingdom that a multitude of facts bearing upon ancient Siam have been brought to light.

Under Prince Damrong's presidency in particular, the National Library became a storehouse for the national literature and began to foster a taste for serious reading through its periodicals, the *Vajirañāna* (monthly 1884-1885 and 1894-1905 and weekly 1886-1894). The Library exerted its influence on the educated public by becoming a most efficient instrument in the awakening of the people to a knowledge of their native land, and to that proper pride in national institutions and traditions which is the best form of genuine partriotism.

Prince Damrong started his literary ventures before the age of 13 and in the same year he served his brother as a cadet and officer in King Chulalongkorn's Bodyguard Regiment. During the decade of his work there, he spent a period away from the world for a few months as a novice at Wat Bovornives Buddhist monastery (where his father had been abbot for 14 years), for disciplinary training as a junior monk (*samanera*). There, a firm impression of Buddhist values - spiritual and temporal - could be imprinted on a young man. At the monastery, although a prince of the blood, he learnt to be more humble, as he was treated equally with the novice commoners, who must rank below a fully ordained bhikkhu, whatever his social origins. Having left the monkhood and the Grand Palace, he started his own household during his teens, and his intellectual creativity in public service started to shine early. King Chulalongkorn said much later that he had noticed that Damrong, since his boyhood days, would one day become a gem adorning the state crown. While a young officer, he started schooling for soldiers, which eventually became modern primary and secondary schools for everyone. Indeed, he became the first Director - General of the newly created Department of Education in 1887 and was promoted to be Minister of Education later on. He did not last long in this Ministry, since the King transferred him to be in charge of the Interior, where he was Minister for 23 years. He did not want to leave Education, for he felt that with education he could be part and parcel with Thai intellectual creativity, which could be healthy, good and useful. The King agreed but he argued that the nation was at stake. Had

Siam been colonized, would the new masters have allowed him to shape the future of Siamese education as he wished? The priority then was administrative reform of the entire kingdom and Chulalongkorn saw no one else who could take such a tremendous responsibility, despite the fact that Damrong was much more junior than most of his brothers. Besides the young princes there was hardly anybody who understood Thai values thoroughly and was aware of the great destructive powers coming from the West. By then the old nobility had largely lost their power base.

Damrong justified Chulalongkorn's expectations. Even while an army offcer, he organized the Royal Survey Department in 1885, so that Siam knew precisely where its boundary lay, which made it more difficult for the French and British to extend their Indo-Chinese and Malayan borders further into Thai territory. Yet they did, by hook and by crook, and took more lands from the kingdom. However, Chulalongkorn followed his father's policy, being willing to lose something, but at all costs maintaining Thai independence and dignity in the proper sense of the words.

While in charge of the Interior Ministry, Damrong managed to reform the entire system of the bureaucracy and provincial administration[10]. An eyewitness stated: "The progress towards efficiency began with the establishment of the Cabinet of Ministers. Prince Damrong's ability enabled him to outstrip easily all competitors, so that the Ministry of the Interior soon developed out of proportion to the other great Departments. Since the desire of the king for progress would not allow for delay, much work which should have been done by others devolved upon this hive of industry and enthusiasm. Indeed, at one time, the Bureau of the Interior so completely overshadowed most of the other Ministries that it appeared either to have swallowed them entirely or to be about to do so. Thus the Departments of Revenue, Police, Criminal Investigation, Forests and Mines were all definitely attached to this Ministry, while the Public Works, Land Registration and Agricultural Departments found themselves unable to function unless the Minister who controlled them received its constant support and assistance. When the necessity for fiscal reform in

---

10 Tej Bunnag : *The Provincial Administration of Siam 1892-1915*, OUP Kuala Lumpur 1977.

the provinces became most pressing, the Ministry of Agriculture was incapable of making the required effort at improvement, while the Ministry of Finance was in possession neither of the requisite knowledge of local conditions nor of the means to acquire that knowledge, and hence, after much discussion and some soul searching, His Majesty confided this very important undertaking to the Minister of the Interior. Prince Damrong at once gave his attention to the matter, and, after a considerable time spent in making inquiries and gathering information from his rural officers, started an experimental Revenue Office in one of the Circles, to work under the orders of the High Commissioner.... This Department proved a success.... The Royal Forest Department and the Department of Mines and Geology, though always in theory forming parts of the Ministry of Lands and Agriculture, were for many years attached to the Ministry of the Interior... both Departments received the earnest care of Prince Damrong."[11]

Damrong's love of education lasted all through his life. Even during his period of Rain's Retreat as a fully ordained bhikkhu at the age of 22 in a provincial monastery near the old capital of Ayudhaya, he noticed country boys could not master the Thai language properly, due to the fact that the old text had to be studied thoroughly before one could be able to read and write. This was all right for those who attended schools in Bangkok, but country boys who came to the temple schools had to spend much time in farming during the ploughing, planting and harvesting seasons. They tended to forget most of what they had already learnt when they returned to school. While a Bhikkhu at Wat Niwet monastery, Prince Damrong wanted to overcome such difficulties, so he wrote a new simplified *Siamese School Primer,* which was in use in most schools in Siam from its publication in 1884, until it was abolished by the order of the new regime against the princes in 1932. Also, when a French Catholic missionary wrote a similar textbook for his school in 1910, Damrong did not regard it as a rival but helped the author improve the manuscript. This book *Darunsuksa* is still widely used among Roman Catholic schools.

---

11 W.A. Graham : *Siam*, London 1924.

Although he was no longer Minister of Education, but because the Minister could not spread modern education to the provinces, King Chulalongkorn asked Damrong and Prince Patriach Vajirañāna, to organize provincial education through the Ministry of the Interior and through the Buddhist monkhood in 1898. This was well established by 1902. Hence, modern Thai education very much depended on the knowledge of Siamese literature and languages, and the old Buddhist temple schools were not being swept away, but were as far as possible being used as the basis of the new scheme. Here new secular knowledge was introuduced, while the old ethics and moral codes were retained. By asking monks to help the state in establishing schools throughout the provinces, Prince Patriarch Vajiranana had the idea of launching the administrative reform of the entire Sangha in 1903.

Later, when Rama VI wanted to fulfil his father's dream by establishing the first institute of higher education – Chulalongkorn University – Damrong was asked to head this project also, since the university was the next step from the School for Civil Servants, started by him at the Ministry of the Interior.

Rama VI (1910-1925) was, however, jealous of Damrong as indeed were quite a few of his brothers and contemporaries, yet he had to depend on the prince on many occasions. When the country was no longer in great danger of being colonized and the provincial administration was working quite well, the King felt that the Ministry of the Interior was too large and the Minister too powerful. In fact there was a proposal that there should be a Prime Minister to preside over the Cabinet instead of the King, who was not as active or interested in the affairs of the state as his father. Rama VI liked the idea but he was afraid that Damrong might be elected by his colleagues as the Prime Minister, so in 1915, Damrong had to retire from the Cabinet, whereupon the knife was applied and the Ministry was stripped of much of its power and prestige. However, the King asked him to continue developing the National Library (and by the next reign the National Museum as well, which eventually became the Royal Congress) to preserve Siam's traditional culture and encourage creative innovation in the arts and sciences. Many Siamese men of letter were inspired by Damrong and the institution he created to encourage would-be authors and scholars. Some of them, like Phya Anuman and Prince Dhani, imitated him excellently in their scholarship. Phya Anuman succeeded him in taking charge of the National Library in the 1940's and tried to start the National Archives and National Portrait Gallery, as Damrong wanted them established (only the National Archives had come into being). Prince Dhani was successful in making Thai museums known to the international community of scholars, and he was later elected chairman of the International Commission of Museums attached to UNESCO.

Even when Damrong undertook the burden of the Interior, wherever he went he studied and wrote books, since he was an accomplished scholar, historian and archaeologist, a quality not often found in a statesman. After his resignation from the cabinet, he devoted more time to study and research. Being interested in the Siamese cultural heritage, Damrong looked back into the past after having his full share in shaping the Siamese future, from the implementing of administrative reforms to fostering the ideas and academic institutions that guide modern intellectuals[12].

He, himself, wrote many serious books of deeper schoarship. He also created a new fashion, the production of works on historical, as well as other subjects for distribution at cremations and on birthday celebrations and so forth, for that was the only way that old manuscripts could be published without subsidy from the treasury. He usually wrote a scholarly introduction to any volume and would even write an obituary for the deceased as well as a biography of the living. Among his publications which became classics were *History of Siam: Second King of the Bangkok Dynasty* (1914); *Commentary on the History of Siam: Ayudhya Period* (1914); *The Establishment of the Siamese Buddhist Order in Ceylon* (1914); *Chinese Porcelain in Siam* (1917); *Siamese Embassies to Europe in the 15th Century* (1918); *Our Wars with Burma*, two volumes (1919); *Treatise on Siamese Drama* (1923); *History of the Administration of the Buddhist Brotherhood in Siam* (1923); *A Visit to Angkor* (1924); *A History of Buddhist Monuments in Siam* (1926); *Siamese Musical Instruments* (1928); and *Ranks of Royalty in Siam* (1929). All of these titles underwent many editions and some titles were translated into Khmer, Dutch, French, German and English. Damrong's writing relied on written

---

12 S. Sivaraksa : "Damrong" in *Samaggi Sara*, publication of Thai Students Association in U.K., 1957.

material, Thai and foreign, as well as archeological evidence and inscriptions. Furthermore he collected many oral statements from his contemporaries, especially his seniors. Oral tradition was much stronger than written statement, and had he not recorded these statements, most of them would have been lost. Also, if the manuscripts in the royal library had not been published, they might have perished as happened at the time when Ayudhya was destroyed by the Burmese in 1767[13].

Publishing activities reached a peak in quality during Damrong's presidency of the National Library. Thai books, accurately printed with the best kind of paper and bindings, were sought after by the educated elite. Siamese scholars were encouraged to do research work on Siamese, Chinese and Indian languages and culture, and foreign scholars (German, French, Brahmin, Khmer, Burmese and Chinese) were employed in the National Library. One, George Coedes, became world-famous and regarded Damrong as his foster father. Even in scholarship he would not dare to contradict Damrong unless he was doubly certain that the Prince made a slip somewhere, somehow. He and a Laotian scholar said the uniqueness of Thai intellectual creativity was due largely to the princes, especially to Damrong. No other Royal House contributed so much to the nation as the Chakkri Dynasty, and no king produced more able children than Mongkut. In his writing, Damrong tried his best to preserve his father's memory in the most appropriate way[14].

When the foreign residents wanted to study Siam and her neighbouring countries in depth and propagate their findings in lectures and publications, Damrong encouraged them. Hence, the Siam Society was founded in 1904 and its first semi-permanent home was at the National Library, under the Vice-Patronage of Prince Damrong (King Rama VI himself was Patron) and the *Journal of the Siam Society* is now fairly well known to those who are interested in Oriental Studies.

---

13 Prince Damrong Rajanubhab : *Raichu Nangsu Phranipondh,* (List of Books written by His Royal Highness), Bangkok 1962.

14 Prince Damrong Rajanubhab : *Kwam Songcham,* (Memoirs) Bangkok, 1962.

Damrong was on the whole popular among commoners and princes alike. He maintained cordial relationships with all whom he knew. He was fair and kind to them and would be helpful to anyone as far as possible. Among the foreign community, in particular, he was a favourite. He was always mentioned favourably in the foreign press at home and abroad. This sometimes annoyed Rama VI who felt that he should receive more credit and attention. The King regarded himself as a scholar, a man of letters, and an able administrator, with a much better education than his uncle, since he had been at Oxford for his further education. After all he was a king. Under one of his pen names, the King even wrote articles and a play attacking Damrong and he suspected Damrong of doing likewise against him. In fact, after his teenage days, Damrong never returned to journalism and he never replied to the King's attack.

Until the end of his reign, Rama VI never realized that Damrong remained a loyal subject all through. In the King's will, there was one paragraph mentioning Damrong as a man of deceit, without principles or religion. Had he had a son who would succeed him, and had Damrong been nominated Regent, the next King would have no territory to reign over. Luckily this will was not revealed publicly, as Rama VI had no son and his brother, Prajadhipok (1925-1935) who ascended to the throne, wished to have Damrong's services. Hence he returned to power once more, as a Supreme Counsellor of State, which was higher than a cabinet minister. He also remained President of the Royal Congress, in charge of the National Library and Museum which he had made famous in the East. In fact, he proposed that at least one commoner should serve on the committee of five Supreme Counsellors of State, but his proposal was not accepted at any time in the reign. This was one of the causes which brought an end to the "absolute" regime of the Chakkri Dynasty, which was accused of being only a clan, which controlled the whole destiny of the growing nation. The King however, wanted to grant a democratic constitution to the people in April 1932, the 150th anniversary of the dynasty, in Bangkok. However, Damrong and other princes, as well as American advisors to the royal government cautioned His Majesty that the people were not ready yet to rule themselves. Hence the government appointed senators, mainly from the ranks of experienced Civil Servants, to experiment with democracy, and tried to arrange for municipal elections at local levels to pave the way at the national level. This was thought to be too slow by the new Thai intellectual elite outside the royal power base, so they managed a successful *coup d'état* and ousted the old regime in June 1932.

On the day of the coup Damrong was arrestsed, together with other senior princes, to bargain with the King, so that the promoters of the *coup* could get what they wanted from Prajadhipok. Unless he granted them amnesty and a democratic constitution, they would kill all the princes. They got what they wanted and the princes were released. A year after, there was an unsuccessful counter-coup, and Damrong was in mortal danger once more, so from then onward he went to live in self-exile in Penang for almost a decade.

This time he was really released from all obligations, and the new regime wanted to destroy what he created by replacing his Royal Congress with the new Royal Institute. The National Library and Museum were lumped together into a small Department called Fine Arts. The new Director-General, Luang Vichitvadakarn, was a pseudoscholar who was known to be an admirer of Prince Damrong, but who could change his principles overnight and who could alter historical facts, literary evidence and even religious reasoning for short-term political policy. Therefore the Fine Arts Department and the Royal Institute were developed into a Congress for National Culture, which fostered patrioism, at the most chauvinistic level. Through the Congress for National Culture, the Prime Minister, Field Marshal Pibulsonggram, ordered Thai citizens to change their national dress by enforcing that all ladies must wear hats if they wished to visit public offices, otherwise they would be fined or imprisoned. Men must wear trousers, jackets and neckties. Married couples should kiss each other before going to work. Above all, everyone must follow the leader, i.e., the Prime Minister, whose portrait was displayed at all cinemas before the films were screened, and everyone had to stand up to salute it. "Siam", too, became "Thailand", the reason being given that "Thai" meant free, yet it was combined with an English word "land"[15]. It was this same

---

15 Thamsook Numnonda : *Thailand and Japanese Presence* 1941-45, Institute of Southeast Asia Studies, Singapore 1978.

man, Pibulsonggram, who announced that he would order his soldiers to shoot Damrong if the prince entered Thai teritory!

Damrong did not mention any grievances or bitterness. He was calm and patient as he was during the reign of Rama VI. He forgave and tried to forget those who made life difficult for him, for he believed in the Buddhist law of Karma, that by good deeds alone could evil thoughts, speeches and actions be overcome. When Pibulsonggram's predecessor, Colonel Phya Phahon, who was the military leader of the 1932 coup, asked for his forgiveness to join the holy brotherhood temporarily, as is customary in Siam, he not only forgave him but sent his eldest daughter to present a set of robes to the newly-ordained bhikkhu.

While in Penang, Damrong wrote quite a number of books and much correspondence, (but not a word did he mention of politics) which were eventually published. Quite a number of them were even better than those he had written while he was President of the National Library. He was by then in his seventies, and was more mature and detached, yet his mental ability had not declined. He had more time to check his sources, although it was more difficult to get books from Bangkok. However, Phya Anuman, in the National Library, who had to bend with the wind of the new regime somewhat, managed to supply books to the Prince, and tried to implement his policy and ideas at a lower level. In fact it was Phya Anuman who tried hard and successfully to make the Prime Minister realize the importance of Prince Damrong culturally, and that he was now harmless politically. Besides, one of Damrong's sons, who worked in the army also won Pibul's confidence. Hence Damrong was allowed to return to Bangkok during the last year of his life, only to see that Bangkok was flooded and bombed and was full of Japanese soldiers.

He and his brothers worked hard, with honesty and dignity, to preserve Siam from British and French imperialism. They built up the idea of a nation-state by centralizing provincial administration and awakening the people to a knowledge of their native land, making them proud of their native land, making them proud of their national institutions and traditions. He lived long enough to see the new masters of the nation, the commoners of his own race who were corrupt and hypocritical, and who were satisfied with shallow and cheap patriotism. They let the country be occupied by foreign troops but proudly proclaimed that they managed to maintain independence and integrity. What then was endogenous Thai identity? The new dress, the new name of the country, like Singapore becoming Shonun, and the blind following of the dictator? Damrong must have asked all these questions quietly. However, he never mentioned a word about the territory lost to France and Britain during his brother's reign, territory which was returned to Thailand by Japan during the war. He must have realized that it was a show or mockery to history and reality.

Of the new leaders of the nation, he had trust in Pridi Pbanomyong, the civilian leader and brain of the 1932 coup, who was then Regent. When Pridi called on him, the young regent was surprised by the intellectual alertness of the octogenarian prince, who asked him to take care of the country, as he had done.

Pridi was very concerned with the then Japanese occupation and was working hard for the future independence of Siam[16]. Through his Free Thai movement, he managed to preserve Siam's independence, through non-violence and reconciliation, as Damrong had wished. He and his colleague, Khwang Abhaiwong, even changed the name of the country back to Siam and allowed the Thai to lead their lives normally and dress as they felt. If they wished to chew betel nut, they could do so. When he became Prime Minister, he was responsible for the erection of the Prince Damrong Library in the compound of the National Library, as a fitting monument of a great man. Yet Pridi, too, failed to steer Siam and its endogenous intellectual creativity forward, when Pibul once again returned to power through yet another successful coup in 1947, after having been accused of being a war criminal. After the re-establishment of the military dictatorship, with only a short civilian democratic interval, Siam again became Thailand and went from bad to worse. People in responsible positions were no longer like Prince Damrong; they were not respected, since they had no strong principles or indigenous creativity. Even institutions created by Damrong like the National Library and the National Museum became dead objects. Attempts were made to create and re-create institutions in the field of Thai national identity and ideology to replace those created by Damrong, but they all failed. After Pibul's return to power in 1947, he enlarged

---

16 Direck Jayanama : *Siam and World War II*, Bangkok 1977.

the Congress for National Culture to be a Ministry of Culture, with his wife as a Minister, with cultural attachés in most embassies abroad, and cultural officers in all the provinces. However, when Field Marshal Sarit Dhannarat ousted Pibul in 1957 he abolished all Pibul's cultural activities and replaced them with the National Research Council, which was supposed to provide the nation with all the answers to the socio-cultural and scientific development problems.

As far as the present state of endogenous Thai intellectual creativity is concerned, one can sum it up in the following lines, taken from William Butler-Yeats:

"Things fall apart, the centre cannot hold

Mere anarchy loosed upon the world,

The blood dimmed tide is loosed and everywhere

The ceremony of innocence is drowned

The best lose all conviction, while the worst

Are full of passionate intensity."

IV

We may perhaps ask three practical questions:

(a) With such excellent men like Damrong, and his contemporaries, developing the country's endogenous Thai intellectual creativity, together with a solid foundation from his father's generation, for almost one century, how has it come about that now "things fall apart" to such a degree that "the centre cannot hold?"

(b) What were Damrong's own short-comings that directly or indirectly produced the present state of affairs?

(c) Would his threefold characteristics of the Thai identity still be applicable to present day Thailand ?

To answer the first question, one must resort to the Buddha's teaching on the Law of Change. He said nothing is permanent. A nation or a culture is just like a man. It could be better. It could be worse. It all depends on its cause and conditions. A wise man, well versed in Buddhist wisdom, is bound to have less greed, hatred and delusion, and would understand his society better and more realistically. He would be proud of his identity but not boastful. Such a good man tends to evolve a system more beneficial to mankind than to himself. However, there can be no guarantee that any society is bound to be run by good men all the time, however much one tries. Even the best system will decay one day, and will in the end disintegrate and perish. This is not a pessimistic view of life and society, especially to those of us who see no immediate future for the Thai development model apart from the selfish materialistic aggressiveness which prevails at present. We should not feel sad or give up things to fate. One should understand that Mongkut, Chulalongkorn and Damrong helped indigenous Thai culture, personally and institutionally, but soon afterwards, especially from the time when Thai students began to go abroad, the new value systems came into conflict with the older ones. The more prestige given to foreign education, the more admiration given to material comfort and Western technology, the more did endogenous Thai values have to give way. Buddhism became a form of words and ceremony without deep penetration. The present state of Thai Buddhism is very much similar to that prior to Mongkut's reform, if not worse because the current degree of materialistic capitalism will intensify the decline of any spiritual tradition. Having understood this fact, those who believe in spiritual values should not "lack all conviction:". At the same time, they shoud check themselves when they "are full of passionate intensity" for their country and people. In other words they should use the Buddha's advice to cultivate self-awareness, to be mindful towards selflessness and towards serving others, by building moral courage to face the unjust system. With more such men who are proud of themselves, and of their cultural heritage, but are at the same time humble and not too passionately attached to things, a new socio-cultural development alternative in self-reliance can be created.

Regarding Damrong's shortcomings, one must see them in the light of his father. Unlike Chulalongkorn who exerted his influence and power as far and as wide as possible, both Mongkut and Damrong limited their roles to the powers that were. Although Mongkut was king, he was elected by the nobility, who exercised their powers behind the throne all through the reign and until the early part of Chulalongkorn's reign. Mongkut never struggled against that power: either he felt too old or too powerless, or perhaps he hoped to build up a new generation with moral courage by his wisdom and inspiration.

Since Damrong was not king, he regarded himself as a mere servant of the King, a mandarin, who would serve the King at his pleasure. He should have known that the Crown Prince simply could not exercise such autocratic power as justly and ably as his father. Yet, there was nothing to suggest to Chulalongkorn that he should evolve a new system of endogenous Thai culture for the future well-being of the country, apart from relying entirely on the ability and goodness of the King. In the reign of Prajadhipok, this question was asked as soon as he succeeded Rama VI, but there was no definite answer until it was too late[17]. Damrong was occupied with administrative work and writing, all of which was important, yet he ignored the most important issue of the future of Siam; the role of the monarchy and the new system of government in a changing world. Hence the commoners, the promoters of the 1932 coup, borrowed a Western concept of constitutional monarchy to provide the answer for Siam. Since this new elite knew little of endogenous Thai culture, their answer has never fitted in with the Thai political system. Every regime which has run the country since 1932 claimed to be geared to constitutional monarchy. In fact it was not so, nor could they understand a constitutional concept so alienated from their own national identity. Even now, nobody on the national level thinks openly about the future of Siam, the role of the monarchy, or the alternative development models for Thai politics and economics except, perhaps, those who operate in the "liberated zone" of the country. Even so, their model seems to be too much of a Marxian blueprint on the propaganda line to be taken seriously at its face value at present.

As to Damrong's threefold characteristics of the Thai identity, namely that the Thai as a rule love freedom, non-violence and are able to bring out usefulness from any conflicting systems of value, one must restate his dictum. At a time when violence is so prevalent either from foreign aggressors or through oppression from within, the Thai do use violence. When Siam lost her independence, the Thai went to war against the enemy to regain their independence. The present Thai generation were fooled, or

---

17 B. Batson (ed): *Siam's Political Future: Documents From the End of the Absolute Monarchy,* (Cornell Data Paper No. 96) 1974.

fooled themselves, into believing that during the Second World War their country was not occupied by Japan. History repeated itself again during the Vietnam War with all the GI's and American air bases within the country. Nor do many realize the enemy in the present economic system, with multinational firms and great capitalistic countries in control of the destiny of smaller nations and peoples.

With such a realization, if non-violence fails to combat the enemy, then violence has to be resorted to. The shortcoming of violence is that it creates more violence. However, if economic and political independence could be achieved, even through violence, it has to be done. Otherwise, the nation will remain divided, with internal rivalries, which undoubtedly will lead to more violence, more greed, hatred and delusion at the expense of everyone, while those in control of the country's destiny care only for increasing their power and their wealth by being willing to serve the multinational corporations, without any real concern for the public welfare. Once freedom is achieved at the national level, it could be cultivated on a personal level and non-violence would be the order of the day. People could then work for truth, beauty and goodness. Once the Thai have such a sense of endogenous intellectual creativity, they would be able to reconcile and compromise with any stream of culture or civilization. Otherwise, reconciliation and compromise mean losing the more essential part of our identity, by gaining more materially, with its resultant superficiality and mediocrity.

Symposium on *Intellectual Creativity in Endogenous Culture*, Kyoto, Japan. November 1978.

DIRECK JAYANAMA

We regret to record that on the first of May H.E. Nai Direck Jayanama passed away at the age of 62. His Excellency served on an Advisory Board of the Buddhist Association for many years, and he was a regular contributor to Visakha Puja. He was also an advisor to the World Fellowship of Buddhists News Bulletin. At the 5th WFB conference in Bangkok, he took a leading role and was to represent Siam again at the last conference held in Chiengmai but ill health prevented him from participating.

Direck Jayanama was born on 18th January 1905, being the eldest son of Phya Upaipipaksa, a leading judge of the Supreme Court. Nai Direck himself was called to the Bar in 1928 and joined the Ministry of Justice. After the 1932 *coup d'état*, he served in many government posts : clerk to the Cabinet, Deputy Foreign Minister, Foreign Minister (three times), Minister of Finance, and Deputy Prime Minister. As a diplomat, he was appointed Ambassador to Japan, the Court of St James's, the Federal Republic of Germany, and Finland. In the academic field, he was the first Dean of the Faculty of Political Science at Thamasart University, where he received his honorary doctorate. He also held the chair of Diplomacy at that university.

Direck Jayanama was a devout Buddhist. In his public lectures, his books, and indeed his life, one can notice the influence of the Buddha's teaching all through. He was always a gentleman, generous and honest. He was kind to all and bore no ill will against anyone.

Whichever position he held, he always found time to help his fellow human being. And if he could assist in any way to promote the better understanding of the Buddha Dhamma, he would do so. He was perhaps the only Siamese Ambassador who was elected Vice-President of the London Buddhist Society. During his tour in Japan, he tried hard and successfully to bring the two Schools of Buddhism into closer contact. And while serving his last post in Bonn, he travelled far and wide to propagate Dhamma to the German people. His observations of Buddhist activities abroad were always reported to his fellow countrymen at home through his speeches and writings, for which he was well known.

Although his understanding of the Dhamma was not deep, he practised what he knew and what he preached. During his last illness, he submitted himself entirely to the Triple Gem and meditated regularly. As he did wrong to no one, did a lot of good to his country and people, and always tried to purify his heart, he could indeed be called a true son of the Buddhasasana. May he one day reach the other shore.

Visakha Puja 1972.

PREECHA ARJUNKA

Preecha Arjunka is a professional artist with his own special métier. He is not a salaried official, nor a part-time painter, nor a person who works according to the specifications of others. He has over the years developed his distinctive style. He does not follow the latest fashion or the fads of the marketplace or what may be momentarily au courant. On the contrary, his work is consistently exciting to the eye–and ultimately to the spirit.

I consider myself lucky to have known Khun Preecha and his work for more than two decades. Our two families have also been close during this period. His wife, Khun Phimphot, is the grand daughter of Maha Suk Suphasiri, my own teacher at Assumption College, and as a textile designer she is an artist in her own right. They have a deep understanding of each other's work, resting upon their many years of personal and artistic sharing. They have also shared their joys and misfortunes with me.

I have known Preecha and Phimphot since the time I published the *Social Science Review,* and later I had the opportunity to encounter them and their work in the United States. And I followed the progress of their creativity in this country after their return home when I saw the excellence of Preecha's work in the exhibition and permanent collection of the Bank of Thailand and other important institutions. I was fortunate to have some of his work in both my home and office to enrich my own life. Phimphot too has enriched my family with frequent gifts of her designs. We feel specially lucky because these were gifts usually reserved for people like Dr. Puey Ungphakorn and other important former students of her grand father.

The Sathirakoses-Nagapradipa Foundation was extremely pleased to have the opportunity to sponsor the work of Preecha and other artists whom he led in an exhibit to the People's Republic of

China four years ago. In turn, the Foundation was enriched by the gifts of Chinese paintings which Preecha brought back from the People's Republic.

In providing the present exhibit, the Silpa Birasri Institute of Modern Art is marking the auspicious occasion of Preecha's reaching a half-century of life. It is for the pleasure not only of Preecha and his family but for all of us who have been interested in his work during the past several decades.

This exhibit is a demonstration of the aesthetics of modern art, not of its monetary nature. It displays the depth of his expressiveness and creativity. It is a cross-section of his life. We who see and admire it will be stamped by its impact.

On this special occasion, I invite the public to wish Preecha and his family progress, strength, and longevity in his artistic endeavors and in his many other activities.

First printed in UNTITLED 86, An Exhibition of Recent Painting by PREECHA ARJUNKA at Birasri Institute of Modern Art 18th October - 9th November 1986.

THOMAS MERTON

Thomas Merton was perhaps the most well known Catholic monk of this century. During his "lay" life, he underlook varied literary and intellectual pursuits. He was more or less "converted" to seek a deeper spiritual meaning of life by becoming a Trappist monk. Yet he managed to maintain a lively interest in worldly events. He kept in touch with political issues, commented on them, signed various petitions and protests, apart from writing prefaces, articles and books, some of which are very popular among the younger generation, especially *Conjectures of a Guilty Bystander* and *The Seven Story Mountain*.

Someone asked Krishnamurti whether he regarded anyone in the contemporary world as having attained enlightenment. He mentioned Thomas Merton and Daisetz T.Suzuki. In fact, Merton had corresponded with Suzuki for years and they met when the latter visited America. Their correspondence has in fact been published in *Zen and the Birds of Appetite*. Although Merton did not know Chinese, *The Way of Chuang Tsu* and his correspondence with Suzuki as well as his article on *"The Significance of the Bhagavad-Gita"* show that he was one of the few Westerners who really understood the spiritual depth of the East. Yet he had never been to Asia until he undertook the Asian journey, which began from California on 15 October and ended by his passing away in Bangkok on 10 December 1968. On this journey he told an Indian Catholic priest that Zen Buddhism was the last of God's revelations. Indeed there was rumour that he was going to become a Buddhist monk. His biography, *The Man in the Sycamore Tree* by Edward Rice, also mentions the conflict he had with his abbey at Gethsemane, Kentucky, U.S.A. There were also rumours that the electrocution at Sawanganiwas near Bangkok was actually a suicide, as he could no longer stand the tragedy of mankind.

In a way, *The Asian Journal* was edited to show that Merton would however, remain a Christian monk, and go back to spend his last days at his "home" monastery and that his death was entirely accidental. Besides, *The Asian Journal* is a superb document, relying on three separate note books : (a) the public journal, which the author intended for publication, (b) the private journal, which contains an occasional intimate note of conscience or spiritual self-analysis, and (c) the pocket notebook for his immediate notes during conversations, drafts for suddenly-inspired poems, etc, All of these blend into Part I of the book, which took the author to Calcutta (via Bangkok), New Delhi, the Himalayas, Madras, Ceylon and back to Bangkok (via Singapore). His encounters with the Dalai Lama and Tibetan gurus are wonderful pieces of spiritual insight, since these people were all on "the fringe of enlightenment", and their conversations were so simple and straight-forward.

In Bangkok, he met the abbot of Wat Bovornives and Bhikkhu Khantipalo, who also wrote, in Appendix II, 'On Mindfulness'. He had a chance to read and make notes of the Ven. Phra Maha Boowa Nanasampanno's *'Wisdom Developed Samadhi'* (which has now been collected and published with other articles of his by the Sathirakoses - Nagapradipa Foundation as *Forest Dhamma*). His talk at Suwanganiwas on the day of his death, *Marxism and Monastic Perspectives'* in Appendix VII, is also very relevant to our Buddhist brotherhood. There are a few spelling mistakes of Thai names, which are inevitable, since his hand writing was not easy to decipher, and the editors did not know much about this country. Yet they did their job thoroughly, supplying notes on almost everything he wrote.

Part II consisting of Merton's Complementary Reading helps us to understand the man much better, especially towards the last phase of his life. The books he read mostly came from the contemplative tradition of Buddhism, Christianity, Hinduism and Islam. Whatever name one gives to the Real and whatever path one treads upon, they seem one and all to lead to the same goal.

It is a great loss to us that Merton's life came to such an abrupt end, for it would have been of great interest to the spiritual and the learned to have been able to follow his further spiritual explorations.

Thomas Merton, the monk, E.F. Schumacher, the economist, and Eric Fromm, the psychologist, are a few leading personalities from the West who have tried, in their own disciplines, to show that Buddhism has something really unique to offer the modern world, if man wants to survive on this planet earth. Those of us who are familiar with Buddhism in this country may need the *farang* to convince us before we take our own religion seriously, especially when the contemplative part of our culture is very much lacking in this day and age. If we do, we should also learn other spiritual traditions thoroughly, as Merton has shown us in the *The Asian Journal*: i.e. books help, but books alone cannot help us all that much.

ALEXANDRA DAVID - NEIL

Alexandra David-Neil may be considered to be the first Western woman to have studied the Tibetan Vajarayana School of Buddhism and popularised it in the West. Before her there were other Westerners who knew something of Tantric Buddhism and who also probably knew the Tibetan language better than her. However they were of a small circle of Western academics who specialised in Tibetan religion and who viewed it as a confused mix of spirit worship and Tantric sexual ritual.

When Mrs. David-Neil died at the age of 101, Tibet had already been occupied by China for over a decade. With Tibet under occupation, accurate knowledge of the country was very limited and writings concerning Tibet could only reach the outside world in small quantities. However, gradually such works have been forth-coming from a wide range of viewpoints, and with increased quality. Mrs. David-Neil can be regarded as one of the most clear-headed writers on Tibet, and additionally, she wrote from a standpoint which is of great value both to Buddhist scholars as well as to social scientists. Her idiomatic style of writing is found to be easily readable for those who are interested in Tibetan religion in the West. For these reasons her books have become very popular for English and French readers throughout Europe and America. Up to today many of her books, some of which are 50 or 60 years old, are still being reprinted. It is a shame, however, that her works are as yet unavailable in Thai translation.

Alexandra David-Neil was born in October 1868. Her father was French, and held strong Republican views. He hated the institutions of the Monarchy and Religion. Her mother however was a devout Christian. They attempted to bring her up to see things as they did, but she showed her rebellious character at an early age and ran away from them. She later studied Sanskrit and Tibetan in Europe, and then travelled to India, inspired by

Mahatma Gandhi's peaceful liberation movement.

It is not known whether it was the impact the East had on Alexandra David-Neil which made her change her ideas when she arrived, or whether other factors were involved, but she gradually lost her interest in Brahminism and eventually sought her refuge in the Buddha. She went to Sri Lanka and India to study Theravada Buddhism at a number of universities, and made comparative studies of Buddhism with other religions.

The first time the young Miss David came to Asia, she did not travel as the other Westerners of the day did. She stayed with holy men, travelled with wandering ascetics and she refused to carry herself as the Westerners did, which was to assume a superiority to the native people.

When she returned to Europe she began teaching at Pritzel University in Belgium and got married to Phillip Neil. However she was unhappy with her married life. Her husband was very traditional in outlook and did not understand her ideas and learning at all. He was also more than 23 years older than Alexandra. As a wife, Alexandra did not enjoy looking after a home and dressing in the fashions of the day, as was expected of her, and so she left Europe for Asia once again in 1910. This was the most important step in her life.

The French Ministry of Public Instruction sent her abroad to study in India where she studied under the 13th Dalai Lama (who preceded the 14th Dalai Lama of today). He had fled his country after the Chinese occupation and had made camp in the Himalayas, along the British frontier (at the Indian border). The Dalai Lama invited her to visit Lhasa, which at that time was a closed city. It had remained so as both the British (for political reason) and the Tibetans (for religious reason) wanted to prevent easy passage across the border.

Alexandra David-Neil tried many times, but without success to cross the border into Tibet, both from the Indian side and the Chinese side. John Blofeld met bell boys at a hotel where she stayed in Peking who thought her strange because she would not sleep on her bed at night, but would sleep on the floor. They did not of course realize that she was devoutly observing the Eight precepts of Buddhist principles she followed.

In those days travellers going to Tibet would have to take a caravan of horses, mules and donkeys to carry the food supplies, clothing, medicines and so on. They would have to arm themselves to prepare against attacks by highwaymen. It would take over a year to reach Lhasa travelling in this way. The travellers would camp on the outskirts of towns to avoid the possibility of arrest or detention inside the town. They could be told to turn around and return unless they were on an official trip or were, for example, part of a group led by Younghusbands, a British soldier who turned towards the spiritual path after having been to Tibet, and who had permission to travel inside Tibet.

Despite these official restraints Mrs. David-Neil managed to get into Tibet by disguising herself as a monk. She disguised herself as a man first in India in order to go to the places where women were forbidden to go. Inside Tibet she disguised herself as a nun. She adopted a Tibetan child who had been ordained as a novice, and they travelled together. They had two attendants to take care of the supplies and their belongings, but spent most of the time travelling on foot as the terrain was unsuitable to use mules and donkeys.

It was not long before she returned to Europe. She spent little time there and she went back once more to Tibet via the Trans-Siberian Railway, from Russia to Peking, and then on to Japan. She travelled to temples set in the holy mountains of China, where the religion and customs of Tibet and Mongolia were still being upheld. She then returned to Europe at the outbreak of the Second World War.

It has been said that Mrs. David-Neil held many secrets for producing magic powers although she herself never openly revealed this ability, nor did she make any mention of them in her writings. Some Westerners have claimed that she once made a flower disappear simply by pronouncing a magic formula. It has also been claimed that after her adopted child died, she used her spiritual powers to maintain contact with him. She lived over a hundred years and still she was able to read without the aid of spectacles. She also had the abilities of a healer and was able to take away pain and suffering from those who came to see her.

Some of her better works in English include *Journey to Lhasa, With Mystics and Magicians in Tibet* and *Initiations in Tibet*. Some of her books have been translated and are available in many Western languages, but unfortunately not in Thai.

The religious and moral standards of the Tibetans are of

great importance. If we are able to reach a full appreciation of them, they will help us to realise the importance of our own traditional beliefs which had existed before we accepted the religion from Sri Lanka. Many of the beliefs and practices of the ancient religion of Tibet are surprisingly similar to some of the findings the Western scientists are coming across today. This is all explained in the introduction to one of Alexandra David-Neil's most important books, which was written by the Head of the French Royal Academy to verify her work.

We might well question when China will ever really understand the Dhamma of the Buddha and the importance of the traditions of Tibet. If this is ever to come about it might stop the destruction of the Tibetan people's customary way of life. Perhaps, however, this is too much to ask of the Communist Party leadership.

Mrs. David-Neil's work has caused many academics to err in claiming that she is a fraud. They write of her reference to certain magic formulas, for example, and to holy men walking on air. But there are others who say that she was always accurate in her writing and wrote only the facts. This reminds me of King Rama Kamhaeng's inscription, which some scholars claimed to be a fake. Therefore, I invited a group of language experts both from the West and from Siam to my home for discussion. Amongst these was Professor William Gedney who maintained that the inscription was genuine. And another Western scholar, at a meeting on the state of Thai Studies in Canberra, made a proposal which goes against some of the Thai academics who have erred in the past. This proposal will be published in the *Journal of the Siam Society* 1989.

Going back to the subject of Tibet, There have been some very interesting accounts on the country written by Westerners who know little of the religion but who have much experience of the country. Heinrich Harrer, an Austrian who took refuge in Tibet from India during the Second World War was one such writer. Whilst in refuge he wrote *Seven Years in Tibet*, a very readable book which also goes through the work of Alexandra David-Neil. It is a valuable work as he was able to stay in the country until the Chinese invasion in 1959.

His recent return to Tibet has resulted in *Return to Tibet: Tibet after the Chinese Occupation,* an extremely interesting work.

In this book he shows us how the Chinese have, sadly, destroyed the cultural and religious life of the country and have attempted to brainwash the people and the various tribes. Every where you walk in the country your eyes meet with Party propaganda posters from China, which propagate political doctrine as well as the current political situation of the country.

It is at least a little comforting to know that Alexandra David-Neil did not have to experience any of this. Recently Arthur Waley was refused entry into China because his interest in the country was primarily to study the ancient poetry of the Tang Dynasty and literary treasures of Tun Huang Cave, rather than in the politics of the country as the Leadership would have wished. These Chinese politicians whose claims that development is all taking place in the name of the people are not even worth listening to. They are only cheating the poeple.

From *Living in Thailand* March, 1988.
Seeds of Peace Vol. 4 No. 3 September, 1988.

VIKAS BHAI

When we mention the name Vikas Bhai in Siam there are not apt to be many people who recognize it. But amongst Indian and other international development workers he is well known as a person who gave his all for, and stood beside the poor. Even though he used Marxist theory to understand the weak and the strong points of society and various religions, he never joined any communist party nor other political organisations. We can consider a person like him rare indeed and he was a close and wonderful friend of mine.

An old Thai saying is "When you meet an Indian and a snake at the same time, you should strike the Indian first". A person like Vikas could easily destroy this kind of prejudice since true friendship doesn't have national, religious or philosophical bias. Most important is to have a basic trust in each other and avoid any kind of back stabbing.

This moral I received from Vikas Bhai and other Indian friends such as Victor Anant, Chakrapani, Swami Agnivesh and Ramesh Gupta etc., even though not one of them is a Buddhist. It's a pleasure that these friends are still with us, though Vikas is gone, having been killed in an automobile accident on December 29, 1987.

Vikas was nearly my age, a big man with a beautiful full beard. He dressed informally, rather like poor, lower class Indian people even though he was born into the Brahmin caste. His father was a progressive man and never had the ceremony performed which would have made Vikas a true Brahmin. So we cannot say he was of high caste but neither can we say he was of low caste since his parents were Brahmins. Vikas was quite satisfied to be "casteless" as it enabled him to remain single and be able to stand on the side of marginalized people, whether they were the "Sudra" or the "Canadala". He could also present himself smartly with high class people. But he really despised the affected mannerisms of all the castes. There are some, who regard themselves as being on the same side with the poor, using the trick to take advantage in the name of grassroot people, the same as high class people who pretend to perform like so called "good people" using many tactics. Being free of a caste label, Vikas was called "Bhai" which means Brother. He was a brother who always made good suggestions and offered others his help without any thought of something in return, whether it be money or honor. International development organizations could not buy him, but could only respect him.

I first met Vikas Bhai when I started "Klet Thai" Publishing House, which was set up in 1972, then we met again to form the Asian Cultural Forum on Development in Bangkok.

We can say that he was the one who assisted this organization in following a democratic course and in keeping it from adopting any dictatorial or fraudulent methods of operation. It was he who requested me to administer the organization for 7 years. And after leaving this position he invited me to join in with the Liberation Religion and Culture program as a way of promoting freedom for people. He was worried about the possibility of politicians and business interests using religion as a tool, especially the new religion of the consumer culture, in which shopping centers become the new temples.

Vikas also pointed out the dangers of leaders of old religions who, no different from other reactionary groups, use their religious base for political control, as in the case of some Muslim leaders in Iran or in some Protestant sects in America.

We should also take notice of some groups of Sikhs and Hindus in India and Buddhists in Sri Lanka and Siam, who, in the name of "love of country" and "love of religion" forget about truth and morality, as in the case of the preacher who said that "it's not a sin to kill a communist".

All the time that I associated with Vikas I received a great deal of knowledge and encouragement from him. I would sometimes visit him at his home in Varanasi. And when I was travelling to other cities in that country, he would often come to greet me warmly.

Vikas was a vegetarian. But whenever he came to Siam he would indulge in every variety of pork, crab and fish, but never beef (showing that some of his Brahmin heritage was still deep in his character). He loved Thai food and would say that Bangkok was both the loveliest and the ugliest city. Thai women, he said, were the most beautiful and Thai fruits the most delicious. Never before had I heard all these things come out of the mouth of an Indian.

But more important was his great sense of humor and his ability to pick out the faults of anyone, including his own hero, Mahatama Gandhi. Moreover he could laugh at himself and the history of his country. Even though he was very proud of Indian culture, when he saw a problem that needed to be eliminated he would want to wipe it out completely.

I belive I'm very lucky to have had a friend like Vikas – he who was not afraid to advise or admonish me. He could accept that I liked his country even though I could never understand it as well as he. And even though Vikas could accept the truth of my belief that the Great Enlightened Buddha was India's greatest gift to the world, yet he couldn't grasp the depth of his teachings.

So now that I'm entering the last period of my life and many of my friends have passed away, I think about Vikas, that if he hadn't met with the accident he might very well have passed away after me. Who knows? At least I believe that had I died first, he would have been able to write me a farewell piece better than this short appreciation that I want to dedicate to him.

"In this remaining time we should conduct our activities to the very best of our ablity", says the Buddha.

From *Asian Action* No. 67/1988.
Seeds of Peace Vol. 4 No. 3 September, 1988.

SURENDRA CHAKRAPANI

I had an Indian Brahmin friend whose name was Surendra Chakrapani. The first time we met was at a meeting held in Penang in 1979. The meeting was organized by the Asian Cultural Forum On Development (ACFOD). He came to greet me and told me that he had heard my name before. Then we talked and made friends with each other very quickly.

He said after the meeting he would go to Bangkok. I asked him where he wished to stay. "I would like to stay with you because I like you," he replied without hesitation and so he did. After that he was elected to be an Executive member of ACFOD. So he had to come at least once or twice a year to Bangkok which is the headquarter of that organization. He always stayed with me. Even though the meeting was over, and other members had left for their respective countries, he often extended his stay and went up country to explore and learn about Thai people's life. This made him aware of Thai culture in various aspects, unlike other foreigners who visit Siam. Consequently my family and most of my colleagues are familiar with him— my wife, children as well as my secretary and even my servants with whom he also made friends.

When I went to India, I could not stay there long as he did in Siam, and I did not stay at his home. However, I sent some of my Thai and British friends to lodge at his house. If I went to New Delhi, he would bring me to have meals cooked by his wife. Likewise he took care of me very well. Or when I went to other cities far away from New Delhi, if possible he would try to meet me. Moreover he would always organize a conference inviting his friends and members of ACFOD who are development workers to discuss ACFOD work while I was Coordinator of that organization. When I resigned from Coordinatorship, it was only him who really understood me and tried to protect my reputation especially when false rumours were spread against me by some ACFOD members.

I have many Indian friends but Surendra Chakrapani was the one who was most concerned about me.

What I was able to learn about Brahmin culture and civilization – besides what I gained through reading and my direct experiences with it– came from him. He used to tell me "Do you know that our God always reincarnates in the Kshatriya caste, for example, Rama, Krishna and Lord Buddha? This is because we Brahmins want to please them, but, in fact, the power behind the throne is always in our hands."

Chakrapani added that sending Thai people to study in western countries is very expensive and makes people admire only westerners, besides being very extravagant which will make those people look down upon their own culture. Some people even don't want to go back to their own country. But by sending Thai people to study in India, they can learn either western or ancient Indian civilization. Furthermore they will learn to economize as well as to be honest and certainly they will return to their country.

His idea is quite good, although the qualifications of those who graduated from India are unfortunately insufficient. In addition he told me, "Don't follow the western culture in connection with permitting your children to select their own partners; it should be parents who select suitable persons for them". He used himself as an example of one whose parents selected a wife for him. This was good, and since then his wife and himself lived happily.

For this suggestion, I could only tell him that our Thai culture is now so far beyond his that we cannot follow that tradition. Even my father selected his wife by himself and so did I. If we were to select partners for our children, surely they would not agree with us, although there are many good things in the old tradition itself.

When I was in gaol, he came to see me and wept! On his return to India, he campaigned with his compatriots to set me free.

When my mother died, Chakrapani held a Brahmin ceremony in New Delhi for her. He took her ashes to scatter under the Sri Maha Bodhi tree at Buddha Gaya, of which I was very grateful.

Although he was a Brahmin, he also respected our Lord Buddha, especially his teachings in relation with self reliance, using wisdom to solve any problem. He prefered respecting the teaching of the Buddha rather than sticking to the myth that he was an incarnation of Lord Vishnu as mentioned in the Brahmin scripture.

The last piece of the work he volunteered to help me with was to hold an exhibition on the Life and Work of Phya Anuman Rajadhon which would be presented at the Gandhi Peace Foundation and the Jawaharal Nehru University. Phra Maha Viro from All India Radio would also help in this venture. But on an unfortunate day there was an overseas call from New Delhi informing us that Chakrapani had suddenly passed away.

The death was perhaps the real happiness for him to leave peacefully from the present world. However, as his friends, we feel difficult to accept that he died so soon and suddenly. He dedicated himself to work with grassroots people especially in Himachal Pradesh – such kind of work has still to be carried on under the guidance of a person like him. Now his wife and children have lost the head of the family which left them in disarray.

In the circle of ACFOD, there may be only a few people who understand him. On the international level, maybe not many realise this loss. But those Indian friends who worked with him during these past three decades will understand his valuable dedication and feel the loss of such a man as Surendra Chakrapani.

For me, it means that I have lost an important good friend for whom I will not find a replacement. When I look back to our friendship over the past decade, we have had love, respect and understanding for each other. Such things are quite difficult to establish, even with the people in one's own nation who speak the same language.

Edited from *Asian Action* No. 69/1988.
Seeds of Peace Vol. 5 No. 1 January, 1989.

SHIGEHARU MATSUMOTO

Only a few Thais know Shigeharu Matsumoto by name. Nonetheless, he was a great man quite well known in Japan, U.S.A. and other countries which are involved in a deeper relationship with Japan. However the Thai elite who have connections with the International House of Japan know that he was the founder and director of the House, up until he passed away recently on Jan 10, 1989.

The International House of Japan was established after World War II with the intention of opening Japan to the world outside and thereby softening her nationalism. The idea was to expose Japanese to the international community and at the same time to give the international community a chance to understand different aspects of Japanese culture. Hopefully this would provide a base for international mutual understanding. Though millionaires like Rockefeller and other leading Americans in diplomatic, business and academic circles contributed a lot to the establishment of the House, without Mr. Matsumoto the institute would have failed to develop such a fine reputation. Nor would it have become a leading place for cultural affairs in Japan, expanding its vision to include other Asian countries through, for example, the intellectual exchange program with South East Asia. Through this venture, many leading Japanese have come to know the people of South East Asia and Siam in particular. Many of the Thai who have been invited are such respected persons as Puay Ungphakorn, Somsak Xuto, Kumsing Srinawk, Kusuma Sanitwongsa and Kanchai Bunpan.

The International House of Japan provides accomodation and a good library for members and others who are interested in the deeper aspects of Japanese culture, though they may not know the Japanese language. It is located in the middle of Tokyo, having a beautiful Japanese garden and good services comparable to any first class hotel, but the rates are more reasonable and the atmosphere more friendly.

Furthermore, the house also arranges academic seminars as they did on the occasion of the 100th anniversary of Thai-Japanese diplomatic relations. In addition to providing academic events, it sponsors exposure trips and many other projects such as the Pacific Youth Forum, which aims at creating friendship among the youth of the Pacific rim, believing that they will be the future leaders in academic, business and political spheres.

We should not forget that the house has become a firmly established institute which has, in turn, helped stimulate the founding of various Japanese philanthropic foundations. Non-government organizations have started to work for peace though they still need the support of the government and big business corporations.

Without a person like Mr. Matsumoto, it would have been extremely difficult for these creative forces to crystalize. From the beginning he was determined to create a new generation among the leaders in business, journalism, diplomatic missions, and academia. He has always had disciples and close admirers in these fields; Mr. Saburo Okita, the former minister of Foreign Affairs and one of the most respected economic advisers of almost every administration is an example. Indeed, some of those who worked with him at the House have become prominent outside their own circle, such as Mr. Meada and Mr. Tsurumi. The former is very well known in France and the latter, among the progressive youth within Japan and South East Asia.

Mr. Matsumoto devoted himself solely to the House without any outside distractions.

He grew up in a family of good lineage. He pursued his studies in the US and Germany as was common for a small elite class of Japanese during the years before and after World War I. When he returned, he took up journalism and became so well respected and influential that he was offered a position as bureau chief in China, where he became acquainted with Chou Enlai.

Mr. Matsumoto had famous friends in literature, such as the Nobel Prize winner, Yasunar Kawabata. Others were prime ministers and leading priests. He himself belonged to Shingon Buddhism, and once took Arnold Toynbee to Koyasan, the holy mountain of this sect.

Accepting the responsibility of running the International House was a personal sacrifice for him, forcing him to reject the ambassadorship that was offered to him. He never lost sight of the importance of creating mutual understanding with other countries. Understanding begets friendship and peace; he did not want to see any more war.

Mr. Matsumoto always humbly said that he was just an ordinary inn keeper. But in fact he was a small emperor in the international circles of Japan. The Tokyo Metropolitan council bestowed on him the the title of "honorable citizen" when he was 88. The Asahi Shimbun published a book written by people all over the world who knew him. His writings in Japanese have been translated into many languages. In any history of Japan after the Second World War, his name will, without a doubt, be mentioned as the creator of mutual friendship between Japan and the international community.

Mr. Matsumoto's wife was actually his cousin. Before and after the First World War, her family had accommodated a few Thai students who came to study in Japan. It was said that a Thai prince was interested in her; this report caused the uneasy Mr. Matsumoto to hurry back from Germany to marry her. The couple lived together peacefully until old age, though his wife passed away many years before him.

This couple were especially well acquainted with Siam. Although, in his elderly years he rarely received guests of the younger generation, he always had time for old friends. He never failed to ask about Dr. Puey Ungphakorn with great concern whenever he met me, He used to say that every country has its share of politicians, businessmen, and writers, etc., but that in each phase of history in any one country, there are never more than 5 persons who are the pillars of the nation, regardless of their position. He regarded Dr. Puey as one of the five of Siam.

When Mr. Matsumoto died, I was in Delhi at the International Center of India. Few people know that Mrs Matsumoto played an important role in establishing that center and making it nearly as lively as the International House of Japan.

Mr. Matsumoto once told me that if we did not mind, he would like to help us establish an International House of Siam. It is a pity that this idea had not yet been implemented before his passing away, though an attempt has been started in that direction. However, what Mr. Matsumoto had done in Japan and the relationship the House has developed with the international community, especially with Siam and other countries in Asia, will help us know the positive side of Japan and make a way for equal friendship and peace in the future.

It would please Mr. Matsumoto if somehow he is able to see the gradual realization of this dream and its potential for the future. May he rest in Peace.

The original Thai version was first Published in *Matichon* Daily 2 February 1989. The English and Japanese translation was published by the International House of Japan as a commemorative volume of its Founder 1989.

III
BACKGROUND TO UNDERSTANDING THAI POLITICS

THE PRIVILEGED ELITE VERSUS THE COMMON MAN

Thai society has always been divided into two groups: the Privileged Elite and the Common Man. The former are not necessarily members of the royalty or noblemen, though many of course are. The Privileged Elite may be further subdivided into classes whose privileges are determined by their respective levels. If a man has a large car with a special emblem attached to the front, or has a soldier as his driver, he can turn left or right contrary to a traffic policeman's orders. Furthermore, if the policeman has any flair he will show his respect by saluting the car and its occupant, further impressing the privileged man with his own power and reinforcing his faith in the propriety and cleverness of his subordinates. If a man belongs to a somewhat lower class and has to drive his own car, but has epaulettes on his sleeve or at least leaves a military hat placed strategically on the back shelf of his car, he may also break traffic regulations at will.

The Common Man has to take the bus to work. While he is hanging out the doorway, the ticket collector feels free to shout at him unceasingly, for the collector knows full well that no Privileged Man would ever be traveling by bus. When the Common Man wants to cross the street as a pedestrian, he must often do so at a crosswalk where all the paint has long since faded away. But he must never criticize this as the fault of government authorities, nor blame the administration for the plethora of potholed roads all over the city. Flooded roads are also supposed to be graciously accepted as small inconveniences which the Common Man must learn to tolerate. Even though a Common Man may have enough money to take a taxi to work, how the taxi driver acts toward his passenger — over whom for the moment he has power — is informative. The Common Men who drive their own cars to work (without benefit of military identification) encounter the power of traffic policemen, who consider themselves Privileged Men when facing a Common Man. They can issue a summons, a fine or a scolding – whatever they like – and if the Common Man has the audacity to bring the matter to the attention of a senior police official, the official without exception supports his bureaucratic subordinate. How many people dare go to the police station to file a complaint? Is there a single Thai citizen who likes or respects the police? We only "like" a particular policeman who can reverse a decision or exert influence on our behalf.

The Common Man also cannot avoid frequent contact with district and municipal officials. Every Thai has an aversion to going to such offices, not only because it is a waste of time but because he knows that he will be ill-treated by the clerk, who is poorly paid and looks on the Common Man as a supplementary source of income. The Privileged Man, on the contrary, would never have had to go to such an office in the first place. He would either have had someone go for him, or he would simply have telephoned to settle the matter quickly. Wealthy people in Siam can use money to obtain all manner of favours from officials.

In every government office the Common Man who comes for assistance is disdained as an inferior being. Officials do not want to waste their time with him. This situation prevails throughout Siam because the administrative branch of government controls nearly all political power, forcing the Common Man to deal constantly with bureaucratic officials in all aspects of his daily life.

If you are engaged in commerce, you must pay a special monthly "tax". When you go to the post office, no matter whether you need stamps, a money order or whatever, you must wait in long lines as if you were begging. When you receive an imported item at the Customs House, not only do you have to wait but you also have to pay addititional bribes according to the personal whims of the customs officer. In depositing or withdrawing money at a government bank, even if it is your own savings account, the process is still made inconvenient and time consuming. If the government were to open public services to free competition, it is unlikely whether a single facility would continue to exist.

When the Common Man becomes ill, those who devote themselves to caring for others have an opportunity to display their power. The ordinary, poor patient eats dirty meals in the public hospital and receives medical treatment reluctantly at best. However, if the Common Man visits the same doctor after office hours at his private clinic he will be received differently.

None of these matters are of any particular concern to the Privileged Man. If he is sick, he can ask for a special room and his doctor will be most attentive. He does not have to pay taxes, or go to the post office. If he travels by train, a special compartment will be provided. Consequently, it is extremely difficult for the Privileged Man to really understand the plight of the Common Man.

All Thais aspire to become Privileged Men, even if only on a temporary basis. When we visit a government office, if we happen to know someone or drop the name of a senior official at an appropriate time, we become a temporary Privileged Man. By doing so, we can cut ahead of the queue or obtain special services. In a hospital, a sick bed can be arranged even if officially there are "no beds available." Meals are more hygenic and nutritious, visitors can come at any time, and all the staff will say "Sir" to you.

In Siam not a solitary Common Man is satisfied with public services. Even in funeral services at the monastery, the monks will not speak politely to the sponsor if the deceased was a Common Man. All this is so discouraging at first glance, but if one thinks a bit further he may feel more in sympathy with the agents of the Privileged Elite: the ticket collector, traffic policeman, district clerk, hospital admissions clerk and monk. Their work is monotonous and they are only carrying out their duties as a matter of routine, seeing their jobs only in terms of money (or as steps to other, better paying jobs). Thus their hearts are not in their work. It is not their fault, but the fault of top administrative officials who permit these people to wield far too much power over the Common Man. In the eyes of top officials this is necessary, for lower level officials must be given certain privileges and a modicum of power to keep them so satisfied.

No matter where one goes in Siam, he will find only these two classes of persons. Only in highly progressive countries are civil servants and lords subject to the power of others. Where absolute administrative power continues to prevail, as in Siam, low ranking officials can exercise power over the rest of us. And so the system of patrons and clients goes on indefinitely.

The Social Science Review, December 1965.

STUDENTS' ROLE IN SOCIETY

The *Social Science Review* Student Edition, which has made its appearance in the book world once before now, although it has not yet had as wide a circulation as it should, has sparked off a great deal of reaction. The article on Music in Kasetsart University, for example, has caused persons in positions of authority in that institution to give support to musical activities in the university in a most gratifying way. All this goes to show that responsible persons in that university are ready to listen to the young people and do the right thing by them. However, the article "Wishing Stone in the University" (Thammasart) has passed without comment from either the teachers or students. It may have been because the subject matter treated in that article is too wide to cause immediate reaction in any particular direction, or it may have been that students and teachers in that institution have been focussing their attention on other things and have not had a chance to properly examine this piece of writing. "Some Observations on Extra-curricular Activities in Chulalongkorn University" caused a great deal of reaction among students. Most of the comments have been emotional rather than rational. Briefly, what they have said about the article is that it is "washing dirty linen in public" (in Thai the expression is "pulling out your intestines to let the crows feed on them"). The attitude is that all our bad points should be kept among ourselves. This shows that our young intellectuals are very much bound up in a group loyalty which is more important to them than truth. Because of loyalty to the group they are ready to accept what is worthless rather than face the facts and find ways of uprooting what is undesirable. This misguided group loyalty has often been the cause of student fights, and it will be harmful even in the students' later lives.

Generally speaking, the criticism on the edition seems to be that it aims to express the anger of the young towards their superiors and towards their institutions, rather than to give knowledge or to entertain. Even the poems reflect anger rather than express humour or love. Those responsible for the magazine must admit that there is a great deal of truth in this. On the other hand, we wish to make a plea for justice to the students. This is the first time that they have had an opportunity to express their independent views, outside their respective universities, without fear of anything, while within their universities they have their freedom restricted. It is no wonder then that they demand this and that, and in rather loud voices. What we must give them credit for is the fact that they use reason and say things with respect to law and order. This way surely is better than allowing their pent-up fellings to explode out of control, causing harm to themselves and society.

However, we have made an effort to amend, and this issue of the Student Edition contains considerably more academic matter. It also gives news of students in foreign countries, invites students to send in questions on various branches of science, encourages them to write and to participate in our quiz for prizes. All this has been designed to sharpen their minds and help them to develop into individual characters, with a love of truth, who will become good citizens of the country and the world.

Having said this much about the production of this magazine, the editor would like to express his personal views in this connection, since this was the first time he had really worked with students and undergraduates. Although the editor was not a teacher, but because he was older than the rest of the editorial board, he was naturally regarded with respect and deference. The editor would like to say how much he admired the sense of dedication, the courage and the wisdom of the young people he worked with. The board had made an agreement that if there should be a dangerous matter involved, the editor should make the final decision. But it turned out that because of the wisdom and good sense of the board members, the editor was never called upon to deal with any such cases. Often the board members proved to be even more careful than the editor himself. All this goes to show that if you give responsibility to young people in the right way, they will prove themselves worthy of it. If, on the other hand, there is mutual distrust, nothing but disaster can result, for all the "anti" feelings will then go and become a subversive force.

It must not, however, be thought that the editor only has

good things to say about his younger colleagues, for they have quite a few faults. Through working with students the editor has discovered that there are very few young people who are genuinely interested in the good of their group or society. Another distressing thing about them is that some take on too many activities. Apart from working on *the Social Science Review*, some were involved in other publications belonging to the Faculty, or a club or the university, not counting other activities outside the university. On top of all this some were on a number of various organizing committees.

The practice of taking on too many activities tends to lead to bad rather than good results. Moreover, it may cause one's studies to suffer. This tendency to take on too much is not confined to young people. One could perhaps say that they follow the example set by the grown-ups. In other words, it is possible that our young people think it respectable to have a great deal on their plate and to concentrate more on the quantity than the quality. It is true that our shortage of manpower is a grave problem, but we must all realize our limitations. Especially when one is still a student one must give great importance to one's programme of study and not allow it to suffer as a result of extracurricular activities.

From their conversations and writing it could be concluded that our young people are more interested in small, insignificant things than in bigger issues of life. They are circumscribed in small circles which they guard jealously against any intrusion. The question of the university authorities stopping the freshmen ceremony, the seniority system, and cheerleading seem to be major issues. And this is because the authorities are intruding into their jealously guarded sovereign state. But they do not spend enough time pondering the question of whether having to take many subjects and not having enough free time to think and study on their own is harmful to them or not. They spend four years at university studying English and end up not being able to speak or read the language. Should they not ask the authorities to do something about this? Or do they think that to make such a demand is beyond their capacity? Most of them seem to want to go into the civil service afterwards. Are there any who plan to volunteer to help the Northeasterners or the Laotians? Or do only people who cannot get jobs become volunteers? What is their philosophy of life? What do they think they are here for? Have our young people ever thought about these things? If so, how seriously? Why haven't they shown in writing what they think to let other people see it.

His Majesty the King once said to a group of students;

"You who are students now will probably, in the future, use your knowledge and the fruit of your education for the benefit of the country. In your study, therefore, you should have a definite aim as to what you want to study and what you want to do later on and proceed to achieve that aim."

How far do our young people follow this piece of advice? Do they take for granted that education attained in this country cannot be of much use, and they must wait for the opportunity to go abroad to be "gold plated". If they cannot go abroad and have no strings to pull, then they have to just hang around some government departments holding temporary positions in the hope that one day they will get permanent post. Once that happens, one becomes part of a big machine, and money, power, prospects and security becomes one's lot, which is what most people want.

The Social Science Review Student Edition No. 2,
September 1966.

THE AVOIDANCE OF BASIC SOCIAL PROBLEMS

It now seems reasonable to conclude that the government will finally accept the principle of sponsoring a nationwide birth control policy, even though one powerful Minister continues to disagree with such a policy. He appears to be the only opponent. The government surely will not allow a single opponent to delay any longer its decision.

In the past, the government has frequently attempted to preserve Cabinet unity "to ensure national security and political stability". This insistence on unity through perfect consensus has produced a distinct lack of strong national leadership. Many important matters remain forever undecided, and hard decisions are deferred until "later". Always accumulating in number and intensity, these problems are like a malignant cancer, which unless immediately removed by an emergency operation, sentences the patient to an early death.

Implementation of a population control policy is only one of these issues. Even if the government does finally accept this necessity, the population will continue to increase daily. But an official policy is a prerequisite for the development of measures to assist the poor in controlling the size of their families. The children of the rich can be cared for physically and materially, no matter what their number, but how are poor children supposed to attend good schools and obtain the education they require? And with inadequate nutrition, even if tuition scholarships were available, how could these children hope to compete with the children of the rich in school entrance examinations?

Even the rich in Siam have to worry about obtaining a decent education for their children. Sending them overseas from childhood on is only avoiding the problem, not facing it. Are we so positive that foreign education is desirable for Thai children? In the long run, is this separation of children from their parents a good thing? Is it not obvious that the student rebellions in Europe and America against teachers and governments are indicative of severe weaknesses in these foreign educational systems? Are we content to forever remain an intellectual colony of the foreigners? As long as the powerful, influential Thai upper class pursues its own interests and those of its children while avoiding our problems at home, our educational system will remain severely constrained and unacceptable.

These problems remain with us because the nation lacks intelligent leaders who have the courage to tackle difficult, controversial issues; there is a lack of honesty in the leadership group as well. Government leaders execute administrative policies which serve only themselves and their clique of supporters, leaving the majority of the population to fend for themselves. The leaders rely on sweet words and superficial deeds to communicate to the people their supposed concern about national problems, but they remain reluctant to deal conclusively with basic issues.

The most important issue facing Thai society is that of social justice. How can any government or society continue to exist in opposition to the principles of social justice? Its existence must be justified on a day-to-day basis when leaders are unwilling to deal with the future in a straight-forward, far-sighted manner.

If we look at Siam as it really is, we can see that our government continues to utilize a system of innate colonialism. The only difference from traditional colonialism is that masters and subjects are of the same nationality. Although the Thai masters have the same dark complexions and black hair as their subjects, their outlook, actions, and way of life make them feel and act superior to and more civilized than their subjects. The very term 'civil servant' implies that they are 'civilized'; this word, borrowed from the West and pronounced by Thais "siwi-lai", suggests a foreign (and superior) element.

The higher the rank of the civil servant, the more he acts like a foreigner among his own people. He can no longer sit on the floor, eat with his hands and dress like a Thai. In order to constantly prove their superiority and foreign-ness, these men refer to foreign textbooks when they have a problem to solve, and whenever possible they travel abroad on "observation tours" or similar ventures. Lower-ranking officials copy their superiors in all respects, patterning their own attitudes toward the masses on the foreign style of the top colonial (Thai) leaders. But real foreigners are considerably better in their behaviour and attitudes than our 'foreign' civil servants, who consider themselves special in every way and superior to the 'natives', who are considered ignorant. They are unable to speak a foreign language, after all, and have no foreign degree after their names. They lack the superficial attributes of modernization. These civil servants rule the country just as the English ruled over India and the French over Indochina. But these western imperialists at least accepted existing laws as supreme to the whims and wishes of the governors.

Our problems are so inter-related that we don't know where to begin in searching for realistic solutions. The National Economic Development Board, National Education Council, National Research Council and other similar agencies face this problem, encumbered by the fact that all are embodiments of governmental powers. NEDB is a little stronger than the others, and although it can't solve all our economic problems, it can at least increase our efficiency in dealing with them. Issues of culture and morality are dealt with only by small, impotent bodies, if at all, despite the fact that these problems are more crucial in the long run, for the society if not the economy.

We are so susceptible to the influence of foreign intellectuals that some of us have been following Nietzsche in claiming that God is dead. Thais today scarcely comprehend their religious or cultural heritage. In a recent seminar on educational planning, for example, there was no mention of the relevance of Buddhism to contemporary education, or the role of monks in educating rural villagers. There was only a brief discussion, demonstrating no real understanding of the issues involved, of a proposal to have monks teach at the elementary level in the public schools. This discussion was so bad that it was an insult to the monks. If today's intellectuals would only look to the past, they would see how strongly their predecessors felt about the dangers of letting the education of our youth slip out of the hands of the monks. The problem for our generation is how to re-combine the patterns of religion, education and culture which are divided into disparate themes in so many foreign lands. We should stop imitating the foreigners and return to the essence in the Thai experience.

However, we are still not even willing to discuss the

philosophy of education, either at seminars on education or in government committees. Thus the really crucial issues are again avoided, just as the Cabinet has assiduously avoided dealing with the issues of population control, the rice premium, taxes on inheritance, land taxes on the wealthy, organization of labourers into collective bargaining units, urban and rural planning, the establishment of a council on the arts, and so on. Since it is possible for the leaders to comfortably retain their positions simply by presiding over one function after another, starting a new agency, convening meetings, receiving visitors, holding interviews and signing innumerable papers, why disturb this situation by thinking about basic problems facing society? As a result, every Cabinet meeting deals with insignificant matters, in a short-term rather than long-term perspective, and with no in-depth analysis. It is time we stopped being so concerned about foreign systems of government – whether democratic or communist – and began to look at ourselves and our own problems seriously.

The first duty of a government is to seek social justice for its people, inducing the people to respect the laws of the land. The people can be expected to respect the law only when the law itself is just and legal procedures are fair. In Siam, however, judicial procedures and practices still over-whelmingly benefit only the rich and the elite minority, exploiting the poor who are the backbone of the nation and its real owners. Who would dare suggest that there is any justice in society?

I am not by any means proposing instituting a system of complete and total equality. I only ask that the rich be taxed more, the poor less, and measures to assist the poor in improving their economic and social status be devised. Even today the government has plenty of information at its disposal to deal with these vital problems. Both Thai and foreign experts have pointed to the superficial development of the country, to the dangers of allowing the vast majority of population to become poorer while a small minority became ever richer and set themselves up virtually above the law. The overdependence of government projects on external support and funding, and the long-term dangers of this trend, have also been clearly pointed out.

If the men who presently run this country cannot see that these are possibly fatal threats to the majority of the Thai population, then they ought to resign. If they insist on retaining their positions without changing their atiiudes or actions, their elimination becomes only a question of time. On the other hand, if they can come to perceive the existence of these problems, they ought to begin immediately to take steps to begin solving them. If they do this, time may still be on their side; but if they wait for this council and that committee to invite experts to express their opinions, they may well run out of time.

Communication with the poor and the dispossessed is far more difficult than with the wealthy and educated elite, but it is desperately required. If the leaders have their own material welfare linked with a system of exploitation of the poor, however, how will they ever agree to themselves changing that system? And what is the alternative? Whatever the government tries to do, it must not defer concerning itself with problems of education, culture and morality. The government must begin to delve directly into the causes of our contemporary problems instead of dealing only with their superficial manifestations. National defence, town planning, sanitation and hospital services are not ends in themselves, but the framework within which people can pursue material and spiritual happiness. Jointly with the people, the government should be concerned about such virtues as beauty, honesty, truth and happiness. If the government does not take the initiative, the people will remain insufficient, the police will still resort to illegal practices to supplement their income; Cabinet Ministers will still engage in private business and commercial activities. In short, the colonial system will remain in operation, and the nation's leaders will remain the people's masters. Such leaders drag the quality of all our institutions down to their own low level. It is not surprising the they permit the mass media to present only the news of which they approve.

In such a situation, one wonders about the utility of even talking about social justice. Perhaps the problem will simply be ignored as was the hilltribe problem in the North – until the Meo tribe turned to the communists. By the time we finally decide to take action, it may not really matter. Things change rapidly. Five years ago, who would have thought that students in Europe and America would take up arms as they now have? Thai students today are throwing bottle bombs at each other; what will they do tomorrow if we don't change our attitudes toward solving national problems?

The Social Science Review, June 1969.

DEMOCRACY IN THE FUTURE

Democracy is a good word. Every country seems to desire this system of government, and even China and Russia claim to behave like democracies although their interests lie in the Communist doctrine. Dictators, too, claim that they are democrats, or at least that the rulers of the countries in question are paving the way for that system. As this word has so much charm, it is only natural for Siam to want to be democratic along with the others, in spite of the fact that the majority of the people do not know yet how good or bad this system of government is and what the elements of the system are.

The resolution of the theorists is that there is only a single form of democracy and there are no other forms. To them, a system whereby no rights and liberties exist, and where there is no way by which the people may cast votes in an election of representatives that could form or overthrow a government, cannot be called democratic system. Some to them dislike the term democracy employed by dictators, so they turn to the genuine form of democracy, which is known as free democracy.

As a matter of fact, the genuine form of democracy is not anything extraordinarily wonderful, and no Thai has ever longed for that form of government. In ancient times, most of the rulers were able to run the country in a manner that made it peaceful and happy. There was then a reasonable amount of freedom and self-government and any changes toward progress usually came from higher-up, including the abolition of slavery, the provision of education and improvement of administrative affairs. The government then did not describe itself as a democracy and it gave those things without being called upon to do so. The people, whether they were of low station by birth or not, stood a chance of being admitted to government service and of climbing to the highest positions. They were given opportunities to trade and to gain immense wealth; and they could profess any religion or creed. The freedom of opinion through the press then appeared to be greater than under what is called the democratic regime.

Then all of a sudden a group of persons staged a *coup d'état* on the ground that it was for the sake of democracy, though the monarchy was then already prepared to introduce the system. After its successful seizure of power, that group of persons did not hand democracy to the people as it had promised. Consequently, a form of oligarchy continued almost continuously; although democratic breezes blew occasionally, they were of very short duration. Once, representatives were successful in overthrowing a government, but that was the only time. On the whole, the political trend was towards a struggle for power.

It is now 35 years since the so-called democratic form of government was adopted. Gotama attained his enlightenment at this age and so the persons in power in Siam should now open their eyes and realize that it is now the time to hand democracy to the people. It is true that they did not clamor to any extent for this system in the past. It is not the best system of government, but it is the only system that provides effective administrative machinery. Otherwise, there will be men who endlessly try to seize power on the claim that they do it for the sake of democracy, of the people or of "Uncle Si and Uncle Sa" (Tom, Dick and Harry). Si or Sa seem to be proper names quoted often lately, and they appear to be more well known than "Phuyai Lee".

Those in power in the country at present should observe the lesson learned by the government of the monarchy. That government wanted to hand a constitution to the people, but, despite its sincerity, it kept on postponing the delivery until another group of persons deprived it of power. Let those in power at present not be careless, just because they have armed power or because they have great friends who have sent mighty forces to help them. Let them be sincere toward the people. What has happened are vague promises and endless postponements. The Siamese, like other human beings, will wait with high hopes. If they are frequently disappointed, their reactions will be increasingly stronger. There is not yet a public uprising, but it is feared that some opportunists may start resisting the government in the name of a "People's Party" as was seen in the past. The result would be that a new swarm of leeches would come in to suck the blood of the people.

To be fair, the present government is one of the best we have had in the so-call democratic period, but it is not as democratic as it is called because it has been in power since the beginning of the Buddhist year 2500 (1957). Some of the Cabinet Ministers used to handle work connected with policies during the times of a former dictator. That it has been in power for such a long time has helped to create stability of government and made it generous enough to listen with a reasonable amount of patience to comments and criticism. It has also agreed to rectify certain shortcomings in response to suggestions made by mass media outside government circles. That is a good sign that it will lead to a democratic administration. Nonetheless, we now must not overlook the fact that the former government had destroyed experienced and good men in newspaper circles or had persuaded them to be on its side by way of appointing so many of them as Constituent Assemblymen that there are almost no good men left behind who have the courage to strongly oppose the government. Besides, martial law is still retained as the last means of pressure. No matter how kind the government is, it can be unkind any time. Only from the press can the government learn whether the blunders in the performance of work and policy planning are serious or slight. For all other influential groups are on the side of the government.

Further, as the government has remained in power for a long time without being required to answer directly to the people or their representatives, it cannot know to what extent the work it has performed is for the benefit of the public, even though every member of the government may be highly intelligent, capable and sincere. If some were without capability and honesty, greater ruin would be brought about more quickly. For example, the giving of permission to the Americans to set up so many bases in Siam will naturally create an obligation that has a bearing on the existence of the entire Thai nation. But the people know nothing about it. The government may have done that in a capable and sincere manner, but it may also be a grave mistake. This mistake may produce extremely serious effects not only upon the government but upon all of the people of this land. In such a case, if discussions are held with the representatives of the masses or representatives of mass media, there might be greater prudence. If all of the people outside government circles should be regarded as men without any wisdom, would that not be an extreme underrating of them?

The foregoing remarks have pointed out the advantages and disadvantages of the present form of government, and, if the government does not promptly offer democracy in the shape of a constitution and election, it is feared that there will be more harm than benefit. It is true that the majority of the people remain uninterested in the form of the government, but the minority, which is displeased with the government's failure to keep its promises, will increase daily in terms of number and anger. It is feared that opportunists will create an unfavorable situation since they have some reasonable excuses to offer.

As for the political theorists who call for a genuine democracy, they are possibly dreaming too much. If they look and really understand the actual situation, they must admit that the constitution, which will be brought out in the near future, allows the existence of "2nd Category" members of the National Assembly. Membership of this category should be improved to be better than at present. Those who are receiving salaries without doing anything, since they were appointed during the tenure of the former government, and those who are incapable, ought to be discharged. The retention of some members of this category is of great importance. Otherwise, the people taking the reins at present would not be able to remain in their positions after the general election. For none of the members of the present government, evidently, would be elected by public opinion. Nonetheless, it is essential to both stability and peace that members of the old clique stay on in the government.

The election of members of the House of Representatives is a necessity, even if the House cannot oust the government and the majority of the people are still not enthusiastic about electing their representatives, since the representatives can constitute another influential group to help comment on and criticize the government in Parliament, thus making certain that ministries and departments perform their work and formulate policies more carefully. It is true that the majority of candidates for election will naturally not have more regard for public interests than personal ones, but those candidates are usually members of the intelligentsia in the provinces who are anxious to play a political role. If they are not allowed to play such a role by constitutional methods, it is feared that they may show hostility to the government through subversion in violation of the law of the country, which seems to have occurred regularly. The important thing is that the government must quickly permit elections and ensure that they are carried out in a clean manner. The government should have no worries, no matter how small the number of the government's followers elected to the House of Representatives may be; it must not cheat in the new elections, nor should it offer bribes to the people's representatives. For those actions would block the way to democracy in the future and also amount to destroying the government indirectly.

The above are suggestions for solving immediate problems. If the government has foresight, it could find ways of allowing the people to elect local representatives to a greater extent and should not allow permanent officials to remain in municipal councils. At the same time, the teaching of democratic principles and techniques should be increased both inside and outside of educational institutions. The institutions themselves ought to grant more rights and freedoms to teachers and students than at present. It is most dangerous to continue the propaganda showing how bad the communists are, when the people still do not know how good or bad democracy is, what its theoretical components are, and to what extent it is being practised in their own country.

This article is based on good intentions toward the government. Should the government not revise its view on democracy, it is feared that genuine democracy will not come about, and that which will replace the present government will be worse than any other political system we have known

Siam Times, April 1967.

CHARTING OUR COURSE

The conduct of most of the teachers, government officials and big shots at the present time brings to mind what King Chulalongkorn had to say in his letter to the Crown Prince, as follows:

"One is not a King in order to gain wealth nor to stamp on others as one wishes, nor to seek vengeance on those whom one doesn't like, nor just to have an easy life. If you wish to be like this, you can do so in two ways – to become a monk is one way, or another way is to be a millionaire. Those who wish to be a King will have to be poor, will have to have patience in the face of happiness and suffering, will have to restrain love and hate, whether these come about in one's own mind or whether they are brought about through someone's insistent babbling, and will have to do away with laziness. The only thing that a King attains is fame following death and a name for maintaining the royal lineage and protecting the people under his rule from suffering. These two basic principles should be kept in mind over and above anything else. If one does not have such intentions, then he will not be able to rule the country."

The above words are 75 years old, but now we still have everyone from policemen to district officials to the higher-ups who want to act as kings and gain great wealth, and also to lead an easy life. Even the majority of the monks are like this. It appears that the higher up a monk goes in the hierarchy the more applicable the King's words become.

With neither the monks nor administrators holding out much hope for us and our future, where are we going to turn unless it is to the monarchy? But this is so high that no one dares interfere with it. And even though the monks have the right to direct the teachings of the Lord Buddha towards the King, they do nothing at present except to stick to the same old type of sermons. And then if others were to attempt to analyze the monarchy, the chances are good that they would be accused of trying to do away with the monarchy, regardless of how good their intentions might have been. Everyone now understands that it is only the monarchy which can successfully join the past with the present and everyone has hopes that this will occur, but as the monarchy is unable to stand analysis, then it is highly doubtful that it will endure.

At present many Thais have given up all hope for the future, and they think of what King Chulalongkorn wrote in his poem (that Ayudhaya fell because of weak kings) and would like to say this same thing, but they still have hopes that Siam will not fall. During World War II another poet wrote in a similar vein about the country, saying;

"Anybody who considers the state of the country at present must also wonder what the future will be. If the Japanese lose the war then what will happen to Siam and how far will she fall? Who will be able to regain her freedom, who is there now who knows the way? Siam is like a ship adrift and from whence will help come?"

But in the end Siam did not lose her independence nor did she lose in the war. Whether this came about because of the good fortune provided by the guardian spirit or because of the help of the Free Thai, we don't know; but anyway the independence wasn't lost. If there is a guardian spirit, the spirit probably did not forsake Siam (even though the name of the spirit has had to be changed in keeping with the change in the name of the country). But no one can tell just how much this rested on good fortune. As for the Free Thai, they certainly no longer exist, and the only thing remaining is the Patriotic Front, but it appears that they are more patriotic towards Red China than they are towards Siam.

These two great poets were most successful in expressing their feelings in times when the country was facing great danger. Now we are faced with a most serious danger. We stand between the mouth of the tiger and the mouth of the bear, and if we were to take the same way out as the "weak kings" in the past did we still could not escape the facts of the situation, So, those who view the crisis say;

"When there is no captain at the helm,

The sailors will be at a loss to know the direction to take.

No one knows what to do, and the suffering increases.

The reason being that they are distant from the Captain,
To whom the people once gave their trust, a trust now discarded".

If the Thai ship has a captain and a ruler who makes use of his wits and is willing to meet the people openly and not just meet them on the surface, and not just follow the principle of adhering to custom and tradition, he should be able to act as the force which will draw together the new ideas to solve the problems of the present time. Apart from this, we have to depend on our good fortune or our guardian spirt, and it's easy to put one's reliance on things outside. This is just like behaving as a child who doesn't know how to grow up, and who always depends on elders. And this makes it easy and everything is alway rosy, especially in this time of development when it seems that everything is said to turn out well. Even with the great number of foreign military coming in to the country, this is passed off as a means by which help is secured, so anything that is wrong is turned into something that is good. So regardless of how much the massage parlours mushroom, or how much the youth discard moral standards, there is no need to worry. Just think that if King Chulalongkorn had taken this easy way out, would the future have extended as far as it has?

Excerpt from *The Social Science Review*,
December 1967.

SIAM VERSUS THE WEST

Farangs, as the Thais call Westerners, have had a significant cultural impact on Siam for a long time. In recent years this influence has become particularly heavy. Perhaps of some benefit to us materially, Western ideas have undeniably affected our way of thinking and altered our customs.

Why has this foreign impact been so far-reaching? To what extent should we Thais adopt these imported manners? Are they compatible with our way of life?

Despite the extreme importance of this problem of adaptation to Farang ways, it seems we have not considered seriously enough the ultimate consequences. Our future may be at stake.

Let us explore the question by examining Thai and Farang attitudes and discover their implications for our future.

Readiness to accept a foreign influence without careful evaluation is always dangerous. For Thais to accept Occidental ways uncritically may be disastrous. But this is what is happening. We Thais are copying from America and Europe without foreseeing the possible results. We can illustrate this by examples taken from our social customs and governmental policy.

We are proud to have been the first nation in Asia to offer television and to install airconditioning in our movie theatres. We rushed to introduce Coca Cola into our homes. Bowling alleys and night clubs, as soon as they open, become crowded centres of leisure-time activity. Several years ago, our well-known dictator, Field Marshal Phibulsongkram, commanded the Thai people to give up wearing the traditional *phanung*. A government order even outlawed the chewing of betel-nut. The name Siam was replaced by the comical hybrid Thailand.

Construction projects in Bangkok attempt to copy the West

but are completed in slap-dash fashion. Forethought is minimal. This is particularly the case with municipal "improvements" such as filling in the city's canals to build wider streets. It is true that Bangkok needed roadway space, but who foresaw that the disarticulation of the capital's drainage system would lead to flooding, stagnant pools and more mosquitoes!

We "solve" traffic problems without thinking whether our capital will be a pleasant or comfortable place to live and move about in. When, in the interests of "modernization", we chopped down our widespreading shade trees, does any one consider the psychological effect on the 2,000,000 inhabitants of a metropolis that has only one park?

In all of this heedless imitation, the writer is reminded of the old Thai preverb: To watch an elephant defecate and then to try to do the same is dangerous. Perhaps the Thais of today are trying to play the elephant, attempting foolishly to follow the Westerners' life style.

Unfortunately, while we have borrowed many things from the West, we seem incapable of copying certain Farang intellectual characteristics, such as the ability to criticise and to evaluate. If simple problems in Bangkok are not being approached with intelligent provision, what can we say of the far off provinces?

If we are honest with ourselves we must confess that we do not copy the Westerners when we are faced with problems which demand concentration, sacrifice and principles.

We are preoccupied with form; we ignore substance. We aircondition our fancy offices while our villages go without schools. Our millionaires compete with Farang investors in erecting luxurious tourist hotels. But they would not think of engaging in a similar competition in building superior universities.

Perhaps we so eagerly grasp at Western culture because we fail to understand our own. We do not really know ourselves. It is distressing that most Thais consider Thai history, literature and art to be the domain of the old or the expert, and of no relevance to the ordinary person. Without understanding our own society, then, we readily accept the external trappings of the West, which we do not understand either.

When King Chulalongkorn paid his visit to Great Britain in the 1890's. *The Times* warned that the Thais might mistake the telephone and other superficial things for the true essence of

Western culture. And, 80 years later, isn't this precisely what is taking place?

One reason, then, for the pervasive Western influence in Siam has been our impetuous acceptance of it. But to comprehend this phenomenon better, we must look into the Westerners' own motives as well.

When the Portuguese, Spaniards, Dutch and French first came to Siam, their intentions were hardly altruistic. They and the English that followed them, sought to establish themselves in our trade and to build forts for their factories, extending thus their economic power and with it their influence over this region. The Americans who have replaced Europe's empire builders may have come on a slightly different pretext, but the majority of them, too, think that we should exchange our way of life for theirs.

This was certainly true of yesterday's colonial powers. The desire to have others copy them appears to be a Western trait. Their religious scriptures declare that God made man in His own Image; but the writer contends that most Westerners act as though they believe the contrary. And it is sure that for those who can create a God, it is little trouble to attempt to mold us as well. Intentionally or otherwise, America seems to be following her European cousins.

Although more and more Westerners come to Siam; and our economy benefits in the short run, the long range effect is undesirable. Economic advanatages go to a few, while the many are faced with rising prices. Tourists may convert their travellers' cheques, but their ready cash induces further erosion of our traditions. American GI's squander their pay, with results unhappily well known.

Nevertheless, even more corrosive in its real, if often undiscerned, effect is the condescension which characterizes many Farang-Thai relationships. Too many of our foreign partners seem to think that we are a people in need of their support and guidance. This is paternalism and it is destructive.

Our present posture of mimicking the West puts and keeps us at a disadvantage by abetting unequal and exploitative relationships. In fact, our present practice of mindless imitation invites paternalistic attitudes from our Western partners. This situation cannot continue without friction. These relationships can only lead to resentment and outbursts of xenophobia. Change for the better will come when we begin to know ourselves and to appreciate our own culture. We must at the same time adopt a more judicious attitude toward the West, to decide critically what aspects of Western culture are beneficial and meaningful for Thais and what cultural characteristics are not.

SIAM: THE MOVE AWAY FROM MILITARY DICTATORSHIP

When the military government of Field Marshal Thanom Kittikachorn collapsed with stunning swiftness in October, 1973, a surprised world watched as Siam began to take on what seemed like a new political shape.

A nation long known for its absolute monarchies, and since 1932 its military dictatorships, appeared to be going against the grain. At a time when some observers said that authoritarian governments were desired by Asians, in Siam the move seemed to be toward more representative and constitutional government.

Demonstrations of thousands of students in Bangkok had been bloodied by heavy military gunfire; hundreds died, thousands were wounded. But the students came to be for a time the symbol of a nation's discontent with corrupt leadership; tens of thousands more students gathered in Bangkok. Suddenly, Thanom, deputy prime minister Prapas Charusathiara, and Thanom's unpoplar son, Colonel Narong Kittikachorn, were out; King Bhumibol Aadulyadej named the Rector of Thammasat University, Sanya Dharmasakti, 66, the first civilian prime minister since 1957. Thanom, Prapas and Narong – now called Siam's "three most hated men" – fled the country.

Did the events of 1973 indeed mean that the Thai people, so long cut off from voice in their nation's politics, would now have a democratic and representative system?

To address this fundamental question, we need to look back to old Siam. It has been said that to understand the present and predict the future, we should know our past. In days of old, the Kingdom of Siam was known as an "absolute monarchy". Despite the myths about the "oriental splendour" of a few hundred years ago and all that connotes, life outside the royal court was comparatively simple. Although the concept of equality was unknown, little polarization existed between the rich and the poor, the powerful and the weak. Because food was still simple and plentiful for all, medicine was the same for princes and commoners alike, and people paid little attention to clothing, not much difference was apparent between the way of life of the rulers and the ruled.

The exception was the king's splendid palaces, yet even within such buildings little interior decoration was seen. People, high and low, sat and slept on the floor. Some monasteries, belonging to the communities and not to any one individual, were as beautiful as palaces. Certainly rich and poor people existed, but money was not the main motive in life. Those with wealth concentrated on looking after their animals and environment rather than exploiting them to get richer and thus more powerful.

In Siamese society social mobility remained fluid. A daughter of a commoner could become queen overnight. The king's descendants returned to common status after a few generations. Polygamy bridged the gap between nobility and the commoner. A bright village boy could realize importance as a monk; if he desired to leave the holy order, he could become a nobleman. Indeed, in a few instances former monks even became kings.

The majority of the population lived far away from the capital, where central authority hardly ever reached them and money was not very useful. Each village was self-contained, with its own food, shelter and basic resources for a livelihood. Thus the majority of the population knew little about riches and power.

Buddhism exerted its influence on the rich and powerful, whose money and power normally did not extend beyond the big cities. Buddhism counseled against attraction to worldly gains. If the king exercised his might against the cardinal teachings of the Buddha, his rivals had cause to remove him from the throne.

Buddhism played an equally crucial role in the lives of the majority of the people. Each village usually had a *wat* (monastery) where the abbot was the spiritual as well as civic leader. The wat played many roles: school, hospital, community hall, cultural center, art gallery, museum. Whatever the village needed and possessed could be found in the monastery.

The monks, entirely supported by the villagers, would always counsel self-sufficiency and denounce greed for more wealth and power. Yet they also urged love for each other. So the villagers usually helped each other plowing and harvesting, often accompanied by song and dance. Medicine made in the home and monastery was distributed free. Gay ceremonies accompanied the building of a new house, a wedding or even a funeral. Work and play went together. If anything was not done with *sanuk* (enjoying oneself), life was not worth living. Although most people were poor, and life expectancy was short, life was lived with sanuk and the people did not feel oppressed.

The ancient monarchical regimes seemed to have little impact, positive or negative, on the people, except in time of war or great famine. In war they had to suffer the national fate; during famine sometimes the benevolence of the rulers muted the consequences. Nature smiled on the Siamese. The land was not overcrowded; if one place became unsuitable for cultivation, it was simple to emigrate to new areas.

The Colonial Impact

Colonial expansion in the nineteenth century began the process of change in Siam. In order to survive as an independent country, we had to adapt to the Western systems. The tactics of our kings (especially Ramas IV and V, also known as Mongkut and Chulalongkorn) prevented our country from becoming a colony of a foreign power, but it did involve a partial loss of national integrity when the great powers, Britain and France, acquired parts of our territory.

At the same time, Siam was opened to other Western powers, and legations were established in those countries to make certain they recognized us as a sovereign nation. Our students went abroad to study Western techniques, and some foreign advisers came to Siam in order to adapt our political and social system to suit what was then required for a "civilized" way of life. The result was a reorganized internal administration, the introduction of Western economic, legal and educational systems, automobiles and telecommunications. Yet the political base of power remained limited to the king and his court.

The new era brought easy accessibility between king and commoners. No conflict resulted as long as the king was just – as was Rama V (Chulalongkorn, who ruled from 1869-1910) – and was perceived to be running the country for the benefit of the people. But if kings failed to do this, as with Rama VI and VII, people with modern political ideas from their new educational perspectives would criticize them.

In 1932 this new Western educated elite successfully took "absolute power" from the king, although the majority of the people were still not involved in political concerns. From 1932 this country has been known as a "democratic" nation. Although the name of the country changed back and forth between Siam and Thailand, little real change occurred in the political or social structures. The king no longer presided over the government, but the political base of power never included the majority of people.

Since 1932 our governments have always declared themselves democratic, but we were generally ruled by dictatorships of one kind or another. From 1932 to 1974 eleven general elections took place, although real power had never been in the General Assembly. Rather, a small group of people who controlled the armed forces reserved the real power for themselves. When a conflict arose among those contending for the position of prime minister, this small group decided. If a peaceful decision was impossible, a *coup d'état* resulted. Siam experienced twelve successful and unsuccessful *coups* between 1932 and 1974.

For fifteen years the ruling elite consisted of key civilians as well as naval and military officers. But from 1947 on the military monopolized the power group. Except for two very brief civilian interludes, the prime minister has also been *ipso facto* field marshal and supreme commander of the armed forces.

The new elite were in a position to strongly criticize the old "absolute" regimes of "feudalism", yet once in command the new power figures soon saw themselves as the new nobility. Although some of those who wielded power meant well for the country, on the whole they looked down on the common people. And when they began to acquire wealth and to live in a Western and princely style, corruption crept in.

The association of government ministers and businessmen broadened the corruption. Accompanying the increased cost of living since World War II, many high ranking officials are known to have acquired wealth by illegitimate means.

Then came the age of United Sates aid, the so-called development help, which meant in effect that money was easily available to "buy" people in authority and tie them to the Western bloc. Thus Thailand, proud of resisting colonialism, found itself led into a neo-colonial period, a time when it let American air bases be established all over Siam.

The Japanese have flooded the country in the past two decades also, buying up economic influence and establishing deep roots in the economy, but, unlike the Americans, not involving themselves in Thai politics. People who resisted this national sellout to the neo-colonialists were labeled Communists, or Communist sympathizers and ostracized or put in prison.

The government of Field Marshal Sait Thanarat used the Communist bogeyman to declare martial law in 1958, and the country was for a decade without a parliament of elected representatives. The press was not free; the educational system directed itself essentially to training civil servants who could serve the government, and the technocrats cared nothing about social justice. The slogan of the period: "Government of the people, by those who know how to operate it for the people." And the prime minister often defended his actions by declaring: "I alone am responsible for the nation."

Development: The Rich Grow Richer

In this political atmosphere, little criticism was heard when national leaders and some international agencies proclaimed that Thailand's national development looked good – the gross national product was increasing at a regular rate. But they did not also add that the rich grew richer. New road systems to areas far from Bangkok? That may look good on paper but it made those areas more accessible to Bangkok bureaucrats and businessmen who went upcountry to purchase land. About 85 percent of our population were land-owning farmers– an unusually large number for Southeast Asia. But quickly more and more became landless. Forestry, mining and agricultural areas, as well as the fishing industry, came more and more to be exploited by the few at the expense of the many.

A huge proportion of the government's expenditures occurred in Bangkok to the neglect of rural areas. And when now landless country folk fled to urban Bangkok to seek jobs, they ended up in slum areas and tightly packed squatter zones. Patriots who resisted this exploitation were labeled subversives; socalled Communists in many areas were simply angry Thais who fought against this loss of their traditional way of life.

While people increasingly felt the whole system was excessively corrupt, enriching the people who ran the government, the government itself went through the motions of granting a Constitution in 1968 and holding another general election in early 1969. Not that any risk was involved; the ruling elite appointed the Upper House had been "bought" already. Yet even this token representation made them uneasy, so in November 1971 they dissolved Parliament and annulled the Constitution.

One of the problems facing any despotic government is the line of succession. Field Marshal (and Prime Minister) Thanom hoped to assure the continuation of his clique which had been in power since 1957 by pushing his son, Narong, as his successor. Narong married the daughter of General (and Deputy Prime Minister) Prapas.

But they made a mistake. By pushing Colonel Narong too far, too quickly, they upset the strong seniority system in the Thai Army. Narong didn't help the plan with greedy, rude and stupid actions. (He once told newspaper interviewers that other than his father, the men he most admired in public life were General Franco of Spain, President Park Chung Hee of South Korea and the Shah of Iran.) Narong's unlimited demands for wealth and power upset the "tea money" system of corruption working so effectively for the bureaucrats and businessmen. The anger of the masses was one thing; but such actions made Narong, his father and father-in-law, unpopular within the ruling group.

October, 1973: Did Anything Really Change?

During the October, 1973 events it appeared that the students and people managed to bring down the corrupt Thanom government. In fact it was the king and the army who forced the three tyrants – Thanom, Prapas and Narong – to leave the country. After the 1932 abolition of "absolute monarchy", the royal court became largely ceremonial. However, in October, 1973 the army brought in King Bhumibol, who enjoys national popularity similar to Queen Elizabeth, to topple the old government.

The result was that no basic changes occurred in our political system. A civilian prime minister was appointed; he allowed freedom of the press. But the army controlled everything, including the police, who continued to check people's telephones, open their letters and watch their movements. One of the 1973 demands produced a new constitution within a year, but it was really no better than any previous version. The National Assembly which drafted it – elected from names nominated by the king – were mostly top bureaucrats and businessmen. Hardly anyone stood for the people, or understood their grievances.

During the first year of the new government, constant rumours of pending *coups d'état* circulated; in fact, the government did resign once, but Prime Minister Sanya resumed his work again within a week with a few new faces in his cabinet. As the new government had no real power, the best it could do was to maintain the status quo.

Still the people, oppressed for so long, began to make demands through strikes and demonstrations and public debate as soon as the new sense of freedom arrived. The government, feeling itself only temporarily in power, could at best pacify the people. But it could not even reform the administration, much less tackle real problems like land reform for the benefit of the majority of Thai farmers.

Real grievances cannot be solved merely by establishing a constitution and parliament. These two institutions help to provide the basic framework for freedom and the rule of law, but as they are now they do not provide for real social justice.

The Thai, even in the time when the kings were sovereign, managed to live with freedom and dignity, as well as be sanuk (remember? "enjoying oneself"). Does our future promise to return these possibilities to us?

Time alone will tell. Although the demands for justice have not been addressed meaningfully, and although democratic institutions are still alien to our soil, we do have now the rule of law, some kind of elected representatives, and an opportunity to talk openly and carefully about the system we want.

If the current government, or one of its type, can last for half a dozen years, we may be able to solve some fundamental problems in the short term.

In the long run perhaps we may be able to find a new political system which can be cultivated in our soil, suitable to our climate and beneficial to our people. Who knows?

Southeast Asians Speak Out: Hopes and Despair in Many Lands. Edited by Barbara & Leon Howell (Friendship Press) New York 1975. Reprinted by kind permission of the Publishers.

INTERVIEW
BY WOLFGANG SCHMIDT
March 6th, 1977.

Schmidt : Mr. Siravaksa, you are a well known man in Thailand. But people in Germany hardly know about you. Could you brief us on your curriculum vitae?

Sulak : Well, I was born in Siam. I was educated first of all in a Protestant school, then I went to a Catholic Secondary School in Bangkok and later I graduated from an Anglican College in Wales. In my work, I became a publisher, I teach at the university and I am involved in social movement in Siam, as well as in Southeast Asia. This is roughly my curriculum vitae. I write books and edit magazines.

Schmidt : You are a Buddhist. Could you briefly explain to us what there is distinctive about Thai Buddhism?

Sulak : Thai Buddhism, to me, works on three levels. The first level is what we call DĀNA or TAHN; generosity or charity or sharing. Human beings ought to share with each other, should be generous to each other, share the suffering and joy. The second step in Thai Buddhism, which we stress is SĪLA, or precepts, that is putting your behaviour right, your speech and your conduct towards fellow human beings and other beings. And the third step is known as BHAVANĀ, or mindfulness, meditation, the attempt to concentrate on the higher things in life, so that you can see the reality in order to achieve salvation, the ultimate, called NIRVANA.

Schmidt : I am wondering whether there is any motivation within Thai Buddhism for (what we like to call) development-aid, something like a Buddhist development theory?

Sulak : You see, Thai Buddhism works very well in the rural areas because Thai Buddhism belongs to the School of Theraveda Buddhism. In Southeast Asia it worked very well for the last 800 years in the rural set-up, and so our development theory is very much a "rural-oriented development theory" in the village concept. Coming back to what I said earlier on, about DĀNA, or generosity. You must help your neighbours, you must help the people around you. If you go anywhere in Siam, Thailand, in the village area you can see the respect for the elders, the care for the poor, the care for the elderly and the sick, and the rich people on the whole are very generous to the poor; the poor have some respect for the rich, so there is no class struggle in this kind of development. But, of course, Buddhism has its weaknesses too, particularly when dealing with urbanisation. So I think we don't have as yet a development theory for the great big urban areas.

Schmidt : Is there a sort of "secularization-intensive" Buddhism or, in other words, what is the relation between Buddhism in a religious society on the one hand, and government and political parties on the other?

Sulak : Again, Buddhism works on a village level; it works at a rather grass-root level. But on high politics, Buddhism tends to support the monarchical concept. That is, if the rulers are good, just and kind, Buddhism works along this line. But at the same time, if the rulers are bad, wicked and so on, Buddhism, or the Buddhist hierarchical set-up, would rather withdraw itself from them, but is not strong enough to oppose them. By historical development, Buddhism tends to be on the monarchical side. But, of course, you have bad kings and their opposition, so you let them fight among themselves. Buddhism would only come out to support good kings; but when there is a bad king, the Buddhist "Church" tends to restrain itself; they keep rather quiet. I think this is the strength and the weakness of Buddhism. As I said earlier on, Buddhism has not developed in the urbanised, cosmopolitan areas. And it is also true that Buddhism has not developed in the political struggle. A lot of politicians, unfortunately, make use of Buddhism, particularly in the Thai case, because we claim that we are still governing in the monarchical way , unlike other Southeast Asian countries which were colonised at one time or the other, and in which Buddhism was involved in mass movements against the colonial power. In our own case, we did not have that. So our set-up is a little bit shaky at this stage.

Schmidt : The Christian Church in Thailand has a minority of not even 1%. What is it to you?

Sulak : Well, you see, Buddhism works with any other religion, with any other people. It doesn't matter how many of them – the Thai Christians number about 30,000 Protestants and over 100,000 to 200,000 Roman Catholics. Well, the Thai population is 43 million; of these 43 million, we have over 200,000 Buddhist monks already. But the numbers don't mean anything. The Christians, on the whole, come from the Western branch of Christianity. It came along with Western knowledge, Western expansion; and has many, many good facets, and many good qualities along with it, and, of course, it also has some weaknesses along with it. Being Thais, whether we are Christians, Muslims or Buddhists, I think we should work together, we ought to share something in common, and we must learn from each other. We learn the differences and we learn to respect each other. I must proudly say, on the whole, the Buddhist in history, and Thai Buddhism anyhow, has been able to tolerate those of other faiths and impress them, inviting them to share with us all along. In the past, the Christians have had a negative attitude toward us, but recently the Christians have come to work with us and truly to share with us. I think this is a very good sign.

Schmidt : You started to talk about indications for a more intensive dialogue between Christians and Buddhists. But where are the critical points in this ongoing dialogue?

Sulak : Well, I think the critical point is, that trust is not fully there. Because in the past, the Buddhists – as I said – were rather willing to work with the Christians but in the past they felt that Christians sometimes made use of this for missionary work and to convert people, and that they tried to do things behind our back. So I think the distrust is there. In my mind, we must build trust all the time. Perhaps starting with a very small group of people, working on something we have in common and then, perhaps having some dialogue or something meaningful and at the same time perhaps sharing some prayer, some meditation together. I think this would be something very meaningful. And it is a good thing that there is now an attempt by Buddhists and Christians to work on something together, on the social welfare thing, visiting people in jail, visiting people in hospitals. As a next step, I feel, there must be a more serious dialogue. And then, as I said, there must be some prayer together.

Schmidt : What about the dialogue between Buddhists, Christians and Muslims? You have a minority of Muslims too.

Sulak : Oh yes we have over one million Muslims in the South particularly. Of course, they are mostly ethnic Malays. The Buddhists and the Muslims have had a dialogue for some time now. There is one famous monk in the South, called Buddhadasa. He and some leading Muslims have been having a dialogue together and, in fact, they have produced books, some of which have even been translated into English. Again it is still a minority movement. But even so, this minority counts a great deal. Some Muslims, Christians and Buddhists have been trying to work together, but not yet successfully.

Schmidt : In Laos, Kampuchea, Vietnam and a long time ago in the People's Republic of China, Buddhism had to deal with Socialism and Communism. This religious, theoretical explanation of Buddhism and Communism, has it occurred in Thailand? And what is the present stage of the discussion?

Sulak : Communism, I am not aware of but there are some leading Buddhist intellectuals who try to equate the pristine teaching of the Buddha with socialism. There is again this leading monk called Buddhadasa. He calls it Dhammaic Socialism, which means the doctrine of sharing, the doctrine of compassion. You must have individual freedom. But at the same time, when you produce, over you basic need, you must share with other people. You mustn't exploit nature, you must not exploit your environment. I think on this line, it has been working. And there is one youth leader, who unfortunately is now in hiding, who has thought a great deal about Buddhist Socialism. He wrote an article, which has been translated into English, but he has not developed much further. I think it is a sign that further development on this line of thought is needed. As it is, it is not thought out clearly yet.

Schmidt : Would you like to make a prognosis about the political future in Thailand, let's say for the next five years?

Sulak : This is very difficult to say. You know at this stage, the government has become very, very dictatorial. They are against any kind of liberalism, there is stong press censorship, they put a lot of people in jail, they lump the liberals with the communists. I don't think this is very healthy, and unfortunately, this will help strengthen the communist movement. Unless they change this tremendously, I fear they will strengthen the communist movement. On top of that, you have the superpowers interfering. The Americans – despite what the new Carter administration is saying – are still involved. And unfortunately, the Taiwanese, Japanese and ASEAN governments are also backing the Thai Government. To them, it is the last stronghold of the so called Free World. I don't think this is very good. The struggle will go on. I don't think it will be over in three or five years. But of course, if we can convince the so called Free World not to get involved and if we could convince the other side, the communists, I don't think the communists are strong enough to take over within three or five years. But if the superpowers from this side have a strong hold there, the communists may have to rely on their superpowers on their side. So civil war will take place; the country could be divided, like Vietnam. But if we could convince the powers on this side not to interfere, to let the Thai settle things themselves, I think the liberation movements and even the communists would realize that they don't want to rely too much on the superpower of the other side either. So, if such could be the case, there might be a chance of a more, well, perhaps socialistic, but a bit more liberal government than, say, Laos or Vietnam. They might even be not quite red. This is my hope, but it may not come true.

Schmidt : There are Christians who ought to be taken seriously, who anticipate that the missionary efforts of Buddhists in Europe challenge the church here and will decisively influence the future of religions in Europe. Would you like to say something about this?

Sulak : You see, being a Buddhist, as I said, we always try to impress those of other faiths. But I can't say anything about the Christian Europeans. If they would share a little bit of my opinion, I think it would do the church a lot of good. These Buddhist movements, I wouldn't call missionary work because mostly they are indigenous people. The Sinhalese monks or the Thai monks who come here, usually look after their own communities. Say I come from England. In England it is the English themselves who are propagating Buddhism, you see? If the Christians would take them seriously, I think, we could learn a lot from each other. I certainly know that some British Buddhists want to learn a great deal from the Christians. I mean they take Christians very seriously and I know some of the German Catholic priests who are writing on Zen practice. There are a lot of things to be learned from each other, paticularly the Buddhist tradition, where the meditation side is very strong. It has been weak, of course, but it is fairly strong yet. And I think this is a bit – if I may humbly say this – that Christians could learn. Buddhists can also learn a lot from the Christians, particularly the radical Christians, about their approach to society. I feel that the Buddhist teaching in the West tends to be too weak on that. They want to withdraw from society. I don't think that is very healthy either, from the Buddhist point of view.

Schmidt: You preached in a Protestant church in England?

Sulak: Well, in an Anglican church, you know, they claim to be both Catholic and Protestant.

Schmidt: Are there sectors or tasks where you feel we should help each other as Christians and Buddhists, or as Thais and Germans?

Sulak: Well, coming back to my point. Point number one is trust. You can't trust people very easily, obviously. But I think we can start with small groups of people, whether Germans or Thais, whether Christians or Buddhists, trusting each other. And from trust comes sharing. You see, using Buddhist terminology, the Dana, is sharing material things, sharing knowledge, sharing spiritual experience. This would be very healthy all around. Because on the other side, there are so many negative things going on. Thais who know about Germany are mainly tourists and Germans who know my country are those taking the Thai girls to Germany. This is a rather negative side, you know. So I think we ought to build on the positive side. Understanding, trusting. And I think committed religious people could do a great deal, if they go out of their way a little bit to make friends with people of other faiths. Making friends with people of other nationalities is not very easy, mind you, because of the cultural gap and all kinds of obstacles. But I think if there is a will, there is a way too! This is also a Buddhist maxim.

Schmidt: You are an editor. Would you tell us the reason why you published German History and Literature in the Thai language?

Sulak: Again I have to come back to my point. I want to build up understanding at all levels. As to my profession, I happen to be a publisher, a journalist, a teacher. I teach to obtain understanding, and publish to obtain a better understanding. I do the same with German people. I do the same with English people, with Americans. I do the same in Southeast Asian Cultural Relations for the Future. We produce booklets and all kinds of things. We publish Thai short stories in English and we hope to do the same in German. And I think, in our small ways, this is hopeful. One way for Thais to know the Germans is through German literature, through their history, and, of course, through personal contacts.

Schmidt : Thank you very much.

Published in German in *der Uberblick du forum* 3/78.
Evarg Verlangswerk GmbH, Stafflenbergstresse 44, Stuttgart.

IV
WESTERN CONTRIBUTIONS
TO THAI STUDIES

AMERICAN INFLUENCE ON BOOKS, MAGAZINES AND NEWSPAPERS IN SIAM

According to tradition, which is to some extent borne out by archeological discoveries, the art of printing was known in Siam and in various other Asian countries long before it was re-invented in Europe. As in China, the necessary characters were cut in relief slabs of wood, inked, and then transferred by hand-pressure to various materials. There was, however, a printing press on Western lines and with a moveable type in Siam in 1662, when Mgr. Laneau of the French Society of Foreign Missions wrote and published at Ayudhaya (the capital), twenty-six volumes of Siamese Christian tracts, one volume of a Siamese and Pali Grammar, and one volume of a Siamese Dictionary. Inspired by this innovation, King Narai also started a royal printing plant within the palace compound at Lopburi. In 1670, Pierre Langrois, another French priest, was sent to help print the catechism in Siamese to propagate the Christian religion.

With the death of King Narai in 1688, there arose a new nationalist movement which rejected all kinds of Western influence. The new King's closed door policy led, in the long run, to the destruction of Ayudhaya by the invading Burmese army in 1767, which burnt all our printed materials and most of our historical records. Yet, the Roman Catholics managed to preserve their printing press up to 1796, when a Thai catechism was printed in Bangkok. But only Roman letters were used for printing the Thai language.

In 1767, the Burmese took with them about 30,000 Siamese war captives to Burma, and from 1813 to 1850, an American missionary couple, the Rev. and Mrs. Adoniram Judson resided in that country, where they came across a Siamese colony in

Moulemain. Mrs. Ann Haseltine Judson, in particular, was so fascinated with the Siamese language that she began to study it, and she eventually translated the "Gospel According to St. Matthew" as well as her husband's Burmese catechism into Thai. She also translated a Siamese Jataka story (Lives of the Buddha prior to his final incarnation) into English.

In 1816, George H. Hough, an American printer, joined the Judsons in Burma for missionary work. He was also very good at casting new type. It is claimed that the first Burmese type was invented by an Italian bishop, Percoto of the Barnabites, who sent Burmese Christian literature to be printed in Rome in 1776. Hough started printing Siamese and Burmese in Burma in early 1817. In 1819 Hough was transferred to Serampore (Calcutta) so he took his crude printing machine with him. Mrs. Judson's Siamese catechism was printed in India in 1819, and in 1828 this same American Baptist Mission Press in Calcutta brought out Captain James Low's *A Grammar of the Thai or Siamese Language*. The press with a font of Siamese type was later purchased by Rev. Robert Barnes of Singapore.

Apart from the Judsons, the Rev. and Mrs. John Taylor Jones of the American Baptist Mission also resided in Burma, and they were later transfered to Siam. Early in 1835, Mr. Jones took his own translation of the Gospel of St Matthew and the catechism from Bangkok to Singapore to have them printed on the Serampore Siamese Press. It is possible that he brought from Moulemein the unpublished Siamese Gospel prepared by Mrs. Judson, and that this manuscript served as the basis of his own translation. It is certain that Mrs.Jones compiled her Siamese dictionary with the aid of the earlier one prepared by Dr. Carl Friedrich Angustus Gutzlaff, the first Protestant missionary who came to Bangkok in 1828. Later in 1835, this now famous first Siamese press was bought by Rev. Dan Beach Bradley, when he travelled en route from the U.S.A. to take up his first mission assignment in Siam; and the first printing job was executed in Bangkok in 1838, consisting of 1,000 copies of an eight-page tract containing the Ten Commandments, with an introduction and explanation, a short prayer and three hymns.

After less than three years in operation, the press attracted the Siamese Government's attention, and on April 27th, 1839 Dr. Bradley turned out the first Government document ever printed in Bangkok, 9,000 copies of a royal proclamation outlawing opium.

His printing kept him in touch with government officials and with commercial and shipping firms, and consequently Bradley was well-known in Bangkok. For a time he published a fortnightly magazine, the *Bangkok Recorder* (1844-1867), and a newspaper, the *Bangkok Calendar* (1859-1872). Both carried material in Siamese and English and both started on July 4th. As Bradley said, "This day is regarded as the American National Day. We take this day as a symbol of the good wishes of the Americans who will share their experiences and new scientific knowledge with the people of Siam. " Apart from the two bilingual periodicals, Bradley also published in English the *Siam Weekly Monitor* (1868-1886) and the *Bangkok Daily Advertiser* (1866). The Bradleys' printing and publishing activities were carried on by Mrs. Bradley even after her husband had passed away, and until her own death in 1893.

In fact, the first Siamese book for which the author received a copyright was from the Bradleys' press in 1861, when Mom Rajothai, official interpreter to the first Siamese Embassy to Queen Victoria, published his poetic account of the trip called *Nirat London* – the publisher's best seller. And it was the US Minister to the Court of Siam, who proposed to the King in 1900 that the Siamese government should pass a copyright law. The American Minister was, of course, interested in protecting American interest, as George MacFarland, son of a missionary and who was himself born in Bangkok, had written books in Thai and English as well as compiling dictionaries and inventing Thai typewriters.

Before leaving Burma, Mr. & Mrs. J.T. Jones adopted an English boy, Samuel John Smith, born in India, then 12 years old, and he was sent to be educated in the USA. There he was ordained and joined the Baptist mission in Bangkok in 1849. From 1869 he operated an independent printing office where he edited and published in English the *Siam Weekly Advertiser* (1869-1886), the *Siam Repository* (1869-1884), the annual *Siam Directory* and in Siamese, *Sayam Samai* (1882-1886), an *English-Siamese Grammar*, a *Siamese-English Grammar*, an arithmetic textbook, a Christian catechism, a *Comprehensive Anglo-Siamese Dictionary* and a Comprehensive Siamese-English Dictionary (which was ready for the press at the time of his death but was never printed). He printed Siamese prose and poetry in great quantities, making the printed page very common and selling presses and fonts of type to Siamese and Chinese job printers, who opened presses everywhere in Siam.

Smith's Siamese periodical, *Sayam Samai*, was started at the time of the centenary celebration of Bangkok. He really wanted to publish one daily newspaper and one weekly magazine of the same name. In fact he could only publish it on a monthly basis during the first year. It became a fortnightly journal in the second year, and a weekly in the third and fourth years, after which it ceased to function.

The American pioneers not only continued their interest in Bangkok, but for years the mission published the only paper in northern Siam, the *Laos Christian News*. No wonder local Thai periodicals started in Chiengmai, our northern capital, before any other town.

After the destruction of Ayudhaya in April 1767, King Taksin managed towards the end of the year to recapture the capital and defeat the Burmese contingent left in Siam. However, Ayudhaya was destroyed beyond repair, and the capital was transferred to Bangkok, and the Royal House of Chakri started anew in 1782, when Rama I succeeded Taksin to the throne. The closed door policy of distrusting Westerners was carried on systematically until 1851, when King Mongkut became Rama IV. Prior to that date, he had been a Buddhist monk for 26 years, all through the reign of his half brother, Rama III. During this period, Western powers were knocking at the door of Siam as they were doing in other Asian countries. Several embassies were sent from the British East India Company, from France and from the United States. The Siamese resisted and yielded as little as they could. Protestant missionaries were finally allowed to enter Siam in 1828.

Prince Mongkut, however, realized the inevitability of encounter with the West. As a monk, he not only studied traditional and religious subjects like the Buddhist Scriptures, astrology and the Pali and Sanskrit languages, but he also learned Latin and English; and through the English language, he could master such subjects as geography, astronomy and natural science, as well as the political history of the Western world. When he realized the importance of the printing press belonging to the American missionaries, he started his own printing operation at the temple (Wat Pavaranives) asking his friends and admirers in the USA to purchase a printing machine for him. When Dr. Bradley cast the new Siamese type in Bangkok in 1842, he offered a set to the Prince and according to Bradley's *Bangkok Calendar* of 1847, the Prince possessed a printing plant, a set of Siamese letters, two sets of Roman letters and two sets of type for the Pali language. Pali, of course, has no alphabet of its own. In Siamese manuscripts, we used old Khmer letters for writing Pali. In Ceylon and Burma, Singhalese and Burmese were used respectively. When Western scholars first published the Pali canon in Europe in 1822, Roman letters were used as is the case today. Prince Mongkut, however, invented a new script similar to the Romanized form called Ariyaka for printing Pali. When his son, King Chulalongkorn, had the Tipitaka printed in 1893 (the first printed version of the entire original Pali teaching of the Buddha in the world), he used Siamese script for the purpose. Soon afterwards, old Khmer letters were discarded for writing the sacred language.

Indeed, when King Chulalongkorn first visited England in 1897, the Royal Asiatic Society presented an Address of Welcome that read, "The society regards with special gratification the advent to our shores of a sovereign who has been a constant friend of education and a distinguished patron of literature.... Your Majesty has shown, throughout your long and beneficent career, an acquaintance with the institutions, the habits and the thoughts of the West, and will appreciate the desire of this Society that the dazzle of Western material prosperity may not blind them to the real value of the great thought in that ancient literature that has been preserved, through so many centuries, by their own Siamese scholars at home.... Your Majesty, yourself a scholar of wide attainments, has, in a manner eminently benefiting the only Buddhist sovereign in the world, taken the best possible steps to ensure a result, not only by your own example and precept, but by ordering the publication, in the alphabet of the Siamese people, of the whole of the Sacred Books of the Buddhists. And this magnificent edition of the Three Pitakas, edited with great learning and accuracy by Siamese scholars, will also be.... of the greatest assistance to those European scholars who are endeavouring to solve the important problem of the real historical meaning and values of that great religion, of which Your Majesty is the acknowledged head.... In all these respects, Your Majesty stands alone among oriental sovereigns. No other has shown so enlightened a sympathy with scholarship at home and abroad, or has done so much to promote that intimate knowledge and intellectual companionship which form the most lasting basis of the mutual respect between the East and West." In fact, copies of the entire 25 volumes of these printed Buddhist Sacred Books were sent to all leading institutions in the West, the USA included, which were interested in the study of Eastern religion and literature.

In 1850, Bradley's Journal also recorded that Prince Amorit, Mongkut's cousin, "....really commenced printing a tract setting forth the claim of Buddhism... He has obtained from us the old printing press which I brought with me from Singapore in 1835. He proposed to purchase it." Prior to that, Mr. & Mrs. G.W. Eddy of Waterford, N.Y. were kind enough to supply Prince Mongkut with ink for his printing purposes. An eyewitness account by an American missionary, Samuel Reynold House, who visited his temple, recorded "several young monks working at the press. One was type-setting, another was folding, yet another was proof-reading. The monks gave us a book printed in Pali, the script of which Prince Mongkut had invented. The book was about the Buddhist Ten Commandments and an explanation."

The following year when Mongkut ascended the Throne, Prince Amorit was appointed printer to His Majesty with the printing press situated in the Grand Palace itself. The King wished to send a young official to be an apprentice abroad so that he could come back to improve the royal printing facility. An American printer, a certain Mr. Cartner, was also hired from Singapore for the same purpose; but he proved a failure. Rev. J.H. Chandler, an American missionary experienced in printing, publishing and journalism in Bangkok, was hired for a time, but he did not get along well with the King. This was different from Dr. Caswell, another American who taught English to the King while he was a monk and who was allowed to preach the Gospels to his Buddhist congregation at the Temple, since the friendship between the two men was sustained. Mongkut not only attended Caswell's funeral, but gave a lot of money to his widow later on. Quite a number of monks also followed the King in leaving the holy order, and some joined the new printing establishment.

Although King Mongkut appreciated Bradley's journalism, he was very much upset by the missionary's attack on him personally and on his country in general. In a personal memorandum, he complained that American newspapers kept praising the USA and its political regime for being advanced and civilized and looked down upon traditional Siamese culture and belief as being backward, to be condemned more than to be praised.

They only liked his innovations, which his people on the whole could not understand. They wanted to encourage him to invest his money in Western technology such as railroads, telegraphy and engineering. He said he was fed up with the newspapers which, either through misunderstanding or real intention, misrepresented Siam to the foreign lands. Yet he did not suppress them, but often wrote letters to the editor, and eventually started his own *Government Gazette* in 1858. The King himself was the editor, and stated that whatever was printed there could really be trusted by his subjects. Unfortunately this periodical lasted only a year, as the King engaged in so many other activities. Yet it was revived by his son, Chulalongkorn, in 1876, and the *Government Gazette* is now the oldest weekly journal we have in the kingdom.

It was not only King Mongkut who was concerned with American missionaries' attacks on the Buddha's teaching. His senior offical, Chao Phya Dipakarawongse, was also taken aback by such rebukes. The old savant, too, was well versed in Western sciences and foreign religions, and he was much esteemed by those who knew him. Although he was Minister for Foreign Affairs, he is best known for having compiled historical records of the Bangkok period. He also wrote a book, extolling the excellence of Buddhism, as a superior religion to Christianity, which obviously no missionary's press would print for him. Therefore, he had his manuscripts cast on slabs of stone and had the book printed that way in 1861. A major part of the book was translated by Henry Alabaster, and published in London in 1871 as *The Wheel of the Law*, which gives a good idea of the Siamese intellectual climate of the period. The book has recently been reprinted in the U.S.A.

When Chulalongkorn succeeded his father to the throne in 1868, he was only 15 years old. He and his younger brothers had received some English education within the Grand Palace and realized the importance of printed books, magazines and newspapers. At first the King was powerless since power was in the hands of the Regent and the old nobility. So the younger generation formed themselves into a sort of political party, which gathered momentum slowly. Its members were sufficiently strong by 1873 to take the lead in urging radical reforms. They began to issue their own newspaper, *Darunowat*, which published a considerable amount of foreign news, proverbs, sciences and articles about fine arts, fables, poetry and drama, as well as general news and much comment on and discussion of reforms that they felt needed to be undertaken in Siam. They formed the Young Siam Society of which Chulalongkorn's full brother, Prince Phanurangsi, was President.

Darunowat itself was published from July 1874 to June 1875 by one of the King's younger brothers, Prince Phrom. It was succeeded by the daily newspaper, *Court* (Sept. 1875 - Sept. 1876) published within the palace walls by eleven of the King's younger brothers, all of whom became famous in the Siamese literary world, as well as for bringing about modern administration both for the Church and State. Without any doubt these young princes were influenced directly or indirectly by Bradley and Smith in particular. Although they were no longer interested in publishing anything as counter attacks on the American missionaries, their books were intended to be much more superior, in accuracy and scholarship, than those produced by the foreigners; and this they achieved handsomely.

Chulalongkorn founded the Vajirañāna Library in memory of his father, who had started collecting books and archeological objects from ancient capitals like Ayudhaya and Sukhothai. His younger brothers and sisters took turns in serving as committee members, and the Vajirañāna Library really became a national library and museum. Until then the history of Siam prior to the fourteenth century was practically unknown. It was due to the valuable research of a small group of enthusiasts, mostly members of the Royal Family, deciphering the annals of neighbouring states and the lithographic inscriptions found in various parts of the kingdom that have brought to light a multitude of facts bearing upon ancient Siam. Under Prince Damrong's presidency in particular, the National Library became a storehouse for the national literature and began to foster a taste for serious reading through its periodicals, the *Vajirañāna* (monthly 1884-1885 and 1894-1905, and weekly 1886-1894). The Library exerted its influence on the educated public by making it a most efficient instrument in the awakening of the people to a knowledge of their native land, and to that proper pride in national institutions and tradition, which is the root of all genuine patriotism.

It was Prince Damrong who started a fashion in producing literary and historical works, as well as works on other Siamese scholarly subjects for distribution at cremations and on birthday celebrations and so forth. Among these may be noted, especially, an able and compendious commentary on those subjects compiled by the Prince himself, apart from biographies he wrote for the deceased. On various occasions he would refer to earlier publications of Siamese prose and poetry at the Bradley's press and note how he had improved on it. It was Damrong, again, who had Bradley's Journal translated into Siamese and published in the Library's monograph series. In 1928, when the Protestant missionaries celebrated their centenary of being in Siam, Prince Damrong wrote the Introduction to their centennial volume in English.

Books, magazines and periodicals were at first in the hands of Westerners and Siamese princes and nobility only. However, with the spread of education and modern printing techniques, commoners who were not in the employ of the royal government also became interested in publishing and journalism. In the reign of King Rama V, K.S.R. Kulab and Thien Wan, in particular, caused much annoyance to the King and the princes, who accused the two editors of being semi-educated men writing for popularity, without any deep understanding of national polity and governance. Both writers, however, claimed a knowledge of English and modern scientific subjects, as well as of foreign lands, no less than an awareness of Siamese traditional culture. Mr. Kulab had his own press and edited a periodical called *Siam Prapet* and published a number of books. He was, however, caught for forging an old manuscript and for mixing facts with fiction. A Royal Commission was therefore set up to judge his literary soundness. As a result he was sent to a lunatic assyulum for a while. Mr. Wan, editor of a fortnightly called *Tulyavipag Pojanakij* (1902-1906) was taken more seriously by the government, and some of his criticisms landed him in jail for a number of years. In this respect, both Thai journalists were also following the Bradley-Smith tradition. The former gave up his journalism because he was sued for defamation and found guilty. Although he was not put in prison, he had to pay a heavy fine. Smith, being a British subject, was sued in Singapore for publishing Siamese literature, which was considered morally corrupted. He too lost his law suit.

Mr. Wan's political writing, in fact, influenced some of Rama VI's thoughts, although the King dismissed it. He also had a liberal impact on later writers, some of whom still think highly of him. His call for parliamentary democracy, in particular, might have sparked the political unrest during the first year of Rama VI's reign, when an unsuccessful coup was attempted by some young army officers.

Periodicals mentioned in this section were all published in Thai. After Smith ended his career as a journalist in 1886, missionaries were no longer interested in journalism, which had become much more commercial; however, the great European powers were interested in it for their own political reasons. The British started an English newspaper, the *Bangkok Times*, in 1887. The French started the *Siam Free Press*, also in English, in 1891. At that time both great powers were very much interested in expanding their empires towards Siam. It was the French Counsul who indirectly forced Bradley to give up his journalistic career. The King felt that the Thai, too, needed an English newspaper for their own cause. Hence, the *Siam Observer* was lanuched in 1903 by a Singhalese in the employ of the Thai Government during the period of unrest just after the blockade of Bangkok by the French fleet, when news was eagerly sought after.

The *Siam Free Press* was forced out of circulation in 1908 when the French were no longer interested in annexing any more of Siam to their Indochinese empire. It was, however, bought by an American named P.A. Hoffman, who re-christened it the *Bangkok Daily Mail*. The *Bangkok Times* and the *Siam Observer* became friendly rivals and achieved a considerable measure of success, establishing themselves upon a firm and sound basis. Both obviously worked in complete harmony with the Siamese Government and were gernerally kept well posted with official news. It was an open secret that they received government subsidies. Later both issued weekly mail editions in English and Siamese for transmission abroad and through the provinces. *The Observer* and *The Times* lasted all through the period of absolute monarchy in Siam, which ended in 1932. (*The Siam Observer* also ceased in the same year.)

What the American missionaries had started in the field of Siamese books, magazines and newspapers, the Thai became competent enough to run fairly smoothly by the end of the nineteenth century.

Apart from Prince Damrong who contributed so much to the secular world of learning, his half-brother, Prince Patriarch Vajirañānavarorasa (who joined the Buddhist brotherhood at the age of twenty and spent the rest of his life in the holy order), did like-wise for the religious world of learning. Like his father, the Prince Patriarch was a scholar of great talent and a prolific writer.

Apart from following his father's footsteps in the reform of the Buddhist Order of monkhood, he also re-established the printing plant in the royal temple, Wat Pavaranives, of which he was abbot. Many books are still being published there, a number of which were written by the Patriarch himself. The Prince had much influence on the education of monks, and together with Prince Damrong he organized modern school education throughout the provinces. His temple itself became the first Buddhist university, and the press became the first university press in the Kingdom. In 1894, he started a monthly called *Dharmacakshu,* which was a focal point for Buddhism. The magazine was discontinued for a period, but has been revived and is still in print, although it has lost much of its intellectual forcefulness.

Dharmacakshu could really be said to be an imitation of *Vajirañána*. The Prince Patriarch also imitated the *Government Gazette* by launching a monthly *Eclesiastical Announcement* in 1903, which is still in circulation.

Some of Prince Vajirañāna's sermons were translated into English, published in book form and circulated to British Burma and Ceylon. None of them contained any attacks on Christianity. In fact, it was Prince Vajirañāna who gave the idea to his nephew, King Prajadhipok or Rama VII (1925-1934), who offered a prize each year for the best essay on the propagation of Buddhism to the young. The essay is still being published annually as a booklet for free distribution among school children. In the announcement for the competition, the King made it plain that essays submitted for the prize should not refer to other religions in contemptuous terms. Early American missionary tracts had always condemned Buddhism contemptuously. The Thai, however, followed a "more excellent way".

It was not only Chulalongkorn's brothers who contributed so much to the printing world in the constructive sense of the word and we have only mentioned two outstanding ones. His sons also helped in this literary tradition. King Vajiravudh known as Rama VI (1910-1925), in particular, started editing magazines and writing essays, plays and poems when he became Crown Prince. Literature was one of his greatest loves, and he was recognized as one of the major Siamese poets of his day. Yet it must be confessed that his style was academic, and apart from patriotic songs, his poetry lacked deep feeling. His knowledge of English was perfect, since he was sent to England for education at an early age. In fact his writing started seriously in that country, where he started a magazine, *Samaggi Sara* in 1901 (in Thai and English) which the Siamese Students Association in England still produces regularly. He was especially impressed with the works of Shakespeare and his translation of three of the master's plays were not only close in idiom and accurate even to punctuation, but were poetical as well. He also translated other English and French playwrights, as well as rendering Sanskrit literature in Siamese. Yet American literature seemed to have no influence on him, although he visited the USA on his way home and admired quite a number of American friends.

Indeed, publishing activities reached the peak in quality during his reign. Thai books with the best kind of paper and bindings were sought after by the educated elite. Siamese scholars were encouraged to do research work on Siamese and Indian language and culture, and foreign scholars were employed in the government. When the foreign residents wanted to study Siam and her neighbouring countries in depth, to propagate their findings in lectures and publications, Vajiravudh and Damrong encouraged them. Hence, the Siam Society was founded under the patronage and vice-patronage of these two members of the royal family in 1904, and the *Journal of the Siam Society* is now fairly well-known to those who are interested in Oriental Studies.

Although Rama VI was an absolute monarch, he was so liberal and liked journalism so much that he wrote many articles under various pseudonyms in Thai and English. The attack on the King in newspapers and magazines, was sometimes so strong, this time by his own subjects and no longer by American missionaries, that he was really hurt. What K.S.R. Kulap and Thien Wan had started in the reign of his father became common during his period of Kingship. The attack was on him personally, on his courtiers and his policy. Very often he wrote back.

The most outspoken newspaper then was the *Chino Siamese Daily News*, published in both the Chinese and Siamese languages. Although the *Bangkok Times* and the *Siam Observers* had been tamed by the end of the last century, the *Bangkok Daily Mail*, in both its English and Siamese editions, was very vocal against the King in many respects. The American editor, Mr. Hoffman, started a very good tradition on an ethical code of conduct for the Thai pressmen, by refusing to let his authors or columnists be known to anyone but himself, not even to the King, since those who wrote articles criticizing the King were more often than not H.M.'s relatives and officials! However much displeased the King was with what he called an outraged attack on him and his administration, like his grandfather King Mongkut, he read the printed words with care. In fact, it was Hoffman's editorial that carried much weight in the King's decision to follow the American nation in declaring war against the Central Axis powers during the First World War; and Siam derived much benefit from the war. The *Bangkok Daily Mail,* however, criticized him so much that he eventually bought it.

Unlike his brother, King Prajadhipok did not like writing much, yet his liberal upbringing in England made him not only tolerate the newspapers, but also encourage some of his close friends and officials to write articles regularly. However, he found the *Mail* drained so much money from the Privy Purse that he sold it to his father-in-law, who employed an American Jewish journalist, A.A. Freeman, to edit it. The paper then became much improved. Later on, a very able Thai, Louis Girivat, became editor. Under his editorship a lot of leading Thai writers were trained.

Both kings, Rama VI and VII, as their father had done before them, subsidized some newspapers and were friendy with some journalists. But journalism then, like book publishing, was still in the hands of the educated elite. Both Kings did not care much for the popular press which they thought vulgar, but tolerated it and did not take the popular newspapers seriously. As for quality journalism, of which there was quite a bit, Rama VII read it attentively. He once remarked: "If any criticism is constructive, the government must act according to its suggestion. If the criticism is nonsensical, we should not take it to heart, since the writer has made a fool of himself already, and what he writes people will soon forget."

In fact it was in the USA in 1931 that King Prajadhipok announced his intention to grant a constitution to his people, and on his return to Bangkok in October of the same year he called a press conference and allowed his secretary to describe his trip to America and to outline some future policies for Siam – the first time that the royal Siamese government dealt with the press as such. Could this be attributed to the experience the King gained in the USA? Unfortunately his relatives and his American advisers then thought that the public was not yet ready for democracy.

When the colonels forced the King to become constitutional monarch in June of 1932, one of the charges made against the princes was that the royal government used secretive methods in running the country. The rulers, they said, took care not to let the public know what they were doing. The people (i.e., the educated military and civil servants who were not informed) felt that what was secret must be bad. Occasional public statements of policy or plans were made, but they were not of great value to the public, since they were usually issued in English. The accusers felt that the King cared more for improving his image among the foreign community. For example, his intention to grant a constitution was first annouced abroad, and important government statements were published in English papers and then translated into Siamese which followed the English idiom and were often unintelligible to the people. Hence, misunderstanding arose between the King and his subjects.

The irony is that after "democracy" dawned in this coutry, there was less freedom for the journalists. One year after the people's government was installed, the Press Act of 1933 was passed to make the newspapers harmless to the Administration. In 1932 alone, after the Revolutionary Party came to power in June, there were ten occasions in which a newspaper was closed either temporarily or permanently. From 1933 to 1934, there were seventeen occasions in which the government found it necessary to close a newspaper. An American author at that period observed: "It may be concluded, then, that Siam has very strict censorship of the Press. There is no freedom of the Press in Siam in the sense that there is freedom of the Press in the United States. All important news is sifted through the government Press Bureau. Not only is it heavily censored, it is often quite late reaching the public."

Although the age of the Princes was over administratively, some members of the Chakri Dynasty still played prominent roles in the publishing world. Prince Bidya started a daily *Pramuan Wan* and weekly *Pramuan Sara* in 1935. At about the same time, his brother-in-law, Prince Wan (who later became the first Thai Ambassador to the US after the war and was eventually the first Asian President of the UN General Assembly) published the *Prachachat (Nation)* daily and weekly. Prince Bidya, himself a poet of repute, represented the liberal conservative line, while Prince Wan, having joined the democratic regime, offered more liberal progressive ideas. The latter in particular coined many new words hitherto unknown to the Siamese language, for instance: Constitution, Revolution, Political Science, Proletariat, Reform, Political Party. These concepts had never found expression before in Thai. (On the other hand, words did exist before 1932 for such terms as Government, Privy Purse, Cabinet, Education, Taxes and Legislation, most of which were created by King Chulalongkorn, his brothers and his sons.) The two princes, the products of Cambridge and Oxford, apart from being great scholars and prolific writers, managed to train quite a number of dedicated Thai journalists, some of whom are known to have sacrificed their lives for the freedom of the Press and of the Thai people. Others of course made use of journalism as a stepping stone to a more ambitious and remunerative career. Prince Dhani, cousin of Prince Wan, having been removed from the portfolio in the Ministry of Public Instruction, became the first Thai editor of the *Journal of the Siam Society*. Indeed, all the three princes contributed articles for this journal. The Society still publishes a number of scholarly books, most of which are in English.

By then, there was no American influence in the Siamese publishing world, so to speak. The new regime more and more admired and imitated Germany, Italy and Japan. British interest in the *Bangkok Times* also faded away gradually, as we must remember that the *Bangkok Times* had a close connection with the royal government and it ceased its operation entirely by 1941.

Up to the end of the Second World War, American interest in Siam was mainly for the sake of the Siamese. The missionaries were still the largest contingency. American businessmen were very few and the American legation was very small. Up to then, the Siamese regarded the Americans as their best friends. Not only did American pioneers in Siam help them in publishing, medical and educational activities, but the USA also never claimed any colonial interest in this country, and she, as well as an American editor in this country, persuaded the Siamese Government to join the First World War on the side of the Allies. As a result of the war, American advisers to the Siamese Foreign Ministry helped to persuade their government to treat us as an equal partner; and because of the American example, other Great Powers also gave up extraterritorial rights in Siam.

The Thai democratic government became more and more dictatorial. They even forced the Thai people to give up their national dress, in order to imitate Western fashion so that the country could be really regarded as civilized; and the name of the country, too, had to have an English word attached to it, since Siam reminded the new leaders of the ancient regime; hence, Thailand was declared the name of the country and it joined the Axis Powers during the Second World War. The Thai minister in Washington, D.C., however, refused to deliver the declaration of war to the USA, which thus did not consider that a state of war existed between the two countries. After the war, the American Government tried hard to persuade and put pressure on the British and the French (who wanted to punish Siam for fighting the war against them) to leave the Thais alone. In fact it was the American press as well as some American citizens, concerned with the independence and integrity of Siam, who helped the Thai mission which was sent to the USA especially for this purpose. According to a member of the Thai mission, it was he who persuaded the Americans to trade more directly with Siam, not via London as hitherto, and emphasized that American capital should immediately be invested in Siam before other Western nationals had the chance to re-establish themselves there.

Soon after the Second World War, the Siamese dream to have the Americans become more interested in their country was really fulfilled. Former missionaries, like K.L. Landon, even became advisers to the State Department. Landon's wife wrote the bestseller on Siam, *Anna and the King*, (unfortunately it was a distorted picture) which became *The King and I*. Former members of the OSS became businessmen and journalists in Bangkok and some became scholars of Thai culture. The Legation in Bangkok, with very few staff members, was raised in status to an Embassy and its activities expanded as Americans became more and more involved in this part of the world.

Up to the Second World War, the American public hardly knew that Siam existed. Those who knew it, loved it and wished it to remain an independent kingdom, preserving its friendliness, tolerance, dignity and way of life. They would have been overjoyed if the Siamese had chosen the path of freedom and democracy, but they did not want to force their way of life on the Thai. Although Dr. Bradley sometimes criticized the Thai severely, he respected them and admired them. (In his own Journal he kept confessing to God his own failure for not being able to convert the Thai to Christianity). And in fact as we may recall, it was the American advisers to the Royal Siamese Government who cautioned the King against granting a constitution to his subjects.

As the US interest in the world grew, while great European empires were shrinking, America became a neocolonialist power, whether intentionally or otherwise. Although she claimed that she did not want to extend her power, her interest in protecting the Free World against communist expansion meant that she wanted to maintain and, if possible, to expand her brand of capitalism. Siam was an ideal country to be picked up early enough to be an American stronghold on the mainland of Southeast Asia. The Siamese had to be taught to fear and to hate the Communists and to admire the American way of life. To do that the US Government was even willing to back the Thai dictator who had once declared war on the USA and who was at one time a war criminal. By backing this man, Field Marshal Pibulsonggram, who re-entered Thai politics via an army coup in 1947, the USA began to manipulate Thai politics directly and has been doing so ever since. Three successive Field Marshals ran the country with full US support until October 1973. A civilian Prime Minister who served a short interim period also had to be approved by Washington.

During this period, the Thai public was given information on only one side of the story. The US Information Service was very active in supplying local editors with the latest "facts", plus ready-made commentaries in Thai, Chinese or English. The friendly Thai editors were frequently invited to meet American VIPs, to visit the USA and her allies in Asia. Training courses and seminars for journalists were often arranged in Bangkok and other provinces by USIS in conjunction with the Thai Public Relations Department or the Thai Press Association. A Press Foundation was established with American money to award prizes to Thai journalists. A John F. Kennedy Foundation, in memory of the late President, was also launched to encourage Thai authors to produce the best books possible. At one time, *Time* magazine even had a project to train all future leading Siamese editors in the USA. Apart from USIS and *Time,* the Thai journalists were encouraged to make use of and look up to AP, UP, *Newsweek*, and *Reader's Digest* – not to mention shady publications and news agencies supported by CIA money. All of these were not US Government organs, but could not be said to represent anything but the American interest.

Any journalist or writer who was not friendly to the Thai or the American Government could easily be branded as a

Communist or fellow traveller. And in the period 1958 to 1973, no new Thai newspaper was registered, while any periodical could easily be closed down at the will of the government. Journalists were very tame. Those who fought for freedom of the press were either in jail (many of them without trial) or in exile abroad. Some, of course, had no other alternative but to join the Communist insurgent movement. In fact, at one time USIS had a list of friendly and unfriendly editors, and the Thai police were sometimes told by American Embassy officials to look out for or even to arrest Thai journalists. One Thai novelist whose short stories were supposed to be political could not even join such a learned institution as the Siam Society, for some Council members thought the author was too dangerous. In fact, he was nearly arrested. USIS always managed to have at least one of its officials attached to the Society and similar organizations. (A US Cultural Attache once even edited the *Journal of the Siam Society*. Even today, USIS has its connection with the Siam Society.) But if any Thai author wrote anything against the Communists, such a book would receive tremendous applause. That is why USIS saw to it that Kukrit Pramoj's *Red Bamboo*, a mediocre novel, was translated into 18 languages.

    USIS was, of course, active in other mass media as well. But radio, moving pictures and television are not within the scope of this paper (although USIS and Voice of America still have a share of "control" over media). It should also be mentioned that USIS founded libraries in the provincial towns, all of which were much more attractive than those run by the Thai authorities. USIS, as well as other American agencies like the Asia Foundation, supplied books in English and Thai (many translations of which were commissioned or subsidized by them) to leading editors and to almost every library, especially in schools and colleges, in the villages and the monasteries. Some professors also received books, magazines and "information sheets" regularly through the courtesy of American "philanthropic" organizations. During this period, Thai academics and administrators were, on the whole, trained en bloc in the USA. American teachers and researchers, as well as advisers and administrators – not to mention military personnel – penetrated through all our institutions. US institutions of learning established independently in this country (like the American University Alumni Association) or attached to the Thai establishment (like Indiana University), one way or the other served American interests rather than learning per se.

As the US belongs to the great liberal and democratic tradition, however imperfect it may be, and however arrogant and selfish her government may have become, some of her citizens still think highly of the American ideals of humanity, equality, and freedom, and are willing to fight for them. Some Americans have been very vocal against their own government and even their own way of life. Some of the Thais who went to the USA for their education returned home as strong critics of US policy and its activitees in our country and in the world. Unfortunately, not many of them had been well educated enough to see beyond the glitter of American materialism and capitalism which hides her real exploitation behind the scene. Some Americans in Siam, such as Peace Corps Volunteers and even ex-GIs or those who defected from the Armed Forces, also informed us of their country's weak points and wickedness. Some even became first-rate journalists and writers who collaborated closely with their Thai counterparts. Again, there were not many of them.

One good point about the Thai regimes was that they had been in power successively for so long that they became relaxed and did not take the press as seriously as they did at the beginning. Besides, the bureaucracy had never been very effective, especially in dealing with foreign literature. Thus even in the early 1960s, some British and American "subversive" books, magazines and newspapers were being sold in Bangkok fairly openly – these printed materials USIS would never have dreamed of sending to their Thai friends. In 1963, some American agencies in Bangkok even helped a group of Siamese educated elite launch the *Social Science Review*. As no newspaper or magazine had been registered since 1958, this was supposed to be an academic quarterly with no social or political bearing on the Thai society. The Review eventually became a monthly, and functioned as a platform for Thai intellectuals to express their views freely. Criticisms of Thai-American relations in the sixties were first published in the Review, which was the first Thai magazine to reveal the presence of American air bases in Siam. Some creative writing also first appeared in the Review before they were published in book form. With the *Social Science Review* as a base, a secular University Press was launched with American Public Law 480 assistance. Some members of the Association of the American University Presses were very helpful to this new venture on a personal basis.

However, the Franklin Book Program was not really interested in Siam. Finally, a bookshop was established and it became a place where liberal authors, columnists and academics met regularly with committed students, who wanted to free Siam from dictatorship and American domination. It has been claimed by some political scientists that from such a small beginning, the dictatorial regime of Field Marshal Thanom Kittikhachorn was eventually overthrown one decade later by the Thai students and people in October 1973; and the Field Marshal had to seek political asylum from his patron in Boston.

Having been brainwashed by American information almost exclusively for about three decades, the public and the elite who believed in maintaining the status quo still clung to the idea that our best friend and ally would always protect us against the communist regimes, which expanded across all the Indochinese states. They are now our next door neighbours in the east and the northeast. American military and economic aid, as well as US troops within our country, were all for our benefit. The bombing in Vietnam, the military intervention in Laos and Cambodia, were for the joint benefit of the Free World. The capitalistic approach to development must be our solution. If only corruption among Thai officials could be eliminated, the Thai Government backed by the great American nation would be effective in maintaining "law and order" for the benefit of our country.

Even after the events of October 1973, when the Thai Government was supposed to have become more liberal and democratic, the American propaganda network was still very effective. Having been in the "game" in this country for so long, Americans even knew how to spread rumours before they appeared in print. They also had many Thai propagandists on their payroll directly or indirectly, some of whom are famous authors. Anyone who was critical of either the government or of the Free World could easily be branded as a communist. Indeed any "anti-American" was normally denounced as anti-monarchy also. It was claimed that those who wrote about the poverty and oppression within Siam or about the exploitation of the minorities in the USA (be it in an article or a novel) were not necessarily communists, but they paved the way for the communists to take over.

Those who were committed to freeing their country of American domination became not only fed up with such accusations (and in some cases, assassinations), but with their own experiences with the Americans during these decades. This made them realize that the US brand of capitalism and free enterprise might only be good for the Americans and for the few local elite who were willing to trade off their country and their people for their own benefit and for the benefit of developed countries like Japan and the USA. Indeed, it was through reading some US books and magazines written and edited by concerned American scholars, that they reached this conclusion. Hence, these people sought an alternative to the American model.

As far as the printed network was concerned, the Communists were at a disadvantage since they could not distribute their literature openly during the last regime. Even immediately after 1973, books on Marx, Engels, Che Guevara and Castro, as well as magazines on the New Left, came mostly from the USA. It was only later that the Thai version of Mao Tse Tung's writings came directly from the People's Republic of China, as the law against importing anything from that country was not lifted until the Thais established diplomatic relations with Peking in 1975. By then Thai translators, authors and editors had managed to produce a lot of local books and magazines with a strong socialistic message. There was a student newspaper which claimed to take a socialist stance, but bombs were thrown at its editorial office, so that it had to cease its publication. The Americans and their friends, of course, confused the issue further, not merely by their accusations that all these people were communists, but also by producing Thai books and magazines which were supposed to be socialistic or even communistic, but which in fact distorted socialism and communism as best they could.

Those who committed themselves to the socialist ideology, although many of them were converted, or could come out in the open only very recently, published a lot of material to propagate the success of Peking and Hanoi. Either by choice or by force of circumstances, they attacked the Thai and the American governments very strongly, seeing no single good point, not even in the remote past. To these people, the past has not been relevant; what they want is not to understand, but to reform the society. Unfortunately, the Thai literature on socialism and communism thus far seems to be rather shallow. It is mostly propaganda (even in the novels), rather than containing real scholarship or literary value, and the authors rarely even understand their own Thai society. They can only analyze things from the Marxian approach.

They seek a quick and ready-made solution, as do their opponents who cling to the American view. These people believe that once Siam becomes a socialist state, all social ills will be easily cured. Even those who are not so naive argue that with an American presence (like we have now) we shall never be able to find our own solutions. By establishing a socialist regime, problems would not be easily solved, but at least there would be a chance of solving them. These people seem to ignore the Chinese, Vietnamese and Russian domination, or they feel they are competent enough to deal with these foreign powers who are at least on the same ideological wave length. Or could it be that the devil we do not know appears to be milder than the devil we know?

The Siamese world of letters at this stage seems to be sharply divided. Even among the same religious community, strong opinions are expressed differently in print on these two lines of approach; and accusation seems to be the order of the day. We cannot minimize American negative influences on this issue. Yet what Siam needs at this stage is books, magazines and newspapers as much as we need honest criticism on them – not to mention our own kind of creative writing, free of propaganda from either camp. We need facts and information per se. The Thais should be allowed to read Marx as well as Jefferson, Thoreau or Gandhi. USIS never had any writings of Jefferson, Adams or de Toqueville translated, not to mention Paine, Irving, Poe or Longfellow. Dean Rusk's and Henry Kissinger's statements (while the two men were in power) were of course always translated in full. USIS only published books which said how wonderful Lincoln, Jefferson or Washington were, not what these men actually thought and wrote.

Thai thinkers and writers should be allowed to study both liberal and communist thought and they ought to be allowed to study these ideologies in depth and dream about them. If they were allowed to study their own society, perhaps from a Thai Buddhist, and not from an American liberal or a Chinese Maoist standpoint, the Thai world of letters would be much enriched. The Thais might even be able to find their own solutions by establishing friendly relations with their communist neighbours and thus learn a great deal from them. The Thais might also be able to maintain friendly relations with the United States, as well as with the Western world and also learn to respect it. In the past, the Thais managed to preserve their independence because of their dignity, modesty and flexibility. The US even helped them towards that end. Now the US has said she would like to help us, but our experience has taught us that she has been a hindrance rather than an aid. And by making us their junior ally for three decades, the American Government has made us lose our confidence. We have become materialistic, superficial and lacking in self respect. With such characteristics, we cannot even produce any first rate literature – not to mention other political, social, cultural and spiritual implications. If the USA would only leave us alone, or allow us to be ourselves once more, we should be able to develop our own thinking, writing and publishing for our own benefit, and perhaps for the benefit of the outside world. If we have a chance to do it ourselves and are unable to do it, then we only have ourselves to blame.

Paper prepared for the 1976 International Conference *THE UNITED STATES IN THE WORLD* September 27-October 1, in Washington D.C. at the Smithsonian Institute. It was published in *The NATION* Sunday 15, 22, 29 October 1978 with permission from The American Studies Association and the American Council for Learned Societies.

Bibliography

Thai

Ampai Chandrachira, *The Evolution of Printed Books in Thailand* (Bangkok, 1973).

Phya Anumanrajadhon, *Memoirs*, Vol. I (Bangkok 1967).

M.L. Boonlua Depyasuwan, "Turning Point in Siamese Literature" in *Wanwithayakorn* Vol. I (Bangkok 1971).

George Coedes, *History of Thai Letters* (Bangkok 1926).

T.H.R. Prince Damrong and Prince Vajirañāna, *A History of Wat Pavaranives* (Bangkok, 1922).

Department of Fine Arts, *Periodicals and Newspapers Printed in Thailand between 1884-1973: a Bibliography*, 5 Volumes (Bangkok, 1970-1975).

F. Hilaire, *"Printed Books in Siam"*, in *Darunsuksa*, Vol. IV (Bangkok, 1921).

Kachorn Sukhabanij, *First Steps of Newspapers in Thailand* (Bangkok, 1965).

Royal Institute, *List of Journals Published in Siam* (Bangkok, 1931).

S. Sivaraksa, "Books and Newspapers", *Siamese Writing* (Bangkok,1967).

English

F. Bradley and G.H. Feltus, eds., *Abstract of the Journal of Rev. Dan Beach Bradley*, Ohio, (1936).

Buddhist Association of Thailand, *Visakha Puja* (Bangkok, 1963).

Direck Jayanama, *Siam and World War II,* translated by Jane Keyes (Bangkok, 1976)

Sodsai Khantivorapong, *History of the Siam Society* (Bangkok, 1976.)

G.G. McFarland, ed., *Historical Sketch of Protestant Missions in Siam 1828-1928* (Bangkok, 1928).

K.L. Landon, *Siam in Transition* (New York, 1939).

D.C. Lord, *Mo Bradley and Thailand* (Michigan, 1969).

Virginia Thompson, *Thailand: The New Siam* (New York,1941).

POLITICAL SCIENCE : A SIAMESE RESPONSE TO WESTERN STUDIES

I have two shortcomings: (1) I have no formal training as a political scientist (I don't know if that's a blessing or not); and (2) because of problems with the Canadian postal service, I did not have Anderson's paper until this morning.

I must say that I always find Ben Anderson's papers of great interest; every piece of his that I have ever read has been stimulating and challenging. For example, his 1977 article on the social and cultural aspects of the October 6th coup fascinated me. Yet I could not bring myself to agree with him, especially with his class analysis of the Thai society. His paper here under discussion puts me in a similar predicament. To contradict him, one would need to do a lot of homework. But at the same time, I feel I cannot simply let him get away unchallenged.

My reaction is deep-rooted. Perhaps this is because he took a position from a rather Marxian standpoint, whereas I having come from a bourgeois Bangkok background, and being royalist and traditionalist at heart, see things differently. But I think that fundamental questions of East–West, Thai–non-Thai may come into it too. You see, in the West you take politics to be amoral. But from my upbringing, I regard politics as something moral. So the role of the monarchy must be a moral one. Of course, there are some shortcomings. I shall return to them later on.

Concerning what Anderson said about Thai uniqueness: my grandfather having come from China and having been an assimilated Thai, I'd like to point to that as Thai uniqueness. I agree with Anderson that one ought not accept unchallenged the idea of Thai uniqueness, but rather understand and go beyond it. However, I believe that several things ought to be said about Thai uniqueness; we must not merely bypass it.

I agree with most of what Anderson said, but I feel he went a little too far. Some of his statements need more factual substantiation to make them fit his theoretical framework or his analysis. I do agree with most of his opening remarks and his conclusion, though. Since he was writing about the work of Westerners, Anderson did not mention *The State of Social Sciences in Thailand*, a survey commissioned by and published by the Social Sciences Association of Thailand (1974); however, that monograph would on the whole confirm his statement on the weak and sad state of serious writing on political science in and about Thailand.

I would like to add in parentheses here that one point on which Anderson and I agree is a preference for the name Siam over Thailand. (Pridi and the princes also agree on the name Siam, although their motives may be different.) Nevertheless, I find that Anderson tends to look too positively toward what he regards as the progressive element, and perhaps too negatively toward the traditionalist and the royalist. Pridi, for example, is much more complex a man than to be branded merely a "progressive Thai statesman." Jit Phumisak, too, is a much more complicated character than his worshipers (and he has been canonized particularly by those who claim to represent the masses) or his admirers make him out to be.

I certainly like Anderson's four axioms and counter-axioms; they are all thought-provoking. But, as I said earlier, to do him justice one would need more time to argue against his points. What I can do here is merely to point out briefly and superficially major disagreements I have with some of the ideas in his paper, and raise some questions.

For instance, I find his treatment of the Thai military as "mainly a means for internal royalist consolidation... [and] in addition, an emblem of modernity" a bit too neat a formulation. I think applying it to the reigns of Rama V and Rama VI stretches it back just a little too far. Admittedly, from the reign of Rama V to 1932, the Thai Army did not have to fight foreign aggressors (except the Ho, who attacked Luang Prabang, which was then part of the Thai kingdom). But to the ruler, the fear of foreign aggression was still real. The thought of using the army to suppress the people is a quite late development in the Thai mental attitude. I agree that during the colonial period Siam should not be compared with Japan; I never wanted to compare Siam with

Japan anyway. But to merely compare Siam with a kind of sultanate in Malaya, I feel the case is being stretched a bit too far there also.

It is fashionable among some progressive Thai writers nowadays to claim that Chulalongkorn's abolition of slavery was merely a matter of self-interest (his own and that of his class), rather than an act of magnanimity for the good of the kingdom and its citizens; Anderson seems also to be of that opinion. Unfortunately, Chulalongkorn has been too much praised; but it is too extreme not to give him the credit due to him. The monarchy may be a hindrance, from the Western nationalist point of view. After all, nationalism is a product of the West; indeed, the idea of nationlism in Siam was instigated by Vajiravudh, who got the idea from England. (He also got his anti-Chinese ideas from England. This is brought out very clearly in a paper written by a Cornell student, Karen Silverstein; she traces how he got his ideas regarding the Chinese as the Jews of the East and so on). Not until recently did the Thais ever regard the monarchy as a hindrance to their national progress. By "Thais" here I mean all writers, including some who have been put in jail by the monarch, for example Tianwan, who, while expressing himself very clearly on Thai nationalism and Thai progress, never ceased to be loyal to the throne.

I would like to know the basis for Anderson's statement that "the coup leaders came close to abolishing the monarchy; but in the end they lost their nerve." In my own reading of the coup of 1932, and in my conversations with many of the coup leaders, there was no intention to abolish the monarchy. In fact, most of the leaders, including Pridi Banomyong, had strong respect for the monarchy. Contemporary feelings against the monarchy must not be extended too far back into history; antimonarchy sentiment tends to be present only after 1976– even the Communist Party of Thailand never said anything against the monarchy before then.

I also have some major disagreements with Anderson on minority and national integration, on stability and instability. Unfortunately, I do not have time to go into those subjects in detail now. However, I would like to point out that I do not see any model state nowadays, including the United States, that is stable. Another matter I wish I had more time to go into here is my idea of "backwardness"; those of you who have read my writings will be aware of it. I do not accept the Western concepts of "progress," "development," "modernization," and so forth. What I find weakest in Anderson's paper is his treatment of culture and politics, and of the Sangha. He does not do the Sangha justice.

Anderson's quoting from the *Area Handbook* (Smith et al. 1968), merely because it supports his argument, does not convince me. In the Kalama Sutta, the Buddha taught that one must not quote another's words simply because they happen to agree with one's own ideas, even if the words be those of the Buddha himself. Indeed, there has been much artistic and cultural deterioration since the reign of King Chulalongkorn, even at the beginning of the Bangkok period. Some would argue that it took place even earlier. Yet the Chakri kings and princes and people did a great deal for conservation and restoration, including new creativity in the Bangkok period. The artistic stagnation took place only in the last two or three decades. Anderson makes much of Sunthon Phu's fall from favour coinciding with the accession of Rama III; in fact, most people realize that Sunthon Phu was very well looked after by the second king of the reign, Rama IV.

Despite my disagreements with him, I have been much enriched by my reading of Anderson's paper. His recommendations ought to be taken seriously. My own modest proposal would include the following points:

(1) Western scholars, especially political scientists, ought to know the Thai language better, and consult more Thai writings. I have been very much encouraged about historians and about anthropologists; their knowledge of Thai has become much better. But I don't see that much knowledge of Thai among political scientists. Although Anderson is a newcomer to Thai studies (after his mastery of Indonesian studies, including Bahasa Indonesia), he has a significant command of Thai; I wish I could say that of other foreign political scientists. If Western scholars would consult more Thai sources, Akin Rabibhadana's M.A. thesis, *The South Organization of Thai Society in the Early Bangkok Period, 1782-1873* (in English, published in 1969 as a Cornell Data Paper) useful as it is, may cease to be a classic to the foreign scholar. In the field of political science, Thai writing is not all that outstanding; yet there is much information that could be gleaned from various books, pamphlets, and so on. Admittedly, during the 1973-76 period there were many propaganda tracts coming out; but some good works were also published, by people like **Saneh Jamarik, Chai-anant Samutwanich, Koson Srisang, Kramol**

Thongtammachart and Likhit Dhiravekin, to name but a few.

(2) Having mastered the Thai language, Western scholars ought not to rely only on written records, which seem to be safest by Western standards. A political scientist ought to consult, take into account, and rely on oral tradition too. Also, the traditional viewpoint ought to be taken more seriously than heretofore. This point is made very clearly in Richard O'Conner's recent thesis on Thai urbanism (though it is written from an anthropological, rather than a political science, perspective). He has shown great respect for the Thai viewpoint. In his argument on the monarchy, religion, and the nation which, unfortunately, is being badly misused by the right-wing element nowadays, O'Conner traces back and reminds us that we ought to take seriously these national institutions. I happen to agree with him.

(3) A political scientist, or any social scientist, should not study Thai politics or anything Thai merely to enhance a theory or to prove one point against another. One may eventually get to that, but a Ph.D. dissertation should not be just another step in building up a theoretical ladder, one way or another, at the expense of Siam or any other area studied.

My last plea, therefore, is that scholars, particularly foreigners, ought to be more modest, more willing to listen to different views and with more tolerance, and with cooler hearts.

Comment on Benedict R.O. G. Anderson's *Studies of the Thai State: State of Thai Studies* in THE STUDY OF THAILAND ed. by Elizre B. Ayal, Center for International Studies, Southeast Asia Program, Ohio University 1978.

Supplementary Bibliography

O'Conner, Richard A.
Urbanism and Religion: Community, Hierarchy and Sanctity in Urban Thai Buddhist Temples. Ph.D. thesis, Cornell 1978.

Paitoon Sayswang (ed.)
The State of Social Sciences in Thailand.
Bangkok: Social Sciences Association of Thailand, 1974.

Silverstein, Karen.
Chinese-Thai Relations and the Beginnings of Anti-Sinoism in Thailand: 1824-1910. Cornell Asian Studies Graduate Seminar paper 1977.

Full citation of works not listed in the Supplementary Bibliography at the end of this Comment are to be found in Anderson's Bibliography.

V
NEW CRISIS : VIEWPOINT FROM THE LATE 1980'S

ON SOUTHEAST ASIAN MODERNIZATION

Past and present trends of modernization

The lands of Southeast Asia, fertile and rich in natural resources as they are (or rather, were), could undoubtedly provide sufficient food and a simple pleasant life for their inhabitants. Why, then, are 60 per cent of the children in rural Siam suffering from malnutrition? Why are the small fishermen on the coast of the Malaysian peninsula finding it difficult to survive? Why have millions of Indonesian peasants migrated to the slums of Jakarta? And why have so many Filipinos left their farms to be migrant workers in the Middle East and elsewhere?

There is an old Siamese saying: "There is rice in the fields; there are fish in the water". This saying does not simply describe the abundance of food resources available to the populations of the region in the past, it also aptly describes the simple life of self-sufficiency that existed among village communities of Southeast Asia before the advent of colonialism and neo-colonialism. In those days, the communities farmed their own land and wove their own cloth. They were governed and protected by their own institutions: the family, the community and the seniority system. Production was carried out by means of co-operation rather than competition, and was geared to self-consumption, thus maintaining the unity and balance of nature.

I do not wish to imply that this was an idyllic life, free from suffering and exploitation. Of course there was disease, natural disasters, warfare, cultural repression of women, etc. Also, village communities were not living in complete isolation; with the establishment of state power structures, land rights came under the control of the king or state rulers. Village communities were required to pay taxes and could be enlisted to dig canals, fight wars, etc. Nevertheless, the relationship between the state and the peasantry was of a special nature in that the state dealt with village communities as a whole rather than with individuals or families. This allowed village communities to largely maintain their own independence in carrying out their production and in dealing with their own problems.

Colonialisation and semi-colonialisation by the Western powers brought about a basic upheaval in the village community production system. Buying and selling of commodities was introduced at the village level, resulting in the decline of traditional village handicrafts, and a change from agricultural production for self-consumption to agricultural production for national and world markets. The self-sufficiency of village communities was gradually destroyed, while market forces over which the communities had no control dictated the economic and social changes in the lives of the peasants. The establishment of agricultural export markets brought larger proportions of agricultural land under the direct ownership of the local aristocracies, thus increasing the numbers of share-cropping tenants. At the same time, foreign companies took over large tracts of land to establish rubber, sugar-cane, coconut and banana plantations, thus creating a new class of peasants – agricultural labourers.

During the past fifty years, colonialism has been replaced by neo-colonialism and "modernization". National governments who took over from colonial governments have continued and accelerated the penetration of market forces and capitalist systems of production throughout the rural areas of Southeast Asia. Rural development policies have concentrated on extending and strengthening infra-structures and on promoting investment in agricultural-related industries. Modernization has forced the peasants to depend on the market for clothing, electricity, water, fuel, construction materials, fertilisers, pesticides, livestock and agricultural tools.

Undoubtedly, "rural development" and "modernization" as carried out by most of the Southeast Asian countries has brought about more efficient agricultural production and an average increase in the income and standard of living of the rural population. But the costs have been extremely high. Most of the benefits have fallen into the hands of the wealthy few, the upper and middle classes, such as the exporters, traders, landlords, plantation owners, agri-businesses, rice and teak-mill owners, farmers with large land-holdings, and businessmen, professionals and high-ranking government officials in general. Economic growth has brought about a comparative growth of the upper and middle classes. Rural development has developed new power structures at the local level in rural areas. The growth of the elite has led to an ever increasing demand for consumer goods from Japan and the West. This, in turn, requires higher agricultural exports and greater exploitation of the actual agricultural producers.

Modernized agriculture has brought about large-scale depletion of natural resources. Forests are rapidly disappearing and with them much wild-life. The mud-fish and edible frogs that thrived in the rice fields and served as a rich source of food for the peasants are being killed by the use of chemical fertilisers and insecticides. Large-scale trawler fishing is depleting fish stocks and destroying the livelihoods of small fishermen. It should be noted that the huge appropriation of natural resources and the resulting upheaval of the balance of nature has been mostly for the benefit of the "advanced" societies in Japan and the West, and for the privileged elites in Southeast Asia, not for self-consumption by the agricultural producers themselves, the peasantry of Southeast Asia, who form the vast majority of the population of the region.

The plight of the peasants has actually been worsened in many respects by rural development and modernization. With population growth, the loss of natural resources, and their increasing dependence on market forces, they are finding it more difficult than before to obtain enough food for their own subsistence. They find it necessary to sell their produce at whatever the market price is, in order to pay their debts for supplies used in the production process. Many do not have enough produce left for their own consumption throughout the year and have to buy food from the market, thus increasing their debts. Their problems are multiplied during years of drought or flooding. The trends are common throughout the region. The wealthy farmers with enough land to produce a surplus easily obtain bank loans to modernize their production and benefit from government support schemes. But they are a small minority of the rural population. The agri-buinesses are also flourishing and gradually extending their operations to the more remote rural areas. They run their own farms or plantation through the use of hired labourers working at subsistence wages, or supply the raw materials and technology for groups of farmers to carry out agricultural or livestock production on their own land, and then purchase the produce from the farmers, deducting their loans of raw materials. While they do benefit some of their contractors in that the farmers may receive higher incomes than before, they have, in fact, placed the farmers under their control, since they tend to monopolise the markets in their areas of operation. They also drive the small farmers further towards bankruptcy.

As for the vast majority of the rural producers – the middle-peasants with only sufficient land to feed their families, the poor peasants with very small plots of land, the share-cropping tenants who lose up to half of their produce as rent, and the agricultural labourers, they are finding it increasingly difficult to survive. They have no bargaining power concerning market prices, land-rents, and daily wages. To obtain loans they have to resort to the local traders and money-lenders to which they pay exorbitant interest rates. Their costs of production are increasing in respect to the income received from their produce. The peasants of Southeast Asia are, therefore, plagued by mounting debts. (In Siam, for example, the five million rural families have accumulated a total debt of over US$1,000 million while the average annual cash income per family is only US$170.00).

Under these conditions, it is not surprising that malnutrition is on the increase among food producers, and that a large proportion of rural families can no longer survive on agricultural production alone. Poor peasants are gradually losing their land through debt, and millions of peasants flock to the cities each year to seek seasonal or year-round employment. Young girls work as servants, unskilled factory workers, or are forced into prostitution. Children work illegally in small work-shops under the harshest conditions. Some of them are even "sold" abroad. The men do heavy labour for low daily wages.

The massive influx of peasants to the cities (in Bangkok, the population has increased three million to five million in a period of only three years and the same is true of Manila and Jakarta) clearly spotlights the misery of the rural population. But migration to the cities does not solve the problems of rural poverty. Industry is not well enough developed to absorb the rural population. The workers from the rural areas receive barely sufficient wages for their own subsistence. Only a small proportion manage to send back money to their families. Living in the slum areas, they are faced with rising urban unemployment. Many are forced to resort to crime.

The worsening situation of the peasant has contributed to the growing strength of many underground revolutionary movements in the region. In retaliation, the governments have introduced repressive measures such as martial law, detention without trial, censorship, and violations of many fundamental human rights. Most of the Southeast Asian governments are military or military-backed authoritarian governments. Under these conditions, the peasants are subject to atrocities and find it extremely difficult to group together to protect their common interests and struggle for their rights to a better life. Growing peasant movements have been crushed time after time. Most farmers' organizations such as agricultural co-operatives and farmers' unions are tightly controlled by the governments and mainly serve the interests of the wealthy farmers. When governments form a link like the Association of Southeast Asian Nations (ASEAN), they share repressive methods against the peasantry too. This is also to serve the interest of the richest nations like Japan and the USA.

Women, who form half the work force of the region, have traditionally suffered from cultural repression. In the present age, they are also the objects of extreme economic repression. They carry out the hardest work for the lowest wages. Millions are forced into semi-slavery, working as servants or prostitutes. The Southeast Asian sex-market on which the tourist industries of the region thrive is famous throughout the world. Many of these "girls" have also been "exported" to Europe, Hong Kong and Japan.

So, the results of the rural development policies, as carried out by the governments of Southeast Asia and supported by Japan and the Western governments as well as international financial institutions, have mainly been to widen the gap between the rich and the poor, and to increase the misery of rural populations for the benefit of local elites and the wealthy societies of Japan and the West.

Alternative models for modernization as it should be.

The present trend of development is wrong because people at the top equate modernization with Westernization and the gross materialistic values of a consumer culture. The poor have been educated or brainwashed by schools or mass media to imitate the rich, who must lead their lives luxuriously, wastefully, and exploitatively. The modern man must, therefore, be employed in urbanized and industrial societies. He will have no time to be alone or to be with nature; he will have to think like others, be busy and live superficially. Hence, the status quo is maintained at the expense of social justice and personal liberation from greed, hatred and delusion.

Not only the poor suffer, the rich are also unhappy. All feel insecure and afraid of death, old age and loneliness.

Those who want to do good or be good, can only do so on the surface, in the name of philanthropy, charity or academic symposium, which only leads to more volumes of publications, while the vicious circle remains the same.

The only solution for the present human predicament is to challenge the present trend of modernization fundamentally – beyond the material approach to development – otherwise one will merely jump from the predicament of capitalism into the dilemma of communism. Fundamentally, there are no human rights nor personal happiness for creative artists in state socialism either. To be recognised materially in the so-called Free World, one has to be a commercial artist or a researcher for big enterprises (not for truth). Likewise, in the socialist countries, one has to be a clever propagandist for the regime. This is human degradation.

Human development towards truth, goodness and beauty must be the order of the day; one must return from the profane to the sacred. Luckily, in Southeast Asia, the spiritual tradition is still available from Buddhism, Hinduism, Islam and Christianity, not to mention indigenous traditional beliefs.

It is true that institutional religion as well as local witch doctors can be harmful to the people, but if we can apply the essential teachings of the Great Traditions of the Buddha, Christ, Mohammad, and many saintly masters to the present society as a hard core value, this will be the science and art of human development, taking into account collaboration not competition, respect for other beings – seen and unseen – and not exploiting each other or the natural environment. Not expecting too much for livelihood, one would have more time for others. One could also be alone with oneself and with nature. What is needed is education beyond the intellect; emotional growth should exist side-by-side with intellectual pursuits.

If one can develop personal self-awareness through *zazen,* prayer or meditation, one could restructure one's ego to be less selfish, more selfless. One will then be in a position to listen, to be aware and to see things as they really are. One will not be biased by Western scientific theories of growth and complicated technology which make us all think alike, and try to live alike.

One good trend is that some leading Western thinkers like Ivan Illich, E.F. Schumacher and Fritjof Capra have now realized the limits of Western science and technology, which have become materialistic and exploitative. Now a body of writing is emerging to show that there can well be a convergence of both Eastern thought and the viewpoint of New Physics, and that this could be the promise of a holistic world-view which could well constitute nothing less than a "paradigm shift" of far reaching consequence. Among the works which treat this convergence of Eastern thought and the New Physics, a few can be mentioned: F. Capra *The Tao of Physics;* J. Needleman, *A Sense of the Cosmos;* A de Reincourt, *The Eye of Shiva;* R.G.H. Siu, *The Tao of Science;* H. Smith, *The Medium, The Mystic, and the Physicist.* M. Talbot, *Mysticism and the New Physics;* and G. Zukav *The Dancing Wu Li Masters.* A provocative introduction to this convergence can be found in L. Leshan's *Forgotten Truth.* Leshan depicts the strikingly similar maps of reality which have been charted by the mystics, Christian and Asian, who have known well the mysteries of inner space and inner-connectedness and the physicists who are learning much new about both the worlds of the very large and the very small.

In Southeast Asia we have many examples of the "very small" reaching out for development at grass roots level already.

In the Philippines, for example, non-violent actions among some Christians have made the regime in that country more democratic, although it will take that country a long time to get rid of the subconscious Spanish and American domination. The Peasantren in Indonesia is an Islamic education alternative using indigenous culture and looking for modern utilization with real self-reliance within their own culture. The Sarvodaya Shramadana movement in Sri Lanka is applying Buddhism to awaken local inhabitants at the village level and make them proud of their local culture. They do this through appropriate technology to survive meaningfully with dignity. The movement hopes to awaken people individually as well as collectively, at national and international levels, so that different trends of development may be learnt by all. In Malaysia, ALIRAN, a national, non-partisan action group is involved in raising social consciousness and encouraging social action that will hopefully lead to social justice.

In Siam, more peasants are now cultivating self-reliance — using traditional methods and culture — avoiding an export or sale orientation, and refusing chemical fertiliser and machinery. They may be poor, but no longer in debt, so ploughing and harvesting may become a time of joy and real participation once again. Some monks use meditation and Buddhist ceremonies to help the poor start their work mindfully and selflessly; hence, collective farms, rice banks and buffalo banks are now possible in many areas.

These trends are not perfect and may make a lot of mistakes, but if the spiritual values of each tradition and locality could be put to use for our contemporary society, diversified approaches to modernisation or post-modernisation may be possible. We may even develop our own science and philosophy beyond those dictated by Newton and Descartes.

The danger is whether the superpowers, the multi-national companies, the World Bank, IMF and even the Asian Development Bank, will allow us or not. Often this outside power is unseen, using outmoded Western science and education to brainwash our Asian elites to oppress their own people who wish to avoid the present oppressive system.

Will a gathering of scholars and intellectuals like this be able to help our small people live with dignity and look for development alternatives, with spiritual values at their base, so that the world will be positively different and meaningful, especially for the multitudes who should have more power to decide their own future? If it can be so, the chance for the survival of Planet Earth will be more assured.

Presented at the International Symposium on
Science, Technology and Spiritual Values
An Asian Approach to Modernization

(Sophia University and the United Nations University 25 – 29 May 1987 Tokyo, Japan).

THE RELIGION OF CONSUMERISM

Introduction

Sulak Sivaraksa, 55, married with three children, is a lawyer, social analyst, non-violent campaigner, lecturer and educationalist. He is the director of the Santi Pracha Dhamma Institute of non formal education and research alternatives and chairperson for the administrative committee for the Thai Inter-Religious Commission of Development. He is a member of the international board of the Buddhist Peace Fellowship. He has had a number of books published in English including *Siamese Resurgence, A Buddhist Vision for Renewing Society, A Socially Engaged Buddhism*, and *Religion and Development*.

In August, 1984, Sulak, an internationally respected activist for peace and social justice, was arrested by the Thai government on charges of *lese-majeste* (offending the Thai monarch) for comments he made in an interview. It was during a period of martial law in the country.

There was an international outcry over his arrest. Amnesty International, peace organizations, aid agencies, religious leaders, universities and lawyers around the world and in Thailand protested vigorously over his arrest. Sulak made such statements in the interview as : "I think the King should be looked upon as a human being who exercises his power judiciously but is nevertheless fallible. If I wish to attack the 9th King, I must write during the reign of the 9th King. I don't have to wait for the next."

In a country where there is reverence for King, country and religion, Sulak's comments were seemingly used as an opportunity to close his voice. After his arrest he was held for 5 days in a top security detention centre. He was due to be tried in a military court and faced between three and 30 years imprisonment. There would be no appeal after sentencing and observers would not be permitted to witness the trial.

Commenting on the international response, the Thai interior minister said at the time: "The law is Thai law. Foreigners must not interfere with our judicial process."

On November 30 Sulak and two co-defendants, the interviewer and publisher, appeared in court and were informed by the presiding judge that the public prosecutors wished to withdraw the case.

Commenting afterwards Sulak said: "It was a good period to test my spiritual strength and to learn to appreciate my friends and wellwishers, both at home and abroad. Prayers were said for us regularly by Buddhists, Christians, Hindus and Muslims. We must really help other victims of injustice as we all live on this tiny planet earth."

Sulak interprets planet earth's contemporary crisis in both spiritual and social terms. He speaks out against nationalism, corruption, capitalism, communism and consumerism. He speaks for the application of Buddhist principles to social reality, the necessity to support and protect the poor, the renewal of the countryside, the establishment of rural co-operatives, and the value of constructive criticism.

Not surprisingly, he has regularly been in trouble with the authorities and powers over the years. In 1976 while speaking overseas, he read in *The Times* newspaper in England of a warrant out in Thailand for his arrest. At the time, during a military takeover, his bookshop in the heart of Bangkok and right oposite his home was raided by the police and army, accompanied by television and press crews. Thousands of his books were burnt rendering him almost bankrupt.

At the present time in Thailand there is a fledgling kind of democracy and a greater opportunity to write and speak one's mind. The authorities and Thai society seem to be developing a begrudging appreciation of Sulak's outspokenness. One person said of Sulak: "Sulak is like a gadfly in the ear of the government." Throughout many changes in government, King Bhumipon of Thailand has to his credit constantly maintained contact with his people in Thailand by spending months of the year visiting the rural areas listening to their voices of concern, making notes on the spot, and telling politicians and civil servants what he hears.

I met with Sulak at his home in Bangkok, where he has lived for the past 40 years. While we met there were many visitors. He was just completing arranging for a small party of monks and lay people to travel to Sri Lanka to speak against violence and to raise more voices for non-violence in the conflict between the Sinhalese and Tamils.

Interview with Sulak Sivalaksa

CT : You have been educated in Thailand and England. In recent years you have seen the enormous impact of Western consumerism on Thai society. Please say a little about the impact.

SS : You must realize that Thailand - which I prefer to call Siam - was not colonised which is a blessing. But we have been more harmed than those countries which became colonies of the West. At least our neighbour, Burma, which was colonised, resists Western consumerism. Unfortunately Thailand never resisted the West because we thought that we maintained our independence.

CT : So Thailand has felt that it retained its independence yet you imply that Thailand has been colonised in a different way.

SS : Precisely. First we were colonised intellectually by adopting a Western way of living. We thought that we preserved our political independence. At first these Western intellectual colonisations only took place among the Thai elite in Bangkok alone. The rest of the country was more or less free from this form of Western colonisation partly due to Buddhism and to our indigenous culture.

CT : When did this influence of Western intellectualism begin in Bangkok?

SS : Sir John Bowring came here in 1855. He forced the open door policy and so we signed the Bowring Treaty with England. King Mongkut, internationally known in "The King and I," was a Buddhist monk for 26 years. He was wise because if we did not open our country we would be colonised by the British. So he opened the country to the British. At the same time he invited the French, Swedish and Germans to balance the situation. So politically, although we were not equal to the West we felt superior to our neighbours who were colonised by the French, British, Dutch and Americans. Our first downfall was to look down upon our neighbours. We thought we were equal to the West. In fact, we wanted to be equal to the West, so gradually we followed the West. We invited the English lady, Mrs. Anna Leonowens, to teach children here. King Chulalongkorn sent all his sons to be educated abroad. When they came back they still retained their Buddhist heritage and Thai culture. But they admired the Western way of life. They gradually introduced Western education, Western medicine, Western technology and Western administration. Correspondingly this reduced our indigenous education and culture. Buddhism as the state religion became formal like the Church of England and lost much of its sanctity.

CT : There has been an acceleration of the values of consumerism in the last twenty years.

SS : Thirty years! At least the old culture maintained a certain *noblesse oblige*, but the new elite, who are devoid of traditional culure just want to be rich and powerful in the name of development. They just want to expand in every direction, including cutting the country up through road building. In the old colonial system the British and the French tried to maintain themselves. They thought they would be in this part of the world forever. On the one hand they had to respect us and on the other they had to maintain the environmental balance. The West thought it could get our timber forever! They replanted the trees so there was not much destruction of the forests. But then the Americans came. They had a very short term view. They wanted to get the natural wealth of the country out as quickly as possible. The American period coincided with the development of Bangkok and the rest of the country. The American period came with the age of advertisement, the age of consumer culture which claims to be a universal culture. So a decadent Western culture was brought to Thailand alongside sexism, violence and use of drugs by the young. If you come to Bangkok now you can see the new kind of temple in the form of a department store. People flock there.

CT : Bangkok looks just like any Western city. One goes outside of Bangkok and one can still sense rural Thai society. Is the shadow of Bangkok penetrating into the rural traditions?

SS : Yes, unfortunately. Development is another word for greed. Our city people never owned land up-country. We never had absentee landlords before. In this age of so-called development, the developers want more land and so destroy more forest. Our education teaches people to admire the urban life, the civil service and business. So obviously we brain-drain our rural areas. If you go to the villages today you find old people. The young are leaving the villages for the capital. Those who have mental ability and ambition have to come to Bangkok. If you cannot compete in Bangkok you may go to the Middle East to sell your labour. We even export our women as prostitutes to Germany, Japan and Hong Kong. The minds and bodies of the young are exploited.

CT : These are all signs of the erosion of a society. Isn't there a danger of idealising traditional rural society and values? And seeing just faults in Western consumerism and its values?

SS : There is a danger if you romanticize it. Rural society was not all that ideal. But it was self-sustaining. People respected one another, the young respected the old. In every Thai village there was a temple which was a centre for spiritual, educational and cultural activities. The self supporting village had been functioning for at least 700 years in this way. It wasn't ideal but it worked. The Buddhist philosophy has as a central principle that it is noble to give (*dāna* in Pali, the early Buddhist language) rather than take. We may not have been very good Buddhists but we practised generosity. We offered what we could to each other. We use the word *sanuk* which means to enjoy our life in a relaxed way. Traditionally for the Thais, play and work was part of life. Competition wasn't admired. Co-operation was valued. This approach worked. In this view those who lived a virtuous and ethical way of life, like the monks, were very much appreciated. At the same time there was respect for other life forms such as animals, birds, fish and trees. Within my lifetime I have seen these thing change greatly.

CT : Why is it that self - supporting, self-sustaining societies have simply not been able to withstand the pressure of consumerism? Why is it that consumerism is the predominant religion? Why is consumerism so powerful that it eats into every worthwhile value?

SS : You have got to realise that consumerism represents greed. We all have greed within ourselves. Consumerism also works with those in power. In fact power represents aggression and anger. And we all have that. On top of that consumerism works side by side with the new educational system, which teaches you to be clever but not wise. In fact we create delusion in ourselves and we think that it is knowledge. Unless we understand the three root causes of greed, aggression and self delusion, you get bogged down. Consumer society works like magic on the mind. It deceives you into believing in the value of consuming more, going faster, living in greater convenience. It sounds wonderful but you do not realise the cost. I feel that once people realise the negative aspects then the situation can change.

CT : Are people realising the negative aspects?

SS : One of the good things about this country is that more and more people are realising the negative aspects of consumerism. Which is linked with feelings of elitism, power, and a sophisticated kind of education, science and technology. There are positive aspects to the consumer society but there seem to be more negative aspects. Once we realise this we can resist it.

CT : There are then two realizations. One is the inner one with regard to greed, aggression, delusion and ignorance, and the second is the realization of the impact these tendencies and forces have on society and the planet.

SS : Precisely.

CT : You work in the field of social change. You see the impact inwardly and outwardly. What kind of responses do you experience?

SS : Being a Buddhist, I have to see everything with *upāya*, that is with skilful means. The Buddha taught that the first thing to be aware of is *dukkha*, unsatisfactoriness or suffering. Once you understand that consumerism brings *dukkha* then you find the causes for *dukkha*.

CT : The friend who drove Venerable Nagasena, Venerable Paññavuddho (two Buddhist monks) and I here today is a businessman in Bangkok. He was cheated two years ago by a business partner of one million baht ($20,000). He is still suffering today over the situation.

SS : Unless the man looks into himself and into the causes, the suffering continues.

CT : Are you employing the Buddha's insights into human existence in a social setting?

SS : You have to do that. You have to translate the essential teaching from your spiritual tradition to confront the modern period. Otherwise Buddhism is nothing more than a decoration, which most governments would like it to be. Paying respect to the national religion and holding big ceremonies may be useful but at the same time could be more harmful. But if we apply the skilful means of the Buddha to understand suffering and social reality and the way to be free from suffering through mindfulness, non-violence and Buddhist practices, then there is the possibility of overcoming suffering, both personally and socially.

CT : What are the skilful means for social change? What actual vehicles are you using to make that happen? How do you connect with concerned people?

SS : The good thing about this country is that it has been a Buddhist kingdom for a long, long time and is one of the few left. Buddhist heritage is available in almost every village, although many villages have succumbed and only the form is left. But there are still many villages which have the form, content *and* local spiritual leadership. I know this country. I live in the capital and I have been exposed to the West. My job is to tell people of the ways available to overcome their sufferings and unsatisfactoriness in life. I work on myself and my society. I look to spiritual leaders, who have mindfullness and awareness themselves. I have met quite a few who try to have a positive answer.

CT : Can you give me an example of engaged spiritual leadership?

SS : In Surin province in the northeast of Thailand (the poorest region of the country), an abbot remembered that when he was young, people were also poor but he sensed that there was more happiness at that time. The people related to each other much better and there was that *sanuk* feeling among the people. In the environment, there was plenty of jungle and the elephants roamed the region freely. The people were free and were able to rely on themselves and the environment. They produced food for their families, for the monks and nuns. What was left over they sold. They had the four prerequisities of food, clothing, shelter and medicine. In the last 30 years through constant development there are more highways and roads. The jungle has disappeared, the elephants have disappeared except for the elephants kept for tourists to photograph. The people suffer.

CT : What is the abbot's response to all this impact upon Surin?

SS : The abbot said that something is seriously wrong. Consumerism means capitalism, which means money comes first. "Our local resources go to Bangkok, the multi-national corporations and then to the super-powers," he said. "This is useless and wasteful." He felt that there must be a way to confront it. Meditation must not only be for personal welfare but must be collective. There needs to be collective mindfulness. We need to confront things together and solve things together. He said that we must use the old traditons.

CT : Are people expressing interest in that approach of establishing the collective?

SS : Oh yes. This is a success story. When he started, people didn't believe him. Being a monk and meditation master, they would come. He pointed out to them what went wrong. He said "Let's try alternative ways of living." He even used strong words like "communal farming". In this country consumerism came along with anti-communism. Here, if you use such concepts as communalism or communal farming then you can be accused of being a communist. But when a monk, who is pure in conduct of body, speech and mind, speaks this way, he arouses interest among the people.

CT : Obviously the role of the monk is an important role in terms of renewal of deeper human values.

SS : The old customs and values must be translated into the contemporary setting. Today people are suffering a great deal. People were told that their traditional values were no good. They were told not to use the buffalo for farming but instead use tractors. People were fascinated with technology. Hired labour occurred with bigger farms instead of small self-sufficient farms. Then with consumer values people had to go more and more to the money lender to keep pace with developments. The monk had been telling the people that all this brings ambition and competitiveness, brings more and more suffering to village life. The monk said that the people have been brainwashed into this way of thinking and living.

CT : What alternatives is he suggesting?

SS : He is encouraging the people to farm together, to share their labour and join together. Skilful means is applied to every area of rural life including the shortage of rice, the unpredictable weather, and the destruction of the jungle and forests. The abbot said we need to have a rice bank, instead of going to the bank to borrow money. The village temples can start the rice bank and whatever you cultivate, whatever is left over from eating, you offer to the temple. The temple keeps the grain. Anybody in need receives the grain from the temple free of charge. It is a new kind of merit-making translated straight into social reality.

CT : How do the people respond to this?

SS : The temple has become powerful and of service to the people. The next project the abbot started was a buffalo bank. Being Buddhists, we don't like to kill the buffalo. The temple keeps the buffalos and offers the offspring of the buffalo to people who can't afford to buy them. The condition is that the buffalo must be treated kindly. Half of any future offspring which comes must be returned to the buffalo bank.

CT : A beautiful system. Now can we shift from the rural to the city situation. In the early 1970's there was a tremendous growth of political awareness among the student community. The students' non-violent protest ended the life of the government. What has happened in recent years? Are students in Thailand now like many students in the West, primarily involved in getting qualifications and their careers together?

SS : Up until 1973 we were told that we were the last of the free lands. We had to fight the communists and believe in Americanism and consumerism. We had been brainwashed for so long. Young people started questioning that. In 1973 the students rejected the American model, but unfortunately they went to the other extreme, to the Maoist model. Hence in 1976 the military came back into power with the blessings of the Americans and Japanese. They killed our students while many students fled to the jungle and others joined the Communist Party of Thailand under the influence of the Communist Party of China. That bitter lesson taught the students that Communism was not the answer, but a fake. They have come to see that the social way of life of their ancestors, and what the Buddha taught is truly meaningful and can be applied to the present.

CT : You are speaking of the Middle Way between the two extremes of capitalism and communism.

SS : That's right. We must turn society towards social justice. We must change both ourselves and our society.

CT : Don't many young people think of monasteries and monks as old and outdated and not in touch with the modern world?

SS : There are, of course, monks not in touch with the modern world, both in a positive and negative way. Sometimes when they are not in touch they have insight and wisdom to give us. Others who are not in touch with the world hang on to outdated ceremonies. Again we have to use skilful means to distinguish the sheep from the goats.

CT : You have been consistently outspoken in your public lectures, meetings and writings. How free is free speech in Thailand today?

SS : To be fair to the government, compared with all our neighbours in South East Asia, we are much more free. We can speak our mind on almost any subject, perhaps except the monarchy.

CT : Did you tread on the toes of the government when you voiced criticisms in 1984? What you said and wrote brought you before the military court.

SS : The pretext was that I said something against the monarchy.

CT : Well, did you?

SS : It depends how you interpret it. I feel if the monarchy is to survive it has got to survive like the Western kind of monarchy. It is not that I admire Western monarchies. I think they survive because they can withstand criticism. To me criticism is an essential teaching of the Buddha. I criticise the Buddha too. The Buddha welcomed criticism of himself and his teachings. He instructs that we do not accept anyting unless we scrutinize it.

CT : In a healthy society criticism must go into every area, even those areas which are regarded as sacred.

SS : I don't accept sacredness, you see. As a Buddhist, I revere the Buddha more than anybody else. Even so, he is not sacred. I respect him profoundly but even his teachings should be criticised.

CT : When you faced charges for your criticism of the monarchy there was a strong protest from the West over the indictment.

SS : To be fair, the King was also a little bit embarrassed. He himself, was educated in Switzerland. He is a man who would welcome criticism personally.

CT : He does tremendous work for the rural people and the hill-tribes.

SS : Without doubt, he has very good intentions, but with some of his good intentions I disagree. We should be able to spell out differences openly.

CT : You have spoken in this interview about what has happened to Bangkok. Why do you choose personally to live in Bangkok? Why aren't you living in a rural society?

SS : Partly my own roots are here in the city. Former generations of my family were in Bangkok. I feel that my role is as an urban person. I can learn from the rural area for the benefit of Bangkok and I feel that Bangkok is a place that attracts everything from other areas. We must change the people of Bangkok so that they respect the people in the rural areas. That's my job.

CT : For many years you have been an international activist on social and political issues. Will that continue?

SS : As part of my job as Chairman of the Asian Cultural Forum On Development I had to work in the whole region. I feel that if you want social justice in any village you can't do it in one village. The work has to be linked to other villages. One country has to be linked with other countries. The Third World has to be linked with the First World. We have to build up that understanding and use the Buddhist methodology of *kalyāna mitta*, that is "good friends", who are on a similar wavelength and have a similar understanding. We must help each other. The small fishermen must help the working women, the working women must help industrial workers. Somehow we must all start relating to each other.

CT : Are there any messages which are coming from the West which are valuable and healthy? Does the West have any part to play in the so-called Third World?

SS : The good thing about the West is that it is now realising the harmfullness that it has done. This is a very good sign. A monk who has committed harm must ask for forgiveness. Since the 18th century and the Age of Enlightenment, the West has believed it has all the answers. The West believes it must conquer everybody else and nature too. Now more people in the West are saying: "No, our knowledge is limited, our thought does not go very far at all." I think that is very profound. I think that awareness and understanding will help Siam and other countries tremendously. The West is just starting to become humble. More people in the West want to learn from our rural cultures. This is wonderful. Secondly, the West is beginning to explore spiritual depths, not just Buddhism, but also its own Christian background. Christian mystics have very profound things to say to us which the West has denied in the last 200 or 300 years.

CT : The growing recognition of the limitation of Western thought, beliefs and views seems to be the first step towards humility and the willingness to learn from other societies. What else do you appreciate from the West at the present time?

SS : The West has developed a certain kind of method and organisation, a kind of network which we must learn. For example the Christians have the World Council of Churches which brings together Christian activists from around the world. We have the World Fellowship of Buddhists but it just a kind of club. The West is willing to confront the power blocs like the multi-national corporations. This is wonderful. We must learn to organise ourselves in this way, too.

CT : What would you say that the West must truly learn about itself?

SS : The West has to learn how to relate truly in an equal way to the rest of the world. The West must recognize that it has as much to learn from the rest of the world as we have to learn from the West.

CT : In a way you are saying that there is an opportunity for fresh forms of dialogue which is not based on a colonial or patronising attitude.

SS : This is essential. I feel my own drawbacks. I don't know the Middle East. I would like to. I would like to learn from the Muslims. I have learnt from Indonesia which is Muslim and quite close to us. Certain sections of the Muslim community there have inherited from the Buddhist tradition. We relate together quite closely. We have to learn in this day and age from each other.

CT : As an organiser of spiritual and social activism, how do you get by financially? Who gives you the funds?

SS : When you organise at the national and international levels the money comes from the West, mostly from Christian organisations. European Catholics and Protestants have been generous. I tried unsuccessfully to get some funds from the Buddhists of Japan. Fortunately we have been able to raise more money within Siam itself. People usually make merit here by giving money to the temples but too much money is spent on building temples and on useless ceremonies. People are collecting money for increasing social awareness and understanding. I hope that in a decade all the money will come from within Siam.

CT : That will be another expression of self support.

SS : Yes, that's right. I am very glad to talk with you. You are an example of the bridging process between our part of the world and the Western part. You came to learn from us; you also came to teach us. This kind of approach must be developed further.

CT : I spent 10 years in the East, six of those as a Buddhist monk in Thailand and India. I share the same concerns as you, Sulak. Thank you.

An Interview with Sulak Sivaraksa by Christopher Titmuss
February 1988.

THE PROBLEM OF ETHNIC MINORITIES AND STATE: BURMA AND SIAM

Burma and Siam have a common religious heritage, Theravada Buddhism, with strong Hindu and animistic elements.

Traditionally, each of these two states had to have a monarch as a supreme ruler, the apex in the hierarchical society. He was the Lord of life and death. He needn't have been *Kshatriya* by caste, but he needed a Brahmin to appoint him as a King or Raja. Although Hinduism regarded him as a *devarājā*, a divine ruler or a god incarnate, ever since these states embraced Theravada Buddhism about 10 centuries ago, the king was expected to be *dhammarājā*, a righteous ruler. i.e. he became king partly due to his previous good *kamma* in past lives in which he surpassed all others in the state. It was thus appropriate for him to be called the lord of the land, but he must rule the land according to the *dhamma*, the prescribed law of conduct appropriate for rulers. He should have the following characteristics; generosity, high moral character, self-sacrifice, integrity, gentleness, self-control, non-anger, non-oppression, forbearance, and conformity to the law.

These ten prescribed rules are guidelines for the king to follow. He might fall short here and there, but if the shortcomings were serious, they might give an opportunity for the contenders to the throne to take advantage of him. Hence the reigning monarch usually needed the *sangha*, the established holy order of monks, to support him in his royal or worldly conduct. The *sangha* became a buffer between the ruler and the ruled. Some senior monks would be royal teachers, teaching the king and princes various arts and sciences, above all for their ethical and spiritual well-being. Hence these teachers earned great respect from the princely and noble families. (In Burma, the Supreme Patriarch – the *Thathanabaing* – was always the king's personal teacher). At the same time, these monks taught ordinary people in the monkhood as well as the common folk, so they knew the people's grievances and aspirations. Thus, they were in the position to tell the rulers whether such a law was too harsh, such taxation was too severe, and if merit - making, like building a hospital or a canal, would be appreciated by the people as well as being good *kamma* for the king himself.

As Buddhism was not an exclusive religion, it allowed the king and the people to take part in animistic rites, if it helped them to feel good socially, culturally and psychologically. Hence the Nats in Burma and the Phii in Siam play important roles in various functions, both at court and among the villagers. Hindu deities, too, were regarded as converts to Buddism and helped in protecting the state and its inhabitants.

Whereas in the sphere of statecraft, the Brahmin experts (mostly foreigners) would have more to say than the Buddhist monks (mostly nationals), in the sphere of ethical conduct, the monks would have more influence; at least they could restrain people from exploiting each other too much. When they could be very influential spiritually, the state of peace and happiness would be widespread, not only among men, but extending even to all other beings within the natural environment. Buddhism, Hinduism and animism have one thing in common, i.e. men and women must live harmoniously within society and must respect other living beings, including birds and bees, trees, rivers and mountains. Indeed human beings are encouraged to respect even those who have departed from this world, since Buddhists believe the dead ones too are living in other worlds not seen by the living.

Although a king in a Southeast Asian state is only a raja or a minor ruler in the great Indian tradition, each would like to imitate Emperor Asoka, the great protector of Buddhism, who was regarded as the universal monarch - *Cakkavatti*. Therefore, if possible, each ruler would follow duties laid down by the Buddha for a universal ruler i.e. (1) he should subject himself to the supremacy of the law of righteousness, (2) he should let no wrongdoing prevail in the kingdom, (3) he should let wealth be given or distributed to the poor, (4) he should go from time to time to see and ask for advice from the men living a religious life who maintain high moral standards, or to have virtuous counsellers and seek after great virtues.

Apart from these four main duties, details are given separately that the universal monarch should give provision of the right watch, ward and protection (a) for one's own folk within the palace, (b) for the armed forces, (c) for colonial kings and administrative officers, (d) for the royal dependants and civil servants, (e) for house holders, professionals, traders and agriculturalists, (f) for town and country dwellers, villagers and up-country people, (g) for the religious, (h) for beasts and birds.

To imitate a universal monarch, the Siamese and Burmese kings regarded themselves as supreme rulers and took the chiefs of the Shans, the Karens, etc., who wanted to be under their protectorate, as colonial kings. It was customary for the supreme ruler to give more than to take, as it was not for economic advantage but for prestige and merit that the supreme rulers looked after the welfare of others, right down to beasts and birds.

Obviously there were political, cultural and ecological, as well as economic, advantages in just administration according to the traditional laws, but the one who wished to be supreme ruler, or could afford to be, thought in terms of *noblesse oblige* more than anything else.

As late as the early 20th century, when the Prince of Chiengmai had lost most of his autonomy to Bangkok, he still held an annual ceremony for the chiefs of the hilltribes, e.g. the Karen chief would present to him wild orchids and some herbs. In the audience hall, the Prince would accept them as tributes, saying that "As long as the orchids bloom, you shall present them to me as a sign of loyalty. I, on my part, shall give a pledge to you that I will guarantee the well-being of your people so that you should be able to live happily within my land."

Likewise, his ancestors as well as the raja of Kedah, Kelantan, Trenggenu, etc., would send gold and silver trees to Ayudhaya and Bangkok every three years, since they were "colonial kings" who had to submit to the supreme ruler, who in turn would let them reign righteously within their domain, taking political and economic advantages within certain limits of the traditional norms then established.

When the British demanded the Malayan states from King Chulalongkorn in 1904, in exchange for some political advantage for Siam, the King said that those Malayan states were in fact an economic burden to the Siamese government. The British used the states to interfere with our borders all the time. We were in effect giving them the states in exchange for our national security.

The same could not be applied to the case of Chiengmai which the British also wanted to annex to Burma, since Chiengmai had been under the Burmese protectorate for over two centuries. In this case, the king of Bangkok regarded the people of Chiengmai to be Thai and was not willing to sacrifice them or that part of the territory easily, as indeed, when we lost Laos and Battambang to the French it was because their gunboats were threatening us right in Bangkok. We chose to keep two provinces: Chandaburi and Trat. We lost Laos and Battambang to the Western imperialists instead.

For the Siamese king, in dealing with Western powers, it was essential to recognize their might, which may not be right, and for our own survival independently, we were willing to lose extraterritorial rights as well as parts of the kingdom, especially those which were regarded by the West as "colonial kingdoms". We then tried to reform our administration in the light of Western education and civilization, though maintaining our monarchy.

Western democracy was not introduced until 1932 and even then, it was not by the king himself; it still appears only in form, while the traditional monarchy is still very viable. Although our form of government is supposed to be a constitutional monarchy, absolute power is very much maintained, not by the king personally, but by the military, who have usurped royal power since 1932, in the name of democracy. The military also increased its power at the expense of democratic rights in 1947, 1957 and 1976.

Now, the Siamese ruling class has no fear of Western intervention, and it goes as far as imitating Western norms at the expense of our traditional values. In fact we follow Western (including Japanese) economic growth, consumer culture and materialism blindly. Hence the destruction of our traditional social well-being at various levels - including the minorities - plus the ecological imbalance, deforestation, concrete jungles, traffic jams, air and river pollution etc.

Not only do we look down upon our own indigenous culture at various local levels but we also have no respect for our neighbours - the Mon, the Burmese, the Khmer, the Laotians and the Malays. We even feel good creating disturbances on the borders of those countries adjacent to ours for our own national security. Hence we support rebellious groups against the governments of Burma, Lao and Kampuchea. To me, such a policy has no Buddhist tradition to support it. It is unethical and very harmful in the short, as well as the long, run. But it serves the interest of the superpowers like USA and China, and our political elites have become only tools of the superpowers and multinational corporations, knowingly or unknowingly.

I fear our new political elites, mostly in the army - have no real understanding of Buddhism and our cultural tradition, although they think they do. In the old days, the king listened to the foreign Brahmins for statecraft and to Buddhist monks on personal conduct. Nowadays our political leaders only pay lip service to Buddhist and Siamese traditions. They need the monarchy and the religion to justify their legitimacy to rule. They may have the support of the Sangha, but they believe the advice of American experts or that of our nationals educated at Harvard or MIT, who have no roots in our spiritual tradition. Their personal behaviour and norms are conditioned by consumer culture and economic ethics, the survival of the fittest, the more the merrier, the richer the better, the quicker the greater; thus the poor suffer and become victims of political and cultural persecution.

The minorities on the whole are poor. Hence they suffer economically, politically and culturally as never before in our history.

Since Siam changed its name to Thailand, the government decided that all races should be assimilated as Thai. The Chinese on the whole were well-assimilated, partly because they were better off economically, and assimilation culturally gave them political security. Adhering to Buddhism in form offered no threat to the overseas Chiness who have become Sino - Thai. But the contrary is true of the Malays in the southern provinces who do not want to compromise religiously, nor do they want to assimilate culturally. Besides, they do not want to become Thai. The Thai authorities have no idea how to deal with the tensions wisely. They even blame the Arab world for interfering with our Muslim minorities.

As for the northern highlanders, the Thai Government wanted to assimilate them too. Instead of calling them hilltribes, they are now called the Thai of the hills. The government even imitated the Christian missionaries by sending Buddhist monks to convert them to Buddhism, because in the traditional Siamese cultural context, to be Thai is to be Buddhist, and a Thai Buddhist would be loyal to the throne. Hence the Thai national ideology is an interweaving of the three sacred institutions of the nation, the monarchy and the religion.

I personally feel that this policy is wrong. At least the former kings had a better approach to the minorities. They were regarded as "colonial" or "upcountry people" and had "autonomy" within their areas. This included not only those on the borders, but also those in the central plane and within the capital city, where Mon, Khmer, Vietnamese, Tavoys, Lao and Malays were allowed to have their own autonomous areas. If they were Christians, they were allowed to have their churches and had religious freedom according to their beliefs. The Vietnamese Buddhists, too, could practice their Mahayana Buddhism separately from the established Theravada tradition. Although the Mon belonged to the same Theravada school of Buddhism, they had their own identity and hierarchy. They held their Pali examination according to their language and culture, and all these were recognized officially by the king and the court.

I feel that the plurality of cultures and religions within the unity of traditional Siam was healthy in dealing with various ethnic groups as well as in dealing with superpowers, certainly much better than nowadays.

After we Siamese regained our independence from the Burmese destruction of Ayudhaya in 1767, our motto was to put vegetables in the basket and to put people in the state. The Thai gathered peoples from various tribes as far away as Southern China so that they would come to live within their kingdom. For the Thai ruling elites, people were the most important resource for any state. Hence they were lenient to the inhabitants settled within their territories. The Siamese kings did not tax too much, nor did they enforce too harsh a labour on their citizens. Further, when ethnic minorities, especially the Mons, escaped from Burma, they were always welcome in Siam.

Later, the Siamese king used Chinese tax farmers to collect revenues for the government, and employed Chinese labourers to dig canals, etc. This showed that the kings of old did not want to be unpopular with the people. The same might not be the case with

Burma.

The Siamese attitude was on the whole flexible. The Thais were willing to compromise and to change for modernisation (which is now our peril). We have come too far from our traditions. The Thais admire the Burmese for keeping to their tradition, for their courage and sincerity, and above all, their decision to be neutral, which may mean lonely. They have few superpowers to dictate to them nor multinational corporations to interfere with their internal economic independence. They may be poor, but they are proud. Yet many of us feel sorry for the people under the dictatorial regime in Burma, with its haughtiness and petty, corrupt officials. We also feel that the Burmese are unsure of themselves in dealing with various ethnic minorities within the Union of Burma. We should, therefore, look into these issues more seriously.

I must confess that my view on old Siam and Burma is on the whole positive. Apart from some small differences on national identity which I have briefly mentioned above, both countries were guided by traditional norms which, on the whole, suited them.

The king was absolute, but he was guided by the Buddhadhamma as well as the Sangha, to be moderate, and if he was secure personally and politically, he would treat other nationalities well, as one can see in the Toungoo kings, who even moved their capital to Pegu, to live among the Mons. Further, the Thai ruler of Sukhothai even felt more loyal to Bayinnaung than to his own father-in-law, the King of Ayudhaya.

Of course, there were bad and wicked kings who caused great suffering to the people and destruction to the cities, but they did not last long and they never interfered with the natural environment. People's memory of the good old days is to be cherished. And this is not only a romantic approach to the past. Even Westerners who were on the whole not sympathetic to our culture in the past, praised our people, as can be seen from the following British account of 1795-6:

"The Burmans are certainly rising fast in the scale of Oriental nations... They... have an undeniable claim to the character of a civilized and well instructed people. Their laws are wise and pregnant with sound morality; their police is better regulated than in most European countries; their natural disposition is.... hospitable to strangers; their manners are rather expressive of manly candour, than (of) courteous dissimulation; the gradations of rank and the respect due to station are maintained with a scrupulousness which never relaxes. A knowledge of letters is so widely diffused that there are no mechanics, few of the peasants, or even of the common waterman ... who cannot read and write ... The feudal system ... still weakens as their acquaintance with the customs and manners of other nations extends; and unless the rage of civil discord be again excited, or some foreign power impose an alien yoke, the Burmans bid fair to be a prosperous ... and enlightened people."*

This is also supported by an American missionary in 1835-6.

"Temperance (in old Burma) is universal. The use of wine, spirits, opium, etc., is not only strictly forbidden both by religion and civil law, but is entirely against public opinion. I have seen thousands (of Burmans) together for hours on public occasions, rejoicing in all ardor, without observing an act of violence or a case of intoxication ... during my whole (period) of residence in the country, I never saw an immodest act or gesture in men or women ...

Old people are always treated with marked reverence ... Gravity and reserve are habitual among all classes ... Men are seldom betrayed into anger, and still less seldom come to blows ... Thieving and pilfering are common, but perhaps not more so than in other countries ... These crimes ... are for the most part perpetuated by a few of the basest sort ... The inadequacy of the government to the protection of the people makes it surprising that criminal offences are not more common. ... Lying ... prevails among all classes. ... They never place confidence in the word of each other, and all dealings are done with chicanery and much disputing. Even when detected in a lie, no shame is manifested... Never was a people more offensively proud, from the monarch... to the pettiest officer ... The meanest citizen seems to feel himself superior to the Peguans, Karens, Tongthoos, etc., around him. Gradations of rank are most minutely and tenaciously maintained."*

---

*Michael Symes: *An Account of An Embassy to the Kingdom of Ava* London 1800.

Howard Malcolm: *Travels in Southeastern Asia, Embracing Hindustan, Malaya, Siam and China, and a Full Account of the Burman Empire,* 2 vols. Boston 1839.

Unfortunately, what Malcolm mentioned in the next to the last sentence has become a serious source of conflict between the Burmans and the ethnic minorities up to the present day.

At least in the old regime, each ethnic minority would have their chief or "colonial king" to refer to, and he in turn would submit the case of conflict to the supreme ruler.

The Siamese still maintain this tradition. Most ethnic groups have disappeared, except the Malay Muslims and the hilltribes on the border with Burma, who still refer their grievances directly to the king. Being a constitutional monarch, His Majesty sometimes can not even help his "upcountry people"; the bureaucracy and vested interests have become very complex. Nothing can be solved easily by royal wishes or commands.

In the case of Burma, the British came to replace the role of the monarch from 1886-1948. During that period, Britain was responsible for the welfare of the peoples of British Burma. With the colonial administration of divide and rule, the Burmans, who were proud of their Buddhist and Burmese cultural heritage, would be left behind. Other ethnic groups who were inclined towards English education and civilization would be more accepted. So the Christian Karens and Chins and the imported Indians were better off economically and socially than the Burmese, who lost their gradations of rank, which were once most minutely and tenaciously maintained.

In Ceylon, the Tamil speaking minorities in the north and east as well as some of those imported from South India were preferred to the Sinhalese. In Malaya too, the Chinese and Indians imported to that country were better off than the natives.

This tendency helped increase the racial tension within each state, especially after the British colonial period.

In the case of Burma, her independence only meant getting rid of the British raj, with Westminster parliamentary democracy replacing the old monarchy. The top elites of each ethnic minority agreed to join the Union of Burma. It was a wonderful gesture to have a Shan Chief of one state to be the first President of the Union. It was very Burmese, too, to refuse to join the British Commonwealth, which could have been economically and diplomatically rewarding.

However, it was clearly proved that the Western form of democracy does not work in most states of Asia. Even in those countries which still have a parliament, it is not the essence of national polity. In many countries, certain strong men have declared themselves king, except in name. Some even used parliament to support their legitimacy.

General Ne Win was, in fact, not unique when he took over Burma with the strong backing of the army. He, like most Burmese, felt himself superior to other ethnic groups. This means that the Burmans are in fact insecure vis-a-vis other ethnic groups. Hence, their policy towards all the minorities in Burma has been very negative and violent throughout.

What I have said above is a slight oversimplification of the modern period, without even mentioning Aung San. Had he not been assassinated, the history of post-independent Burma would have been different.

Indeed the Panlong Conference on 12 February 1947 was very important in making the Union of Burma different from the old concept of the Burmese "universal monarch" and the "colonial kings" of various ethnic groups. The Chins and the Shan princes worked positively and harmoniously with the Takin movement for united Burma which led to her independence on 4 January 1948. Yet the independence day was marred by the great massacre of "Martyrs Day" on 19 July 1947. Besides, the Red Karens felt that they were betrayed by the British, even by the concept of the Union of Burma, because there had been no real consultation with them.

To be fair, the first constitution in 1947 provided a trial period of 10 years, in case different nationalities wanted to leave the federated states of the Union. Unfortunately, by 1957, many of them wanted to secede. Hence, Ne Win was asked to take over. Although he and the army handed over the government to U Nu, who won a landslide general election afterwards, once the army tasted the supreme authority of running a state, as in the case of Siam and elsewhere, they wanted to return to power, which in the case of Burma, they did in 1962. They have remained there ever since.

At least, U Nu saw himself as a universal monarch of old, who wanted to treat all ethnic chiefs as "colonial kings". Besides, he had an honest and kindly character, and he understood history. He even wanted to support the Sangha in its Sixth Council, following Emperor Asoka, who had patronized the Third Great Council in India and, of course, King Mindon, who held the Fifth

Council at Mandalay. Unfortunately, he was weak politically and his parliamentary democracy was no match for the army under General Ne Win.

Burma may need a strong man, but not for 26 years. Burma like Siam, does not need the army to run its country either. But in the present situation, Siam and Burma need some enlightened people in the army to prepare the army to liquidate its power within the next few years.

For Siam, it is more difficult, since we are much in alliance with USA, China, Japan and ASEAN, and multinational corporations. A strong group of army officers will not be able to change the course of our history.

As for Burma, being truly independent, free from any multinational corporations and superpower influence (perhaps with the exception of China, which still supports the Burmese Communist Party), a group of good-willed and honest people in the army could change the course of history, provided that they see the mistake of parliamentary democracy a la U Nu and personal dictatorship a la Ne Win.

In the case of Burma, the state council consists of not only the leading colonels but also some respectable representatives of the ethnic groups. But the party and the military must take the students' grievances seriously. The farmers and the labour unions, too, should be really consulted, and not in a merely formalistic way. Indeed they should also listen to dissident views. Like those of Aung Gyi.

If the 23 July party's congress could be something meaningful, then Burma may be able to avoid national catastrophe.

From the agenda, it appears that they want to change their economic policy and to amend the party's constitution. It is better to be late than never at all. But if the congress is only a window-dressing without any substance, then the present regime will certainly face a civil war. I hope a change is coming.

The Buddhist middle way of Burma is not to go back to the old kingship, but to learn from tradition to be self-critical, so that public participation is real at all levels. This would curb official haughtiness and petty corruption.

Cultivation for self-reliance in Burma is possible if proper incentive is given.

Burma should avoid industrialization and export orientation as in the case of the Thai failure. The more the Thai want to imitate NICs, the more the majority suffer. Making people crave money and material things in order to have a Western life-style as shown on television, is harmful for Siam.

I think the Burmans have no incentive at all to produce, so the middle way is needed. China could even be a model for this, but one should also take great caution in adopting the Chinese model.

There is something seriously wrong with the Burmese road to socialism. But to abandon it in order to follow the capitalist road to consumerism would be hazardous in its own way.

Burmese socialism is in fact state capitalism with selfish nationalism, which is unhealthy and dictatorial. We should introduce Dhammic Socialism, with less interference from the state, strengthening people's organizations at various villages, and creating non-government organizations to serve, as well as to learn from, the grassroots, where local wisdom is still available. Traditional herbal medicine, handicrafts, etc. are much stronger in Burma than in Siam.

The Burmese must first of all respect the ethnic minorities as their equals, not treating them even as "colonial kings". With this fraternity and tolerance, loving kindness and compassion could grow naturally. There is nothing wrong with the Christian Karens and the Muslims around the Chittagong areas, and with the Shans and the Kachins. They all want to live with the Burmese as equals.

If their view could be established widely, then a national solution could be achieved non-violently. There is no need to kill each other all the time in so many areas, and no need to use the Thai borders to grow opium to buy arms. This is harmful to all concerned. Germans and Americans sell arms to the rebels while Western children suffer from street drugs originating in these areas.

The Thai and the Burmese declare themselves to be Buddhists. But to be a Buddhist properly one must be self-critical in order to be humble and generous. Hence one should not exploit one-self and others. From this basic attitude, one can really respect and trust those of a different ethnic origin, culture and religion.

With trust and benevolence, friendship can be established. The Buddha said in this world, externally, there is nothing more important than a good friend. The Burmese need good friends beyond their own culture and ethnicity. They need the Shans, the Karens, the Mons, the Chins, the Kachins etc.

Fortunately for the Burmese, if they are humble and treat others as their equal partners, the ethnic minorities will reciprocate very readily.

From what I gather from the National Democratic Front, which consists of most, it not all, nationalities of Burma, their demands are fairly reasonble. They only want a democratic government to establish a genuine federation of states with a multi-party system, with autonomy within each state, and equal rights for every citizen of each ethnic group.

After a free general election, the government can decide, with public consultation, whether the country should go along a socialist or capitalist road.

Although the Thai are, on the whole, quite hostile to the Burmese, there are some Thais who are willing to be real friends of Burma. The Burmese need the Thai as much as the Thai need them.

Although it is good for Burma not to associate closely with an Eastern or a Western bloc to solve their national crisis, the Burmese also need real friends from abroad, who do not want economic advantage from Burma in a short term policy, but who want to see Burma as a solution for the world, especially in solving ethnic conflicts peacefully and living together non-violently for self reliance, by keeping the superpowers and the multinational corporations far away.

If Burma could now solve her national crisis non-violently, and set herself on the road to self reliance with Dhammic Socialism as a means and an end, she would indeed provide a model for us all.

Originally delivered as *"Understanding a State and its Minorities from a Religious and Cultural Perspective – the case of Siam and Burma"* in Bonn, 23 July 1988.

First published in *Solidarity*, Manila, No.121 January-March 1989.

ARGUMENTS FOR REAL WORLD DEVELOPMENT: A BUDDHIST PERSPECTIVE

During the past decades, indeed, since the end of World War II in 1945, our One World has remained divided and disunited. There is confrontation on all fronts: superpower confrontation, ideological confrontation, and confrontation between the "haves" of the northern world – the developed industrial countries of the North – and the "have nots" – the third world countries of Latin America, Asia and Africa. Instead of growing internationalism, there is increased and increasing nationalism and parochialism. We are witnessing a major assault on an already fragile structure of international cooperation. Instead of man being his brother's keeper, there is a widespread display of self-centredness, selfishness and cynicism. Regrettably, we are now in what has been described as the "Me" era, under the guise of which a large and growing number of people and nations have abandoned themselves to a special kind of selfishness and to a unique disregard for the claims of social order, particularly at the international level. And nations, particularly the big and powerful ones, are busy causing injury and hardship to other nations, usually the weak and helpless ones.

What kind of world will exist by the year 2000? What kind of legacy will the twenty-first century inherit from this excessively troubled twentieth century, where might has always been right, where the end has invariably justified the means, and the weak have been persistently oppressed by the strong, and man's inhumanity to man, particularly on account of racial and religious differences, has reigned supreme? Not surprisingly, the first five decades of the twentieth century witnessed two savagely fought World Wars; the so called civilized countries were engaged in very bloody combat against one another. Not surprisingly also, there was a widely-held determination that the Second World War must be the war that ended all wars, and that after it a better world must be built. How far we have succeeded in building a better world is a moot point.

Suffice it to say that the recognition of the need for a better post-World War II was an admission that much was wrong, which needed not be wrong and which, therefore, could be altered, if the powers that be were so determined. It was also generally agreed that such a better world would have to be built on the foundation of several ideals: justice, particularly economic and social justice, based on a new economic and social order; freedom, particularly political freedom resulting from the elimination of imperialism, aggression, and colonialism; freedom from hunger in place of the build-up of destructive weaponry; tolerance, particularly racial tolerance, and the elimination of racism and racial prejudice; and concern for humanity, particularly a universal subscription to the ideal of the oneness of humanity and the dignity of man. The extent to which we are today close to the achievement of these ideals and the challenges resulting from our failure to build trust through economic and social development and ecological balance will be our main concern in this paper.

The Promise and Disappointment of Early Post-war Years

First, let us begin with a review of the immediate post-war years. This period saw a vigorous pursuit of the objective of building a better world. The United Nations was established on 24 October 1945, and soon thereafter the Charter of Human Rights was adopted. It was the intention of all concerned that the UN should be a universal organization in the way that the League of Nations was not. And thanks to the organization, the decolonization process, begun in 1947 when India became independent, was vigorously pursued. Thus the UN, which, when it was set up in 1945 had a membership of 51 states, boasted of 159 sovereign member states in 1985 when it celebrated, with appropriate pomp and pageantry, its fortieth birthday. We now have, for the first time in the history of mankind, a truly universal world organization which provides a common forum for the small and poor countries to rub shoulders with the big, powerful and rich ones on the basis of equality on matters of common concern. In fact, in those heady, early post-war years, the emphasis in favour of the emergence of a truly united world was so strong that leaders of thought and statesmen were talking about the need for a world government. Yet it must be acknowledged that this universality of the United Nations has become a source of conflict as the big and powerful nations have come to increasingly resent the dominance of the organization by the small and poor nations. Although a small nation like Siam is now a member of the UN Security Council, still this means nothing as far as decreasing world conflicts goes.

Side by side with the setting up of the United Nations came also the establishment of the World Bank and the International Monetary Fund (IMF), the Bretton Woods institutions. The Bretton Woods system was originally intended to include an International Trade Organization which was negotiated and agreed upon in Havana in 1948. Unfortunaely, its charter was never ratified by the US Congress. In its place was established the less ambitious and more restricted General Agreement on Tariff and Trade (GATT) in 1948. GATT was intended as an interim arrangement but has become the principal forum for multinational trade negotiations. Given its limited mandate, GATT has been unable to address the wider issues of international trade including steps towards organizing commodity markets – all of which the International Trade Organization was to deal with had it been established. Equally unfortunate is the fact that unlike the United Nations, the membership of these Bretton Woods institutions is not universal. Some important planned-economy countries of Eastern Europe, notably the USSR, are not members.

Instead of striving to achieve unity in addressing world economic problems, the Western and Socialist countries, soon after World War II, went their respective ways. In 1947, the US initiated the Marshall Plan for the economic recovery of Western Europe, the nucleus of which later became the Organization for Economic Cooperation and Development (OECD). For their part, the Socialist countries established, in 1949, the Council for Mutual Economic Assistance (CMEA or Comecon). Thus the opportunity was lost to begin the process of establishing a new world economic order which would cut across ideological differences. Although the third world countries joined the Bank and the IMF as they gained their independence, their impact on these institutions, whose control lies in the hands of major industrial market economies through votes weighted by the size of contributions, has remained marginal. In any case, although the post-war years saw the emergence of Asia and Africa into the political activities of the world, they together with the Latin American countries, played very minor roles in shaping the post-war world, particularly in the domain of international economic relations.

By their exclusion, the world polity that emerged was Euro-American centred. Not surprisingly, therefore, the world soon became divided into two unequal halves – North and South. The North, which includes all the countries of Europe, North America and Australasia, (especially Japan) today controls over 90 per cent of the world's manufacturing industry. And as the Brandt Commission on International Development Issues stated:

"...most patents and new technologies are the property of multinational corporations in the North, which conduct a large share of world investment and world trade in raw materials and manufactures. Because of this economic power, northern countries dominate the international economic system – its rules and regulations, and its international institutions of trade, money and finance... The North... has a quarter of the worlds population and four-fifths of its income; the South, including China, has three-quarters of the world's population but living on one-fifth of the world's income."

The high hopes entertained in the fifties and sixties of massive transfer of capital and technological know-how from the North to the South, along the lines of the Marshall Plan which had proved so vital for European recovery, did not materialize. The enthusiasm, which the launching of the first United Nations Development Decade generated, soon faded away as it became clear that the will to bring about basic changes and reform in the world economic system was simply lacking. While no one disputes the fact that economic forces left entirely to themselves tend to produce growing inequality, the rich North has shown remarkable reluctance to acknowledge this basic principle in relations between nations within the world community – a principle that has sadly been universally applied to relations between individuals and societies within a single nation. Countries which have protected the weak and have promoted the principles of justice within their national borders have been half-hearted in their support for, if not downright opposed to, the establishment of a new international order based on justice, freedom, tolerance and humanity. The establishment of the oneness and solidarity of mankind as an axiom in an age whose real achievements were of international application has eluded us because nationalism is fast becoming, as it did during the inter-war years of 1914 to 1939, an omnivorous all-permeating passion. We remember all too well the disastrous consequences of the rampant nationalism of the nineteenth and early twentieth centuries which, combined with the pursuit of oligarchy, degenerated into the bogus concept of racial purity invoked by the Nazis in their pursuit of world domination. And if we are not careful, Japan may again be involved in the Third World War. If that war takes place, there will be no winners, all will be losers as there may not be anybody left in the world!

The Regression to Nationalism and Isolation

There is no denying the fact that the world is today more interdependent than it has ever been. Politically, economically, culturally and socially, the scale and complexity of the links among the countries and peoples of the world has risen sharply during the last forty years, particularly during the first two and a half decades of the post-World War II era, when there developed a strong current of internationalism running through many societies. The Eastern bloc countries cooperated brilliantly to rebuild the war-devastated economies of Europe and throughout the world there was a unique advance in the creation of wealth and income.

But this cooperation, this internationalism lasted only a generation. As the divide between the rich North and the poor South widened into a gulf, the cooperation disappeared and was replaced by confrontation. Successive economic crises, with low or negative growth rates in the North and consequential chronic mass unemployment, bred parochialism in the industrialized countries of the North. And in such circumstances, North-South cooperation plummetted. But even in the industrialized countries, the economic crisis resulted in a widening gap between the rich and the poor and in the dismantling of essential public services with the inevitable accentuation of social tensions.

Unfortunately, by choosing protectionism the countries of Western democracies have shown that old habits, however bad and deleterious they may be, die hard. Although not as glaring as in the inter-war years, economic nationalism has begun to rear its ugly head in our world of today. An increasing number of countries are tightening restrictions upon the entry of foreigners – particularly non-white foreigners. That these actions have been taken by some of the most powerful states proves the veracity of the aphorism that if there is any lesson that history teaches us, it is that it teaches us nothing. Our world – particularly the developed part of it – seems to have learned nothing and forgotten nothing!

The dangers posed by the crisis through which international relations and the world economy are now passing are growing more serious every day. The present North-South divide is not in the long-term interest of our world, as it is becoming clear that major national problems have significant international implications and can only, therefore, be solved through international cooperation. In other words, the international system has become complicated as well as becoming more interdependent with the result that what appear to be national problems – e.g. environment, energy, money, trade and finance and unemployment – can only be solved through international cooperation. The achievement of economic growth and development in one country depends increasingly on the performance of others. As the Brandt Commission repeatedly remarked in its North-South report: "The South cannot grow adequately without the North. The North cannot prosper or improve its situation unless there is greater progress in the South."

The regression to the mentality which prevailed after 1918 must be a source of increasing anxiety to all men of goodwill who believe in peace, justice, freedom, tolerance and humanity. In no area is the regression proving so dangerous and bringing the world so uncomfortably close to the inter-war years as in the crisis of debt, the volatility in exchange rates and the growing menace to free trade. And this regression must be stopped and reversed in order to avert what happened in the inter-war years: the Great Depression and Hitler.

Some Further Economic Obstacles

In view of the gravity of the debt problem, let me devote part of this section to a discussion of it. Whatever the reasons for the huge external debt that developing countries have piled up, one of its main and dangerous consequences is the reverse or negative flow of resources from the poor countries to the rich countries. After 1945 and beginning with the Marshall Plan, there was a one-way flow of resources from the advanced countries to the developing countries to promote their development.

Indeed, this was also the case in the nineteenth century and during the first decade and a half of the twentieth century. Since the debt crisis which broke in 1982, the flows of resources have been reversed. For example, according to the estimates of the IMF, there was a resource flow from the seven largest third world borrowers – i.e. Brazil, Mexico, South Korea, Argentina, Venezuela, Indonesia and Philippines – worth US$32 billion in 1985 to their more prosperous creditors. This was nearly 20 per cent of the entire export earnings of these countries. Interest payments alone from developing countries in 1985 amounted to US $ 54 billion.

These reverse flows, unnatural as they are, and inimical to the economic well being of the world as they are, are being elevated into a necessary system of "adjustment" by the official policy of the industrial countries which are unwilling to assume their proper responsibility for the healthy functioning of the world's economy. Yet, as Lord Lever and Christopher Huhne stated in their book *Debt and Danger* :

"...such abdication of responsibility is singularly misplaced. The world's financial safety and economic health is balanced on a knife-edge. If defaults halt the reverse flow, many of the largest banks in the advanced countries will become insolvent. A crisis of the kind which we have thankfully not experienced since the Great Crash of 1929 would once again be a terrible reality. But if the Third World's debtors continue to generate the large trade surpluses required to make payment to the advanced countries, their economic development, already manifestly inadequate, will be hobbled for a generation. The effort to sustain the large trade surpluses required imposes enormous strains on the world's trading system, as industries in the advanced countries have to make way for Third World exports and resist the adjustment by means of ever more strident appeals for protectionism. Moreover, the very uncertain type of continued payments in these circumstances of rising political pressures in both debtor and creditor countries causes the banks themselves to slow down their lending, adding a further depressive influence to world trade."

It is only the governments and monetary authorities of the industrialized creditor countries that can resolve the debt crisis. For it is only they which have both the resources and the standing to reconcile the interests of both debtors and bankers and by so doing safeguard the world economy. It is difficult to disagree with Lever and Huhne that,

"Debt needs our urgent attention for the threat it poses in itself – but also because it epitomizes a sickness in the West. It is a dramatic crystallization of the failure of Western democracies during the last twenty years to adopt to a world of economic interdependence.... The leaders of the world, whether they be politicians, civil servants or central bankers, have consistently failed to provide strategic thinking. Matters are handled piecemeal with no sense of overall design. The case-by-case approach, justified from one angle, is elevated to high principle. In reality, it is a sign of intellectual bankruptcy, a euphemism for abdicating responsibility for the aggregate results of our actions. "Leave it to the market", we are told, as if financial markets operate in a vacuum and are not powerfully conditioned by the actions of our great institutions."

It is in the mutual interest of all that a solution be found before the debt crisis develops into an incalculable disaster–a situation which might suddenly develop were all the major debtor nations to follow the lead of Peru or even take more drastic unilateral actions.

We have already referred to regression to protectionism in recent years – a development which is an antithesis of the trade liberalization movement of the post-war era. It was realized then that trade liberalization would need to be supported by stable exchange rates. The enormous cost of competitive devaluation and beggar-my-neighbour policy of the 1930s was recognized as something that must be avoided in the new post-World War II era. Hence the creation of the IMF to provide even-handed support in the periods of balance of payments adjustments. Yet three decades and a half after the Bretton Woods system was inaugurated, the stable exchange rate system was abandoned. Free floating, contrary to early expectations, has intensified currency speculation and brought new restrictions to domestic policy through its adverse impact on patterns of trade and production and its immense repercussions on inflation.

Next, we come to the problems of trade deficits. One of the functions which the IMF was set up to perform was to mitigate the injurious consequences of trade imbalances by protecting not only the trade-deficit countries but also their trading partners through balance of payments support. Unfortunaltely, IMF operations are too limited and short-term focussed, as they are designed to solve the problems of temporary deficits rather than of long-term deficits which are inevitable in the developing countries. Indeed, the IMF with its policy of conditionalities is nowdays always the subject of sever criticisms in developing countries.

"My personal experience... convinced me of the colonial status which the multinationals have succeeded in imposing upon Britain. The same is true of the international financial power, now symbolized by the International Monetary Fund", wrote Tony Benn in his book *Arguments for Democracy*. He continued: "Two Cabinets in which I served sent to the IMF for bridging loans, one after the 1967 devaluation and the second in 1976. The IMF sent a team to examine Britain's economic policy and laid down the most rigid prescription for corrective measures to be adopted before either instalment of aid was made available.... The humiliation that the IMF imperialism imposes upon colonial Britain is deepened, rather than lessened, by the knowledge that our government has been compelled to pretend that it wished to follow policies that have in fact been imposed by the pressure of world bankers."

If Britain, once the center of world power, could be humiliated by the neo-colonialism of economic interests, what about small states in the Third World?

Fundamental Problems of Hunger, Malnutrition and Poverty

Susan George began her extremely readable, frank and thought-provoking book *How the other Half Dies* with this incisive comparison:

"The present world political and economic order might be compared to that which reigned over social class relations in individual countries in nineteenth century Europe – with the Third World now playing the role of the working class. All the varied horrors we look back upon with mingled disgust and incredulity have their equivalents, and worse, in the Asian, African and Latin American countries, where well over 500 million people are living in what the World Bank has called "absolute poverty". And just as the "propertied classes" of yesteryear opposed every reform and predicted imminent economic disaster if eight-year-olds could no longer work in the mills, so today those groups that profit from the poverty that keeps people hungry are attempting to maintain the staus quo between the rich and poor worlds."

Hence she concluded that hunger is not a scourge but a scandal.

Now it is twelve years after the publication of Susan George's book. The Hunger Project, consisting of a group of people dedicated to the elimination of hunger and starvation from our planet by the end of the century, came out with an authoritative and comprehensive publication, *Ending Hunger* – an idea whose time has come, whose facts are so horrifying that they should have shocked the conscience of the rich world, if it was not too cynical. Here are some of the horrible facts. In an age where the civilized world boasts that "scientific and technical advances in agriculture have yielded an era in which harvests are now outpacing population growth, producing for the first time more food than the world needs", hunger and starvation take the lives of 13 to 18 million people every year. This works out at an average of 35,000 persons every day, 24 every minute and of these 18 are children. Nearly one billion people – i.e. 20 per cent of mankind are chronically and seriously under-nourished. While it would be comparatively easy to wipe out famine, the more pernicious consequences of malnutrition will be harder to tackle. They will only disappear when real development takes place in the third world.

As The Hunger Project publication has also indicated, there is no other disaster that compares to the devastation of hunger. It has killed more people during the past two years than were killed in World War I and World War II combined. Compared with the disaster wrought by hunger every 48 hours, the Hiroshima bomb disaster was like a child's play, tragic as it no doubt was. When the most disastrous earthquake in modern history, which took place in China in 1976, resulted in about one quarter of a million deaths, the whole world rightly and properly mourned; yet hunger kills that many people every seven days. The Great Hunger Belt stretches from South-East Asia, through the Indian sub-continent and the Middle East through the continent of Africa to the equatorial region of Latin America. About 50 per cent of the world's hungry people live in just five countries - India, Bangladesh, Nigeria, Pakistan and Indonesia. One cannot but agree with the Brandt Commission that "the idea of a community of nations has little meaning if ... hunger is regarded as a marginal problem which humanity can live with".

Towards Ecological Balance and Human Environment

It is evident that our world is caught up in a cycle. Especially in quantitative development, the further it goes the more problems appear, faster than they can be solved, and the technocrats are not able to stop the spiralling because (1) they are afraid that if the quantity is not increased everything will come to a standstill. Or all the systems will go haywire leading to possible ruin. For instance, the population will increase and there will be insufficient food, leading to clashes. Actually in this regard there is enough food, if it were distributed equitably and used without waste. The problem is that those who have the surplus refuse to share it, because (2) they want to maintain the status of the rich. Their hope is that by increasing production most of the poor will receive a portion of the increase, continually raising their standards. But our nature is such that once we ourselves have become more comfortably situated, even though we see some injustices appearing, we don't get much excited about them if they don't touch us too much. Besides, if we do something about them, we might get hurt.

Is it not for these reasons that development has worked out in such a way that the gap has grown between the rich and the poor, and between the wealthy nations and the poor nations? In Siam, since development planning began, a few wealthy people in Bangkok have become continually wealthier, while the people of the northeast have become poorer, not to mention conditions in other parts of the country. And up until now, there has been no indication that my country is considering a change in its development policies, but it goes blithely on following the blueprints of the capitalist economists. If anyone raises objections to these methods or this type of thinking, he is labelled a rabble-rouser, a proponent of communism, or else he is accused of disloyalty to the nation, religion and king. Is it not time that we should speak the truth, and especially those who hold themselves to be religious? We must be honest, and if we are honest, we must admit that this type of development has not added to the happiness of the people in any real human sense, but on the contrary has taken a form that to a greater or lesser extent is permeated throughout with crooked deceptions. Moreover, we must not forget that the increase in production through the use of modern machinery to exploit natural resources cannot go on forever. Oil, coal and iron, once they are gone, cannot be brought back. As for the forests and some wild animals, when they are depleted, if they are to be brought back, it won't be in our time or our children's time. Production on a grand scale not only uses up the raw materials, it also destroys the environment, poisoning the air and the water, the fish and the fields, so that people are forced to ingest poison continually. We do not need to expand further on how man takes advantage of his fellowman.

In short, any country that feels itself so inferior as to call itself developing or underdeveloped, cannot and should not try to raise itself up through this kind of quantitative development in order to put itself on a par with those nations which brag that they are developed.

It cannot do so because, as Everett Reimer has said, if every country was like the United States, "oil consumption would be increased fifty times, iron one hundred times, and other metals two hundred times. And the United States itself would have to triple its use of these materials simply in the process of production itself." There are not enough raw materials in the world to do this, nor would the atmosphere be able to take the change. The world as we know it would come to an end.

You will, no doubt, surmise that I do not agree with that form of development which aims at quantity, and not even that form of development which has as its objective the improvement of the quality of human life, yet still stresses material things. In reality, the latter, too, diminishes the quality of human life.

It is not only that materialism fosters violence, but modern applied science also destroys the values of time and space. To a materialist civilization, time means only that which a clock can measure in terms of work-days, work-hours, work-minutes. Space simply has three dimensions which are filled with material things. That is why Buddhadasa Bhikkhu, a leading Thai monk, says development means confusion, for it assumes the more the merrier, the longer one's life the better, with no thought of measuring the real value of a long evil life as against that of a short good life. This is contrary to the teaching of the Buddha who said the life of a good man, however short it may be, is more valuable than that of an evil one, however long he lives.

As a matter of fact, it is only religion, which puts material things in second place and keeps the ultimate goals of development in sight, that can bring out the true value in human development.

For even in the matter of judging the value of development, from the point of view of ethics and morality, it is difficult to keep material considerations from being the sole criteria.

From the Buddhist point of view, development must aim at the reduction of craving, the avoidance of violence, and the development of the spirit rather than of material things. As each individual progresses, he increasingly helps others without waiting for the millennium, or for the ideal socialist society. Cooperation is better than competition, whether of the capitalist variety which favours the capitalist, or the socialist variety which favours the labourer.

From the standpoint of religion, the goal can be attained by stages as evil desires are overcome. So goals are perceived in two ways. From the worldly standpoint, the more desires are increased or satisfied the further development can proceed. From the religious standpoint, the more desires can be reduced the further development can proceed.

Western civilization erodes Christianity, or at least real Christian spiritual values, and becomes merely capitalistic or socialistic, aiming to increase material goods in order to satisfy craving. The capitalist variety wants to raise the material standard of living of other groups if possible, provided the capitalists themselves can stay on top. The socialist variety reverses it and wants the majority, to oppress the minority or those who are opposed to them.

The value scale of Western-type development emphasizes extremes. The richer the better; the capitalists apply this to the wealthy, and the socialists to the labourer. The quicker the better. The bigger the better. The more knowledge the better. Buddhism, on the other hand, emphasizes the middle way between extremes, a moderation which strikes a balance appropriate to the balance of nature itself. Knowledge must be a complete knowledge of nature, in order to be wisdom, otherwise, knowledge is ignorance. Partial knowledge leads to delusion, and encourages the growth of greed and hate. These are the roots of evil that lead to ruin. The remedy is the threefold way of self-knowledge, leading to right speech and action and right relations to other people and other beings as well as the environment (*Sila* or morality), consideration of the inner truth of one's own spirit and of nature (*Samadhi* or meditation), leading finally to enlightenment or complete knowledge (*Pañña* or wisdom). It is an awakening, and a complete awareness of the world.

When one understands this one understands the three characteristics of all things from the Buddhist point of view: their unsatisfactoriness, their impermanence, and their lack of a permanent selfhood.

True development will arrange for the rhythm of life and movement to be in accordance with the facts, while maintaining an awareness that man is but a part of the universe, and that ways must be found to integrate mankind with the laws of nature. There must be no boasting, no proud self-centered attempts to master nature, no emphasis placed on the creation of material things to the point where people become slaves to things and have no time left for themselves to search after the truth which is out beyond the realm of material things.

In 1929, Max Scheler formulated a remark which is just as true today as then. He said:

"We have never before seriously faced the question whether the entire development of Western civilization, that one-sided and over-active process of expansion outward, might not ultimately be an attempt using unsuitable means – if we lose sight of the complementary art of inner self-control over our entire underdeveloped and otherwise involuntary psychological life, an art of meditation, search of soul, and forbearance. We must learn anew to envisage the great, invisible solidarity of all living beings in universal life, of all minds in the eternal spirit – and at the same time the mutual solidarity of the world process and the destiny of its supreme principle, and we must not just accept this world unity as a mere doctrine; but practise and promote it in our inner and outer lives."

This is indeed the spirit of Buddhist development, where inner strength must be cultivated first; then compassion and loving-kindness to others becomes possible. Work and play would be interchangeable. There is no need to regard work as something which has to be done, has to be bargained for, in order to get more wages or in order to get more leisure time. Work ethics would not be to get ahead of others, but to enjoy one's work and to work in harmony with others. Materially there may not be too much to boast about, but the simple life ought to be comfortable enough, and simple food is less harmful to the body and mind. Besides, a simple diet could be produced without exploiting nature, and one would then need not keep animals merely for the sake of man's food.

In *Small is Beautiful,* E.F. Schumacher reminds us that Western economists go for maximization of developmental goals in a material sense such that they hardly care for people. He suggests Buddhist economics as a study of economics as if people mattered. He says that in the Buddhist concept of development, we should avoid gigantism, especially of machines, which tend to control rather than to serve man. With gigantism, men are driven by an excessive greed in violating and raping nature. If the two extremes (bigness and greed) could be avoided, the Middle Path of Buddhist development could be achieved, i.e. both the world of industry and agriculture could be converted into a meaningful habitat for man.

I agree with Schumacher that small is beautiful in the Buddhist concept of development, but what he did not stress is that cultivation must first come from within.

From the Buddhist standpoint, man must cultivate his awareness or mindfulness – to know himself, in order not to exploit himself. Unfortunately most of us exploit ourselves in the name of fame, success, development or even social justice.

Only when one is less egocentric, would one become humble and natural then one would be in a true position of trying not to exploit others – not only humans, but animals, birds and bees, as well as being respectful to our environment.

Sīla in Buddhism does not only mean ethics for man's personal behaviour, it in fact refers to meaningful social as well as environmental relations.

Environmental consciousness toward improving the quality of life came along with the change in attitude toward industrial and technological progress. The 1970 report, *Toward Balanced Growth : quantity with quality* addressed the potential consequences of new technologies. Specifically, one of the first successes of the environmentalists involved their challenge of the development of supersonic transport. The Three Mile Island nuclear power plant incident of 1979 confirmed a growing public suspicion that development in science and technology requires public scrutiny and control.

The complex situations of the development problem in the 70s were attributed to factors such as limited resources, environmental concerns, the pursuit of material sufficiency for all, and a shift from individual to social responsibility. Most of the goals and problems associated with development and environment have not changed over the past three decades, and many environmental aspects have become more pressing. As was expressed in President Carter's environmental message, the situation is one in which "the projected deterioration of the global environmental and resource base" has become one of the world's "most urgent and complex challenges of the 1980s". In this context, a "World Conservation Strategy designed to make conservation and development mutually supportive" was announced in Washington and other capitals in 1980.

Although the initial upsurge of interest in conservation came in the 1960s and 1970s, "the integration of conservation and environmental considerations into the world development process was emphasized in this new strategy under the conviction that it is essential to the future expansion of dynamic world society." Both the First and Third World nations became aware that "international co-operation is an essential factor both in preserving the global balance of nature and in reducing the damage to the world's ecosystems."

Supporting the conservation strategy, the president of the World Bank issued a statement that the bank was committed to the principle of sustainable development, and pointed out that "...economic growth on the careless pattern of the past century poses an undeniable threat to the environment and ultimately to the very ecological foundations of development itself." The announcement of the marriage of conservation and development was characterized as a response to the desperate human needs of the poor Third World, by abandoning "the elitist Western mould".

Conclusions

Although man is an adaptive creature of evolution, which enables him to cope with environmental changes, the amount and rates of these changes may become so drastic as to overwhelm the ability of human beings to accommodate them. The shortage of resources has become increasingly serious and is essentially worldwide. There is no longer the possibility of choosing dumping sites without deteriorating the ecosystem. Instead, the negative effects induced in the biosphere may be profound and irreversible.

Realizing these facts from the 1960s, we should say that

there have been considerable efforts in the management of the problem (of which the theme may be summarized as the conservation strategy through international cooperation). Did we succeed? Despite this strategy, our senses tell us that we have an increasingly serious environmental problem in the process of post-industrialization. At the moment,it looks as if our traditional approach to the problem is going to lose the race against extermination.

Therefore, in conclusion, we should talk about what must be done to implement the recommendations of the past three decades. First of all, we must admit the inherent difficulty of the environmental problem itself; especially in growing industrial and post-industrial societies where this very difficult project actively involves the natural and social sciences, technology, economics, and politics. However, the present approach is geared primarily toward engineering. Given these facts, discussion on human environmental problems should be pursued on a multidisciplinary range of professions including the scientific disciplines. We have to learn that many of the mistakes have arisen from an overly narrow assessment of technological change in society.

Secondly, the efforts to solve environmental problems should be carried out by governmental and private sectors of a nation together with close international co-operation. Individual attempts to maximize each country's own wealth, although they may seem to bring apparent profits in the short term, can only lead to disaster in the end.

Thirdly, religious people should be aware of these problems. They should have a deep commitment to ecological balance as part and parcel of building trust through economic and social development.

I am happy to report that now there is a joint Thai-Tibetan project under the patronage of His Holiness the Dalai Lama on the Buddhist perception of nature. The project has distributed 3000 books of stories and teachings drawn from Buddhist Scriptures that relate to the environment.

These will be followed by 50,000 others to all Thai monasteries, which are still vital centres of education and social life in rural areas.

Similar literature is being distributed to schools in Tibetan refugee camps of North India. The books – believed to be the first compilation of environmental themes in Buddhism – include vivid tales of monks and lay people who chopped down trees and killed animals, and parables in which the Buddha uses nature to illustrate how life should be lived and how humans and animals are part of the same continuum.

It is hoped that this project can soon expand to countries like Japan and South Korea, which have strong Buddhist roots and considerable resources for fighting environmental problems and a much criticized conservation record, especially in their economic expansion to Southeast Asia and othe parts of the world.

One member of the project explains: "It's going to work in the long run. But it must be inculcated into our children so when they grow up they feel close to nature. Once you love nature, you don't even have to teach about conservation – you nourish it naturally."

In 1855, the President of the United States, Franklin Pierce pressured the Indian chief of the Swami tribe, Seattle, to sell the land of what is now Washington State. To this the chief replied as follows (excerpt from his letter):

"How can love buy or sell the sky, the warmth of land? Such thoughts to us are inconceivable. We are not in possession of the freshness of the air, or the water-bubbles. Every corner of this land, to my people, is holy. It remains holy in the memory of my people; the sparkling pineleafs and the sandy beaches, the mist of dark brooding forests to the songs of insects.

"We know that White Men do not understand our way of life. Our piece of land is exactly like another, because he comes at night to rob the land of what he needs. Land, to you, is not a brother but an enemy. After conquering a piece he proceeds to the next. After devouring the land with his voracious appetite, only deserts remain.

"If I were to accept your proposition, you must do me one thing in return. What is man without other animals? If the beasts were to be ravished, man, too, would suffer and die from loneliness. What happened to animals is also to occur to humans.

"Our god is the same god that you worship. His compassion extends equally to White Men and Indians. This land is precious to him and harming it, therefore, is an insult to our creator. The White Man will be extinguished. If you continue to pollute your sleeping place, some day you will find yourself suffocating amidst your waste. When the buffalos are killed and wild horses tamed, when the sanctified corners of the forest are damaged by the stench of humans, that will be the end of life and the commencement of death.

"When the last Indians are extinct from this land and only the shadows of clouds traversing the plains remain, even then the spirit of my people will be preserved by the beaches and forests. This is because, like a new-born babe listening to the heartbeat in the bosom of his mother, my people love this land.

"After we turn over our land to you, keep in mind that we will continue to love and cherish this land as we always have. After you have taken this land from us, love this land as you do your children, as our god does us, with all your might, and ability and heart. We know that your god and ours is the same. This land is precious to him and White Men cannot be exempted from this commonfate."

This letter would be a revelation not only to the President of 130 years ago, but to the modern man who destroys and pollutes Nature.

Dhyani Ywahoo, Cherokee medicine woman and teacher of Tibetan Buddhism, who has brought together two great traditions in the teaching, has said, "There is a stream of compassionate wisdom of which we are all a part... From that flowing heart comes a great wisdom to which each of us is attuned... So peace is alive within us as a seed, as a song. To call it forth is a practice of clear vision and clear speech. See the beauty and praise the beauty, and wisdom's stream shall flow abundantly in our heart."

Buddhism, through its insistence on the interrelatedness of all life, its teachings of compassion for all beings, its nonviolence, and again, as with native spiritual teachings anywhere, its caring for all of existence, has been leading some Westerners to broader and deeper interpretations of the relationships between social, environmental, racial and sexual justice, and peace.

In this area we are inspired by some examples of such movement like the Sarvodaya in Sri Lanka and especially by the Vietnamese monk, Thich Nhat Hanh, who teaches us to pay close attention to the minute particulars in our actions, as well as to the giant web of all life.

Now let me describe another example of the interrelatedness of peace and justice as it is played out on American soil, and the implications in its emphasis on compassion and the interconnection of all beings. In its inherent nonviolence, Buddhism seems particularly suited to peace and justice issues. Buddhism and native spiritual traditions in any land can lead us away from our anthropocentric position to a caring for the animal world and all of nature. There is a renewed emphasis on the interconnection of all life in modern Buddhism.

An organization that is attempting to move on this awareness in confronting issues of building trust through economomic and social development with an awareness of ecological balance is the Buddhist Peace Fellowship. Begun in 1987 by Robert Aitken of the Diamond Sangha in Hawaii and others, it offers Buddhists a way to take their practice into the world of political and social action.

Its Statement of Purpose proposes:

- To make clear public witness to the Buddha Way as a way of peace and protection of all beings

- To raise peace and ecology concerns among Buddhists and to promote projects through which the Sangha may respond to these concerns

- To encourage the delineation in English of the Buddhist way of nonviolence, building from the rich resources of traditional Buddhist teachings a foundation for new action

- To serve as liaison to, and enlist support for, existing national and international Buddhist peace and ecology programmes

- To offer avenues to realize the kinship among groups and members of Western and world Sangha

- To provide a focus for concerns over the persecution of Buddhists, as a particular expression of our intent to protect all beings; and

- To bring the Buddhist perspective to contemporary peace and ecology movements.

The BPF consists of a national organization composed of independent local groups in the USA, each working on its own projects, as well as a chapter in England. It also has a chapter in Australia. BPF members sponsored a demonstration in San Fransisco for monks, nuns, and writers who are prisoners of conscience in Vietnam, and gathered more than 4500 signatures on a petition that was delivered to the UN Human Rights Commission. It also gathers funds to send to Vietnam for the support of hungry families. The most recent project is the attempt to stop the execution of two Buddhist monks in Vietnam who were accused of associating with an anti-government group. To protest this unjust punishment, Buddhists and others concerned about human rights sent hundreds of telegrams of protest to the Secretary General of the Communist Party in Hanoi, with the result that capital punishment for the two monks has been reduced to twenty years imprisonment!

On one Sunday each month the BPF goes to meditate on the railroad tracks at the Concord Naval Weapons Station in California, where weapons are sent to Central America to be used against the people of Nicaragua; one brave and persistent member said, "Sitting to meditate between the road and the chain link fence, we register a silent protest to the imperialist violence of our government, and the loud horns of passing hostile cars remind us, of the noise of our own minds, the violence and carelessness in ourselves."

The name Thich Nhat Hanh has been mentioned earlier. He is a leading inspirational figure for members of the Buddhist Peace Fellowship.

He particularly stresses nondualism in his teaching, and speaks of "being peace" in in one's own life as part of making peace in the world. He stresses the continuity of inner and outer, calling the world our "large self." and asks us to become it actively and to care for it.

His Tiep Hien Order, created in Vietnam during the war, is in the lineage of the Zen school of Lin Chi. It is a form of engaged Buddhism in daily life, in society. The best translation of Tiep Hien, according to Thich Nhat Hanh, is the "Order of Interbeing," which he explains in this way: "I am, therefore you are. You are, therefore I am, That is the meaning of the word interbeing. We inter-are."

The Order of Interbeing, as it is known among BPF members, is based on Thich Nhat Hanh's reformulation of the Buddhist precepts into fourteen guiding statements, designed to explicitly address social justice and peace issuess, sensitizing the particpant to test his behaviour in relation to the needs of the larger community, while freeing him from limiting patterns. These precepts address issues of mind, speech and body.

The first precept is: "Do not be idolatrous about or bound to any doctrine, theory, or ideology, even Buddhist ones. All systems of thought are guiding means; they are not absolute truths." And in his discussion of this, Thich Nhat Hanh writes, "If you have a gun, you can shoot one, two, three, five people; but if you have an ideology and stick to it, thinking it is the absolute truth, you can kill millions." And : "Peace can only be achieved when we are not attached to a view, when we are free from fanaticism. The more you decide to practice this precept, the deeper you will go into reality and understand the teachings of Buddhism."

Another precept urges us not to avoid contact with suffering but to find ways to be with those who suffer. And another, not to accumulate wealth while millions are hungry.

These precepts create a consciousness of, and a precedent for, social justice and peace work grounded firmly in Buddhist principles, in our individual beings and in our practice of mindfulness. The seventh precept is perhaps the most important, a pivot on which the others turn:

"Do not lose yourself in dispersion and in your surroundings. Learn to practice breathing in order to regain composure of body and mind, to practice mindfulness, and to develop concentration and understanding."

These guiding statements achieve an integration of the traditional five precepts with elements of the Noble Eightfold Path, and I believe Thich Nhat Hanh's decision to elaborate on the traditional precepts came from his observation that one can interpret these to encourage a withdrawal from the world, a passivity in the face of war and injustice, a separation of oneself from the common lot of humanity. In rewriting the precepts he is countering that tendency. In directing us to focus on our interconnection with other beings, he is asking us to experience the continuity between the inner and the outer world, to act in collaboration, in mutuality with others in the dynamic unfolding of the truth that nurtures justice and creates peace.

Some of us are trying to meet this challenge. I hope what some of us are trying to do in connecting our "being peace" within to the outside world, engagingly and mindfully, will contribute to a better world with social justice, non-vioience and ecological balance – the Middle Way for each individual and for the society at large to live in harmony with one another and with nature.

Originally delivered to the World Conference on Religion and Peace as "Building Trust Through Economic and Social Development and Ecological Balance: a Buddhist Perspective" at Monash University, Melbourne, 23 January 1989.

VI
ASPECTS OF THAI BUDDHISM

BUDDHADĀSA BHIKKHU: A RELIGIOUS INNOVATOR OF UNDYING FAME

Buddhadāsa-bhikkhu is an unconventional, unique monk who has broken away from all restrictions of Buddhist sects and institutions in order to find the primordial, perfect, and real essence of the doctrine. His thought is so broad and profound that he is well-known as the Theravadin Nagarjuna.

He is a Mahā-nikāya monk with an ecclesiastical rank of Phra Dhammakosācārya and now the abbot of a royal monastery in Southern Siam. Previously, his work had not been recognized by either the Thai government or the Order. But after he had founded Suan Mokkha Balārāma (the Hermitage of the Garden of Liberation) even the Dhammayutika monks of the highest ecclesiastical rank could not help admiring him and willingly gave him their support. Yet, before his innovation was widely accepted, he had worked honestly, perseveringly and wisely, with his perfect monastic discipline, for quite a long time.

Suan Mokkha is not only a place where Buddhist theories are in harmony with Buddhist practices, but also a place where Buddhist studies can return to the Buddha's original teachings. Furthermore, Buddhadasa and Suan Mokkha are respectively a person and a place beyond the limit of Theravada tradition. Though Buddhadasa adheres firmly to the doctrine of the Pali Scriptures, he still keeps commending Mahayāna teachings and practices. At first, his religious ways of life were insulted, laughed at, and made fun of by his opposers. Nevertheless, he could calmly tolerate being an "insane monk" in his Theravada society and let all the "sane monks" live happily with their wealth and gain. This may remind us of the Venerable Somdet Phra Budhacarya (To)'s words: "When the old monk To was sane, they said he was mad.

But when the old monk To was mad, they said he was sane." If some monks of rank, however, are insane like Buddhadasa, they will certainly be able to make Thai Buddhism more progressive and beneficial than before.

Though Buddhadāsa studies Mahayāna doctrine through English publications, he has been assisted by many Chinese scholars and increasingly praised for his work. Buddhadasa's appreciation of Mahayana Buddhism is not as amazing as his admiration of Christianity and Islam. Most Thais feel that Christianity and Islam are alien. If they really understand Christian and Islamic basic teachings, they will be able to appreciate and live peacefully with Christians and Muslims.

Unlike most Thai scholars, Buddhadāsa has never tried to understand other religions by means of textbooks. He carefully detects the meanings of all teachings in their sources. His intention to work for all religions is quite honorable. Once, he said: "I have three resolutions. First, I will make all religious followers understand one another properly. Secondly, I will make all religious followers understand the essence of their own doctrines. Thirdly, I will free everyone from materialism."

Buddhadāsa respects all other religions. Though he is a devout Buddhist, he regards other faiths impartially. His religious interpretations can be used in Buddhism as well as in Christianity. He explains that the Christian Cross is the symbol of *anattā* (no-self) as it shows a crossing mark on the "I" or "myself." His interpretation of *anattā* in Christianity is similar to that of Professor Masao Abe, a leading Japanese scholar in Buddhist studies. In addition, it implies an expression of Christian mystics. For example, Meister Eckhart (ca. 1260-1327) once referred to God as the Nameless Nothing, i.e., God's isness means "free from becoming" which is similar to the Buddhist suññatā. Eckhart's saying – "Let us learn self-forgetting until we call nothing more our own" –is certainly a move toward the Buddhist doctrine of *anattā*. We may compare his saying to that of Master Dogen of Zen Buddhism:

"When we practice "bare attention" we just see what is there without adding any comment, interpretation, judgment or conclusion. There is just attending. Learning to see in this way is the basic practice of Buddhist meditation. The self does not come into it. To forget the self is to be enlightened by all things."

Similarly, Thomas Merton, a contemporary Christian practitioner, once said: "There is just seeing. Seeing what? Not an Absolute Object but Absolute Seeing. " Whoever understands these words may be able to enter the stream of enlightenment.

If we want to understand the essence of a doctrine, we need to examine the actual practices accordingly. A Christian friend once said:

"We are spiritually paralysed by the fetish of Jesus....His literary image in the Gospels has, through centuries of homage, become far more of an idol than anything graven in wood or stone, so that today the most genuinely reverent act of worship is to destroy that image."

This may remind Buddhists of a Zen teaching: "When you meet the Buddha, kill him," or Buddhadasa's metaphor: "A Buddha image is a mountain on the way toward Buddhadhamma."

Buddhadasa's second resolution is a resistance to Christians' intrusion upon Buddhist faith, i.e., an attempt to convert Buddhists to Christianity. Once, I asked a Christian refugee, in his camp, about the denomination he professed. He answered that his was the American denomination because it gave him many privileges, e.g., to be able to enter the United States sooner, and so on.

Buddhadasa is attacked by a considerable number of Buddhists, especially in Sri Lanka. Some Buddhists criticize Buddhadasa's generosity and express their concern that his work may be artfully used by Christians. Some Christians use certain passages of Buddhadasa's work to propagate their own doctrine. They do not realize that a good relationship and understanding among different religious followers should begin with mutual respect, honesty, and modesty.

In Sri Lanka, Buddhism was damaged by some Christians economically, politically, educationally, socially, and culturally. Sri Lankan Buddhists, however, could survive because some leading Christians, such as Rhys-Davids, Colonel Olcott, and so on, left their own faith for Buddhism.

Fortunately, Thai Buddhism has never been rudely trampled by others. The duty of all Buddhists is to be careful with their own properties and actions. They should support good Christians and follow the way of Buddhadasa. His work is attacked merely by narrow-minded people. Among generous people, on the other hand, his fame is widely known. I have known many Westerners and Japanese who teach Comparative Religion. All of them who know Buddhism well enough always know the name Buddhadasa. Even Professor Hans Kung of Tubingen University, Germany, who is a leading Catholic theologian, used to discuss the dhamma with Buddhadasa at Suan Mokkha.

Any religious propagation which disregards morality in its procedure will never retain its essence. If a religious follower does not understand and respect other religions, how can that person really understand his or her own religion?

Buddhadasa's resolutions encourage us to help one another eliminate selfishness and egoism. Those who have read Buddhadasa's writings and are inspired to work with one another for peace and justice are certainly sharing the same path toward the Ultimate Reality. The world today is burning in the flame of war, greed, hatred, and delusion. These are dangerous tools of Satan. Thus, we need to cultivate mutual understanding and respect and fulfill Buddhadasa's resolutions in order to attain purity, justice, and peaceful happiness together.

Translated by *Ms. Bhadraporn Sirikanjana*
Seeds of Peace Vol. 4 No. 3 September, 1988.

VISAKHA PUJA 2509 IN SUAN MOKKHA

Suan Mokkha (meaning the Garden of Liberation) is in Chaiya, Suratdhani Province, in the south of Siam. There lives a leading Buddhist monk, the Venerable Buddhadasa, who is well-known throughout the kingdom for his upright behaviour, originality, outspokenness and profound scholarship in the Buddhist scriptures. Some of his writings have been translated into English and he himself reads English as well as Pali.

Whenever he comes to Bangkok, multitudes of people turn up to listen to him at the various assembly halls. And he usually travels to Bangkok at least once a year to give a series of lectures to high court judges and university students. He also broadcasts a short sermon daily on the Army Radio Network.

Suan Mok (kha) is indeed a forest suitable for those who seek liberation from life's suffering. Its one hundred acres are full of trees, hills and brooks, where birds sing and flowers bloom everywhere. Here monks and laypeople can really tread the path pointed out by the Buddha.

This year the Venerable Acāriya Buddhadāsa wanted to celebrate the Buddha's Birth, Enlightenment and Passing Away on the full moon day of May – a month earlier than the Visakha Puja.

On that day it was not quite sure whether the gods would be kind and grant a dry afternoon for the traditional ceremony. However they decided after the thunder of their deliberations to steer the impending storm elsewhere and merely sprinkled us with a few drops by way of blessing.

The morning had been fine and not too warm and had seen many faithful householders from round about, and some disciples of the Venerable Acāriya from Bangkok, come bringing ample offerings to fill the bowls of the thirty or so bhikkhus in residence.

Now the time had crept round to about four o'clock in the afternoon with both the bhikkhus and two or three hundred laymen and women assembled on top of Pudthong Hill which is in the centre of the *wat*, the spot which is consecrated for assembly – there being no temple.

The bhikkhus were of all ages and from different places. Some were resident, some visitors, some old, but most fairly young. Some wore the yellowish-brown robes dipped in jackfruit dye which is the traditional colour worn by the jungle-dwellers, while others were more brightly clad in orange robes, the garb of the town-dwelling bhikkhus. Most were Siamese and from the southern provinces but three Western bhikkhus were to be seen, two from Germany and one from England.

After the preliminary arrangements were complete, everybody gradually sat down. The laypeople were ranged along one side of the hilltop, the ladies being led by two or three nuns in white robes, while the men sat apart and were headed by the Nai Amphur, an important local government official.

Over the whole hill, both sides and summit, there grew a canopy of lofty trees cleared of the usual tangle of creepers. During the clearance work and upon the very summit, a number of bricks were found indicating that in ancient times a stupa had stood there. These bricks had been carefully collected and arranged around the bases of several trees and now supported a number of mouldings of ancient Indian stupas and other Buddhist symbols which have been copied with fidelity and artistic success by the bhikkus here. All the hills round about are said to be crowned by stupas; we had visited one on the Hill of Mrs. Nair which, of unique style rather like a pagoda and built of very fine bricks, certainly merits restoration.

After the Venerable Acariya had taken his place on a large round stone with the rest of the bhikkhus seated near him upon mats, the Refuges and Precepts were requested by the laypeople and given by him. Then followed the *desanā* or instruction in Dhamma which dealt with the meaning of Visakha and Enlightenment. After nearly an hour, during which both bhikkhus and laypeople sat silently absorbed in the discourse, the Venerable Acariya concluded by giving the meaning of the circumambulation ceremony which the laypeople were about to make and by saying that they should concentrate their minds while doing so on the virtues of the Lord Buddha.

By this time the light was beginning to fade and the candles shone out in the hands of both young and old. All carried sticks of incense and many had brought flowers from the village or had plucked twigs of the wild jasmine which seemed to have begun flowering specially for this occasion. The small and regular shaped bushes full of scented white stars stood all over the hill. The flowers, representing Impermanence, incense, the fragrance of Virtue, and a candle, standing for the light of Wisdom, are the traditional offerings made on every Buddhist shrine.

The circumambulation around the edge of the hilltop proceeded while the bhikkhus chanted the ancient Pali passages in praise of the Lord Buddha, the Dhamma and Sangha, and then blessed the assembled laypeople wishing them "all fortune" (*sabbamangala*).

The laypeople having sat down again, the Venerable Acariya suggested that they should now chant the evening *puja* which they did phrase by phrase, first in Pali and then in a Thai translation, and all from memory. This finished, they also chanted the Dhammacakkappavattana Sutta (Lord Buddha's first discourse) and the Atthangikamagga Patha (the Noble Eightfold Path) also in Pali and Thai in the same way. This concluded, they recited the verse which was the last words of the Lord Buddha, again in Pali and Thai, and then laypeople chanted a long Pali dedication of merits to all beings wherever they are living.

During this time of about an hour and a half, the bhikkhus were offered a sweet drink and then sat silently in meditation with the Venerable Acariya.

When all chanting was completed, it being by now quite dark, and the forest gathering lit only by the flickering candles, the Venerable Acariya asked that these should be extinguished for fear of forest fire.

May all beings wherever they dwell extinguish the fires of desire for fear of continued wandering in Samsara.

Written with Bhikkhu Khantipalo *Visakha Puja 2510* (1967).

AN INTERVIEW WITH
BUDDHADĀSA BHIKKHU

Sulak Sivaraksa: Venerable sir, I am preparing the publication of a special issue of *The Social Science Review* on the theme of Buddhism and Thai society today, so I came down here to ask you a few questions.

Before going into that, I'd like to express my opinion on certain activities of the Sangha. As I understand it, the dissemination of Buddhism in the old days, first by the Lord Buddha, was carried out in two ways: 1) by exemplary practice; 2) by preaching. At that time preaching meant speaking to a public audience. Later, writing and printing came into use. Now radio, television, cinema, etc., have come into existence. Therefore, I understand that Buddhism should adapt itself to catch up with the times. It's apparent that you're making some improvements here at a more advanced stage than anywhere else, for instance, by the use of a Spiritual Theatre. That's my impression: it might be right or wrong. Accordingly, I beg leave to ask you, sir, for your opinion on this and its purpose insofar as the future dissemination of Buddhism is envisaged.

Buddhadāsa : The purpose, particularly in respect to the Spiritual Theatre, is something similar to what you've just mentioned, that is, to improve and bring things up to date. The word "improve" has a wider sense, and suggests many ways of application. So we've selected some and put into practice as much as we possibly can, bearing in mind the fact that people lack interest in Dharma (or Buddha's teaching) or Buddhism, and furthermore, apparently show such an attitude that they even turn their backs upon it. So we wish to change that attitude of disinterest, and think of how to set about doing it. Firstly, a significant principle in Lord Buddha's words came to our minds;

that Dharma is fine and pleasing in the beginning, in the middle and in the end. The Buddha himself preached with the aim of making it so, to make it enjoyable to the audience and to give them courage to try it out. In short, preaching Dharma should give satisfaction and make the audience feel attracted to its practice. Thus, the fear that Dharma is unattainable and unsuitable for laymen would be overcome. We therefore come to the conclusion that preaching Dharma is to be made enjoyable, serious and entertaining. The word "mahorasaba" (entertaining) is said, in its Pali origin, to mean "entertainment", which gives pleasure to the audience. We call it a cinema for short, but it is intended to be a theatre, so it is named the "Spiritual Theatre". "Theatre" conveys the idea of entertainment, and "spiritual" signifies the element of mind, that material things can't touch, that is to say, a matter of dealing deeply with mind and soul on the basis that mind or soul is more significant than body. If there is any development at all, mind should be developed more than body; satisfaction obtained in the mind from this is more profound than for the body. General entertainments, such as cinemas, and theatres in the world are but temptations. They give no relaxation, but make the mind tired. As this is the case, worldly theatres are not an entertainment for the mind, for they torment it. Dharma is by itself an entertainment for the mind and not a material or worldly entertainment. When one has an interest in Dharma and really upholds Dharma one finds delight, pleasure and strength. But this is quite different from worldly pleasures. It's the sort of pleasure that makes the mind satisfied, peaceful and purified. For that reason, we call our plan a "Spiritual Theatre".

Sulak : What kind of procedures will you use? You say that it's not a cinema but a theatre, so what are you going to offer to the audience? And another thing, don't you think the place is too far away for interested people to come here?

Buddhāsa : To such a question, I'll have to answer within the existing conditions: first, the plan is still in its experimental stage; we can't boast of its practicability and exactitude. In certain respects, this place is appropriate for a matter of mind and soul, so the interested public should give up some of their comforts. The place as such is a necessity, a foundation and a background for the required procedures. It has many things quite different from those in Bangkok, so different that we speak of hearing a sermon in the stones and trees; while sitting by a stone or a tree one can hear its murmurs. The natural solitude shall lead us to a certain feeling as these words written at our dining hall: "Solitude is a resting place of a struggling soul". It's not easy to find a place in Bangkok as peaceful as this. If we had enough money and managed to set it up in Bangkok, it would not afford us natural amenities. In fact, we can't afford to set it up in Bangkok, and a suitable site can't be found. So it is in this place. If it's far away, let's think of the reasons mentioned before. Second, people who wish to understand Dharma must forsake something, that is giving up work, family and wealth for a period of time in order to gain a new kind of mind that is able to grasp the meaning of these worldly possessions. It would be much better if they could sacrifice their lives, that is to say, they make up their minds that while living here they've no fear of being attacked by bandits, nor of being murdered, nor of being killed by wild beasts. This is because one should do some forsaking as a foretaste of abandonment, even of one's own life. Thus resolute, that kind of mind is ready to understand that the "Spiritual Theatre" is not too far away.

Sulak : What would the audience get when they enter the "Theatre"?

Buddhadāsa : Now then, when referring to the Theatre, we should know that it's as yet to be completed. The main principles, as already decided, are to allow the audience to learn Dharma unconsciously, intensively and with enjoyment. The two principles will help them unconsciously to learn the profound Dharma with enjoyment. But which things are to be put in has posed a problem from the beginning. We've turned it round in our minds for some time. Now we have solved this problem in a wider frame of reference; we'll select some of the things unknown to this country and put them on show to the best of our ability. We've chosen unfamiliar sets of sculptures and paintings that do not exist in this country. When on view, they will give the audience excitement and satisfaction. Such will serve the first purpose to learn Dharma with enjoyment. As for the second one to learn profound Dharma we'll choose subject-matter that stimulates profound thinking and high intelligence. It'll need some thinking before one can understand these subjects, so we'll call it enigmatic in the same way as certain paintings or pictures. They never lightly explain themselves to viewers; if asked, they simply keep silent; they make viewers think and rethink. For example, I've been asked nearly a hundred times about the meaning of a cluster of five posts erected at various places, and my answer is always that one should think this riddle out for oneself. The chosen paintings will be a source of stimulation to deep thinking. So far as this kind of painting is concerned, we're not up to the desired standard yet. We have to turn to those of a Zen sect for the time being. They have done better than us. Thus, one set of paintings shows the students in the manner of Zen; other sets, though not of the Zen sect, are of paintings that will be food for thought. All chosen paintings must possess prescribed qualities as such. As for sculptures, viewers would admit on the spot that such and such things never existed in this country before. In each painting or piece of sculpture, there won't be any image of Lord Buddha; he will be symbolized by nothingness. One has to ponder why Lord Buddha is symbolized by Nothingness. Nothingness is Lord Buddha, and incidentally this belief coincides with that of the Zen sect. Time and again, they say that Dharma is Nothingness, Nothingness is Dharma, Buddha is Nothingness and Nothingness is Buddha. We think it best to choose a set depicting the life of Lord Buddha. In summing up, everything on show must stimulate thinking. Viewers must love thinking and food for thought. The use of intelligence as an enigma is simply good food for thought.

Sulak : On that point, I do agree with you entirely. When one comes to think of our present educational system, one realizes that they hardly teach people to think. I agree with the principle that this place will help the public to think for themselves, but at the same time I'm worried about the majority who don't know how to think. Reverend sir, do you aim only at thinkers, or at making this place useful to those lacking interest in thinking as well?

Buddhadāsa : Your question is rather personal: whether we'll manage to help people from all walks of life or only a certain section has been considered long before. The problem still remains with us. Anyhow, whatever we do next we'll keep it within our limitations. Thinkers would find it easy to understand those things we've in mind, while those who don't like thinking and those who are unable to think for themselves would find it beyond their understanding. Anyway, we'll first tackle thinkers or ordinary intelligent people, and if time permits and anything can be done we'll extend our activities to other sections. In this connection, one should be aware of the fact that there are many kinds of thinking methods. We must at least accept what Mahayana holds, that everyone possesses an ingredient or element of the nature of

Enlightenment in himself; crudely speaking, even a dog has such an ingredient. Now, we'll put this view that everyone has the nature of Enlightenment to test. With some people, this nature is ready to flower or has only a very thin and delicate covering. Lord Buddha himself admits that some living beings on earth have very little dust in their eyes and a single touch would make them see light. Of some others, the covering is thicker. Ways and means to crack the crusts have to be found in order to bring them to light. Mahayana, particularly, maintains in the same manner as Zen, that everyone, even a dullard, can be brought to light. It depends on the capability of achariyas (teachers) to use proper devices to crack the crusts, thin or thick, with a variety of delicate or crude methods. We'll experiment with these successively. However, we have to begin with intelligent people, because this is necessary to prevent our work from becoming a failure. So our hope lies in the intelligentsia. Do take note of the fact that the people taking great interest in Suan Mokkha, whether they come down here or not, are those who understand the information and publications we have put out. It just shows that they have as much intelligence as us. When we first came and lived at Suan Mokkha, some people said that we'd gone out of our minds, but some agreed that we've done the right thing. It was just like that, then. Intelligent people are fortunate that they may enjoy the benefits first, and those who branded us madcaps will come after. It's surely true that they'll have a chance to enjoy the benefits as well, for we've been doing things and seeing to them for some time. Don't worry about this so much. Don't think of any further division. Think farther; if the intended methods are used in a similar manner to Zen we almost need no division of people into the intelligent and the unintelligent. We can treat them as separate identities each by different but appropriate methods or procedures. Some of them need a procedure so drastic that, in a well-said comparison, the skin of their heads about the size of the palm of the hand has to be peeled off before they can feel anything. Thus, their feelings can be reached.

Sulak : Now I understand, reverend sir. The aim is at the intelligentsia, but at the same time the moderately intelligent or unintelligent may benefit from this place as well, can't they?

Buddhadāsa : That's about it.

Sulak : As I understand it, I've previously imagined that this would be something like a European "Church Hall", but despite incompleteness, it would have something intellectual or something signifying wisdom for people to see, for example, a mural painting depicting the life of Lord Buddha without his image, or a garden or a boat nearby with paintings on the inside. And the next step, I presume, would be the screening of films, and Dharma-riddle slides on light and profound themes, including lectures and preaching. It would be like that in this place, wouldn't it, sir?

Buddhadāsa : Speaking of films and slides, we don't think we could do better than those who have done so much in this respect, yet we've those things in mind and expect to use, to make and to improve them, in our best possible interests. But our very hope lies in another direction, that is, the natural surroundings in Suan Mokkha. We want the people to live near to nature, to understand it, to sit for hours amidst nature. Even those who are moderately intelligent and begin by seeing films, paintings and sculptures, etc., should be encouraged to try sitting by a stone or a tree, to sit amidst nature alone in silence. We want them to experience that sort of thing and to benefit from it.

Sulak : This calls for a question: it seems to me that Buddhism has divided ways of life into two kinds: Gamavasi and Aranyavasi, a division which had probably been made during its early phase in Ceylon. Gamavasi are those who live in town; Aranyavasi, outside it. While I'm here I feel I'm an Aranyavasi. But the Spiritual Theatre is here! On entering the place, I feel it's rather modern and up-to-date. Almost all modern ideas have been used; electric lighting, water supply and its own electric generator. The next step might be to have air-conditioned rooms and all that. Yet outside is nature: clumps of trees and scenery. I feel it's rather like Gamavasi within Aranyavasi. And another thing, reverend sir, you've mentioned at the beginning that Dharma learning would be done in the company of pleasure. Could the two things go well together, sir?

Buddhadāsa : I think we've to consider the meaning of the word "pleasure". Don't forget we always add the word " spiritual" to it. The pleasure of mind or a spiritual pleasure is one thing, worldly pleasures of the masses are another. Whoever gets through to whichever pleasures would be satisfied just as much. A devotee to his spiritual pleasure can be as much absorbed in it as a devotee to worldly pleasures is. They say ascetics and monks can be intensely absorbed in meditation and concentration amidst nature and wild beasts, being absorbed in a spiritual pleasure. As a verse goes: (roughly rendered)

So deep, deep in fine meditation,
Body immobile like a petrified one,
Precepts in mind while living on air,
And finding ever-lasting happiness there.

This verse is a good example of spiritual pleasure. As for modern equipment and means, don't jump to the conclusion that they would be used in the current manner. We'll use them as a spiritual means or a means of the soul. Whatever they are, electricity, radio or other things, they'll serve as a means to help people to understand the spiritual matter of the soul. Suppose we make a film, it must be on something that makes people understand a spiritual matter. Paintings, sculptures or other things must promote understanding and spiritual pleasure. A division based on this equipment or means is not practical. All this equipment would be a servant to spiritual matters. Therefore, everything would become a spiritual matter as is needed by Buddhism. Then, we must come to an understanding with people involved and show everything in its proper light.

Sulak : In summing up, whatever the pleasure, if we've conscience or awareness, all this equipment is but instrumental. Reverend sir, is that what you mean?

Buddhadāsa : Exactly. It all depends which direction one's mind turns to. If one's mind turns to material things, the equipment would be used in a material way. If one's mind determines to go deeper into a spiritual matter, all that equipment would be used in a spiritual way. All this could therefore be used both ways.

Sulak : So this means that we can leave alone the Four Requisites used since the early Buddhist era. In the present time many things other than those Four Requisites such as modern gadgets and all that are allowed.

Buddhadāsa : Speaking of the Four Requisites, naturally they are physical and material things. Clothes, food, a living place and medicine are material means. Machinery and mechanical things have been more progressively made, and they help to improve material means. But here we must think carefully. Spiritual means are more than that. To speak of the Four

Requisites is to refer to a physical matter. A physical life is not a spiritual thing yet. We therefore can confidently claim that, with only the Four Requisites man cannot maintain a life above an animal state. If wrongly used, they would make man more like an animal, for he is firmly attached to them. In becoming a much more complete man, he must have means Nos. 5, 6, 7, 8. Or if we don't put them in a row, we may count them as another set of means, Nos. 1,2,3 being spiritual means. The original four means which people know, seek after and pay most attention to, are physical matters. At most they can give people well-being or physical comfort. If, in an unguarded moment, people fall slave to them, their minds consequently become degraded or morally debased, and cause encroachment or advantage taking all round. So we'd better be careful. The four original means have their own merits and demerits. The means Nos. 5,6, 7 and 8 are for the mind or soul; they must be different from, and opposite to, the original ones. That is to say, they are props to the mind to reach a clean, enlightened and peaceful state. The three words, clean, enlightened and peaceful are the objectives of Buddhism or a summary of the whole purpose of Buddhism. Cleanliness is purity without evil or secrets; enlightenment, knowing things worthy of human knowledge thoroughly; peace, being peaceful individually and collectively. If the mind is not for cleanliness, enlightenment or peace, the state of being of man is not complete nor developed in the right direction. The four original means to which people are so much attached have no power nor quality to help their minds to reach a clean, enlightened and peaceful state, nor to help them to live normal lives. It's not sure that those living this sort of life would have clean, enlightened and peaceful minds. They're inadequate and mean so little for mechanical progress. The more the four original means are sought in excess, the more difficult it would be to guarantee peace in this world. It's likely to result in turmoil rather than a normal situation, and it tends towards a blind passion for pleasures and excesses. As for excesses, I'd like to remind everyone that whoever seeks, possesses and consumes in excess must be regarded as an evil person. These excesses being ignorance, a misunderstanding and an evil as always are the causes of disorders and different sorts of encroachment or advantage-taking. We must know the quality of moderation. Things made for more material progress must be kept under control. Some people think that the mind becomes healthy only when the stomach is full. Even non-Communists agree to that, as well as Communists. As regards the non-Communists who believe so, I'd like to say that both non-Communists and Communists proceed in quite a different way to that of Lord Buddha. We'll have to control these things within moderation, not to live only with physical comforts, but to add spiritual happiness as another part of our lives. We must regard it as a most significant part of man for it's the quintessence of mind, the core. The body is only an outer covering; however healthy, pretty and fine it may be, it's still a covering. Mind can be healthy and fine through Dharma. A body with a healthy and fine mind is complete to the core; in that state of being man is complete. When man is complete as such and exists in the world, then we can create peace to reign supreme in it. If man is healthy only in body and not to the core, it's a serious mistake, and he is not able to create peace to reign supreme in the world. However advanced material progress may be with machinery and mechanical things in plenty, there'll be more disorders than ever before. Those are my impressions of the Four Requisites or original means.

Sulak : Now I understand. This is one place that has certain procedures to better man, to make him seek more after a spiritual happiness. Some other places also have their own procedures. For instance, in some countries, they use political means to help religion. Some countries are much in the limelight now; in Japan, for example, they've a new sect claiming to be Buddhist, called "Soka Gakkai". And, in France, Roman Catholic priests have recently used a procedure of social work, that is, these priests have formerly spent their lives in the same mode as our monks, and even now still live in chastity, but they stay among the people and work for the people in close contact. Reverend sir, do you think our monks should do the same?

Buddhadāsa : Frankly speaking, I entirely disagree with the idea. And I'd like to give you something to think about; monks should not directly take part in social work or any public development work for it's a duplication of work and a matter of bringing coals to Newcastle. Monks should concern themselves in helping people to be spiritually developed and delivered, so monks must assume the duty of spiritual leaders and continually look after people on the spiritual side of their lives. They must not be involved in making material things for people themselves, but should be the protectors of people from unhappiness, troubles, ignorance and delusions in their work. This is the most important point; whatever nationality they are, whatever language they speak, people must have some unhappiness or difficulties in the course of their working lives. For instance, they misunderstand the meaning of life or work. People as such live in hell on earth. Monks shouldn't interfere with their work, but should try to reform their character and minds until they understand the meaning of life and work, love their work and find happiness in it; to work is to be happy. Then they feel they reach heaven on earth. In detail, man usually is a defeatist, defeated by greed or love of gain, by anger and by delusion or evil designs, lust, desire etc.; living in unhappiness and torment as if he were in hell on earth. Monks should not directly go in and help him in his work, and lessen his poverty, but make him wise in fighting against greed, anger, delusion, lust, desire, etc. and make his mind clean and robust; he'll be in good mental health not suffering from neurosis nor psychoneurosis, nor having any suicidal tendency, and such like. In this way, we'll be doing an incomparable service to him, far better than a monk who applies for a job in social work or joins in such work as kitchen gardening. That's not a proper thing to do.

Sulak : If a monk does not go in for this sort of work, how can he encourage the people concerned, sir? And suppose a group of devout laymen who do this work invites him to the thresholds of their houses. I've noticed such a thing; there's one in Bangkok, the Christian Centre. The Centre has a hostel for Christian students. The procedure is this; train students to make good and send them to visit and help friendless patients in different hospitals. Apart from that, academic activities are organized, lectures or discussions on various themes, sometimes on worldly subjects beyond the scope of Christianity, on political issues, on literature and language teaching, as well as worldly entertainments. At present, we've none of these activities in our wats. If our devout laymen would do the same, would you also sir? If you would, reverend, sir, what sort of procedures would you suggest?

Buddhadāsa : We must hold that monks are always spiritual leaders and guides; if they can form a group to give guidance and help to people in all respects, this would be a creative service to their spiritual high-mindedness. I've already mentioned that monks could do it in this manner and it's their very duty. If laymen would be willing to play a supporting role under monks' guidance, it would be for the better. But we must draw some sort of a borderline as to what comes under the scope of religion, monks, devout laymen, the Buddhist Association, and the Young Buddhist Association. Whatever it is, if true to form, it must be a spiritual concern. Suppose one visits a prisoner; one doesn't need to bring food for him, but may do some other things to uplift his heart. Or, if one visits a patient in hospital, one doesn't need to bring him some sweets, fruits or flowers, but can do something else to ease his mind or to give him spiritual comfort. Monks may also bring with them some sweets and flowers, for those things may serve some purpose towards spiritual leadership. Duty as such shouldn't be put on their shoulders, for monks mustn't amass material wealth and their duty is not in making any material contribution. So, if we're going to have a Young Buddhist Association, etc., and send its young members to visit prisoners or patients, it should be a duty principally related to spiritual service with material things becoming something trivial. Or, if we're going to organize a library, literature and academic studies, we'd have to make sure that, in giving this sort of service, these things always bring an adequate spiritual return, and that they shouldn't be concerned only with something material and worldly. As it is today, things are already going a worldly way; if we're not careful, they will become more worldly. We must take care to turn some of their aspects towards a spiritual end. We agree to the point that we should have an association or other organ to give different services in social work as they generally do, but not blindly. They usually only know and aim at material results. They never try to improve their minds. What, then, do they expect to give to others? So, we agree with you I must say. But the heart of the matter or its principle and procedures must be as I've explained.

Sulak : Another thing that'll come to monks; obviously, it seems to me that, in foreign countries, priests or Christian organizations keep their eyes on different universities. If they find anyone showing any sign of faith in God or Christianity, they'll persuade him or her to come over to further the faith. After being ordained, he's carefully trained to remain thus for the rest of his life and to devote himself to God. This, I notice, has not been done in this country; in the past, there was no cause for anxiety since education here had been based on a single principle, that is, learning through monastic life. Among those people entering monkhood, some still prefered the worldly way of life to the spiritual one, and, when leaving the monkhood, they used the knowledge they had gained to do useful work for the nation and community. Some were strongly possessed with the faith and stayed on to devote themselves to Buddhism. At a later period, education was divided into two branches, lay and ecclesiastical. Their purposes have become farther and farther apart. If the ecclesiastical branch has no programme to induce leading lay intelligentsia to come into Buddhism, though some of them are strongly possessed with the faith, I'm afraid, in the future, we may find fewer leading highly intellectual monks on the ecclesiastical side than those intellectuals on the lay side. I might be wrong, reverend sir, what do you propose to do about it?

Buddhadāsa : I've noticed it for some time. I'm rather worried about it. In the future, there would be only mediocre monks in our wats and those living under the guise of religion. The latter may be clever or cunning, but only at taking advantage of religion. If only this type remains in our wats the religion would be doomed. But, on looking at the other side of the problem, we see that it's like Fortune's wheel turning to its own tempo. Now, the tempo or the turn of Fortune's wheel is just that, like the way of the world. It has changed to such a state, so it may change for the better in the future. We aren't too worried, but realize that the situation must be saved and certainly prevented from becoming worse. We have to find out why the intelligentsia ignore wats and turn to the worldly way of life. It's a time in which the world is advanced in its material aspects, with so many distractions and temptations everywhere; therefore people turn to all sorts of material things. The intelligentsia find easier opportunities and amass more wealth. The consequence is disastrous. They tend towards the same direction, and this tendency becomes a fashion among the majority of the whole world, both ecclesiastical and lay. But it's not so bad as if it were a fixed feature or tempo. One of these days, when unhappiness or suffering appears on the scene, people will be disillusioned with the worldly way of life despite their riches, glamour, extravagance and pleasures. We know that there are more neurotic cases, more prisons, more hospitals and more psychopathic cases in the streets of civilized countries. When the majority of communities open their eyes to these aspects of life, particularly from the angle of civilization, or simply from the viewpoint of the European, so far as material progress is concerned, Thai people will follow their footsteps. The Europeans realize the danger and the crooked path. The rank and file will then turn more and more towards a spiritual way of life. Now, we can only ask whether in such delusion and atmosphere we should even attempt a discussion or interpretation of Dharma and religious subjects? This may catch up with the tempo and make people realize the danger from the material world and turn to religious teaching. No matter which religion it may be. Whoever is a good Buddhist, good in the sense of being true to form and not sham, may be a good Christian or a good Muslim. A good Christian is one who practises his faith truly according to the original teachings of Christ. Teachings other than that aren't part of the practice of a good Christian, for they may be different from, and contradictory to, the old or original one. A good Buddhist may be as good a Christian as Jesus Christ could have wished, or as good a Muslim as Mohammed could have wished; minor details shouldn't be brought in to mix with these. Thus, being able to be a good Christian or a good Muslim is regarded as part of being a good Buddhist. This is to show that, with any religion, we have an equal opportunity; each has his own religion already. And the stupidity of universal ignorance gives people a few hard slaps in the face until they turn to their own religions; then, they take a new step towards a spiritual path again. The timing would be just right. When the majority of the people in the world take that direction, monks and novices in our wats will increase too. So the intelligentsia would come in, and the wats would have the intelligentsia or brilliant monks again. And the number of the mediocre monks and humbugs would be gradually reduced. Fortune's wheel is turning in such a way, and now it's just like that. It would be foolhardy to resist it with any force; if we do, it'd be like levering up a big log with a thin plank, or trying to break something stronger than us. We have to wait for a ripe opportunity or a suitable time. All we can do now is to slow down the trend and to divert it towards a better direction little by little. We should set our sights on doing just that.

Sulak : I'm not sure what you've said would be possible. Maybe I'm still young and inexperienced. If we're waiting for the Europeans to turn to us to receive them with open arms, the situation would be beyond redemption. By the way, you mentioned at the beginning that the Spiritual Theatre is suitably located here far away and deep in the forest. I'd rather see it in the city. In the old days education and all the good things were in our wats, that is to say, wats were not only seats of learning, but also parks for our children to romp about, they were everything a social centre should be. I must say, wats are now no longer what they used to be, nor do they fulfil the duty they used to perform. So I believe it's most necessary to have this Spiritual Theatre to attract people to come in and find enjoyment as you've said. At present, we've not done anything in this direction; we've not found suitable persons to train to be good and solid monks, nor thought up any way to keep them. Moreover, some have been put down in one way or the other, and when the rein has become slack, some good monks have left the monkhood. It appears that most of our brilliant monks usually leave the monkhood. I'm worried about it. But you've said that what we can do now is to slow down and to wait until Fortune's wheel turns to our advantage. I wonder whether there's anything better than that?

Buddhadāsa : Speaking of "Fortune's wheel", we mean something more powerful than us and we just can't stop it. But we may be able to slow it down, or to put it off a little bit. If we're wise enough we can do quite a lot. We can't just turn it back all of a sudden, we must rely on timing, it's timing. Anyway, this doesn't mean that we won't do anything at all, but that we mustn't be sad or in despair. We should realize that such a thing is like that and at the same time we must try our best to find a solution. We do our best to slow it down or to improve the situation. As for the location of the Spiritual Theatre in the city. Oh, yes, of course. But only up to a certain level. Spiritual affairs must exist at least on two or three levels. When more peace is needed one must practise in a forest in the same way as in an initial meditation in a forest. It would be easier than to do it in the Theatre; this doesn't mean that the practice should never be done in the Theatre at all. Therefore, the Spiritual Theatre activities can be organized in the city, but they must be at a much lower level, which is better than nothing. The city doesn't understand the thing, for no city people have even applied for it. They are not prepared to organize wats into spiritual places. For example, when we said a wat should organize a new Buddhist association, some people laughed at the idea. If it can be organized, we wonder which wat would do so. Wats in the city centre would never accept the idea of turning themselves into places of solitude, nor to be the seats of Buddhist associations, because the people concerned are selfish; they live in wats just to feather their nests. One can't reorganize and drive them out, for they wouldn't have it. We'd like to say that the city people are still blind to, and ignorant of this; they're not prepared to force the issue properly. If it goes on like this, we won't be able to organize a place of solitude in the city. No matter which way it's organized, it's still better than not at all. We support anyone who would do so. It is result may only be up to a certain level, but it's not possible to expect anything like what's being done in the country, at a mountain, in the forest around here. It's hardly possible to organize a park in our sense; if it is, it must be somewhere other than in a wat, for monks of that wat wouldn't have it. They keep the ground for building new houses to let and to bring in some money for the maintenance of their wat. We should take this point into consideration.

Sulak: Yes, sir. In Bangkok, it's definitely impossible. Yet it could be done in some other cities; it would be easier at Chiengmai. In the past, all wats were so beautiful and surrounded by walls. At present, new houses gain ground upon those walls exactly as you've said. But I feel that, in some places, they follow your good example. At Chiengmai, they're doing so, and, at Wat Cholprathanrangsarit, Nondaburi, they're building a spiritual hospital. All this will be making a gradual progress like you've said. Sir, I've another way. It may be slow but with an extensive result; that is, in the education system. Up till now, ecclesiastical education has followed the nine standards of scriptural studies. The whole nine years is such a long, long time, I believe. Prince Vajirañana once revised the teaching and examination arrangements, and scriptural student monks came into existence. It seems that there has been no revision since then. Later, the Maha Mongkut Royal Academy and the Maha Chulalongkorn Royal Academy were set up. They're all well-intentioned institutions. But I feel that the set education programme tends too much towards the way of the world, and the result is not up to expectations. On the other hand, the customary misbelief in some quarters is that a monk should be ordained at a very young and innocent age, so he may become a solid monk, grow up in rank and remain in the service of Buddhism for the rest of his life. This attitude should be put right, I believe. In my opinion, one should pass through worldly experiences before entering the community, as Europeans usually do. There should be a pre-ordination training and strict post-ordination training. Reverend, sir, what do you think of the education?

Buddhadāsa : Improvement is necessary without a doubt. We've lived close to it and seen that it needs improvement in so many aspects that we're in despair. There are so many things to do before we get to our objective of monks or wats being spiritual leaders. At present, they're not. Apart from that, teachers at schools and colleges, who should be spiritual leaders as well, are not. Improvement measures pose a hard problem. Teachers should perform the duty of spiritual leaders, but they become sick and deluded themselves. Wherever they are, in wats, at home or at school they all look up to wealth, honour and fame as the highest attainments. Wealth for pleasure from the satisfaction of the five senses. Such is spiritual degradation. Their souls are almost like those of hell-inhabitants, for they're completely deluded by satisfaction from the five senses, and they lead people on to a wrong path to become slaves to material or physical things rather than to be independent of them. Just think of that! How are we to help them out of such an intoxication as blind as being overcome by opium, marijuana or other sorts of habit-forming drugs? It won't be an easy job. What we can do now is to adopt one of Lord Buddha's principles, that is, keep on trying to improve the situation, in the hope that some section of people may benefit from what we're doing for them, and be brought back to their senses or to the fold. Lord Buddha preached Dharma of a high degree in the hope that a small section of the people could understand it.

Sulak : I do believe your attempts will be successful. They cover various techniques: lectures, preaching and pamphleteering. You've set up a lay college at Chaiya. But what about an ecclesiastical college? I wonder why you don't set it up too, considering its sure direct results.

Buddhadāsa : Surely, if that could be done, it would be successful. And it should be set up too. But we have to think of our available resources: physical, mental and material. We're conditioned by so many things. On the other hand, if we do too many things, we'd achieve very little indeed. So we make up our minds to only deal with certain things. Then we do them as solidly as possible, and take care of ourselves. We agree to what you've said, but that's beyond our resources.

Sulak : There's another way. Two weeks ago a missionary came to see me at the office and we discussed a few problems. He said worriedly that in the future this country would suffer the same fate as other European or foreign countries, which we would see as material progress. It would loom larger over us; people would be more and more drowned in material things, and life would be much more rapacious. Then, he asked me about an antidote to this downward trend. As we see it, many people are deluded, even administrators, educators, education planners and students. But I see there's only one way, a gradual improvement. What I'm doing now is: I've been trying to recruit youth from five or six universities to do something worthwhile, but only a very small number have responded. In doing things, we'll observe Dharma principles, and do some social work and whatnot, but we'll not set ourselves up as an association. We expect no gains whatsoever. We're not sure whether we will succeed or not, anyway. If we have a permanent office and our activities grow wider and wider, we will succeed in the long run. Another way is what the Europeans call "retreat", meaning that one should find time to go and stay in a forest for, say, 3, 5 or 7 days in a year. This method, I believe, would be successful. Since the early days, a man of 20 or 21 years of age must enter the monkhood for a prescribed period of 3 months, usually during the Rain's Retreat period. Now we should apply this procedure in a new way, that is instead of 3 months, he is asked for only 7 days. A monkhood practice as such, by laymen in each year would help them to get a little closer to Buddha's Dharma, to understand the meaning of contentment and to see the dangers of different evil designs and deeds. If the number of those people is increased and a place to accommodate them can be found, the community as a whole would be improved. Do you agree, reverend, sir?

Buddhadāsa : We agree, of course. We've thought of that before. We mean that to solve the major problem bears a characteristic similar to belling the cat. And which mouse would dare? It's an attempt on the impossible. What's left for us is to do whatever we can. Those who clearly see the problem and have a mutual understanding should come together for the time being, then, their number may be increased. The solution to the problem, universally, would have to be approached in a similar manner. So, don't despair or stop doing something worthwhile. We should keep on trying within our limitations. One day we'd have an adequate number of such people, and then we'd think of people in general. Before our hope is realized, we may die many deaths; we won't live to see the fruit of our work. Yet, we should do our best for mankind. It's for mankind, by man and not by a single individual. So it must certainly be done. Do get together people with a mutual understanding into a small club until the right time comes of its own accord. When one sets up something, he has certainly to come into conflict with the majority. He may meet with opposition, may come to some harm, or anything can happen to him. So he must be prepared to make some sacrifice. Don't force it too much lest we come to harm too soon. So we must make a point of this, and take care not to create so much misunderstanding that others get rid of us. We won't work so as to get into that awkward position and, thus, our work is possible. The seeds of the third and fourth institutions are then sown. Even if ten of us fall, there may be another ninety or so of us left.

Sulak : Reverend sir. Apart from this, I wonder if you've got any other suggestions? Some people have suggested "Brahmadanda" or a measure of indifference towards the society, that is, a treatment with non-viloence, but with an indifference towards wicked characters giving them no welcome nor criticism but civil disobedience.

Buddhadāsa : We won't have enough to enforce Brahmadanda for we're in the minority. Only people in the majority can enforce such a measure upon those in the minority. Actually, we're up against a majority of some magnitude, so that sort of a measure isn't possible. The only thing to do is to make an effort to bring them back to their senses or to make them view things in the right light. This is the principle of Buddhism. Everything is conditioned by Sammāditthi. Sammāditthi means a right view or attitude. Therefore, we must cultivate a right view or attitude among ourselves as well. The problem of the world with its war and killing as now, is due to the lack of a right view or attitude. Sammāditthi covers things from insignificant matters up to Nirvāṇā. An agency or club or association for continually cultivating the right view or attitude should be set up. A Sammā ditthi association as such should exist at all times; it would take root, grow, gain strength and lead to something else by itself in the same way as other creeds, political creeds, religious creeds, if it's done in the right manner.

Sulak : Sir, I've benefited quite a lot from what we've discussed today. I hope that your statements will be of some benefit to the community as a whole too. I beg to thank you most kindly.

Visakha Puja 2510 (1967).

CONVERSATION WITH AN ABBOT

Recently I went to Uthai Thani (Pali: *Udaya Dhani*, "City of the Dawn") a provincial town in the middle part of Siam, about 300 kilometres from Bangkok. The town itself offers no special attraction to tourists. Indeed it is quite difficult to get there. The nearest highway and railway station is 26 kilometers away. Then one has to go on an unpaved road and cross a ferry before one reaches the town, which is situated on a small inlet of the Chao Phya River called Menam Sakaekrung. Up to a few years ago the only communication with the capital was by steamer. Now the town is still comparatively peaceful. Most people are farmers, and they live in house boats. Television has not yet become popular, but wireless sets are already doing their best to upset the peace.

    Although the town is an old one, it has no distinguishsed historical records. In recent years, however, it produced two well known figures, similar, in degree, to Alcibiades and Socrates of ancient Athens. The former is disliked by the town folks, while the latter, being a Buddhist monk, is greatly respected and admired. This *bhikkhu* was in fact of Chinese descent, and rose to the rank of Vanarata, which was second only to the Supreme Patriarch – *Sangharāja*. And as the name signifies, holders of this title are in charge of all monks who are "delighted in forest-dwelling". The Maha Thera was abbot of Wat Maha That (Pali: *Mahā Dhātu*, "the Great Relic"), one of the biggest monasteries in Bangkok. His elder brother was also a local abbot and bhikkhu in charge of all monks in the province. The two brothers did much for the religious and educational welfare of the town. The local abbot, by his upright behaviour and strict discipline, would encourage young men to join and remain in the holy brotherhood. Should they show any promising sign, he would send them for further instruction under his younger brother's guidance in Bangkok. Wat Maha That at that time nursed many monks from

Uthai.

When I was there I met an elderly man who, like many others of his contemporaries, was ordained by the late chief abbot of the town, serving one year at Wat Pichai (Pali: *Vijaya*, "Victorious Monastery") under him, and who was later sent by him to the Great Relic Monastery in Bangkok, where he stayed for five years before disrobing. I asked him whether he knew the late Vanarata well.

"Yes, of cours," he said. "As you know, he was a native of this town. We still think very highly of him. Mind you, when I went to Bangkok during the First World War, he was not abbot then. His predecessor was still very much in charge, despite the fact that he was in his eighties."

"Did you know the old man?" I asked.

"Well, not really," he replied, "He was not the local boy from here, you know? His title was also Vanarata. He was the thirteenth abbot of Wat Maha That. His personal name was 'Dit, a shortened version of the Pali Pandit and he was very wise too. His religious name was Udaya, but that had nothing to do with this town. In fact, he was born in Ayudhya, our old capital, about 150 kilometres downstream from here. However, I had a memorable conversation with him once."

"What was it all about? Please tell me."

"In fact, someone requested me to ask him a question. I've forgotten now who that person was. Yet, I plucked up my courage and went to ask the old abbot. As you know, junior monks on the whole stand in awe of their senior, especially if he is learned, pious and upright. I am glad I was brave enough to go and see the abbot and put the question to him face to face. As soon as I arrived, I knelt down and prostrated three times in our usual manner, then I sat down and raised my palms and asked him. 'Sir', I said, 'We young monks are amazed, that you, in your old age, are still able to manage the affairs of the Wat and of the Sangha. You are still mindful of all things and are very well informed in almost all subjects. We wonder why you are still able and why you have never been deceived by the external world. Someone really wants to know whether you have a special principle which guides you all through your life'."

"To this he smiled, asking me the name of the inquisitive person. I must have told him, but I cannot recollect who it was.

The abbot nodded his head, but did not reply to my question. Instead, he said, 'If the Germans win the war, I don't know what will happen to the *Sasana* (Religion). At present, Prince Patriarch Vajirañana is also very ill. It will be a bad day for Buddhism, if anything happens to him now. In the past when a monk beat the gong at four o'clock to call us to our morning prayer, dogs always barked and bayed at the sound of the gong, but I have been noticing lately that they do not do so now. Is this a good or bad omen? I do not know'."

"His mind was not at all at rest. It was wandering, and I thought that he must have forgotten all about my question. But, having paused for a while, he suddenly said, `Now, as to the question you put to me earlier on. Your friend wanted to know whether I had any principle upon which I based my entire life. The answer is "Yes." As a matter of fact I have three principles. I recite them forward and backward, day in and day out, and I find them very useful for my life.'"

'First of all, I know the Mulakaccayana grammatical text well. I recite it every day just to keep my Pali knowledge alive. This text may now be considered old-fashioned, but I used it when I started studying Pali. I learnt it by heart then, and still know it now. This is very useful to me. Despite the fact that our young scholars nowadays study modern Pali grammar written by no less a person than the Prince Patriarch himself, often they turn up to me and ask me to solve grammatical problems for them. By being perfectly aware of the old text, I can give them the right solution. Otherwise these young monks would have a poor opinion of me, thinking that the abbot is old and forgetful. He no longer knows his academic subjects. Once a junior monk thinks badly of anyone, especially his senior, he treads on a dangerous path, which will lead to his downfall. In fact, monks should always cultivate compassion and loving kindness to all beings. And it is essential that he must always be able to look up to his senior and teacher. In order to help my brethren in the holy order and to maintain my academic background I always keep this principle in mind.'

'Secondly, I know all the Patimokkha rules by heart. On the fortnightly Uposatha day, when a monk recites the Vinaya rules, I am always perfectly aware whether he makes mistakes or not. Knowing the bhikkhu's codes of behaviour is essential to all those who are in the holy brotherhood. I have risen from a layman, from a novice to a fully ordained monk, a junior abbot to the rank of

Vanarata. In the entire Sangha of this realm, I am second only to the Prince PATRIACH. I would not have been able to become all these, if I did not follow the holy disciplines for monks. Should I break a major rule, I would cease to be a monk straight away. Should I break only a minor rule, I would still become impure. Monks must certainly lead a pure and blameless life. By reciting this Patimokkha, I examine myself as I go along. If I find that by deed or by word, I have committed sin wilfully or otherwise, I would bear that guilt in mind and declare it to the Sangha and ask for their forgiveness in order that I may again become pure and worthy of the holy brotherhood.

'Thirdly, I always recite the Mahasatipatthana Sutta daily. This is essential for developing mindfulness. It is useful to monks and laymen alike. Such a recital will help one to be detached from the world, to be mindful about all things, and then one will not be misled by appearances. This Sutta can help one to reach reality − Nibbana.'

'These three principles I alway bear in mind. I recite them consecutively, one after another, forward and backward, every day and night. I always recite these when I am alone. When someone comes to see me − be he a guest or a novice who takes turns to read a book or newspaper to me − I stop my recitation. When he has gone, I resume my recitation from the place where I left it. I have been using this method since I was a young monk, and it has kept me content, calm and happy in the holy brotherhood up to now.'

'You may go now and tell your friend about my three principles in life'.

Visakha Puja 2507 Annual Publication of The Buddhist Association of Thailand 1964.

BUDDHISM AND SOCIAL VALUES

To talk about religion is very difficult in Buddhism as religion is "sasana" which translates as "teaching". It could be teaching from Christ, teaching from Mohamed, any teaching, but for us the teaching must be the teaching of truth. Dharma is taught also in Hinduism, but Dhamma in Buddhism relates directly to the truth that made Siddhartha Gautama become the Buddha. The first of the Four Noble Truths of Buddhism is suffering. In our context any religion which does not deal with suffering is not worthy. It is just an escape from suffering.

To know how to confront suffering is not enough. You must know the cause of suffering; that is the second truth. Once you know the cause of suffering then the third is the cessation of suffering, getting rid of suffering. And finally the fourth truth is really the whole fabric of Buddhism known as the Noble Eight-Fold Path; in fact it is the way to get rid of suffering. This is, of course, not exclusively Buddhist; anybody can use it; it is common to many traditions; Buddhism does not have copyright on it. To get rid of suffering is what "liberation" means. The word "moksha" again a Hindu and Buddhist word means "liberation". To be liberated means "nirvāna" (or "nibānna") the stage of cessation of suffering. Hence liberation is the key word in Buddhism. If we do not lead our lives towards liberation it is not worth being a Buddhist.

Anybody can be a Buddhist in this sense, because unlike in other religions you do not have to declare that you will join Buddhism, you do not have any special rights or privileges if you actually join. If you want to it is O.K., if you do not want to it is also O.K. This is the strength and weakness of Buddhism. There is no dogma in Buddhism. You are not required to believe in anything; you are told to challenge every teaching, even if it is the teaching of the Buddha, the word of Buddha, any sacred scripture, unless that teaching helps you to realise the truth, leads you to liberation and shows you the way to do it. That means that to be liberated, you must be able to get rid of the three root causes of suffering.

That is, first of all, greed and lust which go together. Then hatred which tends to link with power, evil and all kinds of affinities. These two are very important but the worst one is delusion or ignorance. Many people think they are clever, but in Buddhism, unless you understand the reality of things you are ignorant or deluded. You are deluded because you have egocentricity or selfishness. Selflessness, and how to overcome selfishness, is the key in Buddhism.

In order to get liberated from suffering, that is to overcome selfishness, every human being should first of all know who he himself or she herself is. We tend to feel that we are somebody permanent or great. In Buddhism that is delusion. If we get up in the morning aiming at changing the world and doing all kinds of things we often fall back into anger, greed and delusion. That is why if you want to practice Buddhism, first of all every person has to find out who he or she is. That is why meditation is important. Reflect for five or ten minutes on how to restructure your mind from a selfish being to a selfless being. That is not easy but it is essential.

That is the first step if you want to be a seriously-practising Buddhist. It is related to the second step. If you restructure yourself to be less selfish you can relate to others. The less you exploit yourself the less you exploit others. Exploitation always begins with exploiting oneself. Those of us who smoke very heavily should realize how they exploit themselves and others. Maybe sometimes we think we have to do it because we are nervous. How you exploit yourself and how you exploit others always goes side by side. Thus personal development and social development must be side by side. You cannot play one against the other. The understanding that Buddhism is only to calm ourselves is wrong. The more calm you are the more society remains unjust and selfish. You should be calm in order to be mindful and to tackle injustices in society more meaningfully. So in this way personal liberation and social liberation must go side by side. We have a three-fold "step": first, mindfulness, which is known as "samadhi". Samadhi is reflection for constructive self criticism. The second is "sila", that is the precept of how to deal with society and not to exploit others and oneself. You can do that properly only when you have wisdom, "paññā" or "prajñā". All this is relative unless you see the truth, unless you get rid of selfishness. Then all these relative values, "sila", "samādhi" and "pañña" become absolute values.

When you are no longer selfish then you can really be liberated. But on the way towards that state you can also be on the way of liberation. We respect others more. For instance, there is a Tibetan tradition of meditation on your enemy. Because your enemy is the best friend you have. I find that very difficult because I have so many enemies. Without them you are without challenges. You feel sometimes they say many bad things about you, sometimes true, sometimes false. However you have to attempt some change, trying not to hate the enemy, so that the enemy can become your friend. But unless you have wisdom you do not know how to change the structures. To kill the enemy is not a help. You have to kill hatred and the system which creates hatred and exploitation. That is the essence of the liberative element in Buddhism as I see it.

The man Gautama became Buddha because he had liberated himself and he wanted to liberate the society. When he became liberated he became the Buddha, the Enlightened One and Awake One. He discovered the "dhamma", the truth. He and the truth became one, the "Buddha-Dhamma". You may identify "dhamma" with god in the Christian sense, I suppose, not as a person but as an universal law which is justice and truth. If we understand and walk along the Buddha-Dhamma we walk along the path of liberation.

But you cannot do that alone, and therefore the Sangha was founded. The Sangha is the ideal Buddhist society, founded, first of all, among those who had become enlightened and liberated. It was also founded to help people who wanted to be liberated and to join the Sangha. And eventually the Sangha became divided into four categories: one is the monks, a very bad translation of "bhikkhu", the second one the "bhikkhuni" for whom I do not want to use the word "nun", as unfortunately this word has become regarded as lower. Male and female monks are equal. The laymen and laywomen make up the third and fourth categories and are all equal too. To be liberated means not to exploit anything at all. You have to become a bhikkhu or bhikkhuni in order not to exploit at all. But in our daily lives unfortunately we have to exploit, we have to kill animals for our living. We do not kill directly, we kill indirectly. Even those who become vegetarians kill vegetation which also has life. So the vegetarians are not generally better beings than non-vegetarians. Of course it is good to be a vegetarian, it is good not to smoke, but it does not mean that one is better. I remember that Alan Watts, an Anglican priest who became a well-known Zen practitioner and proponent in California, once said that the reason he became a vegetarian was that cows cry louder than cabbages. You see, if you go to the extreme not to exploit you might end up like those religious teachers during the time of Buddha who ate fruit that had fallen from the tree because to pluck was also violent.

Thus the idea of the monkhood is that their lives should be an example of non-exploitation. They do not earn for their livelihood as they have no family; they live in a community owning nothing except the minimum essential three pieces of robe and so on. However if you look at them from a Marxist point of view they exploit the lay people that have to support them. But if they are no good we do not support them. Yet, their life is supposed to be good, their life is supposed to help us because it is spent doing nothing. For in Buddhism, meditation that is meaningful has to be full time. You should not do anything else; you contemplate to reach the truth, and that is most important. The best poets are those who are idle. The same with thinkers. Those of us who are lay persons try but we cannot; we have to compromise; we have to earn a living compromising with violence.

This is where the interrelationship of religion and culture can be seen. Religion ideally means no exploitation at all. But you have to build up a culture where some exploitation takes place. In the Thai context we ate fish for our survival. We did not eat pork until we came across the Chinese; we did not eat beef until we came across the Muslims. In Sri Lanka the serious Sinhalese Buddhists do not even eat fish, although there are a lot of Christian and Muslim fishermen. Whether that is good or not is another point. Sometimes to avoid the issue, you take fish. The monk cannot even till the ground, he cannot cut the tree; their community is supposed to be an example because fraternity is communal. Almost everything is owned jointly and in common–fraternally, equally, democratically. However, when we talk about democracy we mostly do not look at our own model but at the Western model. That is why most of us failed. We should look at the Sangha as the model of democracy for our society. That was the idea of Buddhism. The Sangha is a model but it sometimes also compromises. Sometimes there is no communal ownership, and sometimes monks even own private companies. That is where Buddhism becomes Buddhism with a big B. However, as long as the monks remain mindful, as long as they work against greed, hate and delusion, they are on the right path. Lay persons are supporting them and are supposed to be guided by them spiritually. Each one of us is weak because we are selfish but each one of us can walk on the path of liberation with a stronger spiritual basis, that is how you can test in society whether you make society more meaningful, more peaceful, more just. I think that is the whole idea of Buddhism.

Buddhism is not claiming to be exclusive. If you take Buddhism seriously it is quite good. But most of us are not very good so we have to compromise. Again, the strength and weakness of Buddhism. To be liberated you need your own strength alone. When you are weak you need some other help. That is why when Buddhism came here it mixed with animism, both positively and negatively. Positively it means that our people respect the river, the tree and the mountain. The Buddha also said you must live in harmony with nature. So we walk along very well with animism. And when Hinduism came we walked with Hinduism because some of its Gods can help you. We even converted Hindu Gods to Buddhism; we are very good at that! Even in the state ceremony, God Shiva and Vishnu come down to pay respect to Buddha because Shiva and Vishnu, in our opinion, are not yet enlightened and liberated; they mix with their wives, and Shiva tends to get very angry, and so on.

To summarize the first part of my argument, in Buddhism you must walk individually toward liberation but cannot do so unless society is peaceful and righteous. Buddhism works best in small communities. In Siam you can see many temples where monks live. Although the monks also compromise, they are still an example for us; they eat less, they possess fewer things than us, they lead a celibate life and spend their time meditating on the truth. Of course they also work on indigenous medicine, they teach and so on; the stress is always on the individual in community, with a harmonious natural surrounding.

Regarding the state, the Buddha said the state or the king is like a snake; you should keep them at arm's length, but you cannot get away from them; do not kill them as that would be violent. Handle the state as you handle the snake; be kind and cautious. If you want to deal with the snake, go behind it, not in front of it.

Regarding trade, a rich man can also be liberated, but as in Christianity it is more difficult for a rich man. That is why a monk does not own anything; he can be liberated easier. But if you are rich it depends on how you acquire your wealth. If you acquire it righteously you might achieve liberation, but if you do not do so you will not achieve it. If you spend your wealth selfishly, that is also wrong. You must spend it generously. The richer you are, the more you can be generous. And generosity in Buddhism means first of all to be generous with your property. But that is only one and not even the major aspect of it. Generosity means to be generous with your time and with your mind which you should share with others. That is much more important. Similarly, charity in Buddhism *(dāna)* means giving away, but not only wealth. You give away selfishness while the most meaningful gift to others is giving the truth for liberation.

This is the basic teaching of Buddhism. Buddhist culture came to be built that way. Unfortunately (or fortunately) some 300 years after the Buddha, as the Christians had Constantine the Great, we had Asoka in India. He was converted to Buddhism because of non-violence. He did wonderful things, sending Buddhist missionaries out and so on. But unfortunately he somehow made Buddhism a state religion and became the protector of Buddhism. Buddhism became too close with the state. He forgot that Buddha regarded the state as a snake. I think that (plus Muslim persecution) is the main reason why Buddhism disappeared from India. Sri Lanka became the home of Buddhism but the Sinhalese fought with the Tamils. And when the Sinhalese king killed the Tamils some monks compromised: "Your majesty, killing the Tamils is not bad, they are the enemies of Buddhism. It is no more than killing a half-human being."

In becoming so close with the state and with any culture Buddhism could become a kind of ethnicity. Anybody who is not Buddhist is not right. I think that is a very great weakness because it does not help liberation. Also when Buddhism compromises with other isms, Hinduism, animism etc., it can be positive and negative. Unfortunately it now compromises with socialism in Laos, Vietnam and China. I see this as more negative than positive. Why? Because you can compromise with animism, Hinduism or any ism provided you know precisely your part of liberation. The Sangha are people who spend their time liberating themselves to help us lay persons liberate ourselves. When Buddhism becomes a kind of priesthood performing rituals and ceremonies, it degenerates; Buddha was against rituals of any form. You can perform a ceremony, but be mindful about it. Just like clothing; of course you have to dress but be mindful about it. We have to eat but must not be over indulgent. Buddhist ceremonies are customs; you can say prayers and meditate, you can sit down, you can stand up. All this is not essential. But once they become a tradition or culture, Buddhism formalizes into a state religion.

Before colonialism the state was relatively powerless. The king at Bangkok was only king in Bangkok, the king of Ayudhaya was only king in Ayudhaya. Even in Suphanburi, only one hundred kilometres from Ayudhaya, they developed their own principality with autonomy. Besides that, Buddhism also deals with the king, the Sangha deals with the king, so the king cannot be too greedy, and therefore the lifestyle of the king was not so much different from the common people. But when colonialism came, things changed tremendously in a negative way. Although this country was not colonized politically, we were colonized intellectually. We have adopted a new religion, not Christianity as was the case in the Philippines, but materialism. We worship the white man as the new priest. Worse than the white men are the Siamese who have been educated in Europe and America who they think they are Buddhists because they adhere to forms and rituals. But they do not realize that to be Buddhist means to be liberated. It means to share and to understand the suffering. But they think they are Buddhists because they pay respect to the Buddha image, go to the temple and give offerings. To me that is a great danger, because all these values which we get from the West– aggressiveness, conquering nature, superiority, money, technology – look down upon the old Buddhist culture. Western medicine, Western dress, Western food, to me anything against the old culture is very harmful. Because the Thai were not colonized, we developed a kind of Western colonial administration. With centralization, Bangkok became more and more powerful at the end of the nineteenth century. On top of that our own people learned from the colonial advisors (though not masters) to make our Sangha become like a Buddhist church, a national church. The Siamese had a Buddhist kingdom before, but they made Buddhism a state church like Anglicanism. They passed three successive laws regarding the ordination of a Buddhist monk; an ordination by decree, by the law and the state. For the first time the state got more and more control over Buddhism. In the name of resisting colonialism we finally colonized our own country, even colonized our own Buddhism, our own religious hierarchy. Hence Buddhism became part and parcel of the state and worst of all it legitimized the state. The trinity we inherited from the British (God, king, country), we changed to religion, monarchy, nation. All these three must be there; this is a great danger. It limits your vision to liberate yourself, it ties you to the status quo and it only helps the top ten percent. The monkhood, particularly the hierarchy, feels that we are a wonderful Buddhist country as now even Westerners are becoming Buddhist. But are we doing the right thing? If so, then for the wrong motives? When we develop nationalism so much, Buddhism becomes nothing different from conservative Christianity or conservative Islam, it becomes nationalistic. Cardinal Spellman once said that to kill the Vietcong is no sin. Now we also have a monk in Siam, whose name is Kittivutto, who said to kill the Vietnamese and the communists is no sin. He has, of course, no tradition to support that. But right-wing Buddhists are supporting him.

Then there is the movement of Santi Asoka which has very good press coverage abroad. The new governor of Bangkok, Major General Chamlong Srimuang, belongs to this movement. He is vegetarian, eats only one meal a day, and is a wonderful man. But this makes Buddhism fundamentalist, which we never had. "Be good, and if you are good like me you can be liberated." I think that is rubbish because to claim to be good is very dangerous in Buddhism. If you think you are good that is egocentric. You have to be humble and you have to change society. In Buddhism we must understand the society. Chamlong says that the people in this country are poor because they are lazy, because they are gambling and drinking. My answer is that they drink because they are poor, they need to escape and drink is sometimes their only hope. Santi Asoka claims to lead a Buddhist way. But if you are fundamentalist and think you are the only way, there is something wrong. Because in Buddhism we believe that there are many ways—even within Christianity, Hinduism, or Islam – to progress along a liberative way, become less selfish and develop more loving-kindness.

Another movement is called Dhammakaya which is very powerful. Again, like movements in any other religion, Dhammakaya compromises with capitalism. However they have helpful meditation. But it can also be harmful because when you concentrate you become mindful and then you can exploit people more neatly and cleverly. In Buddhism mindfulness must be "samma - samadhi", it must be rightful meditation: meditation for selflessness, meditation for service, meditation in order to understand suffering and to get rid of suffering.

So there are quite a number of negative elements in this country making use of Buddhism. Buddhism has become part and parcel of the state, dominated by the military. Buddhism has become part and parcel of capitalism. Even the temples have become rich for the first time in history; they now get a good amount of money with which they build more big temples, which, however, do not really help the people.

Although there are a number of Buddhist examples against liberation there are nevertheless also wonderful liberative examples. The most important one was started in 1932 by Buddhadasa Bhikkhu, calling himself servant of the Buddha. He has pointed to what went wrong with Buddhism even before the colonial period. He said it started in Sri Lanka, when we divided the monks in two categories, the learning and the meditative; the learning ones being recognized by the state as scholarly, and the meditative monks living in the forest. He said, "That is wrong. You must synchronize those two; those who study must also meditate, and those who meditate must also study because otherwise you may meditate but you go off on the wrong track making amulets or claiming to have supernatural powers" Regarding society, Buddhadasa said that one has to deal with the state but the state should be less powerful and materialistic. In his book *Dhammic Socialism* he said that all socialist societies are wrong because they have state capitalism instead. Dhammic socialism means that each community should be more socialistic, should be self - contained, and should be more decentralized; it is very similar to Gandhi's village republic. But you must have mindfulness and collaboration, not competition.

In 1960, the Venerable Prayudh, a young monk from Supanburi province communicated the essential teachings of the Buddha with a social dimension. He and Buddhadasa Bhikkhu have a tremendous appeal with the young people. People are now coming back to Buddhism in a big way. Because up to then they saw Buddhism as something related to state ceremonies, as something dead or conformist, but now they realise that Buddhism is beyond the state. In his book *Looking to America to Solve Thailand's Problems* he said that we follow the Americans far too much, and they interfere far too often. Yet also in America there is a movement to change people's lifestyles. We should look at all aspects. When we look at the West we usually look at the materialist aspects only but never look at the liberative elements. But more importantly, he said, we should look into our own culture. Our Buddhist culture has enough liberative elements to free ourselves from mental colonialism

There are of course, also lay people who are very helpful. I should first mention Dr. Prawase Wasi who was the vice-rector of a very prestigious university, a medical doctor, and an expert on blood—one of the most expert in the world. If he had developed that more he might even have received a nobel prize. Just as important for him, was to work with monks reviving indigenous medicine. For the first time the state is now recognizing that there is a lot of potential among the monkhood. They are still the custodians of indigenous culture. He got the Public Health Ministry and his own medical science university to recognize the monks and train them in curing. The WHO hopes that by the year 2000 there will be health for all. This country is the only one in Asia where the WHO hopes to achieve this aim because Prawase is working with the monks. In WHO circles they say that in China they have bare-foot doctors, but in Siam they have bare-headed doctors. This potential was ignored when we introduced the new education system which told us that our traditional medical system was no good. People in the countryside said "We do not have a hospital while in Bangkok they have built big hospitals!" But they are only for the rich while the poor have to go to the monks.

There are not only remarkable laymen like Dr. Prawase, there is also a lay woman, Ms. Chatsumarn Kabilsingh. She feels that we must revive the order of female monks; they were here for 800 years but then disappeared. Her commitment to revive the female order helps a good deal. Because now the poorest of the poor join the monkhood as they cannot even afford to go to school. But by putting on a yellow robe people respect you culturally and you can have an education. And if you are clever you can move from your village to the town, and from the town to Bangkok. The community supports you while the state does not. They even send you to be educated in India. Now if we can revive the female monkhood I am pretty sure a lot of prostitution will disappear. They sell their bodies because they have nothing else. Now luckily the first Thai woman ordination has taken place, fortunately or unfortunately, in Los Angeles. It has to be done there because the hierarchy here is still very conservative. Perhaps they also feel threatened. In a way it is good that it started in Los Angeles because in this country we blindly admire the West. If we start female ordination in the West and then come home with it, it will be accepted much easier. The most important thing, however, is the up-country monks. They have now realized that in the name of progress and development the state told them to believe that economic development was good. The monks have realized that this is all a lie. They realize that their lives have become much worse: the environment is spoilt, the animals have gone, there are more roads and dams and more electricity. Yet only the rich reap the benefit. To counter the wrong trends of development, these monks who are working with the people, bring Buddhism back to life for the masses. Meditation has become collective meditation, meditation with social analysis. They want self - reliance, not growing for sale, and they are reviving their old traditions. Instead of using tractors, they work together with buffaloes. What we need now in this country is to link all these liberative elements together, spreading the message of those up-country monks of whom we have more than twenty now. Seri Phongphit, our Catholic friend, has written a book on them, *Buddhism and Alternative Development : Religion in a Changing Society*, but he mentioned only a few cases. We have to link them into a movement which is our first priority now. Secondly we have not yet tackled the urban problem: how Buddhism can be meaningful in the urban setting.

In Bangkok, Buddhism has become very ceremonial. How can we help in the urban areas? Twenty percent of Bangkok is now slums. We have a monk now working in the slums, but moreover we have to have some Marxist analysis to understand society. Because in Buddhism you can take from any ideology. So while we are firmly using the Buddhist way, we need to understand how exploitation in our society works. We have to link all this together into a movement. That is why we have to learn from other ideologies. We must learn from other traditions because nowadays Buddhism alone is not sufficient. We have to learn from the

Muslims, the Hindus and the Christians. In this country we luckily do not have many antipathies against the Christians. We are working together. Of course the conservative Christians and the conservative Buddhists do not like that. On the one hand they join together to support the status-quo, on the other hand they are afraid of losing their own followers. But we who live and work on the liberative elements have to work together to help liberate ourselves and our societies. Therefore you have to build up a culture. In Supanburi, for example, there is a Buddhist temple on the river bank. In front of the temple they have a lot of fish but nobody would dare to fish there; also birds are all safe in the temple grounds. But once you feel that respect for life goes too far, and this is what happening in this country now, where the new educated elite comes and tells us that respect for life is rubbish, then we kill all the insects with DDT! Thus we have no environmental balance any more. We cut down the trees because we do not believe in the spirit of the tree. In the name of development the new god is money. People who have respect for life are regarded as naive, but in fact nature as a whole has a balance. We have to be very perceptive. That is why mindfulness is very important in being friendly and in understanding. I think those who come from a different culture which has little respect for life and nature cannot understand that.

With regard to the relationship between Marxism and Buddhism I have the feeling that those who claim to be Marxist, many of them in Sri Lanka, just want to make Buddhism a kind of Marxism. In Vietnam, Cambodia and Laos, Buddhism must go along with socialism. This is dangerous. The same is true for China. But I think we have a great deal to learn from Marxism (analysis of society and class structures for example), but we must be firm in our Buddhist understanding first and we must liberate our minds. Our way is a non-violent way while Marxism is a violent way. Nevertheless we should understand and learn from it. It is no harm to learn. Even in South Korea they now have liberation theology but it is "Minjung" theology from their own Korean perspective. I think it would be desirable for Buddhists who claim to be progressive to inherit some Marxist insights from a Buddhist perspective. This is the difficulty with Buddhism: sometimes we compromise. In Kampuchea they go along with the socialist state. But to me that is not even socialism. The same with capitalism: Buddhism here is compromising too much. We have to study capitalism with care and caution. I mean it is easy to condemn capitalism outright. I think if we are to work on liberation we have to ask ourselves how we can make the state less powerful. You cannot change the state but at least you must be able to resist it in your own community. To me the state is like a disease. Thus you have to build up enough resistance against the disease. That is why mindfulness is so important. You have to build up your own community and your own organization not to be tempted by this disease.

Similarly, capitalism, multinationals and consumerism are diseases against which we should build up our communities (all religions have failed so far). We have not yet succeeded in building up a new culture. We talk so much about liberation but do not ask ourselves why in Latin America they have been successful. And I think they were successful because they offered a new culture. When a bishop gives up his palace that is something! It is too easy to say "get back to the roots"; you should change your lifestyle and mental attitude to be more simple. That is why Gandhi was successful. He changed his lifestyle. He changed his attitude and he was fairly radical. I think if we want liberation we have to be radical. But so far we have not been able to build up a new culture. The culture you see everywhere is a feudal culture. We claim to be progressive and very scientific but it is a feudal culture. Siam is the only one which has not done away with the monarchy system. But if this system is going to remain it ought to be the Buddhist concept of monarchy, that is, elected by the people, serving the people, near to the people, with the people and in righteousness. Otherwise the people have the right to overthrow the monarchy. This is all in the Suttras. We need a new culture with a spiritual dimension. I think this is where we are different from others when we talk about liberation, religion and culture. Other philanthropic organisations, Marxists and socialists are much better than us in many repects but I think they lack that spiritual dimension. But I feel the need for this dimension is coming back. If the Green Party is to survive, and I hope they do, I think they will reach this spiritual level. The Christian Democrats have become reactionary. Or you have a Buddhist party as in Sri Lanka which is also nationalistic and lacks spiritual depth. We do not want religious political parties exclusively, we want a spiritual dimension in politics and society. Why should we not take from Mahayana and from Christianity?! In this area you cannot have only one religion anymore. At one time the missionaries told us that they had the only religion! Now some Buddhists seem to have adopted this opinion. But we have to coexist and we must learn from each other. But we can only learn from those who are on a similar wave-length, struggling with the people to overcome problems.

At the same time, however, you cannot get away from organized religion. You cannot destroy the system, yet you can and should be aware of the system; even the bishops are, for the most part, very old fashioned and very conservative. Also in this country the hierarchy is very old fashioned, and some of those in the Sangha are very good with wonderful minds and hearts but they do not really understand that they are giving blessing to capitalism instead of building up awareness.

Each community, firm in its roots, related through a movement within and outside the country, should try to bring together Buddhists, Christians and Muslims, all those who work for liberation. It has to be done. At the same time we must develop some common culture of simplicity. Socialism in England failed because they could not produce a new social culture. They still used the feudal culture. Capitalism also uses feudal culture to oppress people. Unfortunately when socialists have no culture they become capitalist themselves. I see that in Australia very clearly: the Labour Party in power on a capitalistic venture. And that is also why our commitment to religion fails. We think of our own religion too much in a tribal way, Buddhism with a capital B has become tribal; Sinhalese Buddhism against the Tamil. Unfortunately Christianity has also been tribal with selected people, chosen people. It used to be the Jews but now the white men are the select ones. For me this is fallacy. Christianity appeals to me because of the aspect of universal love, and the image of Christ appeals to me because he sacrificed himself. In any religion we have universal love in order to overcome suffering. We can be together.

Finally if we want to work on liberation we have to study the media very seriously. Religious media, as it is now, is only good for propagation. But we need media for liberation. How can we get the media to be more useful for liberation? Most important of all, however, is education. If we can reform our educational institutions to be liberative and not so conservative that would have a tremendous impact. But even this is not enough. We have to build up more awareness and therefore we need more alternative education and alternative media, we need alternative lifestyles and, indeed, we need to change our attitudes and focus more clearly on liberation.

Liberation Religion and Culture : Asian - Pacific Perspectives, Proceedings of an ACFOD Seminar, Asian Cultural Forum On Development, Bangkok 1989.

RENEWAL: A BUDDHIST PERSPECTIVE

Speaking from a Buddhist perspective, witnessing would obviously include spiritual renewal, spiritual strength and personal growth. At the same time, it must lead to environmental balance and ensure social justice. In both aspects, i.e. personal renewal and social renewal, we take Peace as our mission and goal.

In working towards that peace, we have to look at our realities. First we must understand who we are and what our society is. We also have to know our region and the world we live in. But, we start with ourselves. For we can be easily misled if we do not know who we are. For example, by nature people are egocentric and very selfish. We talk a great deal about love; sometimes we mean it, most of the time we do not. We have to know the reality about our ego. And so we are encouraged to be self-critical, i.e. how selfish we are, the weaknesses we have, whether we are controlled by greed, hatred or delusion, etc. Only when we are critical can we have a chance for our spiritual renewal, spiritual growth and liberation. Hence, the primary concept in Buddhism is self-critical awareness. There is a Pali word we use which means "you must know who you are". That is why meditation is so very important in Buddhism. The effort is directed towards study of the self.

The next important element is to know how one relates to one's society. In the Siamese Buddhist tradition this was easy and simple. Society was mostly agrarian, and in this country people were fairly homogenous, belonging mainly to one religion. Each village had a temple. People were proud, happy and self-reliant. But sometimes there emerged corrupt kings and their courts were therefore also corrupt. But then Buddhism played an important role to change that situation and it was successful in doing so. Because greed, delusion and hatred are seen as evil in Buddhism, so the kings tried to be righteous rulers. By culture and tradition the king had to be in touch with the people.

But things have changed tremendously, particularly since the Second World War. The present Siam is no longer what it was. It has become earthly Thailand. When I was young, Bangkok was a conglomeration of villages, now it has become a big city. Slums have begun to spread in the last 30 years. Buddhism, which has been practiced for over 700 years, seems to have lost its way and its strength. It does not know how to deal with the emerging complex industrial society. How can we then give Buddhist witness?

Let me try to clarify what I mean. In the traditional society the precepts of Buddhism, for example, "not to kill" "not to steal", etc., could be easily followed by the faithful. Looking at food habits, for instance, even until recently the main Siamese diet was rice and fish. We did not eat pork until we became acquainted with the Chinese culture. We started eating beef only when we came in contact with the Moslem culture. But now when we talk about "not killing", we also see the existence of so many slaughter houses. The whole meat market system is dependent on it. Then again, the precept tells us not to steal. But we have the multinational corporations which control, to a large extent, the whole banking system, the armament race and the armament sales. On the one hand we have the precept but on the other hand we are not sure how to go about following it. The precept thus becomes a mockery. So unless we re-examine our traditions in the light of our present social realities, the social system, Buddhism, or any Religion for that matter, becomes a kind of decoration for the "new religion" which could be Consumerism, Capitalism, or Communism.

Hence, when we talk about renewal and "knowing one's self" we also emphasize the need to understand society, because we have an obligation to relate appropriately to society. In this effort, we need to look at the present world order, the global system, the north-south relationship, etc. We need to focus our attention on our economic, political, and social structure. For example, in the economic system we need to understand how the rich become richer and the poor become poorer. Unfortunately, most poor people do not even know how they are being exploited. Political issues become important because the situation today is such that masses of our Asian people are being exploited. Even worse is the condition of minorities; ethnic minorities and religious minorities. Unfortunately, some minority communities in our contries wish to relate only to the party in power and the rich in society in order to assure their security. Cultural issues need also to be looked into, for there is a cultural exploitation going on. To me, the most important of them now is the "Consumer Culture". This is like a new "religion". When one goes to Bangkok and enters those large department stores and those entertainment establishments, one knows what I mean by cultural exploitation!

We have to be aware of and unite ourselves against these ungodly trends. As you know, many of these trends are fostered and controlled by multinational corporations. We must therefore understand the system we are in, and in doing so we, as Buddhists, try to go back to our roots in Buddhism. We try to go back to the Buddha to see how he wanted us to renew ourselves.

The encouraging fact is that in this country there are signs of people going back to their indigenous cultures. That is the only way to transform the situation. In this effort we must learn to live in loving kindness, to be compassionate and truthful. And we must unite not only amongst ourselves, Buddhists, but also with people of other faiths. In our multi-religious context, this is of great importance. To be a good Buddhist in the multi-religious context means we must respect our friends who are Christians, Hindus, Moslems and people belonging to other religious faiths.

Of course, we must also remember that in all the great religions there exist followers who are open to renewal on the basis of their respective faith, and there are also others who maintain a negative outlook in these matters. Among Buddhists, too, there are people with negative outlooks. They are not hindered in exploiting the poor for their own benefit. Even religious leaders in the name of religion or nationalism, engage in activities that are irrelevant and often detrimental to the people. For example, some religious leader are reluctant to conserve or preserve our lofty traditions. I think this is also true in Christianity. But in each religion we also find good people, people who wish to liberate themselves and the entire humankind.

In concluding I wish to once again emphasize that in Buddhism each individual must endeavour to be self-critical. Self-examination or self-awareness is primary. No one can help you to reach that; you have to reach it yourself. The religious teachings can only point the way. So, we examine ourselves and see how relevant we are in society and how well we can grow to be meaningful in it. In this task we must have good friends. Good friends could come from the Buddhist tradition, Christian tradition, or any other tradition. When these good friends come together they can work towards common goals. They can agree to disagree. They agree to work together although they may belong to a different religion and a different ideology. And we work together to destroy the unjust systems, in a non-violent way, in a peaceful way... so that peace and justice can prevail.

Witness in A Multi-Religious Context, Report of the YMCA Seminar, Chiengmai 27-31 October 1986.

PAÑÑĀNANDA BHIKKHU

Formerly the dissemination of Buddhism in Siam was organized by a central policy-making body under a Sangha Councillor, and there were provincial propagators as well as district propagaters to carry out the policy. But there were no impressive or permanent results until disseminating organizations were set up in accordance with the Sangha Organization Act of 1941. When the new Sangha Organization Act of 1962 came into force the various disseminating organizations were dissolved. The enthusiastic dissemination of Buddhism has entered a new phase this year (1966). Buddhist missions have been sent out to different remote provinces, the results of which remain to be seen.

In fact, the dissemination of the Buddha's teaching has been practised since the time Buddhism became firmly established in India, as is mentioned in the words of Buddha: **cāratha bhikkhavē cārikam' Bahujanahitāya bahujanasukhāya.**

Sanghas in the past and in the present have followed these sacred words and carried on the practice sporadically, subject to their own ability and industry. As a result, Buddhism has spread into, and become firmly established in, many countries. But the dissemination has been carried out by Sanghas on an individual basis rather than in compliance with any planned procedure originating from the administrators of the whole Sangha body. They sometimes have received co-operation from the administrative authorities, sometimes not, and some have met with strong opposition.

If anyone asks who is the most popular disseminator of Buddhism in Siam today, he is likely to get one and the same answer: Venerable Paññānanda Bhikkhu. Almost every Thai, including those who are not interested in Buddhism, must have heard of his name. There must be millions of people who have listened to his impressive preaching. The subjects of Dharma he chooses are simple and suitable for the practical life of laymen, and his interpretation is simplified so as to make the subjects more comprehensible to the popular audience. On certain occasions there are harsh words in his preaching, particularly against misbelief and misapprehension of the Buddha's teaching on such matters as alcohol drinking, gambling, necromancy and spirit houses. His preaching in this respect has sometimes caused a reaction among senior members of the community. The Sangha circle has regarded him with suspicion, and some high-ranking monks have shown their distaste to such action. It might be due to professional jealousy; maybe they consider he has gone too far, or that the fruit of such preaching will never last.

Laymen who have met Venerable Paññānanda Bhikkhu feel that he practises what he preaches. He is an exemplary monk living a simple life and having no ambition for higher status, quite unlike certain high ranking monks whose preaching is one thing and practice is another, or those who disregard their Buddhist precepts and monastic discipline so as to indulge in moneylending, and letting and purchasing articles. As for Venerable Paññānanda Bhikkhu, gratuitous money received from preaching is given to public funds, and money received from other religious functions is saved up for publishing religious tracts to distribute among the masses. He devotes himself to sacrifice and maintains a moderate disciplined life. His feelings are calmer than his words. He feels no attachment to gains, honour or fame; he regards worldly possessions with indiffirence. Although his living abode is crowded with things as if he were a collector, he looks upon them with detachment. In addition, Venerable Paññānanda Bhikkhu has spent his life more on preaching tours than on staying in his wat. He has taken a catnap on the long distance coach more often than having a comfortable sleep at his abode. This may, to some extent, have caused the administration in his wat to weaken, but he has already set up rules of procedure for all his monks and novices to follow. For instance, a lady visitor is not allowed to come and see any monk in his living room; no monks are allowed to have money in their possession, their necessities being supplied by parental benefactors or others; the lay recitation used in all wats in his jurisdiction contains an accompanying translation in the style of Wat Suan Mokkha so as to convey the meaning of the passage and to make the belief more comprehensible to laymen. When in residence, Venerable Paññānanda Bhikkhu preaches every Buddhist observance day and on Sundays. People from far and near flock to listen to him. Apart from this he preaches on radio and television. His religious addresses have been recorded and published in various periodicals, and they have also been printed for free distribution and for sale widely among the public.

Many people have met him, listened to and read his religious addresses, but very few people indeed know his life on account of the fact that he has hardly mentioned anything about himself. One who wishes to search for information about Venerable Buddhadasa Bhikkhu will find it an easier job because his writings contain profound thoughts which have evolved in different phases, and do reflect, to a certain extent, his own life. Venerable Paññānanda Bhikkhu's religious addresses are meant for the masses in general, and they remain so regardless of the evolution of his thinking and age. Thus, his preaching does not reflect how his thinking has evolved, nor how he has set about his work, in spite of the fact that he has been a persistent propagator thoughout his monastic life, and has devoted himself to bringing the Buddha's teachings to the public since his entry to the monkhood. In his approach to conveying the teaching to the masses he has made use of all modern means. So it may be said that he is quite an up-to-date preacher, and that he succeeds in employing worldly means for spiritual good.

Venerable Paññānanda was born in the year of the Hog, B.E. 2454 (11 May 1911). His first name is Pan and the family name Snehcharoen. His native town is Pattaloong, and he comes from pure Thai stock. He was educated in the same manner as most provincial boys, that is, in the provincial government school and he finished Mathyom 3 (Grade 9). After graduation, he entered the teaching profession as a local school teacher in his home town. An abbot persuaded him to become a Buddhist novice, and he received lower ordination at the age of eighteen. On coming of age (20), he became a bhikkhu and took residence at Wat Nang Lard, near his home, Tambon Guhasawan, Pattaloong, for the prescribed period of three months during the Rains Retreat. Then, he went to study Buddhist scripture in Nakornsridhamaraj. As his lay name is Pan, his preceptor gave him the monk's name of Paññānanda, meaning "one who takes pleasure in knowledge". This given name suits perfectly his character and mind. It was not long before he had made a name for himself as an outstanding ethical debater whose words were highly persuasive. He was then frequently invited to take part in religious discourses in and around Nakornsridhamaraj. In his opinion, a preaching method as such produces very little effect upon the public. It is a demonstration of the debater's ingenious arguments rather than an interpretation of ethical concepts and their applications that penetrates into the minds of the popular audience. He himself realized that his knowledge of the Buddha's teaching was not yet enough, and that he wished to know far more to enable him to read the Scripture in its original language.

At the time Pali study had not reached the southern provinces of this country, so he decided to come to Bangkok to study it. He took residence at Wat Samphya and studied Pali under the Venerable Phra Dhammapaññāpati (then Mahā Fuen, a graduate of the 9th standard) for 5 years. As a result, he passed the examination and became a graduate of the 4th standard, enough to be able to read the Buddhist Scripture in its original language fairly well. As he had no wish to acquaint himself further with the scriptural knowledge, he did not continue his study up to higher standards. Now, it happened that Mahā Nguem Indapañño, a graduate of the 3rd standard, residing at Wat Padumagonggā who also came from the southern provinces, had given up his scriptural study and gone back to his native village at Tambon Poomriang, Chaiya District, Surat Thani. There, he began, in accordance with the Buddha's teaching, to lead a much more strict way of monastic life at the old Suan Mokkha and issued a periodical entitled *Buddhasanā*; he also wrote Buddhsit tracts in an original style. These captured Mahā Pan's (now Venerable Paññānanda Bhikkhu) imagination. So he left Wat Samphya in Bangkok for the new way of monastic life at Suan Mokkha. For one year he tasted the scriptural truth as well as its practice, and made himself a worthy follower of the Buddha. Thus he was one of the pioneers who took residence at Suan Mokkha with Buddhadasa Bhikkhu Indapañño. This association has since strengthened the tie of respect for Buddhadāsa Bhikkhu. He calls Buddhadasa Bhikkhu "Elder Brother" and continues his methods of practice at Suan Mokkha up to the present day, including, for example, the publication of books, the setting up of a printing press and of libraries, monastic modes of living, and the proposed plan to set up a spiritual hospital similar to the "spiritual theatre" under construction at Suan Mokkha. The lack of personnel is the major difficulty in setting up a school as a Buddhist centre.

In essence, Venerable Paññānanda Bhikkhu is a propagator more than anything else. Despite his knowledge of Buddhist scripture and his experience in practice and applications, it was apparent that he could undertake to disseminate the Buddha's teaching only in his own country, for his knowledge of foreign languages was still inadequate for preaching abroad. After residing in the south for a few years, he took an opportunity to spend a period of three months at Wat Kampongko, Perah State, Malaya. At Wat Kampongko he had a chance to improve his knowledge of a foreign tongue. His reputation as a devout, learned, and up-to-date Buddhist monk led the Buddhist circle in Malaya to invite him to stay and preach among them. He therefore accepted their invitation and stayed at Wat Pinbang-orn, Penang, for a period of time.

During his sojourn abroad, Venerable Paññānanda Bhikkhu occasionally did his preaching with the help of an interpreter. Although it was difficult to ascertain the satisfaction of his audience, he felt that he had gained more experience in acquiring knowledge of a foreign language for the benefit of his fellow countrymen. After returning to his home country, he went to India and Ceylon for almost a year. Then he went to stay in England for many months, and also made a tour through many other European countries. Wherever he met Thai students abroad, their faith in Thai Buddhist monks was reaffirmed. In addition, he has encouraged his monk followers to further their studies abroad in spite of opposition from the Sangha body and senior members of the community. While many monks sent to further their studies abroad by other persons leave the monkhood as soon as they return, Venerable Paññānanda Bhikkhu sent Silānanda Bhikkhu and Vivekananda Bhikkhu to further their studies at Nalanda University for six years. The two learned monks still remain in the Order and render useful service to Buddhism with their knowledge of foreign languages to this day.

Silānanda Bhikkhu came to the faith by accident or probably by the influence of Venerable Paññānanda Bhikkhu. He was born and raised in Penang by a Thai mother and an Irish father. He speaks many tongues, including various Chinese dialects, English, Tamil, Hindi and Malay. As his mother was a Buddhist, he entered the Buddhist monkhood at a Thai wat in Penang for a period of three months with the intention of leaving the monastic life like other young men. It happened that Venerable

Paññānanda Bhikkhu went to take residence there in 1947, and on preaching tours he was accompanied by this newly ordained monk as an interpreter. When Chao Chuen Siroros of Chiengtung invited Venerable Paññānanda Bhikkhu to set up a Buddhist centre at Chiengmai like the one at Suan Mokkha, Chaiya, he asked Silānanda Bhikkhu to accompany him to Chiengmai. So Silānanda Bhikkhu went to his motherland for the first time. He has stayed on to serve Buddhism ever since. Later, he went to take residence at a Thai wat at Buddhagaya, and then came back to manage the existing Buddhist centre at Chiengmai. He is also the forerunner of the Nanda group of monk followers of Venerable Paññānanda Bhikkhu. Apart from Vivekananda mentioned above (now residing in India), there is Dhammananda Bhikkhu, a preacher, orator, and propagator like his superior (but not as profound as his superior), and Vimuttyānanda Bhikkhu, more of a thinker and writer than an orator, who is responsible for the publication of *The Buddhists* issued in Chiengmai in the same manner as *Buddhasāsanā* by the Dharmadana, a group at Chaiya.

In 1949, Venerable Paññānanda Bhikkhu set up a Buddhist centre at Wat Umong outside the city of Chiengmai. Consequently, he revived Buddhism there and raised the standard of morality among the populace considerably. The previous abbot, Venerable Phra Srīvichaya, had been famed and respected for his building, maintenance work and mysticism, but Venerable Paññānanda Bhikkhu brought the essence of the Buddha's teaching to the public. He did not do any maintenance work on the historical buildings, yet conserved Wat Umong in the best condition with peaceful surroundings, worthy of the name Arama. He was also the patron in the construction of a Buddhist centre in the city of Chiengmai. The dignitaries of Chiengmai, from the Governor and Chief Judge to the Christian contingent lent their hands to the cause. Many senior monks in the northern region took a dim view of his work. In the end, they did co-operate, however nominally.

Although Venerable Paññānanda Bhikkhu was born and raised in the southern region, he has done a tremendous job for the improvement of the status of Buddhism in the northern region. Some improvements were revolutionary, some were a change for the better counteracting those for the worse, and some were a stimulation for a beneficial revival. His work during this period produced more substantial results than that in later years. He has still not been appointed a propagator of any province or district in the northern region. He was not promoted to any higher ecclesiastical position. In fact, he never seeks for any title or honour and he is satisfied with his given name of Paññānanda, without any additions. When he was appointed High Abbot he was entitled to the name Phra Paññānandamuni. But he still uses his old name, Paññānanda Bhikkhu, and this has confused even highranking government officials, so much that some of them address him as Phra Paññānandamuni Bhikkhu. Today there is a multitude of high abbots. As he has not been the High Abbot of a royal wat and holds no post in the Sangha Council, he has hardly used his official fan. It is said that once when he was invited unexpectedly to a royal opening ceremony of the Bhumibol Dam, his official fan had to be searched for. It was found at Wat Mahadhatu where it had been left since the day he received it.

The incident of his appointment as a High Abbot carries a strange ring; it is said that Phra Vimaladhamma (Arj Asabha), Sangha Councillor in charge of the administration department at the time, impressed by his work, had proposed in the midst of opposition from certain members of the Council, that honour and title should be conferred upon Venerable Paññānanda Bhikkhu. A certain Councillor mentioned that Venerable Paññananda Bhikkhu had not done anything significant, as if he himself had done something better! Another Councillor suggested that he should be promoted only to the rank of Phra Kru. Only when the Councillor in charge of the administration department had reaffirmed the merits of Venerable Paññānanda Bhikkhu did the Sangha Council condescend to propose his name designate for a high abbot. This was the first time that the Sangha Council recognized his work. His acceptance of ecclesiastical honours has given rise to comments in certain groups of his monk and lay followers that he should have nothing to do with honours or fame. He himself holds that the spiritual world is outside self; it is all right if one is not attached to it. Again, when he was appointed preceptor, the procedure was contrary to the set regulations of the Thai Sangha.

It seems odd that the Thai Sangha has employed such a strange device in encouraging a good man. In those days, kind words of encouragement had come forth only from the Supreme Patriarch who was then Somdej Phra Buddhagohsācāraya and had no influence in the administration of the nation's faith. When he became Supreme Patriarch he was very old and weak; certain high ranking monks took the liberty of wielding their own control over the Sangha body. As for the present Supreme Patriarch, when Paññānanda Bhikkhu happened to be received in audience, he was given a set of Burmese monk's robes. This gesture served as sufficient encouragement. His appointment as head of the Buddhist Mission for the South covering two regions, indirectly recognized his ability and work in the dissemination of the religion in those regions in the past.

Venerable Paññānanda Bhikkhu resided in Chiengmai Province for ten years. Later the Royal Irrigation Department built Wat Cholpradanrangsarit in Nondaburi Province. When it was completed in 1960, the Department concerned sought a high abbot for the newly constructed Wat. Venerable Khemarangsī and some senior officials of the department made a suggestion to the Director-General that Venerable Paññānada should be invited from Chiengmai to Wat Cholpradan in the same manner as Venerable Buddhadāsa had previously suggested to Chao Chuen Siroros that he should be invited up to Chiengmai. His leaving Chiengmai stirred up comments and feelings of loss in many quarters. But he maintains that he has done quite enough for Chiengmai. The Buddhist centre there has taken firm root; its management is running well enough not to need his support on the spot. Even now, he often goes up to preach at Chiengmai, and is still the president of the committee of the Buddhist centre there.

In taking residence at Nondaburi he has a chance to enjoy solitude, for Wat Cholpradan is far from the capital, but not too far away for those who wish to go and attend his preaching. Wat Cholpradan provides a good base for his going up north or down south for the dissemination of the Buddha's teaching. In the capital, he usually resides at Wat Mahadatu with his good friend, Phra Devavisuddhimolī, and he lectures at the Royal Mahachulalongkorn Academy from time to time. Apart from this he has other lecture programmes at the meeting halls of various government offices. So far as broadcasting is concerned he preaches on the radio at the Armoured Corps Station every Monday (7.30 p.m.) and Wednesday (6.00 p.m), and at the Kaset Station every Sunday (7.05 p.m.).

At present (1966), Venerable Paññānanda Bhikkhu is fifty-five years old, and has been in the monkhood for thirty-five years. He is worthy of his position as a senior and learned monk, following the monks' precepts, keeping well and healthy, rising early, speaking very little, preaching a great deal, working steadily, and continually travelling far and wide. If there were ten monk propagators working as hard as Venerable Paññānanda Bhikkhu, Buddhism would be firmly established in the minds of the masses. If an organization for the propagation of Buddhism is envisaged again, it would be a good thing to have Paññānanda Bhikkhu taking part at a policy-making level. What we have learned now is only that the Department of Religious Affairs has invited him to be a member of the Committee on the Buddhist Mission to England. It is deemed desirable to think far beyond that and to make the most out of such a good man by requesting him to lend his hand more and more. As he has no love for gain, his service would cost us nothing at all. If we leave him to work for a cause single-handedly and have no long-term plan, there will be no follow-up for his good work.

Visakha Puja 2510 (1967).

DHAMMAVITAKA BHIKKHU

It is a great loss to the Siamese Sangha that Bhikkhu Phya Nararatana Rajamanit passed away on 8th January 1971 at the age of 74. To be a Phya – an equivalent to a knight bachelor – at the age of 25 and a Privy Councillor at the age of 27 is indeed a great worldly achievement. Yet at the age of 28 the Chao Khun decided to take the yellow robes to dedicate the merit to His late Majesty King Vajiravudh, under whom he served as an ordinary page, rising to the position of Master of the Royal Bed Chamber. His friends and relatives thought he would be a bhikkhu for the customary three month period. Yet he remained in the Order for the rest of his life, altogether 45 Rain's Retreats. At his ordination, he was given the name of Dhammavitako.

Phya Nararatana's family name was Cintayananda and his personal name was Truk. He was born on 5th February 1897, which happened to be the full moon day of Magha Month. His mother delivered him soon after offering food to bhikkhus in their morning round of alms collecting. Both his parents were devout Buddhists. His father, too, spent the end of his life as a bhikkhu. He joined the order about 3 years after the Chao Khun. His mother as well as his maternal grandmother also spent the last part of their lives as nuns (upasika) taking the eight precepts, shaving their hair and wearing the white robes, practising the Dhamma seriously.

The late Chao Khun was educated at a temple school and proceeded to Chulalongkorn University before entering the Royal Household Department. While a page, he had the duty of serving high ranking monks who received offerings from His Majesty every week. He thus had an opportunity of learning Buddhism from the Venerable Somdej Phra Buddhaghosācāraya, then Abbot of Wat Debsirindra, who later became the preceptor at his ordination.

Before entering the monkhood, Bhikkhu Dhammavitako was already engaged to be married. The new King also promised him a more challenging and fulfilling position, yet he found more happiness in following the Buddha's eight-fold path.

His meditation practice, his strict diet, and his regular attendance at the morning and evening chantings, as well as his wonderful personality and deep insight in the understanding of the Dhamma, already made him a legend in his lifetime, although he refused to attend any formal function, inside or outside the wat. And he never received guests at his lodging. Needless to say he would not accept gifts, honour or position of any kind whatsoever. He wrote very little and declined to give any sermon to the public, but was willing to talk to those who seriously sought the path to Nibbana.

Although most people never met him in person, the fact that such a bhikkhu existed in the midst of the busy city for almost half a century, proves that Bangkok is still a Buddhist capital despite the changes.

No doubt there are a few more monks like the late Bhikkhu Dhammavitako living among us in this great city, but we must really go out of our way to find them.

Visakha Puja 2514 (1971).

PHRA DHAMMACETIYA: IN MEMORIAM

The Venerable Phra Dhammacetiya (1908-1979) was one of the most renowned Pali scholars in Siam. He had the well deserved reputation as the best professor of the Pali language in the Kingdom. It is very difficult for a bhikkhu (fully ordained monk) let alone a samanera (novice) to attain the Ninth Grade of Pali scholarship, the highest academic attainment in traditional Buddhist studies. Yet, forty-five students of the Venerable Phra Dhammacetiya attained such distinction out of a total number of 150 who have passed this level since written examinations were introduced to replace oral examinations in 1916. Under his tutelge, a samanera passed the Ninth Grade examination in 1960, the first such novice to do so in the present reign. Previously, there had been only two other samaneras who attained such distinction, one in the Third and another in the Fifth reigns. Both eventually became Supreme Patriarchs. (The Venerable Phra Dhammacetiya wrote a very interesting account, "Pali Education in Siam", which was translated and published in *Visakha Puja* 2507.)

At the time of his death, Phra Dhammacetiya was the Abbot of Wat Thongnopakhun in Dhonburi, which is not a large monastery but is unique artistically. (See *Artistic Venture at Wat Thongnopakhun*) As abbot, he spent 10 years restoring the Uposatha (Consecrated Assembly Hall), giving attention in minute detail to the main Buddha image, the altar, mural paintings, carved doors, windows, and roof. He consulted experts in every field – architects, sculptors, environmentalists, archaeologists, and art historians. His wat was a model one in terms of artistic conservation and environmental planning as well as in the exemplary discipline of the resident monks.

He was promoted to be Ecclesiastical Governor of Dhonburi and later Ecclesiastical Governor-General of the Fourth Region, consisting of Nakornswan, Kampaengpet, Pejaboon and Pichit provinces. He assisted the Patriarch of the North for the entire northern part of the kingdom in conducting seminars concerning Sangha administration. Apart from strictly religious subjects, some of the seminars he organized dealt with such subjects as public health, credit unions and the conservation of Buddhist artistic heritage. The objective of all these seminars was to train the provincial Sangha leadership to more effectively under-take their spiritual, intellectual and community service roles in a fast changing world beset by forces of modernization.

His Majesty the King honoured the exemplary life and work of the Venerable Phra Dhammacetiya by graciously raising the status of the urn which contained the late abbot's body from an ordinary urn (โกศโถ)* to which he was entitled by his Dhamma rank to an octagonal urn (โกศแปดเหลี่ยม) which is traditionally reserved exclusively for the highest class (Rawng or Deputy Somdej) of the Phra Rajagana rank. There was no predecence for raising the status of an urn for a deceased monk. His Majesty the King graciously sponsored the cremation rites. H.R.H. Crown Prince Vajiralongkorn graciously represented His Majesty, in lighting the funeral pyre at the Royal Crematorium, Wat Debsirindra, on Monday 7th May 1979.

---

* A rājāgana monk lower than the Dhamma level – Deva, Raja and Ordinary (Sāman) – is only entitled to a golden coffin (หีบทอง). Phra Dhammacetiya first received the royal title of Phra Kittisārasobhana. He was later promoted to the titles of Phra Rājavedi and Devamedhi respectively.

Visakha Puja 2522 (1979).

ARTISTIC VENTURE
AT WAT THONGNOPAKHUN

Wat Thongnopakhun must have been a small monastery in Dhonburi, built during the Ayudhaya period. Soon after Bangkok had become the capital after the sacking of Ayudhaya, Phya Jodukraja-setthi, a rich nobleman who was in charge of all the Chinese merchants in Siam, helped financially to have most of the buildings reconstructed. He also begged His Majesty King Rama III to accept Wat Thongnopakhun as a royal monastery.

In carrying out this reconstruction work, the abbot, Phra Khru Kasinasangvara, supervised almost everything. He adorned the gable-end of the Vihara, where the main Buddha images are installed, with Chinese porcelains, which was fashionable during the reigns of Rama II and III, and the walls inside were merely whitewashed. The doors and windows were also very ordinary. The Uposatha, or the Consecrated Assembly Hall, however, seemed to be his masterpiece. He expanded the original building, which must have been the same size as the Vihara, and added the "sky tassels", which consist of a block of hard wood carved to represent multiple pointed heads of the Nagas in an open fan-shaped position with a piece like a gracefully curved finger pointing upwards, rising above the whole; thus the building consists of a group of glittering spires. Yet these are not unique; they are characteristic architectural decorations for the roofs of Siamese Buddhist buildings. The special features of this building are its doors and windows.

There are five windows on each side of the building and normally the decoration on each window would be the same. But here, the middle windows look like Siamese crowns, or pointed head-decorations worn by actors. The next pair from the centre look like official fans carried by Lord Abbots of the Rājāgana rank equivalent to a bishop. The last pair at the extreme ends of the building represent fans carried by Phra Khru, learned monks of the rank below that of the Rajagana.

The central door in front of the building which leads directly to the main Buddha image in the Uposatha Hall also represents a Siamese crown worn by an actor. So the whole building is really a stage. Not only kings and monks are actors. Even the Buddha himself is seated before a curtain, under the nine tiered umbrella, which is normally only for the monarch. The white umbrella hangs down from the ceilling above the Buddha image. This image must have been made during the Bangkok period, and it is considered to be one of the most beautiful ones of the period. The curtain was painted on the wall behind the image, and it looked so natural that when King Mongkut, Rama IV, came to present Kathina robes to the monks at the end of a rain's retreat, he remarked "Why hang a curtain behind the Buddha image?"

The natural approach to painting was fairly new to Siam, and traditionlly behind the main Buddha image the painting would be on the theme of the three worlds in the Buddhist cosmology i.e. heaven, earth and hell. Khrua In Khong of Wat Rajaburana was the first monk-artist to use perspective in his painting. King Mongkut was very fond of this artist and had him paint European and American scenes on the walls of both Wat Bovornives and Wat Boromnivas. The abbot of Wat Thongnopakhun happened to be a close disciple of Khrua In Khong and he was in the same monastery in Bangkok as his master before he became abbot of Wat Thongnopakhun downstream on the other side of the river.

It must have been King Mongkut's first impression when he made that remark, for when one looks at the curtain carefully, one can see that on the wall above the two back doors of the Uposatha Hall, there are paintings of Indra and the other gods in positions of humble adoration before the image of the Buddha.

Traditionally, the painting on the upper section of the wall opposite the main Buddha image, would be the episode of the Buddha reaching the final stage of victory over Mara, the evil one. But here, the artist painted palm leaves wrapped up in colourful cloths, representing the whole Canon in Three Baskets: Vinaya (the Discipline), Sutta (the Discourses) and Abhidhamma (the Metaphysics). They are all placed on stools, with a Chinese altar in front of them. Underneath the stools, two cats gaze at each other playfully.

The two sections on the same wall, which are divided by the entrance to the Uposatha, have two different kinds of painting. On the right hand side of the main image, the artist painted a tree with three trunks, representing hatred, greed and delusion. He also painted monks who are studying the Canon and who are practising meditation in order to cut down the three sources or causes of sin. The tree with three trunks could also mean the Buddha's teaching which is divided into three sections or baskets. Whatever the meaning, monks must know these three well in order to reach the ultimate goal.

King Mongkut liked the idea behind this painting and he also praised the craftsmanship of the artist. He ordered a court painter to have it copied on the wall of Wat Mahaprudharam, another royal monastery being rebuilt at that time.

The painting on another section of the same wall, however, caused quite a stir. This is what King Mongkut had to say: "Phra Khru Kasinasangvara is a senior monk in charge of a royal monastery. He does not let the royal monastery decay, but has invited the faithful to contribute money to maintain and reconstruct Buddhist monuments in the royal monastery which are better and more beautiful than before. The craftsmanship is unique and the King is very pleased with what he has seen. Phra Khru Kasinasangvara ought to be praised highly for what he has done. He is surely better than those Rajaganas and Phra Khrus who are in charge of royal monasteries, yet have never maintained them, and let them decay. The King feels that Phra Khru Kasinasagvasa ought to be raised to the Rajagana rank with the title of Phra Nanarangsi, Lord Abbot of this Royal Monastery, but looking at one panel of the painting in the Uposatha Hall, which is between the central door and the northern door, opposite the left hand side of the main Buddha image, the King found it disturbed his eyes. The painting illustrates the life of Prince Vesantara, the previous life of the Buddha-to-be. In this section, Indra and Phusti, his wife, are together in a turreted palace in the heavenly garden full of goddesses, who are plucking flowers and fruits from various trees. Some are bathing in the lotus pond. But there are seven of these goddesses who are not properly painted. (1) One lady lifts her skirt right up to her buttock in a position to pass water. (2) One lady opens her skirt right in front of herself. (3) One lady swims with her face to the water, while her buttocks are above the water and there is no cloth to cover them. (4) One lady swims with her back to the water, her body above the water, and she has no clothes either. (5) One lady, having finished with bathing, is in the process of changing clothes, leaving her breast bare. (6) Another lady is also changing her clothes, leaving her buttock bare. (7) One lady falls down and her clothes falls down from her also.

"These seven ladies all represent goddesses. They wear crowns and their decorations are painted with real gold. They are not amateurishly but skillfully painted, and this panel is in the front part of the consecrated Assembly Hall, right in front of the face of the main Buddha image. When the King comes, he would sit in front of this painting, and when the holy brotherhood assembles for their religious function, they have to see this picture until the ceremony is over.

"Are these seven goddesses painted under the direction of the Lord Abbot or did the artist paint them without the Abbot's instruction? What benefits would derive from such painting? Would there be a religious riddle behind this picture? Or having seen such a painting, would one feel pity and be more devout in the observance of the Holy Disciplines? Or perhaps the painter is mad. If mad, why can he execute it so beautifully?"

King Mongkut was well aware that the Abbot himself was the painter. Hence the Abbot was never raised to the Rājāgana rank all through his life, and the paintings had to be altered accordingly.

Aurora Vol. 1 No. 1 October 1971.
Visakha Puja 2515 (1972).

VII
SIAM – SE ASIA – JAPAN

THE SIAM SOCIETY'S 84th ANNIVERSARY

Privately run, and organized in the European tradition, the Siam Society – the oldest institute of learning in the country – is to become a full 84 years old by the end of February 1988.

As a matter of fact, the Society has as its founder a European, who had set it up in the pattern of the Royal Asiatic Society of Britain, and saw, in the course of time, its expansion to India and Malaysia, where its branches are also to be found.

The primary purpose of the Siam Society was to seek, through necessary research study, to learn more about Siam and its neighbouring countries, and to publicize the knowledge thus obtained among members by reading it to them. Later, the Society started publishing its own journal for the said purpose, as, without an office of its own to hold meetings, it had to seek the needed facilities therefore at various places in the meantime. The Society did not have its office until after the 1932 revolution, when Phya Indra Montri (Francis Giles) succeeded in his request for a plot of land from Mr. A.E. Nana, who gave the one on Soi Asoke, Sukhumvit Road, where the office was constructed, and has been serving since then as the Society's permanent home. However, while the meeting hall, the library and various houses have remained intact all along, the land on which they stand has not, since a part of it has been sacrificed, in the name of "development", when widening Soi Asoke was considered a "must" by the competent authorities.

When the Siam Society reached 72 years of age, I had asked Sodsai Khantivarapong to write its history, which has been published both in Thai and English. Yet, the Society remains little known among Thais in general. This is because any attempt at seeking to release those involved from their tendency to submit themselves to foreign domination is bound to fail. I myself made an attempt at it, by offering to reorganize the Society's new council, under the Chairmanship of Phya Anuman Rajadhon in 1969, in a bid to increase the Thai membership to the council for a greater control over it. But the attempt was a hard one, difficult to succeed. In other words, the Siam Society may be described as a small unit in a big society, and with Siam and those, among the leading Thais, being prepared to allow themselves to be dominated by Western intellectual influence, subconsciously following its leadership in whatever direction it may lead, how could one expect a small unit to resist in such a context? And what's more, with some foreigners in control of the Siam Society, being the ones, who have it in their interests to protect and promote, it is therefore natural that these people would be more concerned with their interests, than with seeking to enrich their intellectual knowledge, in depth, of Thai arts and cultures. As such these are the people, who should be regarded more as deadwood or a parasite, than as the intellectual guides.

In any event, those foreigners of the earlier generation are admittedly far more worthy, such as Phya Indra Montri, who was an Englishman, whom I have earlier cited as an example. This English nobleman was widely recognized both for his proven capacity as an administrator, and for his eminence, as the one, who held the highest position, among all the foreigners serving in the Thai Goverment's service at the time. He left behind in Siam a number of descendants, who have all become Thai citizens by now. He was one, who dedicated himself and his time to working in the interest of the Siam Society, and to doing research work in the anthropological fields of his own interest. Thus it is to be regarded as most deservedly appropriate that, on the occasion of the celebration of the Siam Society's 7th 12-year cycle, his portrait will be installed at the function, in commemoration of the great services rendered by him to the Society.

Then there was the decent German, like Dr. Frankfurter, decent French, like Prof. George Coedes, Phra Sarasat Pholakhant (Gerini), Italian, and Mr. Sidenfaden, Danish, all of whom were contributors, to whom we are always prepared to pay tribute, with all our sincerity, for their high academic learning.

It is not that foreign council members of the present generation are worthless, but, in deference to the comparable academic qualifications having now been achieved among the academic Thais, would it not be the proper time now for them to step back, to play a secondary role in the administration of this old institute of learning, particularly the halfblooded ones, who pride themselves on their knowledge of Siam, but whose behaviour is deplorable, mean, and completely devoid of any noble character. Have they ever asked themselves about the advisability of holding on shamelessly to their membership in the council. But worse among them are the ones, who may be described as scoundrels, for their unscrupulous exploitation of the Siam Society for their personal gains, economic, social, and political, and done in the manner, more or less, of members of an outcast society.

To the question of why the academic Thais of the new generation have chosen to stay away from the Siam Society's arena, there are many reasons that could be offered, as follows:

1) Since the time when Prince Dhani Nivat was the Siam Society's president, which was before his promotion to the higher princely title of Krommamuen, it was said that the Society was an arena for scholarly snobbery and this was looked upon by some people as something repulsive. One among such people was Prince Chumbojbhongse Boripat, who refused the Siam Society's invitation for him to be a council member.

2) The Thais of the new generation see the Siam Society as a place for those among the earlier generation, who are members of the royal family, and their descendants, or the pro-West ones. Publishing by the Society of its journal and other publications in Thai, and holding its public meetings, for which Thai is used as the language medium, have proved in the main unsuccessful. Probably, they were inadequate, or belated, while the competitive ones in the field have already proceeded far ahead.

3) There are available now to the academic Thais of the new generation more opportunities and facilities, such as new institutes in the universities, new associations, and others, including the Royal Institute itself (which is also open now to the people of the new generation), and the National Research Council, where they are offered the opportunity to demonstrate their potential, without having to seek to do so at a regular monthly meeting, and having to use a foreign language as the medium, enjoying at the same time the meeting allowances payable to them by the institutes concerned, in return for the benefits obtained by the latter, which may be more than enough to cover the expenses paid, while the Siam Society still continues on with its noble English practice

of working, for which the council members are to pay for all the costs involved, out of their pockets. As such, if the member is not a rich man, or a foreigner, he could not be expected to stay long in the council, with his working on something, from which he could not expect any returns, or promotion, such as from the position of assistant professor to a fullfledged one. Nor could he expect any recognition from the government. In fact, following the expansion into this country of its political and military influences in 1957, the U.S. sought to initiate its role as an academic activist, through the Cornell University, which set its eye on the Siam Society, hoping to activate it into playing a leading role, as a private institute, in the field of social sciences and humanities (both are American terminologies, which have never been heard of in Europe). The idea was considered unacceptable by the leader of the Siam Society at the time, probably because of his conservatism, and nobility. (A highly educated Thai, with an impressive background in English education, who considered himself a good scholar, would not want to be led by Americans!). The American offer of its liberal financial support was therefore rejected.

It seems to me that, once failed in their approach to the Siam Society under Prince Dhani's leadership, the Americans then turned to what could be described as half-baked scholars at the various universities for support for their ideas, especially when the Social Science Association of Thailand was set up in 1956. For its funding, an enormous amount was made available under Public Law 480, with the American claim that the Association had to be made financially viable to ensure its success, working for the consolidation of its research in the fields of social science and humanities. The American offer also included the setting up of a university press, to do the printing work of all the universities, which at that time were to be found only in Bangkok. However, the Americans had again to turn to another prince, who had also been educated in England, namely Prince Wan Waithayakorn, for his help to serve as the president of the newly set up Association. The reason was that the Prince was seen by the Americans to be more progressive and accommodating than was Prince Dhani Another reason was that there could hardly be found at that time academic, American-graduated Thais whose personal repute enjoyed as wide a recognition as Prince Wan's, both inside and outside the country. However, there was yet one Thai, who was acceptable to both the Siam Society and the newly set up Association, and who had been serving successfully as a link between the two princes, one being conservative and the other liberal. This Thai was Phya Anuman Rajadhon, who had never been educated outside the country.

I myself used to serve as a council member of these two institutes, and during my tenure of office, I also tried to decentralize the power of the group holding it as its monopoly. But I am not going to discuss it here, except to tell you that the Americans still had not given up the Siam Society as a lost hope. What it did was to set up at the Siam Society a major research centre, despite the unwilling support of the Society's leader, but with the support of a majority of the council members, who found the prevailing conditions, and the financial assistance offered, at that time, too appealingly strong a force for them to resist. This led to the Siam Society having to revise its aid accepting policy, to make possible for it to accept aid from other surces as well, making use of its agreement of this with Denmark to serve as the basis (in accordance with the diplomatic tradition adopted and followed by Siam in the past). Such foreign financial assistance was largely spent as salary for a European staff member, who was highly paid, but who produced little work that could be accepted as worthy, in terms of its academic value and permanency. This led eventually to Prince Dhani's decision to resign his presidency (an account of which was given in his autobiography).

To claim that there could hardly be found any Thais, who were qualified enough to take up the leadership of the Siam Society at that time sounds quite plausible enough. But after a lapse of 31 years, it is now rather absurd that the Siam Society still has never given any thought to the advisability of employing a highly qualified Thai academic to serve and to work as a permanent administrator. The library, once convinced it would serve the national library's best interest, did not hesitate to employ the service of George Coedes to do the work.

A properly qualified Thai could be found now for the Siam Society, but if its council members are just a bunch of fools without any sense of direction or purpose, not knowing whether they are meant to serve foreign interests, or this country's, it would again be difficult for him to serve the Society successfully. This is the situation, where the Siam Society is more or less a reflection of Siam, which is still lacking the basic moral principle of self dependence, on which self-dignity stands.

Having offered my comments thus far, I now have to offer my commendation on the coming celebration by the Siam Society of the completion of its 7th 12-year cycle. The Siam Society appears to have allowed more self-questioning than earlier. It is making greater efforts at seeking to serve the Thai society now, both in scope and in depth. How successful its efforts are remain to be seen. But the Siam Society has at least succeeded already to the extent that it has as its leader at present, a person who is generous at heart, though rather too readily conciliatory by nature, and he is very much like "Pa" (our prime Minister) in that it would be extremely difficult to find anyone to replace him, if need be. However, the Siam Society's leader is vastly different from the Prime Minister in that he is friendly with all, near and far, regardless of their attitude towards him, no matter how unfriendly to him they might be.

The Siam Society's social promotion efforts currently in progress began toward the end of last year, when it hosted an international seminar on "Thailand's cultural and environmental problems" in Chiang Mai, in August 1987. The participants were mostly foreigners from different parts of the world, and because of this the medium of language used had to be English. However, there was one participant, who did not use it. That was Mr. Sujit Wongtest, who spoke out in Thai, the only one to do so. Hardly any Thai newspapers paid much attention to the seminar, and in their news coverage, they published only a sketchy report on it. The English newspaper *The Nation*, reporting the seminar in its August 30, 1987, edition, published a rather good coverage on it by Mr. Maitri Ungphakorn. His artice was later reprinted in the January 1988 issue of *Seeds of Peace*.

The seminar produced the following results:

(1) It provided a venue to discuss the preparatory arrangements for the commemorative function to be organized to commemorate Phya Anuman Rajadhon's centennial, the first Thai commoner ever to be elected president of the Siam Society, an academic institute, patronized by the King, and founded by foreigners.

(2) It set down the path to be followed by the Siam Society, in its 8th 12-year cycle, which calls for greater efforts at seeking to conserve arts, culture, and natural environment, in a constructive manner, consistent with its committed stand thereto, which

should be more definite than earlier. It was also hoped that the results of the seminar would be published in English and Thai .

One good omen of the seminar was that it was held in the north. This represents a shift of power from the centre, in the manner of its decentralization, and it augurs well for the Siam Society, considering the fact that there is to be found at the Chiang Mai University, the Lanna Art & Cultural Promotion Centre, which could very well be expected to give its full support to the Siam Society's efforts in this direction, as it earlier did, when, in cooperation with the Society and the Sathirakoses-Nagapradipa Foundation, it organized a Thai-medium seminar, under the chairmanship of Phra Boddhirangsi, the deputy provincial Buddhist religious head, on the conservation of temples and religious development, for Chiang Mai's Buddhist Monk Council, to enable it to serve effectively in its role as a community cultural leader. Then taking over the promotional effort made so far, the Siam Society organized another Thai-speaking seminar at its office on the controversial issue of the proposed construction of the Keuan-namjone dam, opposing the said construction project, which it sees as having a negative ecological effect. The Siam Society, in this connection, also communicated its view as such in a letter to the goverment. At the same time, the Siam Society was considering expansion of its activities into Maejam District, to work on the conservation of Wat Pah-dad temple there, following the publication of an article on it by Mr. Anant Viriyapinij, of the Thai Khadii Research Institute, Thammasart University.The article speaks of the dilapidated conditions of the temple, and the urgent need for its conservation. A survey study of the temple had been made by Mr. Fua Haripitak, who sent his son to make duplicated copies of the wall paintings inside it, as a safeguard measure. The article was published in Thai in *The Journal of the the Siam Society* 1987 annual edition.

Further , I was given to understand that a work-coordination plan on art and cultural conservation and development, between Buddhist associations in northeastern Siam and the Siam Society, is under preparation, to provide necessary training for the Buddhist religious leaders who work under it, while the Cultural Development Centre at Chiangmai University also has a plan for palm-leaf scripture conservation, the working of which is expected to lead to more seminars among the monks involved in various northern provinces.

My writing here is simply a presentation of some points of fact and thought, but without any conclusion.

Should the Thais, who are interested in arts and culture, take more interest in the Siam Society, and should the Siam Society's council members be more condescending to listen to the common Thais, one then could expect to find the foreign influence over the Siam Society somewhat decreased. The decent and modest foreign academic members should cooperate with the Thais, whereas the disgustingly impudent ones should be expelled, not only from the Siam Society, but from this country as well.

It is regrettable to find leading people in the country so submissive to the foreigners. All we Thais should demand the right of equality, not only with foreigners, but also with the leading people, many of whom claim to be patriotic and nationalistic Thais, but who think and act shamelessly under the heels of the foreigners.

For proof, take a look at those, garbed in the King-conferred, traditional Thai costume, and find out from which countries were imported the socks and shoes they wear, what brands of imported perfumes and lotions they use, and what are the prices thereof.

Translated from *Silpa Watthanadham* February 1988.

THAI DILEMMA

I think the Thai dilemma at the national level is similar to that of other countries, namely how to bridge the gap between the rich and the poor on the one hand and to adapt the nation to fit in significantly with the region on the other. The Thai government, it appears, has chosen the latter i.e. to play a leading role within ASEAN to help solve the Kampuchean conflict and to promote friendship with the three Indochinese states – not for moral or cultural reasons, but merely for economic motives. The Thai prime minister even said that "We should change the battlefield into a market place." The same motives can be seen in the rush to recognize the repressive regime in the demonic government of Burma. To me, this is a very short-sighted view and will bring much political and cultural tension to the region in the future.

Likewise ASEAN is becoming more and more like JASEAN i.e. we just blindly follow Japan, which lacks moral or cultural leadership. The so-called catching up with NICs is another dilemma for Siam and SEA. The only country in the region which is really a NIC is Singapore, which is very much disliked and distrusted by her neighbours.

I agree with the statement that a country which changes at a national level must first of all look to its own cultural roots, with humility and self criticism; otherwise it could breed a kind of ultra rationalism. We should certainly look at regional and global imperatives, but must not blindly follow the rich, to be swallowed up by consumerism and gross material success at the expense of moral standards. That is, we cannot afford to ignore basic human rights within our own nation, or even in other countries. The Japanese have no right to maltreat the Koreans in Japan, nor the Chinese, the Tibetans. To me this is not a matter to be left to internal politics, but basic human rights which concerns us all.

The success of NICs and the Japanese can in fact be linked to neoconfucianism, i.e. we must work hard for our own wellbeing – our family, our nation and our culture – the barbarians outside our boundaries can be left to suffer. The other countries are of interest to us because they have natural resources for us to plunder, they have cheap labour for us to exploit and they are a good potential market for our products.

Confucianism in fact produces scholars, philosophers, writers, poets and professors, but not intellectuals.

Intellectuals are not, of course, superior beings; they are the ones who can be critical of the establishment fundamentally - be it the government in power or the leading companies who control public opinion. They need to search for new paradigms in national, regional, and global development.

An intellectual must act like a prophet, not like a priest who only wants to preserve the status quo.

Unless we seek an alternative form of development seriously, we shall not find one ; instead we will blindly follow the rich and the powerful who are everywhere morally bankrupt.

My answer as a Buddhist is that we should take the poor much more seriously and confront the problem of suffering mindfully. We must take time to examine ourselves, and not rush towards success or adapt our country to fit into the regional or global destiny, which is like a fast train running with no brakes . Only then is it possible for the world and the region to become subordinate to the local and individual level (of development).

Power, wealth and technology may then become less significant than morality and spiritual commitment to eliminate hatred, greed and delusion.

(A Talk at An Asian Cultural Forum, Keidaren Guest House, Japan 19 April 1989).
Seeds of Peace September, 1989.

RESISTANCE FOR RECONSTRUCTION: A MESSAGE FROM SOUTHEAST ASIA

The other day our Filipina friend spoke about the crisis in her country and the American penetration or intervention there. Some of you might feel that it was a strong presentation, but in fact it could even be stronger.

The U.S.A. not only has a military presence in the Philippines, it controls that country politically as well as economically, and is trying to dominate her culturally too. US neocolonialism there is much worse than during the overt American imperial rule over the islands.

Vis-a-vis the USA, my country is only next to the Philippines. Most of you may not realize that if the worse comes to worst, the Americans will move their military bases from the Philippines to Thailand. That of course is the official name of my country, imposed on us by our military dictatorship some decades ago. Once that half anglicized name came into being, Siam lost most of her indigenous Buddhist values, the essence of which is peace, nonviolence, freedom, liberation and public participation at various local levels. We are still being ruled by military cliques, with democratic window dressing, which means that violence is preferred to nonviolence, war to peace, and developmental philosophy is for the benefit of the top ten percent of the population who are clients of the super powers and the TNCs.

Siam used to be the rice bowl of Asia, full of birds and bees, plenty of natural resources. Buddhism of course taught us to be respectful to all living creatures, including those in the plant kingdom. But Thailand is now the land of malnutrition, with more prostitutes than monks, and child labour exists in abundance. Our forests are disappearing very quickly and pollution problems are very serious. Food poisoning threatens the rich and the poor alike.

Yet, the elites of my country, who are proud that Siam was never colonized politically, follow the West, especially the US, blindly; consumer culture is preferrable to our own traditional and local cultures. Western sciences and technologies are the answer for all individual and social ills. They do not realize that the symptoms of our illness have come from not being ourselves but blindly following other models of development.

You must realize that although the Vietnam war was over more than a decade ago, the Americans still play a nasty role on mainland Souteast Asia. Nor are the Russians better in this respect. And now the Chinese have also come into our area in a big way.

The Chinese used to be closer to the USSR, but now they take a similar stand with the USA. All three Great Powers are involved in armaments and local warfares, while the European and smaller powers follow suit in lesser degree. For instance, the French, and the Germans too, concentrate on selling arms to our part of the world. Even the Thais, acting as agents of those powers, export weapons to South America! Now they are talking of having American war stockpiles in my country. This is very dangerous indeed.

The reason for all this is simple. For the superpowers like the Americans, the Vietnam war is subconsiously not yet over. And our political leaders have been brainwashed by them so the Thais see the Vietnamese as our arch enemy, as over a decade ago we thought the Chinese were our enemy number one. But now the Chinese are very close with us. They back us with money and armaments so that we would interfere in Cambodia. The Americans pretend not be interested in this affair, but in fact give full backing to the Thai and Chinese vis-a-vis that small country, with so many factions and governments; a president of which lives mostly in Peking while his prime minister spends most of his time in Bangkok. Of course the Vietnamese are not blameless, nor are the Russians innocent. But I feel if the Americans are mature, accepting Asian realities with good political leadership, they could reduce many conflicts in this region. Yet I can't complain too much either, because we too lack political leadership. Although we are a small country, in the past we managed to maintain our independence throughout the colonial periods, despite many gunboats having reached our shores, because our kings were wise; they could use diplomacy skilfully and nonviolently to safeguard our national interest with dignity.

I mentioned Cambodia (or Kampuchea) as an example on the micro level. If you look at a wider area of Southeast Asia, you could see that it is divided into the so-called Association of South East Asian Nations (ASEAN), which comprises the Philippines, Siam, Indonesia, Malaysia, Singapore and Brunei on the one hand, and the former French Indo-China on the other.

The former is supposed to be free and democratic, whereas the latter is supposed to be behind the Iron Curtain. In fact, both blocs are comprised of military or semi-military regimes, with few human rights within any state. ASEAN may not admit it, but they are being dominated by the Americans, politically, economically, and now more culturally too - certainly through consumerism. Western Europe, Australia, and New Zealand also follow the American leadership, more or less. (If the Americans could dump nuclear waste in the Pacific, why should not the French?) Now with the Four Modernizations, especially the last one on modernizing armaments, the Chinese are in this camp, and they see the Russians as more dangerous than the Americans.

Since the three Indo-Chinese States, Vietnam, Laos and Kampuchea are being dominated by the USSR, whether they like it or not, China and ASEAN regard them as our common enemies. We are back again to the Cold War period. All ASEAN countries therefore spend most of their national budgets on armaments, which strengthens militarism within the country, and the super-powers as well as the TNCs—all of them involved somewhat in arms productions and sales – are happy. The result is poverty and insecurity within each country. Hence more repression. If people want to be free, to organise themselves as NGOs, to question the legitimacy of the Government or its expenditures, and to find alternative modes of development, through nonviolence, for peace and justice, they are branded as communists, traitors etc, They are arrested, often without warrants, accused publicly and sometimes maltreated physically.

Once the elites are insecure and are selfish, they do not wish to be questioned, they do not want free expression, and they do not want real public participation.

Senators in my country are mostly from the armed forces. You can be an MP if you are rich or are willing to bend along with the American political philosophy of patron and client. Cabinet ministers are controlled indirectly by the National Security Council, or the military, who are in direct contact with the CIA and the American establishment.

Before the Second World War, we had a Siamese statesman named Pridi Banomyong, who believed in peace and nonviolence. He and his colleagues tried hard to keep Siam as a neutral state, but our military leaders colluded with the Japanese and led Thailand to join the Axis Powers. Mr. Pridi, as the Regent of Siam, organized a Free Thai Movement, working closely with the Allies; so after the war, unlike Japan, we were not punished, and he became our national hero - having already been the founder of our democracy in 1932. He also foresaw an indigenous ASEAN, free from any form of colonialism whatsoever. The region would also be strictly neutral and self-reliant. He helped nationalist movements in Indonesia and Indochina to gain their independence. Despite his close ties with the Allies during the war, the Americans later saw him as a danger, especially when they began to be involved in the Korea and Vietnam wars. Hence he was pushed out of power, and his rival, who had been the military dictator and a war criminal, was put in his place. Ever since, my country has been at the mercy of American interests. Mr. Pridi lived in exile 36 years and died in Paris three years ago. If Siam is to be itself free from foreign interference, we have to look back to a man like that and bring the relevance of his message forward to our present age.

Right now our political leaders and those in the consumer business want to belittle us, the people. They want us to follow them like sheep, so that we would feel small in order that they could control us easily. They want us to feel insecure, so that we need their protection. Hence more money for the armed forces. They want us to sell everything cheaply, including our labour, our bodies and our souls, but everything we buy from them, starting from soft drinks, fast food, chemical fertilizers, motor cars, and weapons, are so expensive.

This is supposed to be good for a "free" society. Now the Americans have overtly introduced protectionism to the so-called free trade policy. It will affect most of the things we sell to them, although the Japanese have been doing this long before, and the EEC is following along quietly. Yet we all want to be like the Americans and the Japanese.

To me, it is good not to sell anything to them. We the people should feel good and great to be ourselves, to know our own society, to be proud of our food, clothing, housing and medicine. We should produce for our sustenance rather than for sale. Why should we be brainwashed into spending so much on luxurious goods? Even western drugs are more harmful than most people realise.

The good thing is that in my country, many people are now becoming aware of the danger from militarism, materialism, capitalism and consumerism. We have known the danger of Chinese and Russian communism long before. We are going back to our Siamese Buddhist roots, not for nationalism, but for alternative models of development in order to bring about peace and social justice. We use meditation practice to help us love ourselves knowingly, not selfishly, and to be compassionate towards those who oppress us. We use Buddhist wisdom to understand our social realities and our individual shortcomings as well as potentialities, so that we can have peace within ourselves, being aware of greed, hatred and delusion which may arise any time. Then we can organise ourselves with our friends at the grassroots, or the riceroots, understanding local conditions and culture, so that we will grow socially, and spiritually; material growth should not proceed the social and spiritual dimensions of man.

If we hate our oppressors, we cultivate hatred within ourselves and we shall never really overcome the struggles. Why should we hate our dictators, who should have our sympathy, since they are controlled by greed and hatred more than we are? Why should we dislike the Americans? Indeed there are so many good Americans who want to be with us and would like us to free them from their unjust system too.

The real enemy is within ourselves. We must overcome our own ignorance within, so that we can be enlightened personally as well as socially. We must overcome the oppressive system, not the oppressors. As long as the unjust system prevails there will always be new oppressors. And if we are not careful or mindful, we ourselves could become oppressors, perhaps even in the name of the poor.

I think things will soon change in the Philippines. Marcos will have to go sooner or later. Likewise in my country, we have had so many dictators in the last few decades, but there is no real change for the better. The change will only be meaningful, if we start changing ourselves and changing our friends who could have dialogue with us.

If we start to cultivate peace and nonviolence within ourselves, we could begin to restructure ourselves to be less selfish and to be more selfless. We would change our way of thinking, changing our life style, to be less dogmatic, to be more tolerant, to be less egocentric and to be more humble. Then we would be in a position to listen to the grassroots, to understand our indigenous culture at its best, (though our traditional culture also has its negative aspects) and to restructure our society nonviolently to be a more peaceful one and a just one.

An address at the War Resisters' International Triennial Assembly on the theme of "Resistance and Reconstruction" at Vedcchi, Gujrat India, 31 Dec. 1985 - 6 Jan. 1986. First published in *Asian Action*, May - June 1986.

NETWORKING AND COORDINATING

I was asked to comment on whether it makes any difference if members of the network do not share common development philosophies and goals.

From my own limited experience within Siam and Asia, my simple answer would be yes. Even when you perform relief work, if you have a fundamentally different belief from other NGOs, or even your own government, it is very difficult for you to coordinate with them. When refugees are pouring into your country, or great famine is taking place in your region, it may seem imperative that you do something immediately in the name of charity or humanity. I am afraid that contributing money during times of big disasters, has become quite fashionable as a way for the rich to ease their consciences and many NGOs benefit from a vast sum of money, which usually becomes their peril.

In fact, malnutrition and infant mortality as well as lack of job opportunities in the Third World is to me as serious as an occasional big flood, earthquake or drought. Yet not much attention is given to getting rid of the root cause of this unjust system. Not to mention that arms factories are mostly operating profitably in the North and a great percentage of these arms are sold to the South, at the expense of poor taxpayers, who have no say in the matter.

In my country, we started the Thai Volunteer Service a few years ago just to train young volunteers to work for various Thai NGOs so that those NGOs could become more effective for social transformation towards a just, peaceful and democratic society. Yet, with each NGO's different philosophy and background, we find it difficult to coordinate them. The TVS still performs a useful function of course. Even so, we had to start a smaller networking, called Thai Development Support Committee, so that NGOs with a similar political ideology would be linked together more effectively. But then, the government in most Third World countries would regard this networking as a communist threat. So we have to link them with more right wing organisations for survival, and if one is not careful in this venture, it wastes a lot of one's time and energy and could easily be coopted.

At the regional level, Asian Cultural Forum On Development, tries to work on development philosophy from the bottom up, which is bound to be different from the national policy of material and social development of most countries in the region. Since most of our members are peasants and the landless, small-scale fishermen and working women, we try to express their vision of alternative development models, as well as make the elites realize the importance of indigenous culture and religion, which could be very effective for liberation, socially and individually. It is easier to coordinate within our small network, although we cover a wide area of South, Southeast and East Asia as well as some parts of the Pacific, providing that we can still raise enough money from outside the region to do this networking. For development projects in each area, these member could look after themselves meaningfully using their own local resources.

Although it is difficult to make our impact felt outside our network (indeed most governments often regard our small people as subversive and often we are punished, lawfully or unlawfully) with patience and a nonviolent approach, I am confident that social change will be possible, if more educated elites would listen to the small men and women at the grassroots.

I personally feel the Asian NGO, Coalition for Agrarian Reform and Rural Development (ANGOC) is a useful network. So is Centre for the Development of Human Resources in Rural Asia (CENDHRRA) etc. But ACFOD and ANGOC should not be networking together since we have a different history and ideology, although the rhetoric may be similar. Yet, if need be, we should learn from each other and share some of our useful experiences as well as our frustrations and failures. One good thing with the different regional NGOs in Asia is that we are equal and we do not get money from each other. Regrettably, our regional NGOs in Asia do not have much relationship with our counterparts in Africa and Latin American. If we did, we would learn much from them.

As for the northern hemisphere, we have many relationships, but not on equal terms. Quite a number donate money to ACFOD, TVS and the like, often generously and with good intention. But somehow it is very difficult to become real friends and partners. Institutional constraints on their part, or being culturally alien in the Asian or Thai context, they never feel at home with us i.e. unless we think like them, act like them, or develop in their fashion or philosophical framework.

I agree with Tim Broadhead in his opening address that money should not be the main criteria for NGOs, especially when one looks towards development alternatives. But it still is, which not only divides North and South, sometimes it makes networking in our own national and regional organizations difficult too.

I propose that if we are serious in looking for development alternatives, we should tackle the money problems in a more meaningful way, allowing funds to be spent more imaginatively, that decision and evaluation ought to be participatory by all concerned with social transformation, whether these people are rich or poor.

For those of us who are not so poor, and who think we are fairly well educated, we should speak less and listen more to the indigenous people.

It is indeed difficult to listen to those who do not speak our language or who do not articulate in our way of thinking. Often we listen, but we do not hear.

We should not be too attached to our own prevailing outlook and life style. Trying to be good to the poor is just not good enough, if we allow our system to exploit them.

We should not only look for a neat proposal and a well written report, which we can sell to our constituencies, but we should try to see things as they really are, especially in those areas which we find difficult to comprehend.

With deep critical awareness of ourselves and an unbiased view on development processes of smaller people, we may get to the point that the Buddhists call the Right View. Then we may become a little more humble, and more able to trust, respect and admire those small people who are different from us and who are trying hard to survive meaningfully in their own culture and environment. If real friendship and partnership is possible, then we are perhaps on the right path towards development alternatives for the poor and the oppressed.

(A speech at Development Alternatives: The Challenge for NGOs. 11-13 March 1987, Regent's College, London).

Seeds of Peace Vol. 4 No. 2 May, 1988.

JAPAN IN ASIA: REALITY AND HOPE FOR THE FUTURE – A THAI POINT OF VIEW

The late Emperor Hirohito began the reign of his Showa period with a Japanese expansionist policy in Asia. For most of Southeast Asian nationalists up to World War II, Japan was seen as a hero, in defeating the Russians and being equal to the West - politically and diplomatically, although not yet economically and technologically. Thai and Burmese military leaders in particular would have liked to have seen Japan as a leader, to rid them of the British Empire. Although we Thai were not colonized by the West, we were not treated as equal by them.

Unfortunately the Japanese occupation of Korea and Taiwan was not well-understood by most of us in Southeast Asia. The Japanese military expansion in China was much criticized by overseas Chinese in the region; however, in the early 1930s, the Thai government instructed its delegation at the League of Nations to abstain while every other nation condemned Japanese aggressive intervention in China.

Since then Japan has become more friendly with Siam, which changed its name to Thailand in 1939. She even helped us in settling our dispute with French Indochina, and as a result we gained parts of Cambodia and Laos, having lost them to the French in the 1880s.

The Japanese friendship with our military elite was viewed with some suspicion by quite a number of civilian intellectuals, especially when Japan asked for our permission to station her troops on our soil to fight against British Malay, Burma and India. Had we refused, she would have occupied our country anyway. Still, the Thai military went along with Japan by declaring war against Great Britain and the USA. We even gained four Malayan states which we had returned to the British in the early twentieth century, plus a part of the Shan State.

By then, most thinking people realized that Japan would not be our liberator but our new master - worse than the British, the Dutch and the Americans. It was apparent that Asia for the Asiatic and the Greater East Asia Co-Prosperity sphere were merely cliches and propaganda.

The Japanese businessmen (even Buddhist priests on cultural missions) who were friendly and humble before the war, pulled on military uniforms and grew arrogant, at times even cruel. They all looked down upon us. For us, the solution was to organize a Free Thai Movement, clandestinely, in collaboration with the allies, in order to survive as an independent country after the war.

Since World War II, all countries in Southeast Asia have become independent, one after another, peacefully or otherwise. Yet none of us have forgotten Japan's aggression and brutality during the war. Many of us fear that even modern Japan may rearm to the extent that she could become a military power again.

The change in emperor may be an opportunity for Japan to look for a new constitution - one with more dignity and prestige, with the revival of Shintoism, nationalism and militarism. Although constitutionally the Emperor need not be sacred anymore, culturally, he is still the symbol of Japan and Japan is still a unique country, which feels justified in exploiting the rest of Asia, her unequal partners, economically, culturally and ecologically.

People of my generation who have seen the Japanese aggressive policy in Southeast Asia before and during World War II, regret to say that Japan has not fundamentally changed her attitude. Although she is not against us militarily, she is very aggressive commercially and economically. She does anything to sell her products and get our raw materials as well as our cheap labour - even promoting prostitution and sex tourism. She bribes our politicians. She advertises as she wishes without any sensitive consideration for local culture or social norms of the country. She has joined the western bandwagon of capitalism and consumerism, without any moral or ethical considerations whatsoever. At least western companies and powers have some Christian concern or a

White Man's burden to do something good in other unfortunate areas of the world. Japan Foundation and the like only do philanthropic work in Southeast Asia when the West has prompted them to do so, or when they feel it is advantageous for them to do so in the footsteps of the West - to keep her image clean. One questions whether she is really committed to friendship, as an equal partner, and to learn from us.

Luckily, among the younger generation in Japan, there is a stronger tendency (albeit a very limited one) to question the Japanese model of economic and technological development as well as blindly following great western powers like the US. These people also want to think for themselves and to seek spiritual depth as well as social justice. Some of those in Japan who have Southeast Asian friends, or have been with the poor in Southeast Asia who have been oppressed by their own elites who collaborate blindly with the Japanese for business reasons, have learned our languages and cultures, and respect us and our indigenous ways of living.

If these young people do not sell their souls to the Japanese establishment in the future, perhaps they may act as seeds for something positive to grow, to change Japan to be less of an economic animal, so that the Japanese can become more humane - perhaps not so rich, but such that they may enjoy life more and have real friends in Southeast Asia and around the world.

If these seeds are allowed to grow and become big trees, then the reign of the new emperor will be the beginning of real peace which must begin within and must always exist side by side with justice and compassion. Otherwise peace will be replaced by expansionism and the history of the last Showa period will repeat itself.

Asian Action April - June 1989.
The Japanese version was published by the *Mainichi Shimbun*.

APPENDICES :
ON THE AUTHOR AND HIS VIEWS

THE DOMINANT FIGURE : SULAK SIVARAKSA

An Intellectual is a person who is well-informed and knowledgeable and shows keen interest in society. He usually aspires to improve the society of which he is a part. He views every problem from all angles, and tries not to see merely one side of the coin. Intellectuals can be found everywhere – in the civil service, in universities, among newspaper writers and journalists, but the number of those who are really qualified to be called intellectuals is very small. Among the technocrats in government, too many are concerned only with their immediate field of competence, paying little or no attention to problems and events outside their limited circles. The same applies to instructors, lecturers and students in our universities.

The intellectuals in our country are not playing an active role in present-day Thai society. This is primarily because the number of real intellectuals is very small, and with rare exceptions, our intellectuals, influence seldom goes far beyond their numerical strength. Another reason is that most of our intellectuals feel frustrated and lack the necessary stimulation, since they are usually poorly remunerated. They are also disenchanted because no one seems to listen to them. True enough, the Government at present allows our intellectuals to voice their opinions and air their views, but it rarely listens to them, much less takes their views and opinions into account. This is especially true with regard to the crucial questions now confronting our country: the Government seems to pay no attention at all to the intellectuals' views and sentiments.

The intellectuals in this country will be playing a diminishing role as the political situations in our neighbouring countries deteriorate. Intellectuals will soon find their freedom of expression increasingly limited. The role of mass media will be less prominent and the numbers of newspapers will decrease.

Outside influence plays a leading role in shaping the thinking of Thai intellectuals. Most intellectuals are Western - oriented since most are educated in the West. Even these Western-trained intellectuals have diverse outlooks towards problems which are essentially similar. Those educated in England will think like the English, and those educated in America never fail to cling the their American ways. In other words, most of them take a myopic view of things. Worse still, most of our intellectuals do not understand the Thai society. They do not see things in the Thai context. Some even look down on their Thai brothers. They read only foreign books and magazines, viewing that as a fashionable thing to do. Most technocrats in government know only their special field; they never try to understand the life and problems of farmers, the backbone of our country.

Thai intellectuals are by and large inward-looking. They cannot see things beyond their limited range of sight. Their thoughts and actions mostly centre on the Thai social norms. Take the Cambodian crisis, for example. When we talk about aiding Cambodia, we view the situation only from one side – our side. Few of us try to look at the situation from the viewpoint of the Cambodians. This is due to two reasons: firstly, our intellectuals do not understand Thai society and, secondly, our intellectuals are small in number. Even this small group of intellectuals are often feuding with one another. They cannot take a united stand on problems of common interest and this makes their influence all the more insignificant.

The slow democratic evolution of the society definitely hindered intellectual activities in Thailand. Thai intellectuals are also handicapped by two more factors. The first is that though the Government allows our intellectuals to speak freely, it does not lend an ear to them. The Government casts aside the intellectuals' suggestions and criticism, leaving them without any recourse. The second is that, because of the small number of intellectuals, they are usually saddled with too many responsibilities and have to attend to far too much work. Consequently, they do not have time to assimilate new knowledge and absorb new ideas.

In this columm 'The Dominant Figures' Manit Jeer interviewed three personalities, Sulak Sivaraksa, writer and editor, M.R. Seni Pramoj, Leader of the Democratic Party and M.R. Kukrit Pramoj, Banker, publisher and writer:

Bangkok Post – Sunday July 12, 1970.

THE MEANING OF PEACE
Peace: Always a Means and an End
A Buddhist View on a Peace Movement in the Third World

He receives us in his home in Bangkok, Thailand, a quiet, cool place in the middle of a noisy metropolis. In his yard we see a traditional Thai pile-house, squeezed between concrete buildings. Contrasts.

A few weeks later we meet him in the Netherlands: Sulak Sivaraksa, a Thai Buddhist and scholar, a social critic and peace activist. In 1984, Sulak was arrested by the military, along with many others. He was held for several weeks on an accusation of *lesé majesté* (defaming the monarchy) before his case was finally dropped. Sulak has not ended his activities. Although his last book, *Unmasking Thai Society*, has been banned, a new book, *Siamese Resurgence* was published recently.

Welmoed Koekebakker
An interview with
Sulak Sivaraksa

SIVARAKSA : The main problem in Siam, the main problem to which Buddhism can make a contribution, is the military dictatorship. The military tries to use Buddhism; they use Buddhist ceremonies and popularize them to legitimise their power. They do it very subtly, very cleverly.

That is what I call Buddhism with a capital B, Buddhism which identifies with the status quo, and is even used to legitimise the military; Buddhists who are the main forces of oppression and act as agents of the superpowers.

But in fact the military does not know real Buddhism. They do not really know Buddhist values.

KOEKEBAKKER : What kind of values does the military adhere to?

SIVARAKSA : What they adhere to is Western values. The military is a client of foreign powers and of the transnational corporations who invest in armaments and rob the poor. We even produce arms ourselves now, and we export them to Latin-America!

They want more reliance on Western technologies, they want export-oriented industrialisation. They want to catch up with Japan. But in the name of progress, in the name of Westernisation, our cultural pattern has broken down. Once Coca Cola came....

KOEKEBAKKER : "The organisation you are involved in, ACFOD, Asian Cultural Forum On Development, has been writing on the dramatic militarisation in south east Asia. Do you find the position of the Thai military is very different from the military in other southeast Asian countries?

SIVARAKSA : Yes, a difference is that Siam is a Kingdom. We are the only country left in southeast Asia that still has feudalism. The military uses it. They exploit the King, again, for their legitimation.

A difference with Indonesia for example is that Indonesia was colonised. And the military had to fight for the independence of the country. Here the military is far less suspicious of the white man. No one hits the Americans in this country!

People do not realize the influence of Western technology.

KOEKEBAKKER : What is for you the reason to oppose Western technology? In what way is advanced technology contrary to Buddhist values?

SIVARAKSA : Most people do not dare attack technology. I do. In the first place I attack technology at its roots. It is a Western invention. It is not value free.

The metaphysical issue of technology is: Man is a supreme being. Man can destroy everything in the name of progress, and arms technology is racist. America would never drop that bomb in Europe! They dropped them in Japan. Later on in Vietnam, in Laos and Cambodia. Not A Bombs but very destructive all the same.

And lastly advanced technology belongs to a path of development which does not pay attention to the needs of the people. Robots produce faster, clearly! But they create unemployment. This is all contrary to Buddhist values.

KOEKEBAKKER : What is your main criterion to judge whether a technology is appropriate or unjust?

SIVARASKA : Unjust is everything which makes man supreme. We should distinguish between tools and machines. But we are still in the process of thinking about Buddhist economics and education. Catholics like Schumacher helped us to think in this direction.

KOEKEBAKKER : In your recent book *Siamese Resurgence* you explain your views on development in more detail. I quote a few sentences.

"A very important word in Buddhism is ignorance – *Avijja*. You do not know the right thing, you know the wrong thing. You think you know everything. And yet, your knowledge is so narrow and that is what is so dangerous. Those who built the atom bomb knew a great deal but only in a very narrow way. When you do not relate to humanity you can destroy everything". (S.Sivarksa, *Siamese Resurgence*. Bangkok (ACFOD) 1985 p. 98)

So in what way do your views as a Buddhist differ from the concepts of the military? Can you give an example?

SIVARAKSA : Yes. My concept of development is contrary to the policy of the military government because the government's path only benefits the needs of the top ten percent. Everything is the outcome of this: prostitution, child labour. I believe that development must benefit the needs of the people, the needs of the poor. Our country is called the rice bowl of Asia, but more than 60 percent of the young generation is malnourished! We must struggle against this – against this basic social injustice.

For us in the Third World, more so than in your countries, a peace movement has to be more concerned with questions of basic livelihood. To us it is all related: you cannot have one without the other, peace without social justice. I think the Western peace movement should be more aware of social injustice. It is all one.

KOEKEBAKKER : Would all your Buddhist colleagues agree with you?

SIVARAKSA : Some do, some don't. Buddhists with a capital B, as now removed from the original concept of Buddhism, identify with meditation. These Buddhists pave the way for escapism, or they accept the status quo in society unmindfully. This kind of monk in Siam tells the poor to be complacent about their situation.

But if you practice the essence of Buddhism, buddhism with a small b, you meditate not only for yourself, but to restructure your consciousness in order to restructure human society. Without one, the other will be ineffective. For this kind of Buddhism, meditation and social action are interrelated.

In other words, it is wrong to try to adjust the external world without changing our minds, without training our minds to be free from fear, hatred, and greed. The position of the poor cannot be made better by less dependency on material goods alone.

KOEKEBAKKER : So if Berthold says 'Erst kommt das Fressen und dann die Moral" (first food and then morals) you turn it around? You would say: the principal thing is the moral, the inner condition?

SIVARAKSA : Yes, unless you overcome these false values created by materialism and so-called economic development, the rich will become richer and the poor remain poor.

We have to gain an indepth understanding of the realities of the world around us. It is not right to hate our oppressors; by doing so, we would become hateful. And then, even if we would be able to defeat our oppressors, we would still hate people (he describes an imaginary line in between his heart and his head). The heart and the head must be synchronised.

I was in jail last year. But if I would have hated and feared the military, I would have been more dependent on them spiritually.

KOEKEBAKKER : In one of the bulletins of the Thai Interreligious Commission for Development, *Seeds of Peace* you published a poem by the Vietnamese poet Thich Nhat Hanh: called "Please call me by my true names". This is difficult to understand for people active in campaigns against armaments, let me quote a bit of it....

"Please call me by my true names.

Do not say that I'll depart tomorrow because even today I still arrive.

....

I am the child in Uganda, all skin and bones, my legs as thin as bamboo sticks, and I am the arms merchant, selling deadly weapons to Uganda."

Can you explain what Thich Nhat Hanh means by this?

SIVARAKSA : Nhat Hanh meant that we cannot build a peaceful society unless we overcome hatred within ourselves. We are ourselves involved in the problem. We should (slowly, Sulak describes a circle around his heart) have a positive feeling in here.

KOEKEBAKKER : How is it possible to practice a combination of detachment and concern? Has the arms merchant in the poem reason to see this as welcome evidence of warm adhesion? How can you practice solidarity? Or oppostion?

SIVARAKSA : Sure! Of course opposition is necessary! Buddhism does not ideally want dualism. But in daily life we are confronted with dualism. With violence, with oppression. So of course we should oppose that.

But peace can never be only an end. Peace must always be a means and an end.

KOEKEBAKKER : Would you call yourself a pacifist?

SIVARAKSA : No... though I do not favour a violent way. Is violence as a method justified? Theoretically not. But emotionally, if the time comes I do not know where I would stand. In a situation like in Vietnam, for example? But the consequence of violence is that the victory is full of hatred.

But in a military dictatorship, like Siam, you should never use violence. Even if you do not believe in nonviolence, you should use it as a tactic, because if your use violence, you will never be able to compete with them. But it is not just a question of tactics.

The deeper you're committed to nonviolence, the better it is for yourself.

Disarmament Campaigns Holland, December 1985.

A BUDDHIST IN BANGKOK

Sulak Sivalaksa is some kind of "Black Sheep" among the Bangkok cultural elite. He could be called a dandy, being dressed in old Siamese style, and always carrying a silver-knobbed walking stick. He is both an occasional lecturer at Thammassat University, and a specialist in History, Buddhism, and Philosophy, having translated Plato and Aristotle into Thai. He is also a publisher and owns a bookstore. His life is restless as we will see.

In 1976, after the fierce suppression of the "Democratric Experience" the police stormed his bookstore on Rama IV Road and confiscated and burnt 45,000 books on the charge of subversion. Most of them though concerned subjects such as Philosophy, Economics, History, Thai literature and Buddhism. Khun Sulak sent a complaint to UNESCO but was never given back his publishing house stock.

In 1984 the situation worsened. Following an order apparently backed by the army, Khun Sulak was arrested under a *lesé-majesté* charge and taken into jail. He was accused of saying in an interview that the King of Siam was not aware of the real situation of the country, as he lived in his palace, surrounded by courtiers.

This "crime" is judged in Thailand by military court and is punishable by up to 15 years in jail. He was freed, thanks partly to foreign protestations, and maybe also royal leniency.

Q. Your last book has been titled *Siamese Resurgence*. What do you understand by this term?

The values tend to disappear from Thai society. There is a need for a revival of traditional Thai values.

Q. What are they?

As far as I am concerned, and for most people in Siam it means Buddhist values. This is the core. But it does not mean "one has to be a Buddhist". It means one has to understand the society in which one lives, understand that the survival of society depends on a natural framework, understand that one should, at the same time, have a broad understanding, be open minded, have respect for the others, even those who are different from us, and also be oneself, avoiding following foreign customs blindly (although we are precisely doing this when we adopt western values without proper understanding of them).

Q. You mentioned harmony with nature. Bangkok seems to be the very opposite case?

Yes precisely. It shows that something went wrong. We have ceased to be ourselves and we imitate what is done abroad. Bangkok is a second rate western city. "Progress." means adding ugliness to concrete, money and power, and unfortunately many people have to suffer from this.

Q. Is this concentration of power in the hands of a group not a product of Thai history?

I know it is the way History is taught in this country. But actually it is the viewpoint of the social elites. The reality is that in the Sukhothai era (the first capital of Siam) King Rama Kamhaeng's position was just slightly above his subjects. When the king was not seated on the throne, a monk would sit there and preach while the king himself would be seated among the audience. There was much more equality. The Sangha was then a model of an ideal society.

Q. Are we not very far from this ideal egalitarian society here in Bangkok today?

We are very far indeed. At that time the centre for traditional society was the Wat. The Wat was the centre for spiritual and intellectual life, as well as teaching, medicine, arts.... Of course, this is no longer the case. We have "commercial centres" and "financial centres" instead (linked to international capitalism) and military men who are linked to big powers and the arms industry; all this goes well along with opium and heroin trafficking! Money, power and ignorance are the roots of evil in Buddhist society.

Q. Instead of a revival you speak rather of the spoiling of Siamese society!

My book suggests indeed the need for such a revival, but the path leading to this is very narrow. What we see is actually a wreck, a decadence.

Q. How did this happen?

First of all because we do not know who are we. Secondly because we tend to accept the idea of the affluent society and "technological progress" blindly.

Q. Thai people seem to be very proud of their culture. How come they are so easily tempted by the western way of life?

My opinion is that it comes from the fact that we have never experienced a colonial situation. In Burma they rejected British rule, at the same time they rejected western influence. They burnt their European clothes, and wore their longji again. With Gandhi it was a similar case. He threw away his western clothes, then declared independence. But we, in Siam, have never suffered from a colonial situation. A fact we are very proud of – and this was our first mistake – to be proud instead of being humble. And we also tend to despise our neighbours.

We were the only country in the region able to negotiate on an equal standing with the government in London or Paris. Then our ministers learnt English. They admired western culture, without understanding it. This is the core of the problem; we have copied western materialism, but we have not understood western values and spirit: human rights, liberty, equality ... Something went wrong... We copied a false model! When one does not know where one stands, and one copies someone else's values and attitudes, one is bound to make mistakes.

Q. Then what is left of Buddhism in contemporary Thai society?

We are Buddhists, but only for ceremonies, festive days. This was not the case before. We did not have, as you have, the duty to go to Church on Sunday. There was no duty because monks did not have any special power. People would naturally go to the wat, as it was their monastery, the place where they had been ordained themselves, or where their son would stay, and monks depended on the people too. But, please, do not think I dream of a past golden era, which has never existed. It is not a Buddhist attitude to try to set the clock back in the past. One of the first Buddhist teachings is about change, impermanence.

A free translation from French by Diana Lee & J. Chirstophe Simon

First published in *Seeds of Peace* Vol. 5 No. 1 January, 1984.

IS FOREIGN MONEY GOOD FOR THAILAND?

Outsiders are very keen to buy into Thailand despite laws that forbid non-Thais to own land or hold more than 49% of equity in joint ventures. Foreign investment reached unprecedented levels in 1987. The number of Japanese companies applying to invest has increased almost fourfold in the last two years. In the first week of this year alone, vigorous trading on the stock exhange's foreign board helped push share values up by 15%. Yet some Thais see foreign investment as a threat to the country's sovereignty and cultural integrity.

Is there any use for foreign investment in Thailand?

I don't rule it out entirely but I don't see much need, personally. My basic philosophy differs from that of the present government. They feel the more exports, the better for the country, and that we must catch up with the Newly Industrialised Countries – become like South Korea, Taiwan and Singapore. I don't see the need and don't think it's possible, either. The present policy is export-oriented. We may still sell more rice, but our farmers become poorer and poorer, and our environment suffers. I think we need more self-sustenance and self-reliance.

Which countries do you regard with suspicion for their investment policies here?

Japan is obvious, but it is not so much countries as multinational corporations. They are more dangerous. They seem to have a kind of universal culture.

Would you condone more investment going into agriculture?

In principle I have no objection, but I would be cautious. Money comes from rich nations who don't understand our aspirations. I would prefer to have investment among the Third

World – poor countries coming together and helping each other. People accuse me of being too idealistic, but it has to be on that level.

Can Thailand develop fast enough without this kind of investment?

Developing fast means rich people have more money but the poor suffer more and more. Development means firstly human development, global development, national pride and respect for neighbours. If we poorer countries developed medicines together, for example, we could then reject the Western kind of medicine which we spend so much money on.

Does foreign investment lead to foreign domination?

Yes, if you're not careful. Our leaders are still dreaming. On the one hand, they claim to be very nationalistic; on the other, they let foreign investment and experts in at every level – running everything, including Thai-owned firms. Obviously, you can have some foreigners working in you company, but key positions should be held by your own people.

Is Thailand being sold off cheaply?

Very much so. It will get much worse. People say we should reduce the population, but that's not the issue. The main issue is that we just want to catch up with the Joneses, and only the top 10% can benefit. People suffer more and more.

ASIA WEEK, February 5, 1988.

SANTI ASOKE:
SYMPTOM, NOT SICKNESS

Could the non-conformist views of Buddhist leader Phra Bhodhirak lead him to be seen as a Thai version of the Ayatollah Khomeini?

Is he really an illegal monk?

Has he really violated the rules of the Sangha?

Is this regimented religious group really a rotten apple that will soon damage Buddhism in Thailand as a whole?

For those who are afraid of the monk's political outspokeness, the answers to all of these questions will be yes.

But according to social critic Sulak Sivaraksa and thinker Prof.Prawase Wasi, the fear inspired by Phra Bhodhirak has a real basis.

Even if the cult leader violates secular and religious laws, which Sulak asserts that he has in fact done, it does not mean that Phra Bhodhirak can be simply written off.

It only means that the script will have to be changed, says Sulak.

According to Sulak, Santi Asoke is only a symptom of an illness. And that illness is the weakness of the clergy's failure to communicate with people of the younger generation.

He also suggested that the present Sangha laws and structures must be changed because "they are out of touch with reality."

In the meantime, Sulak alleges there is no question but that Phra Bhodhirak has violated both secular and religious laws.

In the case of the Dhamma Vinaya, Sulak says it has been clearly stated since ancient times where the ordination should be performed, how and by whom. And ordination at a Buddhist centre such as Santi Asoke is simply not valid, he asserts.

An expert on Thai culture and religion, Sulak also says that the Lord Buddha told the Sangha to accept secular laws and to live peacefully according to them, as long as they did not violate morality or the precepts of religious law.

According to secular law, Buddhist monks must be ordained by a senior monk of at least 10 years' standing. They must have certificates recording their ordination, and they must belong to one of the two sects, Mahanikaya or Dhammayuti.

The law also says that legal approval is needed to ordain monks. Phra Bhodhirak has no such approval.

But Sulak points out that breaking the law is not the reason why Phra Bhodhirak is under attack at the moment from the Parian Dharma Association, a conservative Buddhist movement.

"It is because Phra Bhodhirak is constantly attacking the clergy. He rocks the boat. And that is what gets him into trouble."

The emergence of Santi Asoke fundamentalist movement, he says, reflects the inefficacy of the clergy in dealing with the pains of alienation among the younger generation, instead confining itself to performing rites and rituals, and concerning itself too greatly with materialism and capitalism.

The Ecclesiastical Council was set up during the reign of King Chulalongkorn as part of his centralisation of the religious hierarchy, following the secular administrative structure.

At present, there are about 300,000 monks in 30,000 temples across the country. And the proliferating "monks' business" of selling amulets or demonstrating "magical" powers are all contrary to religious law.

"But they have not been dealt with because they know better than to challenge the authorities," said Sulak.

The Ecclesiastical Council is comprised mostly of elderly monks whose main functions now are to give titles and promotions to monks throughout the country.

The time is ripe to find ways to revitalise the clergy and the Sangha, so that they can give spiritual answers to modern social problems, and help steer society away from greed and violence, Sulak says. In other words, cure the ailment afflicting the whole body, rather than simply disposing of the symptom: in this case,

Santi Asoke.

According to Prof Prawase Wasi, the antagonism against Phra Bhodhirak stems mainly from his "thundering" against the clergy and other elements of the Buddhist establishment.

But he stresses that we should look below the surface in order to reach the essence of Buddhist teaching: that is, a return to sharing and an equitable society.

While Sulak agrees that Santi Asoke does more good than harm in bringing about a revival of religious interest in the country, he remains critical of Phra Bhodhirak.

"What he has done is to give society a much-needed moral jolt. Society is too much concerned with greed, competition and materialism. What he preaches needs to be heard."

But Sulak cautions against arrogance.

"The central teaching of Buddha is the eradication of self and of egotism. Phra Bhodirak's arrogance comes from a bloated ego. And that, I think, is dangerous".

Buddhism, he says, also stresses tolerance and peaceful co-existence. And Phra Bhodhirak's antagonism does not accord with a tolerant nature.

Certain of Phra Bhodhirak's practices are also at odds with those of Thailand's strict Theravada Buddhism.

Ancient religious law also prohibits monks from revealing or boasting of any supernatural qualities they may feel they possess. This rule is dismissed by Phra Bhodhirak as conflicting with common sense.

His vegetarianism and the concept of the I or Buddha's reincarnation as a Bhodhisattava – which he claims himself to be– are also more part of the Mahayana tradition than of the Theravada.

"It is possible to accept Santi Asoke as another sect in Siam. But certainly not in the Theravada tradition," says Sulak.

The "holier than thou" attitude also does not have any place in Buddhist teachings, he pointed out.

"The Lord Buddha never said that his way was the best. For example, he did not condemn animism, realising that not everyone could follow his path.

"What he did was only to recommend to people that there

was a better way if one wanted to be rid of suffering.

"Yet Bhodhirak claims that his teachings alone are correct. Everyone else is wrong. That is just against our Buddhist tradition of modesty and compassion".

The recent effort by the Parian Dharma Association to bring Santi Asoke to account is by no means the first.

According to Sulak, the Ecclesiastical Order had set up an investigative committee led by legal and religious authorities to consider the status of Santi Asoke in 1984.

After four years of investigation, the committee agreed that Santi Asoke had indeed violated both religious and sccular laws concerning the Sangha.

The committee then submitted its findings to the security council for action. Much to the Sangha's disappointment, the answer, according to Sulak, was that the controversy was a highly sensitive matter politically. Therefore, the council agreed to put the matter into abeyance, and in the meantime to recommend that efforts should be made to strengthen the Sangha.

In other words, there was nothing to be done. Full stop.

Sulak says it is understandable that the conservative Sangha should be afraid of Santi Asoke's political power because, he says, the cult has been antagonistic all along. But it is another matter to exaggerate this power by describing him as a Thai version of the Ayatollah Khomeini.

The strict demands made by Santi Asoke upon its followers will tend to limit its appeal, in any case, he says.

Also, he stresses that it is necessary to separate Bangkok Governor Chamlong Srimuang from Phra Bhodhirak and to take account of the fact that Thailand's political and social structures have no room for extremism.

"As I see it, the Governor has more chance than Phra Bhodhirak of being politcally powerful. But he has done little to apply his strict Buddhist beliefs to the practices of the wider society, for example, the sale of alcohol. Change doesn't come easy."

Khomeini or not, what Santi Asoke has done is to show how much society wants monks who can communicate with the younger generation.

"It will be a pity if the clergy let this pass without considering it themselves.

"After all, Santi Asoke is but a symptom. We need to cure the illness itself."

by Sanitsuda Ekachai,
from *Bangkok Post* July 23, 1988.

EAST MEETS WEST – A DIALOGUE

Sulak Sivaraksa, a Thai Buddhist scholar, writer, teacher and peace activist, visited Sydney recently. His talks were held in a variety of locations like the Friends' Meeting House in Devonshire Street, the Teacher's Federation Hall, Sydney and Macquarie University, a Thai Buddhist Temple and All Saints Anglican Church in Hunters Hill. These diverse locations reflect the wide range of appeal that Sulak has – to Quakers, Buddhists, Anglicans, development workers, peace activists, teachers, students and other concerned citizens.

Above all his visit made me aware of how little we Australians know about our neighbours. We pay lip service to wanting to develop better relations with our Asian and Pacific neighbours, but in reality, as Sulak justly pointed out, we still largely regard ourselves as a European outpost, with our eyes turned towards either the UK, the US or Europe. Is there little wonder that our community leaders are still talking about 'social cohesion', as if the coulour of people's skin or the shape of their eyes was the key factor involved?

One of the main themes of Sulak's talks was the need of Australians in general, and development workers in particular, to have face to face dialogues with the people they wish to help, so they can understand them and their real needs. He cited examples of such lack of understanding in his own country, where farmers had been given or sold pesticides and fertilizers to improve their crop efficiency. However, although that may have increased the yield to some degree, these chemicals had polluted the waters of the rice fields, so that the fish and frogs – an additional supplement to their diet in between harvests – were poisoned and no longer edible. He was working with such villagers, helping them restore their traditional methods of agriculture.

Education was another area of great importance that we need to re-examine, according to Sulak. He regarded education in most countries to have been a failure, but as he pointed out; "In rich countries they can afford it, but in poor countries they can't afford it!" In the main he considered Western education to be concerned only with the head – not the whole human being. True education is life itself ! When speaking about development education he said: "There was no such thing as a developing country as opposed to developed contries, because we are all developing together." Indeed, this is the most important thing for all of us, to develop ourselves. For in Buddhism, the most important aspect of our humanity is the mind, through which we feel compassion for the suffering in the world, and it is this awareness we all need to develop, regardless of where we live.

On the other hand, the most destructive force in the world today, according to Sulak, is 'consumerism'. In his country and in much of Asia, "the middle classes want to be upper classes and the upper classes want to be like the middle classes in the USA." They all want to consume more and more. Consumer society worldwide is exploiting the valuable resources of the world. It is an example of the three evils of Buddhism – greed, hatred and delusion – and it's time we learnt to question this way of thinking and learn to respect other beings. He told of how some 90% of forests in his country had been destroyed since World War II, not to mention the ecological damage to the planet we are causing through consumerism, something we are all becoming a little more aware of in recent weeks with reports on the Greenhouse Effect and the Ozone layer damage. However, Sulak observed that bodies like religious groups, who were critical of multinationals and of the build up of nuclear weapons, had not as yet spoken out on consumerism. This was in spite of the fact that, "the most important values are created by consumer culture and the people who are most caught up in it are the middle classes." From his point of view, only the poor are not caught up in this process. They are suffering, but their suffering brings them wisdom. We must learn from the poor, we must have dialogue with them as equals.

Also, we need to open up to the South East Asian community, that is already in Australia, they too have much to teach us. Through his work with the Peace Brigades International, the Buddhist Peace Fellowship and other UN and NGO agencies and groups, Sulak was attempting to bridge the gaps through dialogue and reconciliation. He has worked in South East Asia, in Sri Lanka, and in Burma – trying to get opposing sides to sit down and talk to each other. He regards the Buddhist - Christian dialogue as another vital stepping stone to world peace. He feels the latter dialogue is only just beginning, as the World Council of Churches has moved away from the missionary approach to one of tolerance and understanding. In Australia, we still have much to learn about tolerance and dialogue – thank you Sulak for your wisdom!

Ben-Zion Weiss,
Buddhist Peace Fellowslip, Australia, September 1988.

A SOCIALLY ENGAGED BUDDHISM

Sulak Sivaraksa from Thailand (or Siam, the ancient name for his country which he prefers to use) is a Buddhist activist and scholar. He has been involved in work on appropriate development models for countries in the south, interreligious dialogue (including meetings arranged by the World Council of Churches), and reflections on Buddhist contributions to a just and peaceful society. He was imprisoned in 1984 on a charge of *lesé majesté* (offending the monarchy). His latest book *A Socially Engaged Buddhism* is reviewed on p.10. Roger Williamson interviewed Sivaraksa in Australia in January and presents an overview of his latest book.

Roger Williamson : First of all I would like to ask you about your latest book of writings on *A Socially Engaged Buddhism*. What are your preoccupations or current concerns? It seems that you have developed a very dynamic approach to the Buddhist faith.

Sivaraksa : As the title of the book shows, to be a Buddhist nowadays, you must have awareness of society and you must get socially engaged in a Buddhist way, that is you must be mindful all the time. But you must not get away from the society. To retreat is good, to meditate is good, being a Buddhist you must try to make peace within yourself but you must also relate to the social realities.

Unfortunately there is so much suffering in the world and you must try to do whatever you can to eliminate that suffering. To me that is the first teaching of the Four Noble Truths.

So what we are doing now is holding a meeting – the name may not be correct, but we call it a Progressive Buddhist Meeting. We use the term progressive, because we feel that a lot of Buddhists are not progressive enough in terms of being socially engaged in society. For instance, the World Fellowship of Buddhists have prayer meetings every few years and they say wonderful things, pass beautiful resolutions, but have not taken a single stand on any issue. I do not want to ennumerate the many other Buddhist organizations. I think some groups are doing good work, like the Buddhist Peace Fellowship, but in Asia I think this will be the first time that in our meeting outside Bangkok we will have representatives from Japan, Korea, from Vietnam, from Laos, Kampuchea, Burma, Bangladesh, India and Sri Lanka – so I think it could be a good bash. There will also be some members from the Buddhist Peace Fellowship in America and England, possibly from Australia as well.

So I think this meeting, small in numbers, twenty or thirty people, hopes to identify some issues of suffering and what we can do to help eliminate the suffering. At least to help them in the short term, and then perhaps to find the cause of the problem in order to eliminate the suffering in the long term.

For instance, in Sri Lanka, concerning the conflicts between the Tamils and the Singhalese – they need the Buddhist presence to help them. So after the meeting in Siam, we hope to go to Sri Lanka if only for a little time, if it is possible, at least to show them that we are with them, but of course in a non - violent way.

The Thais themselves have a lot of problems. We unfortunately export a lot of prostitutes to other countries, particularly Japan, and we want the Japanese Buddhists to be concerned. The Japanese Buddhists are in a wonderful position if they are concerned. They have plenty of money, but unfortunately they do not hope for too much from the politicians and the big companies. Luckily there are now some Buddhists, unfortunately they are only at the fringes, but they are committed to help us to identify some issues, and then to network together. We hope that these sort of things will be something to help solve some concrete problems, and restore some peace with dignity and with justice.

RW : I am very interested in your own intellectual development because I know that for many years you lived and worked in Britain, so you know the thought-world of Christianity almost as well as that of Buddhism. Can you tell me why you think a Buddhist approach to issues such as development is a particularly appropriate one? What are the spiritual strengths of the Buddhist tradition in you opinion?

SS : That the Buddhists have also been aware, you know, of social issues all along. Usually Great Britain was interested in only a certain type of book on Buddhism, because for Westerners, particularly in the 19th century and early in this century, when they came to Buddhism, they felt it was only meditation, retreat, because most of them came from the upper middle class and middle class and they wanted to forget about their society. That made Buddhism unhealthy.

If you look at the Asian realities, the monks have been involoved all the time, in the Buddhist way, not too involved, a little bit detached, but involved nonetheless, in social concern.

Unfortunately their role has been limited to the rural areas of society, and they have no understanding of the complexity of modern society, particularly at the national level.

That is why people like me, who have been exposed to internationalism, international conferences, can try to understand some of the complexity of urbanisation. We have to bring this home to them in order for them to see that Buddhism will only be relevant if it leads social concern from the micro-level to the macro-level.

For instance, the first precept against killing is wonderful, because even the thought of killing is bad in you. Yet, most Buddhists in many countries are not aware of the armament build-up, are unaware of militarism, so they have to be brought to awareness of this. That is linked to the First precept. The same with the second precept against stealing. Most of us are not aware that in international banking, there exists a kind of robbery, which is legal.

If you borrow money from them they charge so much and they take your money away and yet they give you so little interest. And the money in their charge they can invest in armament factories, they can invest even in drug-trafficking and so on, we have no control.

That is why we have to build up all this awareness. You can go on with all these precepts. My involvement now is to build up awareness among Buddhist leaders at various local levels and try to link them up. And once they are linked up, they can work together and we want to give them more factual information so that they can translate that into their sermons, and make their sermons more relevant to the modern world.

RW : Do you feel an affinity between your approach to

Buddhism and the more radical and committed forms of Christianity? Do you feel any problems with inter-religious dialogue between people who are committed to social justice?

SS : I see no problems between those who are committed to social change, if they have the right kind of motives. The only difference, for instance, with some of my progressive Christian friends, theologians, is only when they are using violent means. I respect them of course, but that is not our way of doing things. We really want to have a dialogue with them, we are not looking for converting them, but we respect them, understand them, but violence is not within our culture, it is not within our belief, our framework.

RW : On the question of violence and the use of violence as a last resort; many more progressive organizations, or organizations on the left, would argue that it is in fact necessary in order to be effective. How would you answer that from your own Buddhist faith and commitment to non-violence?

SS : As I said, I have respect for them, I would like to have dialogue with them, and if they want to hear from my point of view, from my own limited experience, the violent revolutions as they were, have not got a real victory. You can cite Vietnam, you can cite China, the people are still suffering. There is so much suffering, oppression. Because with armed struggle, violent revolution, you must have a cadre, you must have a party, you must have the kind of leadership where the rest are led.

But with non-violent transformation, everybody must be transformed. Of course, this is much more difficult, you see, and this is where you need that religious commitment and this faith, and you have to believe that the other side is as good as you are. You are not superior to them, you just cannot say that capitalism is wicked, but we have to change the capitalistic system. Of course in some cases they kill you, and you have to have that kind of faith to be nonviolent. It is not easy, I know. And of course it also has many weak points—whether to defend yourself—but I feel that this is the only way.

If we use armed struggle, particularly in this day and age, we have to rely on the Great Powers. Either you count on the Soviet Union, the Chinese or the Americans, or else you have got to be involved in drug trafficking, as you can see in the former warfare in Burma. I respect them, these people should be liberated and so on, unfortunately they have to deal in opium and the like, merely for survival, merely to buy arms, but should you help the first world to sell more arms? So I see a lot of negative implications, but as I said, I always respect them.

RW : In what areas do you see particular signs of hope, because, to use a Christian image, we often talk of "the kingdom of God" growing like a mustard seed? The growth is slow and unspectacular, and the growth of the forces of power and influence seems to be so overwhelmingly strong. Where do you see these signs of hope, these mustard seeds growing?

SS : Well, I think this is where I am with the Christians, you see all those gigantic things the devils are doing, they cannot do it all the time. Even now the consumer culture is so strong, but they cannot penetrate too long. People will get fed up with it. You know, you can see signs that people are looking for other different lifestyles. You know you have to think deep in order to go to something genuine. I think people cannot be pleased with greed, hatred and delusion all the time. I believe that on the whole you have wisdom in everyone. You have the seeds of God in everyone. I think that this really is the real hope and the real confidence in humanity.

RW : In terms of your own spiritual development and background, what were the factors that led you to leave London, the secure and, some would say, influential position in London, to come to this much more precarious life that you now lead?

SS : Well, I suppose that Buddhists would say karma, that one thing leads to another. I was influenced then by a thing that a Burmese said, I cannot even remember his name; we were teaching at the London School of Oriental and African Studies together. He just mentioned gently to me that he could not go home but I could, why didn't I try? And I felt the words he said made sense, why not go home and try? It was hard but I did try. Then, of course, I became successful as a publisher, as editor of a progressive magazine. Then again I was challenged by a prince. He said: "Your intellectual magazine is wonderful, you think. Do you know anything of the farmers?" I said, " I don't know anything about the farmers". He said: "Kid, your magazine is intellectual masturbation. The farmers are the hard core of the country, if you don't know how much they suffer while you are eating rice, you see you are playing". Then I had to go and live with the farmers and see how they suffer. Then it dawned on me, you see the first truth of the Four Noble Truths is suffering, that I must understand suffering, to find the cause of suffering, and from there on I have been in hot water one way and another. I still feel that I am in a much better position than they are, but I feel that I have to devote a part of my life at least to the cause of eliminating suffering.

RW : Do you see any conflict in the question of eliminating suffering, between trying to relieve peoples' social and economic needs and hardship and a more ultimate sense of release from suffering in terms of nirvana. Do you see a contradiction? How do these relate together in your understanding?

SS : I think they must go side by side. For instance, if you are in jail, as I was, obviously you want to be released as soon as possible. You can't wait for the elimination of the cause of suffering. You see, recently two Buddhist monks were to be executed by the Vietnamese government. We did what we could. I had a small part to play; they were not released but they got 20 years imprisonment. That is the first step. The second step is that we wish we can have them released by the Vietnamese government without the latter losing face. You have to do that, you see, for each case, and this is where a lot of time is used, it is time-consuming, but you have to do it.

Or to take another example, there are a lot of prostitutes. Some of them cannot even earn a livelihood. What can you do? You teach them English, and they get more money and they get more security. You have to do that in the short term, but in the long term you want to get rid of all prostitution, at least from your own country, since it is related to your own social development, political development, economic development.

To me, all these approaches are leading to the path of nirvana, you see, it may be the bodhisattva path, but I don't want to use such a grand term, but you've got to do that; if you don't have nirvana, or enlightenment as a goal, you lose heart. You have to have a goal in life. Whatever you do, you must also try to uplift yourself, because otherwise it is so much temptation. Sometimes you want to do it for glory and you want to become a hero and so on. No, I think you must be humble to do these things.

RW : For many Christians it is a great difficulty relating the precept of Jesus from two thousand years ago to the complexities of today's social life. How do you make that kind of bridge from the teaching of the Buddha to, for example, dealing with the question of multinational companies, of deforestation, or pollution and industrial waste? How do you make the bridge between the teaching and the demands of social reality today?

SS : Of course, I do not have the solution yet, I'm probing. In my thinking, and I think in most Buddhist thinking, you have to have a clear understanding that the essential teaching of the Buddha is against greed, hatred and delusion, and the Noble Eightfold Path is to be mindful, have right speech, right action and so on. I think that is basic. The other parts are what we will call complementary, some of which may have been useful two thousand years ago, some of which may have been useful one thousand years ago, I think you have to make these things clear. I think most religious tradition probably confuses them. Sometimes you want to interpret it literally – even what was maybe useful two thousand years ago. This is the crux, you see. In the Theravada tradition, they spent so much time on whether the monks should wear the robes this way or that way. This may also be useful or useless, but one must not spend too much time on that. Again you see, my experience in the Christian education, at least in the fifties. You got angry if you spent too much time on High Church, Low Church, two candles, six candles and I hope all this is now over. If you understand the essential teaching against greed, hatred and delusion, then you come to realize that the multinational corporations use consumerism to build up greed in people, and you have to understand the mechanism, and how to undo it. In the Buddhist way they call it pratityasamutpada (codependent origination of events), which means you have to understand all the conditions. Then I think perhaps you can solve problems of disarmament and so on. And this is why I feel that in this day and age, one tradition alone is insufficient. On one hand you use the Buddhist teaching as the main motive for doing things. But there are many things you can learn from Christians – the church has done so much study on the multinational corporations. It would be foolish not to work with them, not to collaborate with them and to learn from them. On the other hand, the World Council of Churches has been good to me, they have talked to me in a very friendly way. The Christians have been very, very slow on conservation of natural resources. So what have the Buddhists been doing? And luckily, we Thai and Tibetans are doing something, joint projects, on the Buddhist perception of nature. We want to share this with others. We want to learn from the

Muslims, on Islamic banking. How could we have something like that as an alternative? Buddhism was aware of that as a need. So these are things we have to learn from each other. And we could even learn from the Marxists – from their way of social analysis. But we must not learn from them the hatred of the bourgoisie or oppressors. We are probing, we do not have the answers yet. But we must, all religious traditions must, have an answer to this, otherwise you just use your religion to go to a Sunday service, to the Vihara, to the temple, and let the world go by, because the new religion is very powerful. The new religion of hatred, that is spiritually the new religion of greed, consumerism, capitalism, and worst of all it is the religion of ignorance and delusion. Education is in a bad state. You teach people only to develop their heads, and you teach them only in a fragmentary way. There is no wholeness in understanding life, so I think we must collaborate; Buddhists, Christians, Muslims and any other religion to tackle the three root-causes of suffering.

RW : Tell me too, in terms of your own involvement as a lay person, how you see the importance of Buddhist monastic life in the approach to the social questions of our time?

SS : Oh yes, I think Buddhist monastic life is very, very important. To me, it is the spring of pure water, because you see, they need not compromise with life. I have to. I have to earn a living, I have to support my family. They don't. Although we have 300,000 monks, many of them may not be that good, many of them compromise. Even if we have five, six or seven persons who don't compromise with the things that we lay people have to compromise with, they can devote all their time to understanding themselves, to understanding the social reality. They can help us a great deal, those who just spend their time meditating, they are wonderful. In all my writing, all my social understanding, I have drawn on them as a great source of inspiration. People like Thich Nhat Hanh in France and some of the monks in my country, I mean, their writing is so original, and so humble, and so helpful, so I think this is for me very important.

RW : Do you ever get worried or frightened that the spiritual resources acting in defence of creation and for justice are just too weak to protect humanity and the planet? Do you think there is a danger of them being crushed like grass under the wheel of a tractor?

SS : No, you see, I believe that if people become more mindful, I think things would change. Of course, the world could be blown up but I believe in the wisdom of the people.

For example, what the Russians are doing now may be fake for many people, but I feel it is something good, a good effort. People may not be excited by Mr Bush as a new president, but you have to have some hope too. Presidents these days are running Super Powers, and at the same time I don't have much faith in them; I have faith in small people. I mentioned two or three monks, to me they are very important. Three or four people here, at a meeting with 600 people, if you have three or four good people coming here, I think that is good. That thing will build up the seeds of peace, they will grow up. No, I have faith, and on the whole, I am not too pessimistic.

RW : In terms of the mechanisms of greed, the institutionalisation of greed in our world today, for example the way in which many of the poor countries in Latin America, in Asia and Africa are producing luxury goods for export to the West, how do you see those mechanisms of greed being reversed? How can you imagine an economics "as though people mattered" to use Schumacher's phrase?

SS : Well, I can't say very much about Latin America because I don't know it. But, I know my country. The government is now wanting to become like the Newly Industrialised Countries, wanting to catch up with South Korea, but I think they will fail. Because when I look at those monks, I mentioned two or three of them, but there are hundreds of monks, many of them are even illiterate, I see them building an alternative, in a way going back to our roots. They are making it more meaningful to contemporary self-reliance on the land, less chemical fertilisation, learning the old wisdom. This has led them to our own culture, to sing songs of collaboration, instead of competition and so on. Of course, this may fail also. But I feel that there is a chance if these initiatives could be translated more into a kind of network, that is why my progressive Buddhist meeting is meaningful to me. Now, even in Sri Lanka, where there is so much fighting, some of the monks even take up arms, unfortunately. But, some live in temples and they are reviving the collecting of food, and the meditation, amidst what is going on now. And now that the Khmer are hopefully going back to their country, we are helping them, we support all this. In this world, in the small area of South East Asia, it may not be counterbalancing, but people want to learn, you see. When they hear that things work, they will do things, they will switch. Then the politicians and the business people will catch up. They will understand the people, once the people are awakened, and we must help to awaken the people, and I think that the people will be able to awaken themselves.

THE MIRROR OF SIAM

In 1931 Winston Churchill's "half-naked fakir" arrived in London. Soon after his arrival, dressed in the simple homespun cotton cloth that was his personal uniform, Gandhi went to Buckingham Palace to take tea with the King. Chided for his dress, he later remarked: "The King was wearing enough for both of us."

That's how Larry Collins and Dominique Lapierre recall one of Gandhi's characteristics in their book *Freedom At Midnight*. The characteristic in question was Gandhi's adamant adherance to his style of clothing, his trademark.

Thailand's leading social critic, Sulak Sivaraksa, like the Indian pacifist leader, has a certain trademark himself. He wears his traditional Thai-style outfit when he's abroad, although he does try to cover up appropriately if it's cold. It's this very "trademark", a word he dislikes, that prompted a question from the audience when Mr. Sulak was addressing the Foreign Correspondents Club of Thailand one evening, as to why he was not riding a buffalo instead of driving a car. The point being that if Mr. Sulak was prepared to symbolically flaunt his national costume, he might as well go all the way.

For this interview, the volatile 56 year old social critic was sitting sedately at a table in the shady garden of his domicile located on Soi Santiparp (Peace), the renowned soi where several of Thailand's leading figures, including deputy Army C-in-C Gen Pichitr Kullavanijaya, have lived at different times. On the table a pot of Chinese tea and some miniature cups were placed next to a couple of books. One of the books, *The Godless Victorian*, by Noel Annan, was about Britain's Leslie Stephen, father of Virginia Woolf and the controversial cleric who turned agnostic.

Sulak Sivaraksa, clad in white *sua moh hom* and navy-blue fisherman's trousers, smiled his impish smile. As always, he was all set and ready for the interview. Any kind of interview, anytime.

"You can call it a trademark, or what, I really don't care," said the "radical royalist," referring to the way he's dressed. "But to me it's not, because I don't push it on other people like Santi Asoke. I look at it only as a personal characteristic," he added, warding off a red ant on his shirt.

As a scholar, and a critic at that, he is in the habit of elucidating his thinking. The simple "yes" or "no" hardly exists in the man's vocabulary. Not even when he was talking to the BBC recently on the subject of the world's monarchies, when the BBC interviewed HRH Princess Galyani Vadhana, HRH Princess Chulabhorn, M.R. Kukrit Pramoj and himself.

It was a programme which Mr Sulak thought was "unfortunate" for him. "I said lots of things, but they used only one line, and that was when I said I couldn't comment on one specific point or I'd be arrested," related Sulak, who in July 1984 was arrested on a *lesé majesté* charge.

On the subject of "trademarks, or personal uniforms, the social critic expanded: "I think it (trademark) is the major problem for Phra Bodhirak which I personally think is so petty. If you want to set up a shop selling the *pa tong ko* (croissant, Chinese style), go ahead, but have a new uniform. You can't have both the cake and not want to eat it. That's worse than dictatorship. Even Deng Xiaoping can be disputed."

Concerning the present ban on the Press reporting on Phra Bodhirak and Santi Asoke, a different question comes to mind. Thailand - land of the free - has always been proud of its tolerance toward religious expression, but is extremely sensitive toward any critical debate on Buddhism. Why is this?

"Because we don't have confidence in our own religion now, and as a result we lack that self-confidence. People don't know where religion is. It's confusing. They don't know if the phallic amulets distributed by Archarn Suan are right or wrong. When confused and lacking confidence, you'll end up attacking other people. A lion facing a barking dog will walk proudly past it, unafraid. Thais in the old days had confidence because they knew their own culture."

One would have thought that part of the Thai culture is in its flexibility – a culture of diversity?

"Only before when flexibility was combined with ethical elements. There was a limit, not now. Thai culture is gentle but it's at the same time strong.

"The strong aspect of Thai culture can easily be seen in Thai women. Look, how many Chinese men became Thais because they had Thai wives. No other countries in Southeast Asia allow that. Once you *saibaat* (offering food to the monks in the morning) you already lose your Chineseness. Being ordained as a monk, to the Chinese, is a terrible thing because you're accused of being lazy. Later on with all the ranks and titles bestowed on the Chinese, that too makes them Thai.

"The gentle part is the weakness. Especially now, a tourist gets off the plane and already he's shown pictures of Thai women money can buy. Even flexibility must have strong points in it," endorses Mr. Sulak, who comes from a Sino-Thai background himself.

The role of social arbiter, who's regarded by the younger generation as the "lamp of the young Thai intellectuals" is not necessarily an easy one to assume in Thai society today. Critics abound, pointing now and then their own fingers at the social critic himself. Arrogant. Controversial. Outrageous. Eccentric. And to some, "no solid intellectual standing."

But for this British-educated barrister-at-law, he stressed his views are "very clear, perhaps as lucid as all the mirrors" he often uses to reflect things cultural, social, spiritual and economic.

In his paper, presented recently in Poland entitled "Tolerance for Diversity of Religion or Belief: Its Importance for Social and Economic Development," he, as always, emphasises the four aspects of development – cultural, spiritual, social and economic. If all four can be integrated then there could be real human development, says the paper. Development can only occur at a pace at which humans and other beings matter, it further points out. In addition to this, the rise of the secular intellectual has been a key factor in shaping the modern world.

Asked to briefly describe Thailand's current situation in each of these four aspects, he pondered:

"It's a pity that these four aspects are bing segregated at the moment. Everything is being thought of in terms of economics. The Prime Minister's policy in turning war zones into marketplaces. The case where shop houses next to Chulalongkorn University campus are being evacuated. Townhouses rise in rural areas. Burmese students are sent back to Rangoon in exchange for the trees in Burma and are killed. These things I'm gravely worried about.

"Development must start from a spiritual level, not spiritual in a religious sense. But we must ask ourselves who we are, and what do we live our lives for. 'Breathe in peace, breathe out happiness,' like the Vietnamese Thich Nhat Hanh says."

From this point, Mr. Sulak believes that people will see the importance of other humans and beings and see that everything is "interrelated". Like looking at a sheet of paper, you'll see it came from a tree, the air, the clouds and the earth. Once ordinary people and everyone have developed spiritually and culturally, other things will follow.

"Politics, which means the power to bargain, will be theirs, not just belonging only to Gen. Chatichai, or Gen. Chavalit," he snapped, wrapping up his thoughts on that particular matter.

Sulak, the "radical royalist," as John Ralston Saul in his *The Paradise Eater,* describes him. Sulak accepts the description, but argues that he's also a "conservative", and that he believes in both "change" and "preservation".

Specifically, he said he respects the traditional system of culture whereby the village and families count with the sangha being the centre. The *rabobe baan* (village, families and sangha) stresses the spiritual and cultural values and economics is a secondary factor. The *rabobe muang* (city, state and government), says Sulak, started in King Rama V's reign. "It, however, deteriorated in Field Marshal Sarit (Thanarat)'s era."

"The old democracy gave priority to the sangha. Democracy today is an imitation of the West," explained the critic, patiently. "The new system doesn't consider villagers smart, only the Western-educated elites.

"I'd like to ask who are the important villagers today? It's the sangha, because they comprise children of the poor who can't afford regular schooling. That's why I try to protect the sangha. I'd like them to be society's model. Today we must all help one another, whatever religion, at the grassroots. Above that, religion too can be turned into an economic tool. I'm not interested in that level.

"Economics theoretically is supposed to be amoral. But in reality it is in fact immoral. It's long been a debatable subject, since Victorian times, like in this book (he pointed to Leslie Stephen's book). How to make economics moral is the point. Schumacher attempted to do that, proving it has to be both ethical and spiritual. Economic theories today exploit the poor, because we still have to depend on the superpowers. Economics today sent Burmese students to Rangoon in exchange for the trees in Burma so they get killed. Economics today sees Japan buying our forests to use the wood to make chopsticks."

Sulak Sivaraksa's point, says he, is that change must come from below, and that all new paradigms take place from the grassroots. That the powers-that-be "dare not touch." He gave as an illustration, the "buffalo bank" set up by one northeastern monk.

"We have to build a base, and that base is the mass, the people. Not in the same sense as the CPT (Communist Party of Thailand) who intoxicated the masses whilst the party itself was the elite. You can see that's partly why China, or the Soviet Union failed. You can respect the people only by having a village system. Deep down, people don't really have respect for the mass, and this slips now and then. Look at our Interior Minister for example," explained the critic, who's also known to be a knowledgeable historian.

Mr. Sulak's educational background and his upbringing have made a "major impact" upon his personality. He was born in Bangkok to a well-to-do Sino-Thai family and the only son of his father from the first wife. He said he was "spoiled" as a child and always "had his way." His elementary and secondary education was at Assumption College, and at the age of 12 he went into the monkhook at Wat Thong Noppakhun and remained in the monkhood nearly two years.

After Assumption, he attended St David's University College at Lampeter, in the UK, and later was at the Middle Temple where he was called to the Bar. Whilst studying, he worked for a short period for the BBC in London. Looking back, he says that the significant influence Britain had on him was the constructive and critical way of thinking as learned from all the classics. "Besides," added Sulak. "Britain is not racist, good friends are more important. Look at Lawrence of Arabia who could die for the Arabs."

He attributed his being a "radical" to having started since

his childhood. "Other kids were reading Pol, Nikorn, Kim-nguan (popular classic comedy series at the time). I went to see the *lakorn chatree* (folk play) which was looked down upon by the upper class," he related smilingly. "But I don't know why I always had to fight with my teachers all the time."

When in the monkhood, he once posted a sign all over the wat attacking one monk who "hit" him on the head - "I woke him up in the morning to open up the temple because it was time to say prayers, and he didn't like it." Another incident which marked a dark spot in his life was when in a rage, he once banged his aunt's head against the wall because she was saying bad things about his mother. He was 10 years old then.

But times have changed the man. Now 46 years later after that event, Mr. Sulak is a totally different man, or so he definitely believes. Even long before he started wearing his trademark attire, he was active in both the sangha and secular worlds. Along with Dr. Puey Ungphakorn and some others he founded the "Society for Conservation of National Treasures and Environment" (SCONTE). He was the first person who organised English sermons at Wat Bavorn.

He has founded or co-founded many philanthropic institutes in the country, one of the more significant being the "Santi Pracha Dhamma Institute" (peace, democracy and righteousness).

For the past two decades he has helped with the sangha almost full time. One important writing was *Khan Chong Song Asoke* (Mirroring the Santi Asoke) in 1982. Said he, "Had Santi Asoke listened to some of my advice, at least I don't think they would have gotten into this kind of trouble." In the early Seventies, Sulak, who by that time had established his name as a celebrated public speaker and writer, founded the *Sangkhom Sart Parithat (Social Science Review)*, a publication which marked a giant step for the intellectuals of the time.

At 56, Sulak is still running hard. He's still acting like society's "mirror". He's still busy "sloughing off" everything, peeling off all the defects. He remains adamant about using the word "Siam" instead of "Thailand", even though it may seem eccentric to other people, because he insists the word is a "neutral term, like Britain, which covers several races," and which was changed because it was "forced" upon the people.

"Despite the fact that Siam was not subjugated politically, she was colonised intellectually, culturally and educationally. The effects of this type of colonisation are almost impossible to reverse," writes Sulak at one point in his paper on "Global Problem Solving: A Buddhist Perspective" to be presented in Mongolia this August.

Mr. Sulak Sivaraksa obviously doesn't see Siam entering a new "golden era." His role is that of an activist on behalf of tradition, against the tidal wave of Western modernisation that the Kingdom is so happily galloping toward.

He is a social critic whose voice will not be stilled; a fervent Buddhist who believes that in self-knowledge and self-awareness are to be found the keys to a modern Siamese drama in which the four strands of life can be woven into a peaceful future.

'In Character' by Kanjana Spindler,
Bangkok Post Frinday June 9, 1989.

LIVING AT SULAK'S

I stumbled upon Achan Sulak quite by accident. As my teaching contract in Japan was drawing to a close earlier this year, I began searching for possible volunteer work opportunities in Asia. Some friends happened to be coming to a conference in Thailand (or Siam as Sulak refers to it) arranged by Sulak and his colleagues, and I was invited to tag along to meet some of their contacts.

Upon arriving, I found that the participants at the conference were all interested in Buddhism and social action — both things I knew nothing about. Though these people and their organizations were all complete strangers to me outside of my two friends, I was overwhelmingly impressed by their commitment and sincerity upon meeting them, and thoroughly enjoyed the four days of discussion which followed.

Although I am not a member of their faith, one of Sulak's budding social organizations with a distinctly Buddhist orientation took me on as a volunteer, and he and his family made room for me in the library of their home.

Most of the four months I've been working, Sulak has been away speaking at various places around the planet. I believe he must be famous in the world of social activism because whenever someone asks me where I'm staying, I usually answer, "with a family". If they ask further, "On a homestay? How did you arrange that?", I have to answer "It's actually the home of my boss's boss. I live in their library." Inevitably, the next question is, "Who?", and the answer almost always brings a soft whistle or note of surprise. This has always made me feel slightly uncomfortable that I should live with the family of a person I have never heard of before, whom everyone seems to know but me.

At any rate, I'd like to relate to you some of what I have observed of this man.

One morning, I was up at 6 a.m. which is very rare for me. Outside in the garden, Sulak was busy scrawling away in Thai. He asked me to join him for breakfast. So I plopped down into a chair in my sarong and T-shirt, still rumpled and bleary-eyed from sleeping. I asked him what he was working on. He said it was a very interesting book on Buddhism in the west by an American fellow. He felt it was extremely important for the Thai people to be able to read this book and was therefore translating the text into Thai. The ideas, he went on to say, contained in the book, were very provocative. I asked him if he agreed with those ideas and he laughed as he replied, "Oh no! Not at all. I just think it's very important for people here to have access to many different alternative points of view."

At different times, he has been described as a social critic, a Thai intellectual, a writer, a lawyer and a leading activist. Seems like he must be a hard being to define. Perhaps every individual is. I do know that he is the chairman of several Thai and international organizations, that he has written several books, has been to and spoken in most of the places I've heard of and many I haven't, has been jailed for things he wrote, owns a bookstore and a restaurant which are run by his wife, is the head of a publishing house which is run by his brother and has a steady stream of assorted visitors coming to the house to see him.

He is a real character — a sense of humour and a good speaker. An excellent showman with a light and charming side as well as a serious, "roll up the shirt sleeves" side that can, at times, become fairly thunderous and enraged. His working style can be fatherly, advisory and full of comradery (I have never seen him with superiors) or it can be like a gigantic, steamroller looming over everyone, storming down the path trying to get the job done, rolling out any inefficiency. If that is the case, you'd better have all your ducks lined up when he calls on you, because if you're "off", even a bit, and stick out, you will surely get crushed down flat. I have a feeling that the path behind him is littered with a few flattened ex-followers who have never really recovered and might be in no real hurry to collaborate closely with him again.

But indeed he gets the job done, and people come to him to ask for his help for just that reason.

Though he seems quite the gentleman — very cultured and intelligent, he can be quite brusque in dealing with people. I'm very comfortable with that because many of my superiors in the past were that way. But I have a feeling that he is not completely comfortable with that and longs to lead a more peaceful life along aesthetic lines.

So far, his books and papers (at least the ones I've read) seem extremely well-thought out and visionary. His is not completely against the mainstream as are many in the alternative community. He often works with and through the establishment, though sometimes by antagonizing it, to promote change.

Lest I forget to mention, the man is driven — a workaholic who in turn demands a great deal from those surrounding him. That and his air of absolute authority instill fear in many of his followers or would-be disciples.

The night before last, a man in his mid-30's arranged a meeting for all those who work with Sulak. It was a large dinner with maybe 20 people crowded around the table, including Sulak's 8-year-old daughter, Ming. The organizer of the meeting, Yai, had worked with Sulak in the past but had separated from him. Many of the younger men gulped back liquid courage in the form of Mekong whiskey.

After awhile, the floor was opened to comments about the group as a whole, and Sulak in particular. It was very informal, like any dinner of co-workers and friends that have known each other for a long time. Yai started off. He wanted to air his grievances and voice his criticism. Others followed suit, and it went on for a few hours.

Comments arose about Sulak's temper, past followers, longtime disciples, his absolute authority and demanding expectations. They asked him many questions and he answered all of them.

What impressed me was the honesty and candor all around the table. There seemed to be very little defensiveness. Spouses of followers also voiced their thoughts. It was incredibly healthy, something I had never witnessed before. Obviously these feelings had been brewing for a long time.

Sulak stated that he does get angry and does demand complete control in order to get things done. Whether that justifies the extent to which he sometimes goes is not for an outsider to judge, but he is human like the rest of us and it seems much more constructive that he and everyone else understands this fact well.

At a brief lull in the conversation, he said gently, "I'm no prophet".

Indeed it seems irresponsible for any of us to force another human being up on a pedestal. It will cause much disillusionment when that person's human flaws are exposed, and we have no right to expect someone to be superhuman simply to fulfill our wishes or needs.

He continued on and talked about the fact that he wants people to challenge him and be critical. That is, according to him, the only way. He says that two of his senior followers, Dr. Uthai and Phipop Dongchai, often talk about him and complain about him, but inevitably they are harsher to him directly and have challenged him countless times face-to-face, and that is why he loves them.

Dr. Uthai, who speaks fluent English and is a hilarious character himself, once mentioned that he met Sulak as a young student. Sulak was the voice that reached many of the young people then. They used to sit on the floor in homes and discuss ideas for hours on end.

Pracha, my boss, who is younger than Uthai, has also said that he met Sulak as a student. It seems Sulak was the political science club prof at the University and was a great inspiration for Pracha and many of his peers. Pracha, who I respect very much, says that they wanted to change the world in those days, and had very big ideas. But I will not be surprised, when all is said and done, if Sulak and his legacy; indeed Sulak himself is the legacy of those before him, do bring about great changes in this world.

Finally, towards the end of the evening, after much food and drink, one young man, perhaps 25 years old, stood up and said, "I am ready to work with you Sulak."

One final observation that I'd like to share with you, happened just a few hours ago. Sulak came into the library last night at 10 p.m. with a stack of papers. I already have loads of work to do, and will have problems getting it done before I leave in eight weeks. It was Saturday night. But that fact doesn't really register with him.

His first question: "Want some more work"?

"Mmmm", I said, "I'm going to have trouble getting the work I have now finished before I leave."

He said, "It's just reading really."

It was a script about an inch and a half thick on this Vietnamese monk's teachings. It's something I wanted to read at some point, although I didn't mention that. He wanted me to proofread it. It had a lot of mistakes in it, but they were mostly just typos. The theme of the text was the interrelatedness of all things and the point is that in order to work for peace, you must first BE PEACE yourself. Well, he asked me to see what I could do. Today, Sunday, I got sick. My body isn't used to Thai food yet. So lucky for Sulak, I had to stay home all day and so had time to proofread. He came in at 4 p.m. to see how I was doing and was happy to hear I was halfway through the pile.

He turned to leave, but stopped just as he was stepping through the doorway to say, "Well try to have it finished by Tuesday, and take care of your health, and .... BE PEACE!" BE PEACE?!? HERE?!? Incredibly funny!

As a volunteer, I came here hoping to be useful. The only way I could contribute was by working hard, since I have no special skills or knowledge. So I was prepared, and am comfortable here in the house of Sulak.

— Sherry Yano June, 1989.

REVIEW OF THE FIRST EDITION

Sulak Sivaraksa, *Siam in Crisis* (Bangkok : Komol Keemthong Foundation, 1980) pp. 462

Sulak Sivaraksa, the always persistent and sometimes abrasive gadfly on the Thai body politic, in the collection of essays that comprise *Siam in Crisis*, has given us his personal critique of Siamese society as it struggles to overcome a "crisis" of national identity. In the initial section, the author, in a series of informative biographical sketches, evokes the richness of Thailand's literary and artistic heritage as personified by such renowned scholars as Prince Naris, Prince Dhani, Prince Damrong and Phya Anuman. Sulak's admiration for these exemplars of Thai culture is not limited to their professional excellence. Scholarly attainment, artistic prowess, technical expertise, must always be complemented by modesty, honesty, integrity, simplicity and virtue in order to demand and warrant respect. These role models in the cultural sphere were exceptionally adept, in the author's opinion, in maintaining their Thai "essence" and identity while at the same time utilizing, to the best advantage, knowledge and experience gained from contact with the West. We are constantly being cautioned by Khun Sulak not to forget our cultural heritage, to understand and appreciate our past if we are to successfully cope, at present and in the future, with the pressures of modernization, westernization, and "cultural imperialism". Khun Sulak castigates the heedless imitation and copying of and the unthinking borrowing from the West. He advises a more judicious selection that will not sacrifice the "quality of life" based on traditional Thai religious, social and cultural values.

As a logical extension of the need to understand our own Thai identity, Khun Sulak pleads for more knowledge and appreciation of our Asian neighbors. Just as the author rails against the paternalism of the West and particularly, what he often perceives as the economic, educational, political, social and cultural "imperialism" of the U.S. and, to a certain extent, Japan, he is similarly critical of Thai paternalistic attitudes towards Laos.

The author eloquently pleads for a more democratic, more equalitarian society. He is withering in his criticism of privilege, abuse of power, exploitation, and corruption. Just as scholars must be virtuous as well as wise, so political leaders must govern with honesty, integrity, and simplicity, ever imbued by the Dharma.

The last section of *Siam in Crisis* is devoted to an exposition of Buddhist principles and values as illustrated in the lives of revered bhikkhu elders. As might be expected, Khun Sulak's choice of role models in the Sangha complements his selection in the lay world. Buddhadasa Bhikkhu, Paññananda Bhikkhu, Dhammavitaka Bhikkhu, Phra Dhammacetiya exemplify not only modern and scholarly attainment but also the virtues of simplictity and humility. Each of these monks is concerned, as is the author, with the problem of applying the Dharma to the daily concerns, problems and needs of the modern-day world. How can the Dharma be made meaningful to the younger generation? How can the Dharma be explained, be spread? Imaginative propagation techniques are discussed. The author displays a deep knowledge and appreciation of Buddhist philosophy, disciplince, ritual, education and art.

Khun Sulak holds up the shining mirror of "truth and beauty" to Thai society and more often than not we see the murky reflection of a society beset by contradictions, a society in tension, in conflict, in crisis. The author is most adept and eloquent as a critic. The prescriptions for reform, for innovation, for change, are less precise. There is a harkening back to a yesteryear when an aristocracy of excellence; moral, professional, academic, reigned supreme while the "common man" enjoyed a relatively just, free and untroubled life.

Khun Sulak, himself, may be viewed as a mirror image of the society he so expressively analyzes. He struggles, as does Thai society, for identity. He faults others for debasing themselves before the coffers of foreign aid, and, yet, he admits he has availed himself of such support and often basked under the umbrella of refuge and protection such foreign support may provide. He rebukes the posturing, the pretense, the posing so much a part of a grasping and materialistic society. And yet, Khun Sulak often postures and poses, uses hyberbole and sometimes intemperate language. Granted it is for effect. One has the impression he often takes a somewhat extreme position so as to elicit a reaction, to create intellectual controversy. The author admonishes his readers to beware of foreign influence, control, authority. And, yet, Khun Sulak has conspicuously benefited from the education, experience, and the personal contacts he has so assiduously cultivated in the world beyond the borders of his beloved Siam. He warns us of the difficult, but necessary, task we face in maintaining our cultural balance, personal integrity and national identity in the face of pressures of materialism and modernization and the threats to security as the international game of power politics is played out. The biting chastisement of the West comes from one who has been fondly labelled as the "last Englishman" by his peers. The author's photograph on the back cover of *Siam in Crisis* symbolizes the identity crisis he articulates with such precision : the rolled umbrella complements the graceful *panung*.

The author's obvious sincerity and integrity tends to offset his abrasiveness, carping, and testiness. A careful reading of Khun Sulak's essays leads to a better appreciation and understanding of Thai culture and of the identity crisis besetting Thai society. It will also illuminate the search for identity that such intellectuals as Khun Sulak have striven for with such determination.

William J. Klausner.
Journal of the Siam Society Volume 69 (1981).

INTERPRETER OF TWO CULTURES

S. Sivaraksa, *A Socially Engaged Buddhism*, Thai Inter-Religious Commission for Development, Bangkok, 1988. 206 pp. (Distributed by Kled Thai Co. Ltd., Suksit Siam, 1715 Rama IV RD., Bangkok 10500, Thailand.)

Sulak Sivaraksa is very well placed to be an interpreter of two cultures to one another. He is a Siamese Buddhist who knows the Western and Christian thought worlds well. He is thus able to describe the important contribution of Buddhist approaches to reverence for life to the current world crisis in ways which those of us trained in Western ways of expressing ourselves can readily understand. In order to give something of the flavour of his work one could say that if Buddhists had theology, Sulak would be a liberation theologian. Immediately that opens up a number of important questions for dialogue. How should Christians and Buddhists relate to one another? What methods are appropriate in the struggle for liberation?

His work is a bold attempt to be true to his spiritual roots and at the same time to expand the horizons of Buddhist social thinking. Buddhism is a way of life which seeks to put an end to suffering. Sulak's analytical skills tell him that suffering is not just caused by what happens to an individual. He sees structural causes for much of the avoidable suffering in the world. In what seems to me to be a completely consistent step, he then argues that an adequate Buddhist response therefore has to address the structures which cause the suffering.

A central chapter in this book is entitled "A Working Paper on a Buddhist Perception of a Desirable Society in the Near Future" (pp. 49-72). This is a programmatic study prepared on behalf of the United Nations University. In it, he both expounds the spiritual roots for a Buddhist social theory and explains some of the reasons why such a theory and indeed the practice has often been lacking within Buddhism.

If understood in an individualistic sense, Buddhism provides strong motivation for an individual personally not to kill, but does little to solve the question of how to protect victims from the consequences of structural violence. Similarly, if the Sangha or community of monks is understood as a community separated from the world, little mitigating effect occurs for rectifying social ills.

Sulak's proposal seems to me to be completely convincing in terms of its approach. To be a consistent Buddhist, once one understands the structural causes of much suffering one sees that effective alleviation of suffering, the Buddhist goal, requires not just personal abstention from killing, but analysis and appropriate action to stop killing occurring. It means not just abstention from theft, but opposition to the identifiable structures and mechanisms which make the poor poorer and the very poor die. Thus the five traditional "*sila* or basic rules" serve as a "framework for building desirable societies". They are as follows: "1) To abstain from killing. 2) To abstain from stealing. 3) To abstain from sexual misconduct. 4) To abstain from false speech. 5) To abstain from intoxicants that cause heedlessness" (p. 59).

To understand these precepts in a structural way means to make the association between killing as the basis for war, the dumping of radio-active waste in the Third World and other ecological problems. It means seeing the link between truthtelling and the distortions of mass media. Right livelihood requires reflection on the New Economic Order from the Buddhist perspective (examples from pp. 66-7). Sulak stresses the importance of meditation, in order to uncover the roots and the effects of damaging social structures, patterns of thought and behaviour. But his religious outlook is not one which ignores physical need. "... Strong international institutions must grow out of responses to actual material needs. Our karmic burdens, our accumulated structures of greed, hatred, and ignorance, are actually precious gifts, for only by working with such material is there an opportunity for liberation" (pp. 68-9). The very international mechanisms which distort and destroy us as people paradoxically also create the possibility of "liberation from the affluent society" (title of 1967 talk by Marcuse) and real international solidarity with people in other parts of the world. "If armament links closely with hatred (*dosa*), consumer culture works hand-in-glove with greed (*lobha*) and lust (*rāga*) out of sheer delusion or ignorance (*moha* or *avija*).

It uses the mass media for advertisement against truth, using falsehood to capture the mind of most people and to look down upon indigenous culture of self-reliance in the name of progress and modernization" (p. 70).

As one would expect, the emphasis is on dialogue and peaceful change, the thinkers cited include Thich Nhat Hanh, Merton, Gandhi and Schumacher. In one of the ironies of the wider ecumenism which is coming to be, he first met Thich Nhat Hanh at a meeting on inter-faith dialogue arranged by the World Council of Churches. As a result, his organisation published *The Miracle of Being Awake*, Thich Nhat Hanh's widely read book on meditation for peace activists. Apart from that friendship which emerged, Sulak rates the meeting "a great failure" – and in an amusing misprint indicates that it "was the first such meeting the WCC had tired" (p. 182).

If you want to discover how one goes from reading law in England to a charge of *lesé majesté* in Thailand, from the BBC and London School of Oriental and African Studies to discussion of such topics as buffalo banks, this is an important book for you. I am pleased to have been involved on behalf of the British Council of Churches in the international and inter-faith network of concern which protested against his imprisonment. It has therefore been a special pleasure to meet with and learn from him.

The chapters in this book are very mixed, some on Siamese Buddhism and personalities, some on self-reliant development, others on Buddhist - Christian dialogue. He learned inter-faith dialogue at an early age with fellow students in Wales who thought he was "not a bad chap" but wondered what would happen to him after he died. His response: "Your God is a just and merciful God. I am sure he will be kind to me. Your people have been very good to me here already, although you are, as you said, imperfect Christians. So your Christian God will be far better to me and to all others than you could really perceive" (pp. 146-7).

To finish with, a truly ecumenical – in the sense of "the whole inhabited earth" – quotation: "India certainly had a prophet in the Mahatma, who combined the best elements in Hinduism, Buddhism and Christianity, for a new lifestyle, which was deeply rooted in the Indian spiritual tradition. Gandhi really searched for a just and sustainable socio-political and economic order. Hence he rejected the Western model of development and its technological arms of oppression. We need to go back to Gandhi, as we should go back to the Buddha and to Christ, with proper historical perspectives and with critical awareness, for their messages to be perceived as relevant to a more just society" (p. 96).

Roger Williamson
Life & Peace Review Vol. 3 No. 2, 1989.

WESTERN CULTURE UNMASKED

For something like a century and a half the Siamese people have been aligning themselves to Western culture, with some peculiar results.

Prior to the reign of King Mongkut (Rama IV) and his 'co-king'Pin Klao, the Siamese looked upon Westerners as a species of Yaksa; hairy, red, drunken and violent, lacking in all the civilized graces but blessed with admirable technical skills, particularly in the arts of war.

King Mongkut and King Pin Klao seem to have been the first (since King Narai) to suspect that there was more to the *Farangs* than met the eye, and that as they had conquered India and Lanka and even humbled great China, the Siamese had better study these strange but in some ways enviable creatures. This was the highly intellectual beginning of Siam's Westernization. Threafter the process speeded up as King Chulalongkorn (Rama V) sent his sons and nephews to study abroad. Some learnt wisdom ; many learnt snobbery.

It was very much a from the top down process with princes becoming English gentlemen, leaving the Natives to Thai indigenous culture, until the 1960s when the massive American military presence here exposed Siamese commoners to the creative and corrosive ways of the West.

The Westernization of Siam was a success in that it preserved the nation from formal colonialism, but cultural colonialism sank deep roots. The most dismal aspect of the process was that it required the Siamese to despise their colonialised neighbours, and to deny the Indo-Lankan origins of their culture. Thus they became cultural orphans.

Another interesting aspect of Siam's Westernization was that it was largely non-intellectual. The princes learnt the sciences and administration but few bothered to enquire into the philosophy behind them. (Even King Vajiravudh, for all his play acting and poetry, was in many ways a 'hearty'.) Of course there have been exceptions, but few of them prospered at home. Prince Prisadang, brilliant constitutionalist and Buddhist scholar, was thrown in the trash bin. Poet and historian Prince Chand Chirayu never received official honours here, though he is praised internationally. Chit Phumisak, Marxist historian and poet was shot when he was thirty six.

In Sulak Sivaraksa, author of *Western Culture Unmasked*, we have another true scholar who has also undergone tribulations and official neglect, but who stubbornly manages to make himself heard. Deeply imbued with his own Hindo-Buddhist culture, he has gone to the trouble of acquiring an understanding of the Greek and Jewish traditions upon which Western civilization is based, and this he reveals in the book under review.

The result is twofold. First he gives a Western reader pride and pleasure that an outsider should have gone to such lengths to acquire true insight. The second effect is alarming because, as an outsider, he can present the face of the West with the clarity of a mirror, unlike the Westerner, owner of the face, who can only imagine what he looks like.

He reminds me of Lin Yu Thang (Son of a Chinese Methodist minister) who could show his readers just what a joke the Christianity taught by the missionaries was, as perceived by the Chinese. This, surely, is a service to humanity, and so is the work of Khun Sulak.

I shall not attempt to discuss the content of *Western Culture Unmasked* except to note that the title is a Thai literary joke and the author's purpose is not to 'unmask' but to explain, which he does lucidly.

He shows how Western thought developed from primitive necessity to great sophistication, how it was used during the colonial period to prove superiority over other cultures, and how its outer trappings were used to confirm the superiority of the Siamese ruling class over the unenlightened natives, despite having over two thousand years of Hindo-Buddhist civilization behind them.

This book should be translated into English so that Westerners may see themselves in an icy clear mirror.

These remarks on *Western Culture Unmasked* lead me to a comparison between S. Sivaraksa and M.R. Kukrit Pramoj, another old England student and bridgemaker between the cultures. They fight bitterly, much to my distress when I first began to read them. Later I realised that had they loved one another they would have become a very tiresome Gang of Two. As vicious sparring partners they bring to light problems and gain the attention of dull people who would not otherwise think.

S. Sivaraksa tends towards the Western fault of pointing the finger of accusation, no matter whom it may irritate. Kukrit has the Siamese vice and cracks his joke, whether true or not, at any expense. Siam needs them both.

Western Culture Unmasked should be translated in western languages. Occidentals would be both shocked and enlightened to see their face as others see them.

Michael Wright
Bangkok Bank Ltd. and, Silpa-Wattanatham Monthly
JSS 1988.

THE MAKING OF THE THAI INTELLECTUAL TRADITION

The first thing about this book that captures our attention is its title: to paraphrase it in English - *"The Making of the Thai Intellectual Tradition,"* The discussion of the subject takes only seventy-three pages. We may doubt if such an encompassing and significant topic can be thoroughly discussed, even in an abbreviated form, within that length. But this is S. Sivaraksa. As usual, his writing is designed to be rather a provocative argument for further studies and discussions than a definitive exposé of the subject.

The book is actually the publication of a lecture which the author delivered at the main hall of Wat Mahathat. The occasion, sponsored by the *Pajarayasarn* Journal and the Institute of Buddhist Research, Mahachulalongkorn University, was held to celebrate the eightieth birthday of Phra Depvisuddhimedhi (Nguam Indapañño) who is commonly known by his alias - Buddhadasa Bhikkhu. This tells us much about the theme of the book. In a sense, the lecture is a discussion of the crucial role which Buddhadasa has played in upholding and enriching what S. Sivaraksa deems the Thai intellectual tradition.

But what exactly is this tradition? This question may first come to our mind. As a matter of fact, the title of the book may even be literally translated as "Intellectual creation in the Thai way." There have been many presentations on other areas of "Thainess" such as ways of living, habits, inclinations, arts, architecture, and so forth. Among them, to recall, is a collection of S. Sivaraksa's views on these matters, published by Kled Thai Press under the title *Yu Yang Thai* (Thai ways of living). We may as well trace these discussions back to one of the earliest and authoritative definitions of "Thainess" given by Prince Damrong

Rajanuphab in his lecture on the characteristics of Thai politics and government in the past. But, to the reviewer's limited knowledge, this is the first time that an attempt has been made to define Thainess in its intellectual sense (that is, without resorting to a specific sphere – whether it be political, cultural, or economic, etc.).

The answer to this question lies in the word *satipanya* itself. Perhaps, to translate the word as "intellect" is to confuse the matter. Although the Thai word generally conveys an idea similar to its English counterpart, it nonetheless implies, in its etymological roots, a specific approach to knowledge. That approach, albeit no longer conspicuous in the day-to-day usage of the word, is the Buddhist cultivation of mindfulness and wisdom.

This is precisely what S. Sivaraksa means by "the Thai way of intellectual creation"; a way of thinking which holds Theravada Buddhist teachings as its perennial core and selectively incorporates other temporal elements in order to strengthen its feasibility in place and relevance in time. The dynamics of the Thai way of thinking, according to this definition, lie thus, on the one hand, in the ability to preserve the genuineness of the teachings and, on the other hand, in the genius in applying them to changing situations.

S. Sivaraksa points to three major innovations and contributions that constitute the milestones of the Thai intellectual heritage.

The first was King Ramkhamhaeng's accomplishment in establishing an effectual model of a Theravada Buddhist state in the Thai social and political contexts of the thirteenth century (A.D.). Under his leadership, the Thais were able to liberate themselves culturally and intellectually from the old Angkorian-Hinduist empire. The King was regarded, not as a god reincarnated, but rather as a benevolent ruler whose legitimacy depended much on his practice of the Dharma. Although animism, superstition and elements of Brahminism were maintained and incorporated into the Thai world-view, they became second and subservient to Buddhism.

The second was the composition of *Traiphum Phra Ruang* (The three worlds according to King Ruang) done by King Lithai, Ramkhamhaeng's grandson. The book, in S. Sivaraksa's words, "was the most important and the most fascinating treatise written from the Sukhothai period up to the middle of the Rattanakosin period." (p.17) It became the major source of the Thai intellectual life for centuries. From the end of the Sukhothai period down to the reign of King Mongkut of Bangkok, the text had survived as the authority on the paradigmatic views concerning cosmology, politics, and ethics. Anybody, who is familiar with Thai mural paintings, knows very well how the influence of *Traiphum* may be seen from those paintings. To put it succinctly for a Western reader, the book was comparable to a concise combination of Ptolemy's astronomy, Aristotle's ethics and politics, and Dante's literary depiction of the worlds. It described the various dimensions of the universe, gave a meaning to them, discussed that meaning in the context of the ethics for the individual, and related these issues to the origin, the legitimacy, and the function of the state.

It was only when the Thais had to face the challenge of Western science and technology as well as Christianity during the high tide of Colonialism in the middle of the nineteenth century that the authority of the text in various fields started to be questioned. The result was the third milestone of the Thai intellectual heritage – the Siamese renaissance under the leadership of King Mongkut. Western science and technology forced the Thais to reconsider their understanding of cosmology; the political threat of Colonialism pressured political elites to restructure the Thai government, which consequently required a new approach to politics; Christianity led many Thais to reexamine their ethics and moral codes. The world was indeed turning upside-down. But King Mongkut and his contemporaries, S. Sivaraksa argues, admirably accomplished the task of carrying the Thai intellectual tradition on into the modern world. They went back to the original sources of Buddhism and redefined various fields of intellectual endeavor as situations required.

Those were the three major intellectual creations and reformations in the past. At present – and this is the main purpose of the lecture – we are now witnessing a new phase of the Thai intellectual tradition. With the downfall of absolute monarchy, a more extensive participation in modern socio-economic trends, and the on-going process of modernization and development, there is a critical need for a redefinition and reinterpretation of the tradition. It was a fortunate incident that in 1932, right before the political change in that year, a young monk, who had just finished his canonical studies in Bangkok, went back to his hometown in Suratthani to found a place for Buddhist intellectual and spiritual activities. Thereafter, he began to interpret Buddhism in a new light and to relate those interpretations to the rapidly changing trends in Thai society. In many cases, he even went beyond his intellectual progenitors. He vigorously criticized Buddhaghosa's exegeses of the original Tripitaka, which had been taken by Theravada Buddhist canonists as an undisputable interpretation of the teachings. While resorting mainly to the original corpus of the canons (as recognized by Theravadins), he nonetheless referred extensively to the interpretations and practices of Mahayana Buddhism. He even went so far as to use the word "God" in his lectures and writings, generating uproars from Buddhists of various backgrounds. Last but not least, he pointed to "Buddhist Socialism *(Dharmikasangamaniyama)*." as a socio-political solution for the current crisis in contemporary Thai society. In many senses, his contributions to the Thai heritage can be seen as constructive proposals for both the Buddhist world and the world at large.

The book is filled with criticisms of the present by means of the relevance of the past. S. Sivaraksa also provides interesting comments on other groups of monks and laymen who have attempted to relate Buddhism to contemporary conditions in Thai society such as the Santi-asoke movement and the school of Dhammakaya.

We may raise many questions about S. Sivaraksa's premises. Is it significant at all to talk about the Thai way of thinking? Is it plausible to define the Thai intellectual tradition by employing only a single criterion, i.e., Theravada Buddhism? S. Sivaraksa makes it clear that, for him, no evidence suggests that there was any major intellectual renovation during the Ayudhaya period. This reminds us of Luang Wichitwathakan whom S. Sivaraksa has always been at issue with. Luang Wichit criticized Ayudhaya, in his lecture on the civilization of Sukhothai, by laying the blame on the influence of the Khmers; S. Sivaraksa did so by downplaying other elements in the Thai mentality. Even the Pali literature of Chiangmai is also dismissed by S. Sivaraksa as a mere imitation of the Sri Lankan literary tradition. But is it necessary to treat the Thai way of *satipany*ā in such an exclusive and selective manner?

This is a provocative and controversial book. It is rich with explanations of the past and insights into the present. The reader will be forced by S. Sivaraksa's bold remarks and conclusions to rethink the way he or she understands the Thai intellectual heritage.

Vira Somboon,
University of Michigan, Ann Arbor, *JSS* 1987.

The following are books which should be obtained, or given to friends who love Siam or want to know more about Siamese Buddhism

- **DHAMMIC SOCIALISM** by Buddhadasa Bhikkhu 142 pp. Bht 80 locally (abroad US$ 4 post free).
- **LOOKING TO AMERICAN TO SOLVE THAILAND'S PROBLEMS** by Phra Rajavaramuni 94 pp. Bht 90 locally (abroad US$ 10 post free).
- **THAI BUDDHISM IN THE BUDDHIST WORLD** by Phra Rajavaramuni (Prayudh Payutto) 178 pp. Bht 100 locally (abroad US$ 2 post free).
- **THE MIRACLE OF BEING AWAKE** by Thich Nhat Hanh 143 pp. Bht 120 locally.
- **MONUMENTS OF THE BUDDHA IN SIAM** by H.R.H. Prince Damrong Rajanubhab. Translated by S. Sivaraksa and A.B. Griswold. 60 pp. Bht 70 locally (abroad US$ 4 post free)
- **POPULAR BUDDHISM IN SIAM AND OTHER ESSAYS ON THAI STUDIES** by Phya Anuman Rajadhon 216 pp. Bht 300 (hard cover, Bht 200 (paper back) locally (abroad US$ 15 hard cover, US$ 10 paper back post free).
- **SOME TRADITIONS OF THE THAI** by Phya Anuman Rajadhon 196 pp. Bht 200 locally (abroad US$ 10 post free).
- **ESSAYS ON THAI FOLKLORE** by Phya Anuman Rajadhon (new edition) 422 pp. Bht 400 locally (abroad US$ 20 post free).
- **SELFLESSNESS IN SARTRE'S EXISTENTIALISM AND EARLY BUDDHISM** by Phramaha Prayoon Mererk 224 pp. Bht 150 locally (abroad US$ 8 post free).

- **ANKARN KALYANAPONG: A CONTEMPORARY SIAMESE POET** 82 pp. Bht 80 locally (abroad US$ 4 post free).
- **BUDDHIST VISION FOR RENEWING SOCIETY** by S.Sivaraksa 276 pp. Bht 120 locally (abroad US$ 6 post free).
- **SIAMESE RESURGENCE** by S.Sivaraksa 492 pp. Bht 260 (hard cover) Bht 180 (paper back) locally (abroad US$ 10 hard cover US$ 7 paper back post free).
- **RELIGION AND DEVELOPMENT** by S.Sivaraksa 81 pp. Bht 90 locally (abroad US$ 5 post free).
- **A SOCIALLY ENGAGED BUDDHISM** by S.Sivaraksa 206 pp. Bht 300 (hard cover) Bht 200 locally (paper back) locally (abroad US$ 15 hard cover, US$ 10 paper back post free).
- **YEARS OF HORROR, DAYS OF HOPE : RESPONDING TO THE CAMBODIAN REFUGEE CRISIS EDITED** by Barry S. Lavy and Daniel C. Susott; 370 pp. 175 Baht (paperback). This title is for sale in Thailand only.
- **SEEDS OF PEACE**, Thai Inter-Religious Commision for Development, 3 issues/year, subscription rate US$ 10 per annum. Vols 1 & 2 (1985-8) bound in hard cover Bht 300 locally (US$ 15 abroad).

THE SANTI PRACHA DHAMMA INSTITUTE

Peace, public participation and righteousness have together been the three ideals of prominent Thai figures in modern times. The combination of these principles was advocated by intellectuals like Thianwan in the reign of King Chulalongkorn, by leaders of the 1932 democratic revolution such as Pridi Banomyong, and by academics and administrators like Puey Ungphakorn. The latter's concept of "democracy by means of non-violence" has also continued to inspire younger generations of Thai society. It is thus not an exaggeration to say that the term "santiprachadhamma (Peace-public participation-righteousness)" represents the pillar of modern Thai intellectual heritage.

The Santi Pracha Dhamma Institute was established in April 1988 as a non-government, non-profit Thai institution with the major aim to promote the pursuit of *Santiprachadhamma* in Thai society. The two main objectives of the institute are, first, to deepen and widen the knowledge and thought on peace/non-violence, democracy, and righteousness, as well as their application to current situations in Thai society, and , second, the search for and develop the human resources conducive to the realization of these principles.

Present activities of the institute consist of the followings.

1. Research - such as Peace Studies and Research Project, Community Development Research Project, Research on Economic Self-Reliance.

2. Training and Teaching - such as Training Program for Newcoming and Prospective Workers of Non-governmental organizations, Teaching of the Languages of Neighboring Countries for the Promotion of Cultural Understanding.

3. Propagation - such as Thai Forum, Exhibitions and Seminars commemorating the 100th Anniversary of Phya Anuman Rajadhon, Publications.

4. Community Activities - such as Wongsanit Ashram Project.

LEGAL STATUS

The Santi Pracha Dhamma Institute is governed by the Sathirakoses Nagapradipa Foundation, a philanthropic organization recognized by the Thai government. The institute, however, has its own separate functions and management.

OFFICE OF THE INSTITUTE

303/7 Soi Santipap, Nares Road,
Bangkok 10500, Thailand
Tel. 233-2382, 233-2792
FAX (662) 236-7783

Objectives of TICD

1. To coordinate work among individuals, groups of individuals and various agencies dealing with religions and development in course of working together.

2. To share experience in and knowledge of religions and development as well as exploring ways and means of working together.

3. To offer training and secure resources in terms of man-power and materials to support and enhance the agencies that need help.

4753/5 Soi Wat Thongnopphakun
Somdejchaophya Road Bangkok 10600
THAILAND G.P.O. BOX 1960
4753/5 ซอยวัดทองนพคุณ ถนนสมเด็จเจ้าพระยา คลองสาน กทม. 10600 ตู้ป.ณ. กลาง 1960